THE ACTS
OF THE
APOSTLES

ABINGDON NEW TESTAMENT COMMENTARIES

THE ACTS OF THE APOSTLES

BEVERLY ROBERTS GAVENTA

Abingdon Press
Nashville

ABINGDON NEW TESTAMENT COMMENTARIES:
THE ACTS OF THE APOSTLES

Library of Congress Cataloging-in-Publication Data

Gaventa, Beverly Roberts.
   The Acts of the Apostles / Beverly Roberts Gaventa.
     p. cm. — (Abingdon New Testament commentries)
   Includes bibliographical references and index.
   ISBN 0-687-05821-X (pbk. : alk. paper)
   1. Bible. N.T. Acts—Commentaries. I. Title. II. Series.

   BS2875.53.G38 2003
   226.6'07—dc21

ISBN 13: 978-0-687-05821-1   2003011641

07 08 09 10 11—10 9 8 7 6 5 4 3 2

MANUFACTURED IN THE UNITED STATES OF AMERICA

In memory of
Raymond E. Brown, S.S.
and
Charles Merritt Nielsen

CONTENTS

FOREWORD

The *Abingdon New Testament Commentaries* series provides compact, critical commentaries on the writings of the New Testament. These commentaries are written with special attention to the needs and interests of theological students, but they will also be useful for students in upper-level college or university settings, as well as for pastors and other church leaders. In addition to providing basic information about the New Testament texts and insights into their meanings, these commentaries are intended to exemplify the tasks and procedures of careful, critical biblical exegesis.

The authors who have contributed to this series come from a wide range of ecclesiastical affiliations and confessional stances. All are seasoned, respected scholars and experienced classroom teachers. They take full account of the most important current scholarship and secondary literature, but do not attempt to summarize that literature or engage in technical academic debate. Their fundamental concern is to analyze the literary, socio-historical, theological, and ethical dimensions of the biblical texts themselves. Although all of the commentaries in this series have been written on the basis of the Greek texts, the authors do not presuppose any knowledge of the biblical languages on the part of the reader. When some awareness of the grammatical, syntactical, or philological issue is necessary for an adequate understanding of a particular text, they explain the matter clearly and concisely.

The introduction of each volume ordinarily includes subdivisions dealing with the *key issues* addressed and/or raised by the New Testament writing under consideration; its *literary genre, structure, and character;* its *occasion and situational context,* including its wider social, historical, and religious contexts; and its *theological and ethical significance* within these several contexts.

In each volume, the *commentary* is organized according to literary units rather than verse by verse. Generally, each of these units is the subject of three types of analysis. First, the *literary analysis* attends to the unit's genre, most important stylistic features, and overall structure. Second, the *exegetical analysis* considers the aim and leading ideas of the unit, deals with any especially important textual variants, and discusses the meanings of important words, phrases, and images. It also takes note of the particular historical and social situations of the writer and original readers, and of the wider cultural and religious contexts of the book as a whole. Finally, the *theological and ethical analysis* discusses the theological and ethical matters with which the unit deals or to which it points, focusing on the theological and ethical significance of the text within its original setting.

Each volume also includes a *select bibliography,* thereby providing guidance to other major commentaries and important scholarly works, and a brief *subject index.* The New Revised Standard Version of the Bible is the principal translation of reference for the series, but the authors draw on all of the major modern English versions, and when necessary provide their own original translations of difficult terms or phrases.

The fundamental aim of this series will have been attained if readers are assisted, not only to understand more about the origins, character, and meaning of the New Testament writings, but also to enter into their own informed and critical engagement with the texts themselves.

Victor Paul Furnish
General Editor

PREFACE

The Acts of the Apostles is a dangerous document. Introduced to many readers as a history of the earliest Christian communities, beginning in Rome and concluding in Jerusalem, it appears to be a harmless account of people, times, and locations. Yet its twists and turns prove captivating, and I have found myself ensnared by Luke's second volume since I first took it up seriously over two decades ago.

This commentary had its origins in a class I taught twenty years ago, but it would never have come into existence without the invitation, the encouragement, and the sheer patience of the series editor, Victor Paul Furnish, and the project editor, D. Moody Smith. The book took shape on diskette and paper during a generous leave for the 2000–2001 academic year. I wish to thank President Thomas W. Gillespie, Dean James Armstrong, and the Board of Trustees of Princeton Theological Seminary, for granting me that sabbatical. My colleagues in the biblical studies department at PTS, a group for whom I am abidingly grateful, protected that sabbatical by taking on additional responsibilities themselves. The Center of Theological Inquiry offered me an uncommon space, one that could accommodate both the feasts and the fasts of an academic project. Wallace M. Alston, Jr., Blanche Jenson, Robert W. Jenson, and Kathi Morley nurtured all of us who were in residence through their uncommon hospitality. The projects of other members at the Center enlarged my thinking on several fronts and made their way into my own work in the form of nagging questions that range from time to the Trinity.

Although I have labored assiduously to make this a commentary on Acts rather than a commentary on other commentaries, I have been instructed at every turn by a distinguished set of predecessors. Among those predecessors, I especially appreciate the theological insights of John Calvin, C. K. Barrett's encyclopedic coverage, Robert Tannehill's grasp of the narrative whole, and the fresh perspectives of Scott Spencer. Along with many other students of Luke–Acts, I find myself enriched and often dismayed by the work of Henry Joel Cadbury, in whose writing on Acts I regularly discover what I had imagined to be my own original insights.

William S. Campbell, Charles B. Cousar, J. Louis Martyn, Scott Spencer, and Patrick J. Willson read and commented on earlier drafts of all or part of the commentary. I appreciate very much the time and energy consumed by those readings, and I know that their questions and suggestions have enhanced the final product. In addition, I have benefitted from conversations with C. Clifton Black, John T. Carroll, Joel Green, Carl Holladay, and Donald H. Juel. I keenly regret that the conversation with my cherished colleague Don Juel was cut short by his untimely death. The Princeton Seminary dissertations of William S. Campbell, Matthew L. Skinner, and John B. F. Miller also taught me much about Acts, for which I am grateful.

The generosity of Princeton Theological Seminary made available to me research assistance from William S. Campbell, Matthew L. Skinner, Lidija Novakovic, John B. F. Miller, and Craig Carpenter. Their relentless and reliable pursuit of a multitude of questions informed and corrected me often, and I hope it proved engaging to them as well. Because they happened to arrive on the scene toward the end of the project, John B. F. Miller and Craig Carpenter drew the unenviable task of confirming a host of references to primary sources and bibliographical details. I am also grateful to Jason Ripley for preparing the index.

As important as are these scholars past and present, I suspect that former students in M.Div. classrooms, continuing education events, and ecclesiastical gatherings will see in what follows the influence of their own lively engagement with Luke's second volume. Although the conversation took place over twenty years ago, I have never forgotten the genuine dismay on the face of the young woman who wanted to know how a God of mercy could inflict death on Ananias and Sapphira. Nor am I likely to read Acts 8 again without hearing the student who wondered what Philip thought when he found himself in Azotus: "Would that be like waking up in Tijuana with a new tattoo?"

Readers of Luke–Acts too often neglect the strand of doxology that runs throughout Luke's work. Raymond E. Brown and Charles M. Nielsen, to whose memory this book is dedicated, embodied the praise of God through their lives of scholarship, teaching, and friendship. I can no longer thank them in person, but I remain grateful to God for their rich presence in my life.

LIST OF ABBREVIATIONS

1 [2] Apol.	Justin Martyr, *First [Second] Apology*
1 [2] Clem.	*First [Second] Clement*
1 En.	Ethiopic *Book of Enoch*
1QS	*Rule of the Community* (Qumran Cave 1)
1QSa	Appendix 1 (*Rule of the Congregation*) to 1QS
11QTemple	*Temple Scroll* (Qumran Cave 11)
4QpNah	Pesher on Nahum (Qumran Cave 4)
4QTest	*Testimonia* (Qumran Cave 4)
2 Apoc. Bar.	Syriac *Apocalypse of Baruch*
AB	Anchor Bible
ABD	D. N. Freedman (ed.), *Anchor Bible Dictionary*
'Abod. Zar.	*Avodah Zarah*
Abr.	Philo, *On Abraham*
ABRL	Anchor Bible Reference Library
Adv. Haer.	Irenaeus, *Against Heresies*
Ag. Ap.	Josephus, *Against Apion*
Alleg. Interp.	Philo, *Allegorical Interpretation*
AnBib	Analecta biblica
Ant.	Josephus, *The Antiquities of the Jews*
BAFCS	Book of Acts in Its First Century Setting
Barn.	*Barnabas*
BC	Beginnings of Christianity
BDAG	W. Bauer, F. W. Danker, W. F. Arndt, and F. W. Gingrich, *Greek-English Lexicon of the NT*
BDF	F. Blass, A. Debrunner, and R. W. Funk, *A Greek Grammar of the NT*
Ber.	*Berakhot*
BETL	Bibliotheca ephemeridum theologicarum lovaniensium
Bib	*Biblica*
BZNW	Beihefte zur ZNW
CBQ	*Catholic Biblical Quarterly*
Contemp. Life	Philo, *The Contemplative Life*
Decalogue	Philo, *On the Decalogue*
Did.	*Didache*
Dreams	Philo, *On Dreams*
EgT	*Eglise et théologie*
Embassy	Philo, *The Embassy to Gaius*

LIST OF ABBREVIATIONS

ETL	*Ephemerides theologicae lovanienses*
Flaccus	Philo, **Against Flaccus**
HTR	*Harvard Theological Review*
ICC	International Critical Commentary
IEJ	*Israel Exploration Journal*
Ign. Mag.	Ignatius, *Letter to the Magnesians*
Ign. Phld.	Ignatius, *Letter to the Philadelphians*
Int	*Interpretation*
JAC	Jahrbuch für Antike und Christentum
JBL	*Journal of Biblical Literature*
Jos. Asen.	*Joseph and Asenath*
Joseph	Philo, *On the Life of Joseph*
JSNTSup	Journal for the Study of the New Testament Supplement Series
JTS	*Journal of Theological Studies*
Jub.	*Jubilees*
J.W.	Josephus, *The Jewish War*
KJV	King James Version
LCL	Loeb Classical Library
LEC	Library of Early Christianity
Let. Aris.	*Letter of Aristeas*
lit.	literally
LXX	Septuagint
m.	*Mishnah*
Mart. Pol.	*Martyrdom of Polycarp*
Mid.	*Middot*
Migration	Philo, *On the Migration of Abraham*
Moses	Philo, *On the Life of Moses*
Ned.	*Nedarim*
NewDocs	*New Documents Illustrating Early Christianity*
NICNT	New International Commentary on the New Testament
NovT	*Novum Testamentum*
NovTSup	Novum Testamentum, Supplements
NPNF	Nicene and Post-Nicene Fathers
NRSV	New Revised Standard Version
NTS	*New Testament Studies*
OBT	Overtures to Biblical Theology
Odes Sol.	*Odes of Solomon*
OGIS	*Orientis graeci inscriptiones selectae*
PGM	K. Preisendanz (ed.), *Papyri graecae magicae*
Pol. Phil.	Polycarp, *Letter to the Philippians*
Pss. Sol.	*Psalms of Solomon*
Qidd.	*Qiddushin*
RB	*Revue biblique*
REB	*The Revised English Bible*
RTP	*Revue de théologie et de philosophie*
Šabb.	*Shabbat*

LIST OF ABBREVIATIONS

Sanh.	*Sanhedrin*
SBLAB	Society of Biblical Literature Academia Biblica
SBLDS	SBL Dissertation Series
SBLRBS	SBL Resources for Biblical Study
SNTA	Studiorum Novi Testamenti Auxilia
SNTSMS	Society for New Testament Studies Monograph Series
Spec. Laws	Philo, *On the Special Laws*
StudBib	Studia Biblica
Syb. Or.	*Sibylline Oracles*
T. 12 Patr.	*Testament of the Twelve Patriarchs*
T. Dan	*Testament of Dan*
T. Naph.	*Testament of Naphtali*
T. Reu.	*Testament of Reuben*
TDNT	G. Kittel and G. Friedrich (eds.), *Theological Dictionary of the New Testament*
Trypho	Justin Martyr, *Dialogue with Trypho*
TU	Texte und Untersuchungen
Virtues	Philo, *On Virtues*
WUNT	Wissenschaftliche Untersuchungen zum Neuen Testament
WW	*Word and World*
ZNW	*Zeitschrift für die neutestamentliche Wissenschaft*

INTRODUCTION

He is the Way.
Follow him through the Land of Unlikeness;
You will see rare beasts, and have unique adventures.
W. H. Auden, "For the Time Being"

Opening the Acts of the Apostles begins a journey that takes travelers beyond domestic borders into unfamiliar territory where passports are invalid and embassies afford little protection. Before Peter gives his first sermon in chapter 2, Luke gathers people from Jerusalem, Asia, Egypt, and Rome. Paul preaches in the intellectual marketplace of Athens, he is driven out of the religious center of Ephesus, and he finds hospitality on the insignificant island of Malta. Not only are the places far-flung and diverse, but the people met along the way both feed the imagination and frustrate the inquisitive traveler. The apostle Matthias and the prophesying daughters of Philip appear and disappear on the road as abruptly as tollbooth attendants. Rhoda and Eutychus enliven the journey with their excitement, on the one hand, and their somnolence on the other. Lydia and the islanders of Malta offer hospitality sorely lacking elsewhere. And Peter, who would seem to be a major figure in the journey, simply disappears without warning or explanation.

Travelers who desire the predictability of an interstate highway system where all roads look alike and every interchange features three gas stations and two fast-food stores will find this journey more closely resembles *A Hitchhiker's Guide to the Galaxy.* Ananias and Sapphira die for wanting only to keep a small nest egg for themselves, but the murderous Saul becomes a globetrotting witness for the risen Jesus. An angel directs Philip to a deserted place during the heat of the day, where he encounters a marvelous Ethiopian eunuch who hears the gospel eagerly. The gift of the Holy Spirit is promised to those who repent and undergo baptism, but it falls on the Gentile Cornelius, along with his family and friends, while Peter is still in the process of explaining Jesus to them.

Customary descriptions of Acts as the story of the church's growth or the story of the spread of the gospel neglect the larger context within which this journey takes place. Although it begins in Israel's leading city, Jerusalem, and ends in the Empire's leading city, Rome, the context of Acts reaches well beyond the cities of the Mediterranean world. Readers who set aside the expectation that Acts is an institutional history, shaped and reshaped by human leaders, will instead see God at work from the beginning until well past the end. God is the one who glorifies Jesus and raises him from the dead, who rescues the apostles from prison, who directs Ananias to baptize Saul, and who insists upon the inclusion of the Gentiles. God sends Paul and his coworkers into Macedonia, heals people through the hands of Peter and Paul, and finally directs Paul safely to Rome. If readers of Acts find themselves in a journey, the major sights are not those created by human hands; they result from the actions of God alone.

The larger context of the Lukan journey also discloses forces arrayed in opposition to God. The Jerusalem religious authorities sometimes act out of their own sense of God's will, and sometimes out of mere jealousy. The Roman official Felix permits Paul to remain in jail in the hope of receiving a bribe. Opposition to God may sometimes appear within the church as well, as when Peter presumes to know for himself what food is clean and unclean, or when the Jerusalem believers demand circumcision for Gentile Christians. Other gods offer opposition, or at least their representatives do, as when the city of Ephesus riots in recognition of the threat posed to the deity Artemis by Christian preaching. Most important, Satan and Satan's agents oppose

God, openly attempting to subvert the gospel or to claim its power for themselves. Elymas or Bar-Jesus, whom Paul identifies as a "son of the devil," attempts to prevent Paul and Barnabas from speaking about the gospel with Sergius Paulus. The magician Simon desires to buy the ability to bestow the gift of the Holy Spirit.

The journey that begins with Acts 1:1 does not end at 28:31, even if Luke's writing stops there. Numerous proleptic references to Paul's witness and his death in Rome signal one trajectory that lies ahead: Paul will testify in Rome and will be executed there. More significantly, since the opening of Acts the story has anticipated Jesus' return. Having traced the fulfillment of the promise of the Holy Spirit and the fulfillment of the witness to Jesus in and beyond Jerusalem, the story anticipates that the third promise, that of the Parousia, also will be fulfilled. As the heavenly messengers instructed the apostles at Jesus' ascension, expectation of that return does not mean mere waiting, but involves obedience of the sort Paul is engaged in at the close of Acts: "proclaiming the kingdom of God and teaching about the Lord Jesus Christ with all boldness and without hindrance" (28:31).

CHARACTERS BEYOND AND WITHIN THE JOURNEY

Despite the title bestowed on Luke's second volume by ancient Christian tradition, from the opening lines of the book readers quickly learn that the apostles will not be in control of this journey. By the end of the first scene, Luke has introduced the activity of God, Jesus, and the Holy Spirit, and their interrelated actions dominate the story. The human characters who inhabit the story—many and intriguing though they may be—are subsidiary to the larger story of divine activity. Luke presents and assesses these human characters in relationship to their place in and reception of the larger story of God. What makes human characters interesting or important for Luke pertains to their response or resistance to God.

God, Jesus Christ, and the Holy Spirit

God

Unlike nineteenth-century writers such as Charles Dickens or Anthony Trollope, whose novels introduce leading characters with extensive histories and character assessments, Luke does not provide readers (either in the Gospel or in Acts) with an introduction to God. Neither does the narrator nor any character speak directly on attributes of God, such as God's omnipotence or God's love. In that sense, Luke's work contrasts sharply with a writer like his near-contemporary Philo, or even the author of the Johannine epistles. Even Paul's speech to the philosophically inclined Athenians begins with God's activity as creator rather than with a claim about divine attributes. (There is one possible exception to that claim, namely the impartiality of God, and that one may be revealing; see below.) Luke is even stingy with his use of titles for God, sparingly using such language as "Sovereign," "God of glory," "Lord of heaven and earth," and "God of our ancestors."

God is the God of Israel. As Acts unfolds, the audience comes to know God through the activity ascribed to God as well as through the speeches and their claims about God. And the first thing the audience learns is that *God is the God of Israel.* Much of what Luke says about God belongs squarely under this initial claim. On Solomon's portico, Peter invokes "the God of Abraham, the God of Isaac, and the God of Jacob, the God of our ancestors" (3:13). Paul insists that he is faithful to "the God of our ancestors" (24:14). These identifications of God are not labels that merely decorate without informing. Peter's Pentecost speech connects Jesus with the prophecy of Joel as well as with the story of David. Stephen's speech comprises a lengthy rehearsal of God's history with Israel. Before Gentile audiences in Lystra and in Athens, of course, Paul does not begin with God's history with Israel, but even those speeches draw heavily on Israel's understanding of God as creator.

Major elements in the character of God in Acts can be subsumed under the assertion that God is the God of Israel. God's initiative for human salvation replays God's repeated initiative to rescue and redeem Israel. God's faithfulness to the promises of Scripture reflects the covenant faithfulness of God in the Old Testament. Even the sending of the Spirit might be understood as contained within the claim that God is the God of Israel, although the Holy Spirit proves difficult to contain in any category.

It is impossible to speak of God in Acts without identifying God as the God of Israel.

Identifying God as the God of Israel is no longer sufficient, however. In the first place, God is also the Father of Jesus, the one who anointed Jesus, who sent him, who attested him through his deeds, and through whose own foreknowledge and plan Jesus was crucified. Most important, God is the one who raised Jesus from the dead. All of these actions not only convey what must be known about Jesus, they convey what must be known also about God.

As important as is Israel's history for understanding Acts, Israel's history never enters the pages of Acts on its own, apart from reference to Jesus. That point is nearly self-evident in Peter's early speeches in Jerusalem, where Israel's history provides the framework within which to explain who Jesus is. But even Stephen's recital of Israel's history finally makes reference to Jesus, and along the way Stephen interprets the patriarchs in language that echoes the life of Jesus. Paul's defense speeches do not include a recital of Israel's history, but they do allude to it, always in order to work their way to the resurrection of Jesus.

Because Luke makes heavy use of prophetic imagery in his interpretation of Jesus, it is tempting to read the history of Israel as presented in Acts as if Jesus were simply one more in the line of the prophets. Yet, however much Jesus is the "prophet like Moses" (3:22), he is more than that; he is nothing less than the agent of salvation. To put the matter sharply, in Acts one can speak of God without invoking Abraham or Moses or David on every occasion, but one cannot any longer speak of God without reference to God's action in Jesus Christ.

In the second place, the claim that God is the God of Israel is no longer sufficient, because *God is also the God who includes the Gentiles, those who are not part of Israel.* Although the early events in Jerusalem anticipate God's radical act of inclusion (2:39; 3:25), this feature of God in Acts comes to forceful expression in the account of Peter and Cornelius in 10:1-11:18. As Peter gradually recognizes what the heavenly voice means when it declares that God makes clean, he interprets unfolding events with the conclusion that "God shows no partiality." The statement is significant as one of the rare occasions when Luke describes God by way of a principle or an abstraction. When Peter rehearses the Cornelius story for believers in Jerusalem, they concretize Peter's abstraction: "Then God has given even to the Gentiles the repentance that leads to life" (11:18). As the witness persists in subsequent chapters, Paul and others frequently characterize their labor as *God's* activity among the Gentiles: they explain "how he had opened a door of faith for the Gentiles" (14:27; see also 15:4, 12; 21:19). God is the God of Israel, the God who raised Jesus from the dead, and the God who is now acting decisively to include the Gentiles. (It is especially telling that the conclusions drawn both by Peter and by believers in Jerusalem are about God rather than about a decision made by the church.)

In yet another way the statement that "God is the God of Israel" does not suffice, because *God is also the God who acts among and through those who are called to believe in Jesus' name.* (The actions of "God" must include Jesus and the Spirit as well; see below.) Divine direction begins with the instruction of the apostles prior to the ascension and extends to the rescue of those caught in the fearsome storm in the Mediterranean. It includes the selection and empowerment of witnesses, specific instructions for their labor, and encouragement of the witness Paul during his captivity. At a fundamental level, the story of Acts is not the story of the church or its apostolic witnesses, but the story of God's actions through those people. This significantly intersects with the claim that God is the God of Israel, of course, since many early believers and their witnesses are themselves part of Israel. They continue to worship in the temple and they teach in synagogues. Yet as believers teach in the synagogue, they teach about Jesus, and they acknowledge and participate in God's inclusion of the Gentiles; those activities make it impossible to subsume God's action in and through the church under the claim that God is the God of Israel.

The place of God in Acts is comprehensive, beginning from the creation and the promises of Scripture, through Israel's history, and into the astonishing present which fulfills those promises in unanticipated and often unwelcome ways. It also extends into the future, as Paul's witness continues in Rome and as the church waits confidently for the return of Jesus Christ. God's comprehensive role means that it should come as no surprise that two small phrases pepper the story: Word of God and Plan of God. "Word of God" or "word of the Lord" are among several expressions Luke employs frequently for the content of the gospel itself (see, for example, 4:31; 13:7, 44; 16:32). "Plan of God" refers to God as the one whose intention and oversight governs the events that unfold, encompassing both the events of Jesus' own life and the way in which the witness moves throughout the cities of the Mediterranean world, stretching in Acts from the Jerusalem ascension of Jesus to the testimony of Paul in Rome (e.g., 2:23; 4:28; 5:38; 20:27).

Jesus Christ

The Fulfillment of Israel's Hopes: Much of the characterization of Jesus in Acts concerns Jesus as the fulfillment of Israel's hopes. Both Peter's early sermons in Jerusalem and Paul's later preaching in the synagogues declare that Jesus is the Messiah whom Israel has awaited. Apart from brief references to Jesus' work as healer, the sermons provide little argument for this claim (beyond the important exception of the resurrection; see below). In Acts, "Messiah" serves less as a title with fixed content than as a way of asserting the connection between Jesus and the hopes of Israel.

Luke's most consistent way of connecting Jesus to Israel's hope is through his resurrection. The early speeches of Peter in

Jerusalem forcefully insist that God raised Jesus in fulfillment of ancient promises and over against the rejection of Jerusalem Jews that led to crucifixion (2:30; 3:18). At Pisidian Antioch, Paul's initial sermon presents Jesus' resurrection as the fulfillment of God's promise (13:32). This identification of the resurrection as the hope that extends back to Israel's ancestors and finds its initial fulfillment in Jesus Christ comes to the forefront again in Paul's final defense speeches (see 23:6; 24:15, 21; and especially 26:6-8, 22-23).

That God sends Jesus as the fulfillment of Israel's hope is an affirmation Luke makes by means of Scripture. The early speeches identify Jesus as the successor of David, albeit a far superior successor, and as the "prophet like Moses" (2:29-36; 3:22). They also draw on the Psalms to interpret Jesus' death and resurrection (e.g., Ps 16:8-11 in Acts 2:25-28; Ps 16:10 in 2:31; Ps 110:1 in 2:34-35). By no means, however, does Luke's interpretation of Jesus through Scripture consist strictly of citations. Stephen's speech recounts the biblical story of Israel in a way that highlights both God's faithfulness to the promise and Israel's rejection of God's agents. Even if the speech does not tell of Jesus' ministry, it unmistakably connects Israel's earlier pattern of rejection with the rejection of Jesus (and of Stephen as well; see 7:51-53). The general references to arguing from the Scripture (17:2) or to what is said in the law and the prophets (3:18; 24:14; 26:22; 28:23) also reinforce this identification of Jesus as the fulfillment of Israel's hope. In a sense, Jesus has his preexistence in Scripture's teaching about him.

Influenced by the work of Hans Conzelmann, students of Luke often characterize his Christology as subordinationist (Conzelmann 1961, 170-84). That label rightly draws attention to assertions such as Peter's introduction of "Jesus of Nazareth, a man attested to you by God with deeds of power, wonders, and signs that God did through him" (2:22). By designating Jesus as a man through whom God acted, Peter appears to be placing Jesus in a subordinate position. Yet the term "subordination" misunderstands the function of the comments about Jesus. In the context of the developing speech, Peter is arguing less that Jesus is subordinate than that Jesus is God's means of fulfilling promises to Israel.

Jesus and God, Jesus and the Holy Spirit: That God sends Jesus in fulfillment of Israel's hopes does not capture all that is said about Jesus in Acts, since for Luke *Jesus is himself associated with God and with the Holy Spirit.* This close association comes to expression in at least three distinct ways in the narrative. First, the risen Jesus is associated with God and the Spirit by means of their shared location. The opening scene of Acts vividly depicts Jesus' ascension to heaven, emphasizing that as his current location ("This Jesus, who has been taken up from you into heaven, will come in the same way as you saw him go into heaven"; 1:11). Peter's Pentecost speech again asserts that Jesus is now "exalted at the right hand of God," from which location Jesus pours out the Holy Spirit on gathered believers (2:33-35; see also 3:21). Stephen's vision of Jesus "standing at the right hand of God" simultaneously testifies to his innocence and prompts the crowd to murder (7:54-58). These repeated assertions of Jesus' location have less to do with geography than with theology; as God was with Jesus (10:38), now Jesus is with God.

Luke associates Jesus with God and the Spirit through their shared location, but he also associates the three by means of their integrally related activities. Multiple passages connect the three with one another, as if they cannot be spoken of apart from one another. The Pentecost speech identifies Jesus as the one who received the Holy Spirit from God and poured it out on those present (2:33). Peter declares to Cornelius and his household that God was "preaching peace by Jesus Christ" and that God anointed Jesus with the Spirit (10:36-37). During Paul's farewell address to the Ephesian elders, he charges them to care for the church, reminding them that the Holy Spirit had made them overseers of "the church of God" which God obtained with "the blood of his own" (NRSV: the blood of his own Son; 20:28).

Perhaps the most emphatic way in which Acts associates Jesus with God is through the frequent reference to the name of Jesus. Healings take place through Jesus' name (3:6, 16; 4:7-12; 16:18;

INTRODUCTION

see also 4:30). People believe and are baptized in his name (2:38; 8:12, 16; 19:5), salvation is declared through the same name (2:21; 4:12), witnesses bear and suffer for the name (5:41; 9:15). Given Luke's knowledge of the Old Testament, this pattern probably reflects something more than the conviction that having a person's name is effective. For example, the psalmist identifies the name of God with God's own power:

The LORD answer you in the day of trouble!
The name of the God of Jacob protect you! (Ps 20:1)

References to Jesus' name and its power actually associate him with God (see also, e.g., Gen 21:33; 1 Kgs 18:24-25; 2 Kgs 5:11; Ps 20:1; Zech 13:9).

Jesus and the Church: If Luke understands Jesus as the fulfillment of Israel's hope and as inextricably related to both God and the Spirit, Luke also understands Jesus to be present and active in the church's witness. Interpreters of Acts have sometimes emphasized the absence of Jesus in Luke's second volume (Conzelmann 1961, 202-206; Zwiep 1997, 182). In obvious and superficial ways, the narrative itself requires Jesus' absence, since following the ascension Jesus can scarcely be present in the same way as he is in Luke's first volume. Some remarkable strands in the narrative undermine that absence, however. In the first verse of Acts, Luke characterizes his first volume as concerning "the things Jesus *began* to do and to teach" (AT, emphasis added). The NRSV obscures this phrase with the translation "all that Jesus did and taught from the beginning," probably because the translators assume that Jesus is absent from the story of Acts. The continuity of Jesus' activity may well be what Luke asserts here, however. Prior to his ascension, Jesus instructs the apostles (v. 2) and identifies them as his witnesses, which implies that their own teaching and preaching is, in effect, Jesus' work. Jesus enters the narrative directly only at Paul's conversion, where he charges Paul with persecuting, not the church, but Jesus himself (9:4). The repetition of this charge in the subsequent reiterations

34

of Paul's conversion (22:7; 26:14) gives it greater force. Two further texts reinforce the presence of Jesus. In Acts 9:34, when Peter goes to the ailing Aeneas, he does not cure him in Jesus' name but announces: "Jesus Christ heals you." And in 26:23, at his climactic defense speech, Paul asserts to Agrippa that Jesus is the one proclaiming light to Israel and the Gentiles. These statements scarcely reflect an understanding of Jesus' absence.

Jesus' Crucifixion: As do other New Testament writings, Acts provides an interpretation of the death of Jesus. Luke clearly affirms both that Jesus died as a result of a human mistake *and* that this death was part of the plan of God (2:22-36; 3:12-26). By contrast with the book of Hebrews, Luke does not draw attention to the sacrificial character of Jesus' death, nor does Luke emphasize Jesus' death as an atonement for human sin. He connects salvation more generally with the comprehensive action of God in sending Jesus (see, e.g., 4:8*b*-12; 5:31; 13:38-39; cf. Luke 2:29-32) rather than with the cross specifically. Luke also does not stress the revelatory character of the cross, by contrast with Paul, for whom the cross unmasks the bankruptcy of human assessment and the determination of God to invade and reclaim the cosmos from the power of evil. In Acts, revelation about the folly of human assessment takes place through the unfolding actions of Jewish leaders in Jerusalem, who mistakenly believe themselves to be interpreters of God and God's temple. It also takes place as the church struggles to understand and accept God's decision to include the Gentiles. Those who are thought to be leaders of the people are unmasked as having misunderstood God's will.

The Holy Spirit

Past, Present, and Future: In Acts, the Holy Spirit arrives as the fulfillment of promises and moves the church into its future. The dramatic entrance of the Holy Spirit at Pentecost serves to fulfill the prophetic word of John the Baptist (Luke 3:16) and the promise made repeatedly by Jesus (Luke 24:49; Acts 1:4-6, 8). Peter's first words by way of interpreting the Spirit's arrival come from the prophet Joel and identify the Spirit's action as the fulfillment of God's own promise. From the beginning of Acts, then, the Holy Spirit that empowers the witness into the future— a future replete with journeys among distant people and places— is also a major sign of God's faithfulness to Israel's past.

Holy Spirit and Scripture: A major way in which Luke displays the connection of the Spirit to Israel's past is through the prophetic voice of the Spirit in Scripture. Peter affirms that the Holy Spirit spoke through the psalms about the fate of Judas (1:16-21). Later, believers in Jerusalem similarly hear the Spirit's voice in Psalm 2 (4:25-26). At the end of the book, Paul identifies the Holy Spirit as the one who spoke through the prophet Isaiah (28:25).

Holy Spirit as Empowering Agent: Most characteristically in Acts, the Spirit empowers believers. At Pentecost, it empowers the dramatic speech that in turn inaugurates the witness of Peter's initial sermon. The significance of the Spirit in these opening chapters of Acts recalls Luke 1–2. There the Spirit "overshadows" Mary in the conception of Jesus, the Spirit fills Elizabeth and inspires her speech to Mary, the Spirit directs Simeon to the temple. The dramatic role of the Spirit in the opening chapters of Acts also recalls the empowering work of God's Spirit in the Old Testament (see, for example, Judg 3:10; 11:29; 1 Sam 10:10; 19:23). The words of Joel quoted by Peter early in the Pentecost sermon indicate that the Spirit's empowerment will be comprehensive:

I will pour out my Spirit upon all flesh,
   and your sons and your daughters shall prophesy,
and your young men shall see visions,
   and your old men shall dream dreams.
Even upon my slaves, both men and women,
   in those days I will pour out my Spirit;
     and they shall prophesy. (2:17-18)

That word is fulfilled, not only by the dramatic events that open the Pentecost scene, but by the response to Peter's speech at its conclusion. Peter's declaration in 2:38 is that the Spirit will empower not a few set aside as a discrete prophesying class, but that the Spirit will be bestowed on all those whom God calls. Although not rigidly consistent in this or other matters, on numerous occasions Acts does detail the gift of the Spirit to believers (see 8:15, 17; 9:17; 19:6).

One way in which the Spirit empowers is through the laying on of hands, a gesture familiar also from Old Testament passages, as when Moses lays hands on his successor Joshua (Deut 34:9). Peter and John venture into Samaria, so that the gift of the Spirit can be bestowed on the Samaritans who have been persuaded by Philip's preaching (8:17), and Ananias lays hands on Saul for healing and the bestowing of the Spirit (9:17). Paul later lays hands on some disciples who have received only water baptism, so that they may receive the Spirit (19:1-7). The frequency of this practice should again not be read as rendering it routine and predictable, which is the mistake made by Simon Magus, who erroneously concludes the Spirit to be a commodity that can be purchased and manipulated (8:9-13, 18-24). That the apostles can lay hands on people and bestow the Spirit also does not mean that the Spirit is at their disposal. Peter and the church learn this dramatically in the Cornelius account, when they watch astonished as the Spirit falls on Gentiles (10:44-48; 11:15-18).

Occasionally, Luke describes an individual as being full of the Spirit as well as joy, faith, or wisdom:

"full of the Spirit and of wisdom" (candidates for service, 6:3)

"full of faith and the Holy Spirit" (Stephen, 6:5; and see 6:10)

"full of the Holy Spirit and of faith" (Barnabas, 11:24)

"filled with joy and with the Holy Spirit" (the disciples, 13:52)

At least the first three of these descriptions serve to recommend the individual who is about to take some particular role. By including reference to the Spirit, Luke indicates that faith, wisdom, and joy are not personal traits of these individuals but actually gifts of the Spirit. In that sense, these descriptions stand in some proximity to Paul's description of spiritual gifts (see Rom 12:4-8; 1 Cor 12:4-11); what these individuals undertake is only possible because they have received from the Spirit gifts of faith, wisdom, or joy.

Holy Spirit as Inaugurator: In addition to its work of empowerment, in Acts the Holy Spirit is also an inaugurator of witness. It directs Philip to go and join the chariot of the Ethiopian eunuch and then sends Philip off to Caesarea after the Ethiopian is baptized (8:29, 39-40). It directs Peter to go to Cornelius's house (10:19-20). On these particular occasions, directions also come from an angel (8:26) and from visions (10:3, 9-16), which might seem to place the Spirit in the role of mere messenger. In other instances, however, it becomes difficult, perhaps impossible, to distinguish the work of the Spirit from that of God. The long journey of Barnabas and Paul begins when the Holy Spirit instructs the Antioch church to commission them (13:1-3). Paul later reminds the Ephesian elders that the Holy Spirit appointed them (20:28). Paul's final journey to Jerusalem and then Rome finds him bound to the Spirit (20:22). The Spirit witnesses together with the witnesses to the gospel (5:32; 15:8, 28); the Spirit witnesses to Paul about his own future (20:23).

Resisting the Holy Spirit: On two important occasions, individuals are accused of resisting the Spirit. Peter charges Ananias with lying to the Holy Spirit and then charges Sapphira with testing the Spirit (5:1-11). Stephen's recital of Israel's history turns into a sharp accusation against his own audience precisely when he characterizes both present and past generations as "forever opposing the Spirit" (7:51).

Perhaps it suffices to say, with the Johannine Jesus, that the Spirit blows where it wishes (John 3:8); attempting to categorize the activity of the Holy Spirit in Acts is futile both theologically and narratively. In these latter examples, where the Spirit becomes the initiator of events and when it is itself resisted, it is exceedingly difficult to disentangle the Spirit from God. In fact, the individual stories would read the same if the agent were identified as God instead of the Spirit. With respect to God, Jesus, and the Spirit, then, they are so identified with one another in Acts that explicitly Trinitarian language seems an inevitable development. Although Luke is not concerned with precisely the same questions that concern later church councils, his story nevertheless moves in a direction that can only be called Trinitarian.

They Were Called Christians (The Church and Its People)

If Luke's second volume begins with the activity of God, Jesus, and the Spirit, it also draws attention to the gathering of those who have rightly perceived that activity. Even before the arrival of the Spirit at Pentecost, women and men come together in Jerusalem to pray (1:12-14). In many places, Luke refers to these people as the *ekklēsia*, "church" (see, e.g., 5:11; 9:31; 15:22; 20:17). Since Luke introduces the term "Christians" to designate those who believe in Jesus Christ, that term also belongs in a discussion of the Lukan story (11:26). Using the term "Christian" should not be understood to separate Jews and Christians from one another, however, since many believers who appear in Acts are Jews *and* Christians simultaneously. Given Luke's understanding that God sends Jesus as the fulfillment of Israel's hopes, it could scarcely be otherwise; Jews who believe Jesus to be the Messiah do not cease to be Jews.

The primary assertion to make about the church in Acts follows from Luke's depiction of God, Jesus, and the Holy Spirit, namely, that the church exists as evidence of God's plan and God's activity in the world. The church draws its existence from God's intervention, rather than from its own initiative. The gathering in Jerusalem prior to Pentecost comes about as a direct result of the risen Jesus' instruction (1:4), and it is the Spirit's arrival that prompts Peter's initial sermon, which in turn elicits the faith of three thousand people. Even Luke's vivid description of the Jerusalem community at the end of Acts 2 stands bracketed by, and therefore interpreted by, Peter's claim that God "calls" people to him (2:39) and the narrator's concluding remark that "the Lord added to their number those who were being saved" (2:47).

Not only does the church come into existence as evidence of God's plan, but in Acts the church's activity is directed and sometimes corrected by God and God's agents. In the story of Philip and the Ethiopian eunuch, an angel directs Philip to a deserted place at midday when no one in the Middle East would travel, then the Holy Spirit tells him to catch up with the chariot of the eunuch, and afterward the Spirit whisks him away to Azotus (8:26-40). Similarly, the risen Jesus commissions the persecutor Saul as a witness and then must overcome Ananias's resistance. Most tellingly, the inclusion of Gentiles comes about by multiple divine interventions and in the face of considerable resistance from inside the church. In a few instances, believers themselves take initiative, as when Peter declares the necessity of replacing Judas and when the Jerusalem community attends to the crisis in food distribution among widows. (Even on these occasions prayer precedes the decisions.) In the vast majority of instances, however, the church takes its orders from God, rather than making its own plans or devising its own strategies. A particularly vivid example of this characteristic of the church appears at the beginning of chapter 16, when Paul and his colleagues want to travel into Asia and are forbidden by the Holy Spirit. They then try to enter Bithynia only to be told not to go there. Afterwards, the vision of the man from Macedonia provides them with the approved itinerary.

Brought into existence and continually directed by God, *the church offers a bold witness to the world.* That witness takes its most obvious form in the proclamation of the gospel throughout the cities of the Mediterranean, beginning from Jerusalem, Judea, and Samaria, and extending to the "ends of the earth" (1:8). Luke frequently characterizes this proclamation as involving boldness of speech, the forthrightness that proclaims the gospel despite contrary and even dangerous circumstances (see, e.g., 4:31; 9:27-28; 13:46; 28:31). In addition, witness occurs when miracles are performed through the mediation of the apostles (see, e.g., 5:12; 9:32-35, 36-42; 19:11-12), as well as when witnesses confront magicians and others who oppose the gospel or seek to commodify it (as in 13:4-12; 19:13-20).

Luke portrays the church's relentless witness through its preaching and teaching, but *the church's witness also takes the form of mutual responsibility in a community of believers.* In the early chapters, the Jerusalem community functions in a number of ways, including gathering for worship, sharing meals, and sharing possessions. Luke displays a group of people connected to one another theologically, liturgically, and socially, and those connections all derive from God's intervention. The description of the community in 2:42-47 begins with a reference to awe and concludes with a report that the Lord added to the community's number on a daily basis.

The formation of Christian community also takes place *outside* Jerusalem, even if Luke does not provide the vivid summary descriptions elsewhere that he does for the Jerusalem community. Nevertheless, such formation continues to play an important role in the story, especially in the depiction of Paul's journey from Ephesus to Jerusalem in 20:1–21:17. There Luke provides three vignettes of community life—the scene involving Eutychus (20:7-12), the farewell address to the Ephesian elders (20:17-38), and the gathering at Philip's home in Caesarea (21:7-14). Each of those scenes anticipates Paul's arrest in Jerusalem, but each also depicts gatherings of believers with strong ties to one another. A major feature of the farewell address in Acts 20 is the responsibility of the leaders to protect the community from harm. Even here, however, Luke calls attention back to divine activity. Paul charges the leaders to responsible action, but he attributes their selection to the Holy Spirit (20:28) and commends them to God's own guidance (20:32).

Prior to and alongside the witness of the church is its doxological response to God's activity. Luke describes believers with a broad vocabulary of amazement, awe, rejoicing, joy, praise, and prayer. Doxology begins with the response to the dramatic invasion of the Holy Spirit at Pentecost and appears in a concentrated fashion in the description of the Jerusalem community at the end of chapter 2. It extends to Paul's final journey, with the thanksgiving he offers before the meal celebrated on ship and his thanksgiving for safe arrival in Rome. Notably, Luke characterizes the Gentiles as responding to the gospel with joy (13:48-52; 16:34; see also 8:8); he also attributes joy to those Jewish believers who witness the Gentiles' response (11:23; 13:52; 15:3). The single comment made about the Ethiopian eunuch after his baptism is that he "went on his way rejoicing" (8:39). The later Christian tradition that the eunuch went home to Ethiopia to proclaim the gospel may not have textual support in Acts, but it certainly coheres with the Lukan story of joyous response to the gospel.

Witnesses and Apostles, Not Leaders and Heroes

In keeping with the assumption that the journey of Acts concerns primarily the church's leaders, their decisions, and their mission, interpreters habitually refer to the figures of Peter, James, and Paul as the leaders of the church, or even as the heroes of the Lukan story. Luke does not use such language for them, however. The eleven, later joined by Matthias, are "apostles" chosen for their assignment. These apostles, joined by others, serve as witnesses. Jesus first describes them as witnesses in 1:8, but they later employ that term for themselves (see, e.g., 3:15; 10:41; 13:31). Preferring the terms "witness" and "apostle" is not simply a purist concession to Luke's own vocabulary, but a recognition that Acts is not a story about human leadership or about successors to Jesus. That view of the book appears to suffice for the story of the appointment of a successor for Judas, since there Peter takes initiative and specifically says that a replacement must be found. Yet the successor who is appointed, Matthias, himself plays no further role. His name never enters the later pages of Acts. Reading Acts as a succession narrative or a story of human leadership becomes even more problematic subsequently. After an angel releases Peter from Herod's prison in chapter 12, Peter goes to greet believers, and then Luke comments that Peter "went to another place," with no explanation of where Peter went or why he left. After Peter makes a final cameo appearance at the Jerusalem Council in Acts 15, not even his name enters the story again. Understanding James as the new leader in Peter's stead also does not do justice to the story, given the slender role James plays in chapter 15 and the single reference to him in chapter 21. As extensive as is Luke's use of the Old Testament, he undoubtedly knew succession stories on which he might have drawn to show the mantle of leadership passing from Peter to James, but he has not used them.

Paul might seem to be the major exception, the Lukan hero *par excellence*, since much of the second half of the book focuses on Paul's activity. And during the extended account of his arrest, captivity, and trial in Jerusalem and Caesarea, he stands alone with no other believers surrounding him. Yet Luke frequently reminds readers that Paul's captivity comes about as a result of the divine plan (see, e.g., 19:21; 20:22; 23:11). The long account of Paul's trials in chapters 22–26 connects them tightly to the earlier references to Paul as persecutor (Schubert 1968a). More important, the two major speeches in this section recite Paul's activity as persecutor, reminding readers that Paul became a witness only after his own intense resistance to the gospel was overcome by Jesus himself (22:3-21; 26:1-23).

"Your Sons and Your Daughters"

Even before Peter employs Joel's words to interpret the Spirit's outpouring on male and female alike (2:17-18), it is clear that this community includes women as well as men. Consistent with the attention given women in Luke's Gospel, the second volume opens with women as well as men gathered in Jerusalem in prayer (1:14). Women regularly appear among believers (9:2, 36; 17:34; 21:5), their homes and possessions serve the witness (12:12; 16:15), and their generosity testifies to the quality of the church's community (9:36-43). Nevertheless, despite the promise that women and men will speak, Luke reports the speech of women only indirectly and seldom quotes them. In addition, Peter stipulates that the replacement for Matthias must be a man (*anēr*; 1:21), and the apostles later stipulate that males should be selected to assist in the distribution of food (6:3). This ambiguity in the story has given rise to considerable discussion with varying assessments as to its implications (Seim 1994; Reimer 1995; O'Day 1998).

Close attention to the relative roles of women and men in Acts can be enhanced by considering the ways in which women and men are treated in other literature in Luke's world. The female characters who appear in much literature contemporary with Luke, such as the *Roman Antiquities* of Dionysius of Halicarnassus or Chariton's novel *Chareas and Callirhoe*, differ substantially from those in Luke's narrative. The women of *Antiquities* and *Chareas and Callirhoe* figure largely as the possessions of their fathers and husbands. Many are described solely as mothers or portrayed in terms of their physical appearance. Seldom do Luke's women serve only as wives or daughters (although see Drusilla in 24:24 and Bernice in 25:13, 23; 26:30). Instead, women are either believers in the gospel, or they are its opponents. In some cases, they act generously with respect to others, as in the case of Dorcas and Lydia. They may also offer instruction, as in the case of Priscilla, or prophetic gifts, as in the case of Philip's daughters, even if we never hear the content of their speech. When Luke introduces female characters, as when he introduces male characters, he places them in relationship to the gospel. What is important in Luke's ordering of things is where people are located in relationship to the gospel, not where they are located in the patriarchy.

Glory to Thy People Israel

Luke's first volume opens with multiple declarations that the coming of Jesus Christ has to do with Israel and Israel's salvation. As early as Gabriel's announcement to Zechariah, Luke characterizes John the Baptist as one who "will turn many of the people of Israel to the Lord their God." Mary both hears from Gabriel and announces in the Magnificat that Jesus comes as the heir "of his ancestor David" and that his birth signals God's assistance to Israel (see also 1:68-79; 2:11, 25-26, 32*b*, 38). That God intends Jesus Christ for the salvation of Israel is a theme that resounds also through Acts, beginning with Peter's Pentecost speech and extending through Paul's final declaration that his own captivity is for "the hope of Israel" (28:20).

Despite this relentless restatement of God's intent to redeem and restore Israel, Acts recounts multiple incidents of Jewish rejection of the gospel and its witnesses. Beginning with the religious leadership in Jerusalem, where the rejection culminates in Stephen's death, this rejection extends to many of the cities in which Paul witnesses. It is not simply that Jews do not believe the gospel, they also plot against Paul in large numbers. Perhaps most troubling are the three scenes in which Paul declares that he will preach no more among Jews but will turn to Gentiles instead (13:44-52; 18:5-7; 28:23-28). The placing of the third such scene at the very end of the book gives the presentation an even more ominous color. The difficult question of Luke's treatment of Israel has produced sharply divided views, particularly since the Holocaust has forced Christians to encounter the ways in which their traditions contributed to generations of anti-Semitism leading up to the slaughter of European Jews (Tyson 1988; Tyson 1999).

Given the complex nature of Luke's story, it is not surprising that a number of issues tend to be tangled up together. Luke's understanding of Israel, its history and its place in God's plan, may be quite different from Luke's interpretation of Jewish law, his presentation of Jews (individual or corporate), or his understanding of the future of Christian witness among Jews. In addition, asking whether Luke's treatment of any of these questions is "positive" or "negative" presumes a simplistic set of views seldom in evidence in this grand story (or in most human experience).

What is clear is that Luke understands Israel to be God's own creation, as the history lesson contained within Stephen's speech in chapter 7 makes abundantly clear. Further, Jesus himself cannot be understood apart from Israel's history. That connection between God and Israel does not necessarily signal a uniform endorsement of Jewish law, about which Luke's view is not easily determined. The question of law observance enters Acts most sharply in relationship to Stephen, the Jerusalem Council's discussion of the inclusion of Gentiles, and Paul. Stephen and Paul both find themselves accused of speaking against the law and the temple (6:11, 13; 21:21, 28), but neither one makes defense of the law or his own law observance an important feature of his response (although see 23:1; 24:1). The Jerusalem Council determines that Gentile believers must observe some basic restrictions having to do with idolatry and sexual immorality, but the discussion does not extol the virtues of the law or the necessity of its maintenance by believers (15:1-35). Paul circumcises Timothy, whose mother is Jewish, but it appears that he does so out of concern for Jewish resistance to Timothy as a coworker, rather than out of a positive commitment to maintaining the law (16:1-3). This pattern scarcely constitutes a ringing endorsement of the law; instead, the treatment of the law appears to serve other concerns, such as showing the injustice of charges against Stephen and Paul or showing the need for Gentiles to avoid blatantly offensive behavior. In other words, the law in and of itself does not seem to be a central Lukan concern.

Luke does display concern for the response of Jews to Christian preaching, and that response is sharply divided. In Acts 2 Jews respond enthusiastically to Peter's preaching, but as early as Acts 3, the leadership in Jerusalem attempts to silence Peter and John. Jews outside Jerusalem consistently divide between those who are willing to hear and those who both reject and attempt to silence Christian witness. In response, Paul three times announces that he will turn to the Gentiles (13:44-52; 18:5-7; 28:23-28). These three declarations, and especially the last one, have been and can be read in diametrically opposing ways. Given that the book ends following the third declaration, which itself follows a solemn quotation from Isaiah, the third may signal the end of Paul's witness among Jews. On the other hand, the third may also imply, as do the others, no more than the prophetic judgment of Israel—that Jews are being called to repentance. Certainly 28:30-31 suggests that Paul will welcome all who come to him, both Jews and Gentiles. As with Luke's double declaration that human beings failed when they crucified Jesus *and* that it was part of God's plan, Luke is able to maintain both that Israel belongs irrevocably to God *and* that many Jews have failed to respond to the salvation God initiated in Jesus Christ.

A Light for the Gentiles

To say that God is faithful to Israel is by no means to say that God is confined to Israel, since as early as the promise of the witness to "the ends of the earth" (1:8), it is clear that the gospel extends as far as humanity can be found. The birth narratives in Luke's Gospel, grounded in Israel's hopes, also include Simeon's canticle in which he declares that Jesus is God's own "salvation," and "a light for revelation to the Gentiles" (Luke 1:29-32, esp. vv. 30-32; see also Acts 26:23). While the story of Paul's stay on the island of Malta does not include proclamation or conversion, it does indicate an interest in the exchange of hospitality even with residents of this cultural backwater.

Cornelius, the Gentile whose conversion forces the church to acknowledge God's inclusion of Gentiles, Luke describes as a God-fearer (10:2). Whether there was historically a distinctive group of Gentiles who gravitated to the synagogue but stopped short of taking the full steps toward conversion is a matter of some controversy, but Luke does not hesitate to speak of Gentiles who acknowledge the God of Israel and who often are found in synagogues (e.g., 13:16; 14:11; 16:14; 17:4, 12; 18:7). That is not to say that all Gentile converts are God-fearers, or that Luke has no place for a mission to Gentiles unless they are already connected to the synagogue in some way (Jervell 1988). The proconsul Sergius Paulus (13:4-12), the Philippian jailer and his household (16:25-34), and Dionysius and Damaris (17:34) are among those who "turn to the Lord," and the text gives no indication that any of them was a God-fearer or proselyte to Judaism.

Among both Gentiles and Jews, the response to Christian proclamation is divided. Luke portrays some Gentiles as understanding and receptive, not only those mentioned above but the ones included in the general assessments of 13:48 and 28:28. Yet the Gentiles of Lystra are fickle (14:8-20), those of Athens are curious (17:21), and those of Ephesus are protective of their deity Artemis and her city (19:23-41). Recurrent references to the many gods served by Gentiles are not surprising, since Luke could not escape knowing that the non-Jewish world was saturated with gods and their worship. Not accidentally, those elements of Jewish law that the Jerusalem Council finds essential for Gentiles are precisely the ones most closely associated with idolatry (15:19-20, 29; 21:25).

After Paul's arrest in Jerusalem, a particular group of Gentiles emerges as crucial for the developing plot, namely, Roman officials. This group includes the tribune Claudius Lysias, the governors Felix and Festus, and the centurion Julius. King Agrippa might also be included in this group, since he rules entirely at the whim of Rome. On the one hand, these individuals appear to assist Paul, as when Claudius Lysias rescues Paul from the mob outside the Jerusalem temple and again when he sends Paul to Caesarea to disrupt a plot against Paul's life (21:31-40; 23:16-30). And Festus and Agrippa agree that Paul has done nothing to merit imprisonment (26:30-32). On the other hand, details in the story also reveal these Roman officials as self-serving, as when Felix seeks conversation with the imprisoned Paul in the hope that Paul would give him money (24:26), or when Claudius Lysias sends a letter to Felix that shades the truth about Paul's initial arrest (23:26-30). These officials do not appear to be aggressively hostile to Paul or his proclamation, but they are also not innocent. This pattern has spawned a number of theories about Luke's desire to defend the church to Roman officials (e.g., Cadbury 1958, 308-316) or Roman officials to the church (Walaskay 1983), but the evidence for either reading is slender indeed. It may be that the ambiguous presentation of Roman officials reflects the narrative's ambiguous stance toward anyone outside the gospel. What matters for Luke is that most Roman officials do not attend to the gospel.

LOCATIONS FOR THE JOURNEY

Unless written in utter isolation from all human contact and destroyed immediately following its creation, any literary work has multiple locations. Because of the complex historical setting in which it came about and especially because of its inclusion in the canon of the Christian church and its long history of influence in the church's life, Acts has a variety of locations that influence its interpretation.

Historical Location of Acts

Twenty-first century readers naturally want to know not only the name of the author but what circumstances in the author's life contributed to the shaping of Luke–Acts. Similarly, information about the audience of Acts and its situation seems an urgent need to contemporary readers. But if Luke has given readers little information about Peter and Paul, he is even less inclined to provide information about himself or his audience, who would not have needed the information in any case. And reading through the narrative for hints about the identity of author and audience is a notoriously hazardous enterprise.

Tradition has identified the author of both the Third Gospel and the Acts of the Apostles as Luke, a physician who traveled with Paul. This identification combines several fragile assumptions. First, it supposes that the "we" passages in Acts reflect the actual travels of the author with Paul, a conclusion that critical scholarship has undermined (see below, "Literary Features"). It then identifies this companion as a physician named Luke, based on references in Col 4:14; 2 Tim 4:11; and Phlm 24. Yet many scholars question Paul's authorship of the first two references, and the third merely names Luke as a coworker along with Mark, Aristarchus, and Demas.

Rather than reading the book through this frail tissue of texts, it is best to work with what can be gleaned from the text of Acts itself, using the name "Luke" in deference to tradition. A masculine verbal form employed in self-reference in the preface to the Gospel identifies Luke as male (*parēkolouthēkoti*; Luke 1:3). Luke is probably well-educated and certainly possesses a keen stylistic ability, judging from his facility with a variety of narrative and rhetorical conventions, not to mention his flair for the dramatic and the vivid. As early as the first scene in Luke's Gospel, he displays his deep knowledge of the Old Testament in Greek form (the Septuagint or LXX), which means that he is either a Jew or a Gentile believer with a long acquaintance with the Septuagint by virtue of an early association with the synagogue (i.e., a God-fearer or proselyte to Judaism before being persuaded by Christian proclamation). Luke's interest in Gentile believers may hint that he is himself Gentile, although that conclusion is by no means certain.

If the author is unnamed, at least one intended reader is named, and that is Theophilus. Both the beginning of Luke's Gospel and the beginning of Acts address him directly. Because the name Theophilus means "lover of God" or "beloved of God," students of Luke–Acts have often concluded that Theophilus represents all believers, but symbolic dedications are not frequent in this period (Alexander 1993, 132-33, 188). It was, however, common to dedicate a volume to someone in the hope that the individual would in turn distribute it more widely, meaning that Luke probably has in mind a larger audience than Theophilus alone (Gamble 1995, 84). That extended audience understands Greek, and it almost certainly consists of Christians, as it is difficult to imagine circumstances in which nonbelievers would read beyond the first few lines. They are either informed about Old Testament traditions, or Luke is taking this opportunity to instruct them. Ascertaining their ethnic identity is difficult, but numerous small details suggest that they are Gentiles or at least that Luke has particular concern for the Gentile believers in his audience. For example, Luke uses "Judea" to refer to the whole of Palestine (e.g., see Luke 1:5; 4:44; Acts 2:9; 10:37;

Fitzmyer 1981, 57-59), and the information about Pharisees and Sadducees provided in Acts 23:8 would be superfluous for Jewish readers.

Regarding the question of date of composition, again there is little evidence. The mention of Festus means that Acts must have been written after he became procurator, around 59 CE, and a date after the destruction of the Jerusalem temple in 70 CE is likely (see Luke 19:41-44; 21:20-24). Further indication of a date after 70 CE may be found if it is assumed, as most scholars do, that Luke drew on Mark's Gospel as a major source for his own first volume, since Mark is normally dated around 70 CE. By the middle of the second century, Christian writers reflect knowledge of Acts, although the first who clearly cites from the book is Irenaeus in *Against Heresies* (ca. 180). This usage of Acts means that it must have been both composed and well circulated by then. Those two end points suggest to many scholars that Acts was written sometime in the 80s or 90s.

Why Luke undertook to write not only a Gospel but an additional narrative recounting God's dealings with and through human witness to the gospel is a significant question, and one for which no single answer is satisfactory. Two features of the story do call for particular attention; namely, the pervasive relationship between the narrative Luke recounts and God's earlier dealings with Israel, on the one hand, and the discrediting of other gods, on the other. If the Lukan audience does contain a number of Gentile believers, then these concerns of the narrative reflect two elements of Luke's purpose. First, Luke wishes his Gentile audience to understand that the story of Jesus Christ makes no sense apart from the context of God's ongoing history with Israel. These believers do not need to become Jews themselves, but they do need to be grounded in Israel's story. Second, Luke's endeavor to show the difference between the Jesus story and the worship of other gods could function to protect these Gentile believers from polytheism (see, e.g., Acts 7:48-50; 14:8-20; 15:20, 29; 17:22-31; 19:23-41). Many Gentiles would naturally assume that Israel's God could be served alongside other gods, since their environment was full of gods, each of whom might convey some benefit and none of whom claimed the exclusive loyalty of worshipers. But Luke fiercely rejects any such assumption. Broadly speaking, then, Luke's purpose might be regarded as catechetical, in that he seeks to instruct (especially) Gentile believers in the fundamentals of their tradition and simultaneously to prevent their syncretizing of that tradition (note the explicit reference to instruction in Luke 1:4).

Beyond all that is not known about Luke and his writings, one thing that is entirely clear is that the historical location of Luke–Acts is in the Roman empire. Every city or region that plays a role in Luke–Acts is under direct Roman control. Within that political world, Greek culture has an ongoing impact, especially in the East, as is seen with particular clarity in the accounts of Paul's experiences in Athens and in Ephesus. The relative stability of the period is reflected in the story's assumption that travel can be undertaken with relative ease, for safe roads were in place throughout the regions involved. Also, despite all the difficulties Paul encounters after his arrest in Jerusalem, the story assumes that there are legal processes in place to which individuals may confidently appeal.

Canonical Locations of Acts

For virtually all contemporary readers, the primary location of Acts is canonical. Its position in the Christian Bible between the Gospels and the epistles says much about the lenses through which the book is read. Because Luke and Acts come from the same author, reading the two together is essential (hence the hyphenated designation "Luke–Acts"). Indeed, much in Acts would make little or no sense without some understanding of the Gospel, beginning with the opening address to Theophilus. Not only does the reader need some understanding of "the events that have been fulfilled among us," but numerous echoes of the Gospel contribute to the significance of many events (e.g., Stephen's vision of the Son of Man recalls Jesus' own words during his trial [Luke 22:69; Acts 7:56]; the various indications that Paul is going to Jerusalem and then Rome recall earlier markers along the way of Jesus' journey to Jerusalem [Luke 9:51; 13:22; 17:11; Acts 19:21; 21:13; 25:9-12; 28:14]).

Readers particularly interested in reconstructing the life of the Apostle Paul study Acts in connection with Paul's letters, but opinions vary considerably on how helpful Acts is as a framework into which Paul's letters can be inserted. These questions will largely fall outside the scope of this commentary (see below, "Orientation"). One commonly held view is that, whoever Luke was and whatever his knowledge of the apostle himself, Luke did not have access to Paul's letters. Luke never mentions that Paul wrote letters, and there is very little indication that Luke knows—or that he draws on—the letters.

The larger canonical context, of course, requires that readers understand both Luke's Gospel and Acts in the context of the Old Testament. Luke would have it no other way. Having observed that God is the God of Israel, one needs to unpack that claim in terms of the history of God's activities with Israel included in the Old Testament. More specifically, however, Luke's own narrative cites, alludes to, and shapes itself around the Old Testament.

Ecclesial Location of Acts

One gauge of the church's understanding of Acts emerges in the use of Acts in the lectionary. In the Revised Common Lectionary, passages from Acts appear almost exclusively during Eastertide, where they replace readings from the Old Testament during that season. Outside of the Easter season, only two brief passages appear in the lectionary; 8:14-17 (Year C) and 19:1-7 (Year B) both appear for the Baptism of the Lord, the first Sunday after Epiphany.

Apart from its limited appearance in the lectionary, the churches turn to Acts largely in discussions of church order. Pentecostals take both their name and their understanding of the necessity of baptism by the Holy Spirit from the account in Acts 2. Churches that affirm apostolic succession, and especially the order of deacons, find arguments for those practices in Acts 6.

The summaries at the ends of chapters 2 and 4 have fueled numerous Christian groups who believe that followers of Jesus must share "all things in common." Diverse as they are, all these discussions treat Acts as something close to a blueprint for what the church should be. Yet, as this introduction should indicate, Acts might be more for the church than a fund out of which to draw elements of church order. Acts might remind the church, especially in times of malaise or crisis, that it does not belong to itself, but to the God of Israel, the God who raised Jesus from the dead, and the God whose witness continues within, outside, and even in spite of the church.

A MAP FOR THE JOURNEY

Literary Structure

The literary structure readers discern in Acts reflects to a large extent their perception of the controlling movement of the book. Those who perceive the geographical spread of the gospel as the paramount feature of the story draw on the programmatic statement of 1:8 and often propose a structure conforming to the locations mentioned there, such as the following (Krodel 1986, 47-49):

I. Introduction: Easter to Pentecost (1:1-26)
II. Part 1: The Witness in Jerusalem, Judea, and Samaria (2:1–9:43)
III. Part 2: The Witness to the End of the Earth (10:1–28:28)
IV. Epilogue

By contrast, those who understand Acts as the story of the central figures Peter and Paul often posit a major division at chapter 13 as follows (Marxsen 1968, 166):

Part I. Peter as Main Figure (chapters 1–12)
Part II. Paul as Main Figure (chapters 13–28)

Numerous other analyses exist, but most of them combine features of these two approaches, reading Acts either as the story of the gospel's geographical spread or as the story of the gospel's witnesses (e.g., Brown 1997, 280; Fitzmyer 1998, 119-23).

Neither of these strategies for understanding the literary structure of Acts suffices, however. Acts does, of course, depict the spread of the church's witness, but if Luke's primary concern is to show geographical movement, it is difficult to understand why Paul arrives in Rome and meets believers who are already there, without a word about how the gospel itself arrived there. Given the massive importance of Rome for the world of Luke's day, it would seem obvious that a chronicle of the geographical spread of the church should attend to that arrival. There are comparable instances elsewhere, such as the reference to believers in Lydda and Joppa, locations not earlier mentioned (9:32-43). Similarly, on Paul's final journey to Jerusalem, he seeks out disciples in Tyre (21:14), although nothing has been said earlier of a mission in Tyre. And partitioning Acts into two parts, one of which concerns Peter and the other Paul, functions only by ignoring the pivotal story in Acts 9 of Paul's conversion. It also overlooks Peter's role at the Jerusalem Council in chapter 15.

A more nuanced approach is required in order to attend to the dramatic development within Acts. In the story Luke tells, two events emerge as climactic, namely, the inclusion of Cornelius in 10:1–11:18 and the final defense speech of Paul in chapter 26. The first signals, in terms that cannot be ignored, that God intends to extend the gospel to Gentiles. The second employs the declaration of Paul's innocence to state in Luke's fullest form God's commitment to extend the gospel to Jew and Gentile alike. In both cases, the events that precede pave the way for these crucial moments and the events that follow work out their implications (see Commentary). Taking these two pivotal events as keys to the Lukan "map," the following overall structure emerges (see Table of Contents for individual units):

Prologue	1:1–2:47
Part I	3:1–15:35
Preparation	3:1–9:43
Climactic event	10:1–11:18
Denouement	11:19–15:35
Part II	15:36–28:31
Preparation	15:36–25:27
Climactic event	26:1–26
Denouement	27:1–28:31

Literary Features

One of the reasons the journey through Acts remains a lively one is that Luke draws skillfully on a large and diverse storytelling vocabulary. He makes use of a variety of techniques and employs elements from both Jewish and non-Jewish storytelling traditions.

Frequently a character enters the story briefly and with minimal introduction, disappears from sight, and then reappears when that character has a larger role to play. An example is Paul, who makes a brief entrance (as Saul) at the death of Stephen (7:59-8:1, 3), then disappears and returns in chapter 9 in the role of Chief Persecutor. Events in Acts replay earlier occurrences in Acts, as well as occurrences in the Lukan Gospel, as when Paul performs miracles that resemble those earlier carried out by Peter (cf. 5:12-16 and 19:11-20), or when Paul's determination to go to Jerusalem and then Rome replays Jesus' journey to Jerusalem (cf. Luke 9:51 and Acts 19:21). Repetition enhances the drama of major developments; for example, the Cornelius account of Acts 10:1–11:18 contains numerous internal repetitions, and Paul's conversion is narrated at three distinct places in the book (chapters 9, 22, 26). Numerous Old Testament recitals of God's history with Israel shape Stephen's recital in Acts 7, Peter's healings of Aeneas and Dorcas recall the miracles of Elijah and Elisha. The speeches of Acts reflect Greco-Roman rhetorical conventions, just as the storm and shipwreck of chapter 27 are features familiar from the popular literature of the period.

Encountering such an array of vivid stories, speeches, and summaries, readers understandably want to know where Luke acquired his material and how he has shaped it to his own purposes. Assuming that the preface to Luke's Gospel governs both Luke and Acts, Luke himself indicates that he has drawn on previous accounts (Luke 1:1-4), and scholars have labored with great diligence to distinguish the sources Luke employed (oral or written) from his editing of those sources. A frequent proposal, for example, is that the early traditions stemming from the church in Antioch constituted one of Luke's sources, just as another source may have stemmed from the traditions of the Jerusalem church. One major difficulty with such proposals is readily apparent: unlike the multiple Gospel accounts, which may be compared with one another, there are no parallels to the Acts of the Apostles. Some passages in Paul's letters may touch on events included in Acts as well, such as the apparent parallels between Galatians 2 and Acts 15, but these instances are few and notoriously difficult to compare with one another. Another problem with any source theory is that Luke's own vocabulary and style pervade the book, reflecting at a minimum his free editing of any sources employed.

The "we" passages might appear to offer an exception to that general assertion. In several places in Acts, and without notice or explanation, the narration shifts from third person into first person plural (16:10-17; 20:5-15; 21:1-18; 27:1–28:16). The first such passage, for instance, abruptly moves from the travels of "they" (Paul, Silas, and Timothy) through Phrygia and Galatia, to the determination that "we" should cross into Macedonia (16:6, 10). Not surprisingly, most readers of Acts conclude that these passages reflect the use of an eyewitness account, either that of Luke himself, or that of a companion of Paul that somehow came into Luke's possession. Even the "we" sections, however, reflect a literary style and perspective coherent with the larger narrative, and recent investigation into the practices of ancient historians undermines the notion that a shift in narration indicates a shift in sources (Campbell 2000).

It is best to acknowledge frankly that, whatever sources Luke had, they are no longer available for analysis. That conclusion does not mean Luke had no sources for Acts, but it does mean that the interpretation of Acts is on more solid ground if it refrains from speculation about Luke's treatment of earlier sources, either written or oral.

Especially because Acts has no literary parallels in the New Testament, interpreters have undertaken to classify its literary genre among other ancient writings, in the hope that understanding the genre would facilitate understanding the larger purpose and function of the book. The logic here is persuasive enough. Just as contemporary readers need to know the difference between a poetry anthology and a telephone directory, they also need to know in what literary category Acts belongs. In actual analysis, however, the genre of Acts has proved elusive. Some interpreters insist that Acts should be read as the continuation of the Lukan biography of Jesus, so that it narrates the successors to Jesus (Talbert 1977). Others propose that Acts should be shelved among historical monographs (Palmer 1993), or general histories (Aune 1987, 77-157), or apologetic histories (Sterling 1992), or ancient novels (Pervo 1987). The problem arises in part because most distinctions among genres are not as clear as those between a telephone directory and a poetry anthology; many such distinctions are quite difficult to maintain. In addition, features common to each of these genres appear in Acts, which means that a decision in favor of any one genre necessarily overlooks other important features of the work.

ORIENTATION OF THE COMMENTARY

The uniqueness of Acts as the only New Testament writing that narrates the activity of the apostles after Jesus' ascension, the creation of communities of believers in Jerusalem and beyond, and the travels of Paul as a Christian witness, makes it especially important for those engaged in reconstructing the history of early Christianity. For some interpreters, that means the history Luke himself depicts (i.e., the origins of Christianity in

Antioch or in Corinth) and the quest is to identify the extent to which Luke provides an accurate depiction of those events; for others, it means the church as it exists when Luke writes sometime in the late first century. A number of fine commentaries address these questions, and the bibliography at the end of this book provides some guidance in locating helpful treatments of historical questions.

In this volume, the emphasis lies elsewhere, although the approach taken here is not ahistorical and certainly not antihistorical. Occasionally historical questions do come to the fore, especially when they impinge on a literary or theological matter. It is difficult, for example, to appreciate the crisis at Ephesus apart from an awareness of the centrality of Artemis to life and culture in Ephesus. Generally speaking, however, readers will find this commentary absorbed with questions about Luke's theological perspective as it is conveyed in his narrative, as those questions have too often taken a backseat to what might be called the quest for the "historical Acts of the Apostles."

Whatever information Luke had or did not have, he has shaped his story in a particular way. As Amos Wilder once wrote, all stories "posit a scheme or order in the nowhere of the world" (Wilder 1983, 360). The question that drives this volume concerns the order Luke posits on the chaotic and colorful realm of the world, an order he refers to as "the events that have been fulfilled among us" (Luke 1:1). For that reason, the commentary lingers over details of narration, introductions of characters, matters repeated and others neglected, while it slights the task, for example, of reconciling Luke's chronology with the details supplied by Paul's letters. Convinced that the scheme Luke posits on the "nowhere of the world" has everything to do with the God for whom nothing is impossible (Luke 1:37), it invites contemporary sisters and brothers of Theophilus to follow along in the great journey of the Way.

COMMENTARY

"You Will Be My Witnesses" (1:1–2:47)

The opening chapters of the Acts of the Apostles propel readers immediately into an amazing series of events. Following a brief glance backward at the Gospel of Luke (1:1-5), including a retelling of Jesus' ascension (1:2, 6-11; cf. Luke 24:50-53), the narrator moves quickly to the gathering of Jesus' followers in Jerusalem (1:12-14) and the selection of a replacement for Judas (1:15-26). The outpouring of the Holy Spirit at Pentecost then compels Peter's public proclamation of the gospel (2:1-36) and elicits an overwhelming response from Jews living in Jerusalem (2:37-47). As with the first two chapters of the Third Gospel, here Luke introduces threads that will run throughout this vibrant tapestry: the fulfillment of prophecy, the power of the Holy Spirit, the apostolic witness to Jesus, and the formation of Christian community.

Preface (1:1-11)

The preface begins, as does that of Luke's Gospel, with first-person address to Theophilus. Unlike the Gospel, however, with its clear transition from the preface (1:1-4) to the story of Gabriel's annunciation to Zechariah (1:5-25), the preface to Acts has no such clearly demarcated ending. On the contrary, even with the NRSV's help in smoothing out the Greek, readers may find themselves bewildered by sudden moves from first person ("I wrote") to third person ("Jesus did and taught") and from indirect discourse ("he ordered them not to leave Jerusalem") to direct discourse ("you heard from me"). Compounding this literary muddiness is the fact that the Greek offers no clear syntactical markers to designate the rounding off of the preface. These features sharpen the question: Where does the preface end, and where does the new story begin?

Commentators disagree concerning that question, with some identifying the preface as vv. 1-2 (Krodel 1986, 51; Conzelmann 1987, 3-4; Palmer 1987, 427-38). Others take vv. 1-5 as the preface (Lake and Cadbury 1933, 2; Bruce 1990, 97, 102). Still others identify vv. 1-8 (Haenchen 1971, 144-47), vv. 1-11 (Johnson 1992, 23-32) or vv. 1-14 as the preface (Barrett 1994, 61-64). Despite the literary difficulties within vv. 1-11, they constitute a sense unit that recalls the ending of Luke's Gospel and prepares for events in Jerusalem. Verse 12 marks the beginning of this new (or continuing) story, with the apostles returning to Jerusalem and joining other believers there.

Within the preface, vv. 1-5 are linked together somewhat loosely by conjunctions and a relative pronoun in v. 3 (obscured in the NRSV). These verses move from the opening address of Theophilus toward a scene in which Jesus instructs the apostles. The ascension itself (vv. 6-11) constitutes a discrete scene. Here the apostles question Jesus (v. 6), find their question rejected (v. 7), and then receive a promise about the Holy Spirit and their own role as Jesus' witnesses (v. 8). Verses 9-11 repeat this pattern, as the apostles stare into heaven (as if asking when Jesus would return, vv. 9-10), find that question also rejected by the heavenly messengers (v. 11*a*), and then receive another promise about Jesus' eventual return (v. 11*b*) (Gaventa 1982, 35-36).

◊ ◊ ◊ ◊

With the opening words, Luke connects this new volume to the Third Gospel. Theophilus, to whom Luke also dedicates his Gospel (Luke 1:3), reappears here, again with no hint as to his identity. The name itself means "lover of God" or "beloved of God," prompting the suggestion that Theophilus is not an individual at all but represents all believers. The name is well-attested in this period, however, and symbolic dedications are not (Alexander 1993, 132-33, 188). Perhaps Luke addresses an individual Christian, but through him a larger audience (see Introduction).

In Acts 1:1 Luke describes his first book as concerning "all that Jesus did and taught from the beginning," a characterization that appears to overlook most of Luke 1–2, in which Jesus himself does and says little (apart from 2:41-52). Yet the function of the birth narratives is to introduce and identify Jesus so that Luke's audience will comprehend what Jesus "does and teaches." Perhaps more puzzling than the apparent oversight of the birth stories is that the Greek, when translated somewhat more literally than in the NRSV, speaks of "all the things that Jesus *began* to do and to teach." Someone who had never read or heard a Gospel might anticipate that Acts would supply yet more stories about Jesus' miracles or accounts of his teaching. These are not forthcoming (although note 9:34; 26:23), but Luke does regularly identify the apostles as Jesus' witnesses (e.g., 1:22; 2:32; 3:15; 5:32; 10:39; 13:31), and they carry out miracles in Jesus' name (3:6, 16; 4:7, 10, 30), so that "all that Jesus did and taught" does not cease with the ascension, but continues in the new community. Indeed, Acts ends with a glimpse of Paul teaching "about the Lord Jesus Christ," which strongly suggests that teaching is one of the traits that binds the church to Jesus (28:31).

Verse 2 introduces the apostles. Later Luke identifies them by name (v. 13), but here he identifies them only in relationship to Jesus. The Greek is ambiguous, leaving it unclear whether "through the Holy Spirit" describes Jesus' instruction of the apostles or his selection of them. Luke's emphasis on the role of the Spirit is such that this ambiguity need not be resolved, since neither action would take place apart from the Spirit's presence (cf. 4:25).

With vv. 3-11 Luke expands on the brief summary of vv. 1-2, but the expansion conflicts in some striking ways with the parallel scene at the close of Luke's Gospel. According to the Gospel, the risen Jesus appears to the "eleven and their companions" in Jerusalem on a single occasion, in which he eats (24:36-43), offers instruction (24:44-49), and then leads them to Bethany where he ascends (24:50-53; cf. Acts 1:12). The impression is of a single event, even a single day, rather than the forty days mentioned in Acts 1:3 (and only here). In addition, Jesus' saying about the apostles as witnesses comes as part of the teaching in Jerusalem prior to the ascension itself (Luke 24:48) rather than immediately preceding it (Acts 1:8). The Gospel makes no reference to the presence of two men dressed in white, as mentioned in Acts 1:10.

On the other hand, the two accounts share certain important motifs. Jesus' prophecy regarding the witness "to all nations, beginning from Jerusalem" (Luke 24:47-48) returns in the promise that the apostles will be witnesses "in Jerusalem, in all Judea and Samaria, and to the ends of the earth" (Acts 1:8). The expectation of power from the Holy Spirit plays a role in both accounts (Luke 24:49; Acts 1:8), although they order and articulate the expectation differently.

The differences between the two accounts probably reflect the locations and needs of each. At the conclusion of the Gospel, the story of the ascension focuses on Jesus himself—his fulfillment of scripture, the divine necessity of his death and resurrection, proclamation in his name, his impending gift of the Holy Spirit, and his departure. Although Jesus continues as a central preoccupation in Acts, the focus shifts to the community that Jesus authorizes, a community that gathers and acts in his name. For that reason, perhaps, Acts 1:1-11 imagines a protracted period of instruction and expands the story, including Jesus' promise of the apostles' witness and the promise of Jesus' Parousia.

According to v. 3, one focus of Jesus' teaching during this forty day period is "the kingdom of God." This recalls Luke's Gospel, which regularly characterizes Jesus' preaching as that of the "kingdom of God" (e.g., Luke 4:43; 9:27; 13:29). Acts uses the expression to refer to the preaching of the apostles (8:12; 19:8; 28:23). The fact that the book closes with Paul's continued proclamation of "the kingdom of God" suggests its ongoing importance for Luke as a feature of the church's work (28:31).

The demand that the apostles wait in Jerusalem for the promised gift of the Holy Spirit stretches readers back to the beginning of Luke's Gospel. It also anticipates not only Pentecost but much that lies ahead in Acts (e.g., 4:23-31; 10:44-48; 16:6; 19:1-7). In Luke, the Spirit is active well before John's preaching (Luke 1:35, 41, 67; 2:26), but it is John who first declares the coming baptism of the Holy Spirit (Luke 3:16). Significantly, in the context of John's proclamation, that baptism appears to be one of judgment rather than the empowerment that occurs in Acts 2.

In v. 6 the apostles speak for the first time, asking Jesus whether he will now restore the kingdom. Restoration of the kingdom refers to Israel's political independence, which sometimes prompts interpreters to identify the disciples' question as reflecting short-sighted or flawed messianic expectations (Dunn 1996, 9-10). Yet Luke's own story forthrightly declares at the outset that Jesus will occupy the throne of his father David (Luke 1:32-33), so that the question is not an occasion for reshaping the apostles' understanding of the Messiah. Instead, the question has to do with time and who controls it, as the answer in v. 7 indicates.

In addition to identifying God as the sole determiner of the time, Jesus once more promises the Holy Spirit and declares that the apostles will become witnesses "in Jerusalem, in all Judea and Samaria, and to the ends of the earth." The story that follows conforms so closely to this statement that it serves as something like a table of contents for the entire book of Acts. The apostles will first witness in Jerusalem (2:1–8:3, then in Judea and Samaria (8:4-40; 9:32-43), and later well beyond those regions.

When exactly the witness reaches "the ends of the earth" is unclear. The "ends of the earth" could refer to the Ethiopian eunuch, who comes from a region far from Jerusalem and romantic in the eyes of Luke's readers (8:26-40). Or perhaps Cornelius, the first Gentile convert, marks the movement to "the ends of the earth" (10:1–11:18). Given the importance Luke attaches to Paul's trip to Rome, and the difficulties attending that journey, perhaps Rome itself marks earth's end. Yet the overwhelming political significance of Rome makes it a better candidate for the center rather than the edge of the world. Perhaps the "ends of the earth" even lie beyond the boundary of Luke's story, awaiting the witness of another generation that will continue the work of preaching and teaching unhindered (28:31). The ascension itself Luke depicts in language calculated to signal its importance. In biblical narrative, clouds often accompany occasions of divine activity, as in Moses' encounters with God (Exod 19:9, 16; 20:21; 24:15-18). Similarly, divine messengers often accompany major events in Luke and Acts (e.g., Luke 1:11, 26; 24:4; Acts 10:3). That here there are two such messengers only heightens the significance of the occasion.

The words of these two messengers reinforce Jesus' command that the apostles return to Jerusalem; they are not to dawdle here but, presumably, to do what has been commanded. In addition, however, the messengers declare that Jesus will return. Their words have a near humorous quality, as they identify Jesus "who has been taken up from you into heaven," as if the apostles have somehow forgotten who he was. Three times they refer to heaven, underscoring that as the place of Jesus' presence (see also 3:21; 7:56).

◊ ◊ ◊ ◊

These verses reintroduce characters and themes from the Third Gospel but, more important, they constitute the overture to the Acts of the Apostles. Luke touches on several of his grand themes here, if only briefly: the Holy Spirit, the apostles as witnesses to Jesus, and the geographical movement of that witness.

Behind and within all these themes stands the most important conviction of the story—that God is the prime agent in what happens. What Jesus teaches is God's kingdom (v. 3). John and Jesus have told them to expect the Holy Spirit, but it comes as "the promise of the father" (v. 4). The restoration of the kingdom, similarly, comes about only when God determines it (v. 7). Strictly speaking, despite its traditional title, Luke's second volume concerns neither the apostles' actions, nor those of the church as a whole, for behind everything stands God's plan.

The promise of Jesus' return (v. 11) raises the much-disputed question of Luke's eschatology. In his highly influential study of Lukan theology, Conzelmann argued that Luke writes to a community whose eschatological expectation has faltered, and he interprets the role of the church as a substitute for the return of Jesus, now projected into an indefinite future (Conzelmann 1961). In light of the other promises made and fulfilled in Luke–Acts, it is more appropriate to understand v. 11 as a reliable promise, instead of as an indefinite postponement of Jesus' return (Gaventa 1982, 37; Carroll 1988, 126-27).

Preparations in Jerusalem (1:12-26)

Two distinct literary units depict the community's obedient response to Jesus' instructions. The first, vv. 12-14, takes the form of a summary describing the group, its place, and its activities. Several such summaries follow in Acts, and they often mark significant developments in the church's life (e.g., 2:43-47; 9:31; 12:24). The second unit, vv. 15-26, a scene rather than a summary, contains a narrative aside that interrupts Peter's speech (vv. 18-19) but provides the reader with crucial information.

◊ ◊ ◊ ◊

Returning to Jerusalem (1:12-14)

The summary description of the community gathered in Jerusalem notes that the apostles returned there from "the mount called Olivet" (v. 12; cf. Luke 24:50 which locates the ascension at Bethany, a village on the east side of the mount of Olives). The fact that Luke specifies the distance from Jerusalem suggests that he does not expect the reader to know either Olivet or its location. In addition, the reference to sabbath law implies that the reader has some acquaintance with Mosaic law.

With the ominous exception of Judas, the names on the list of v. 13 are identical to those in Luke 6:14-16. Here Luke has altered the order slightly, however. Significantly, Peter's name is followed by that of John rather than Andrew, perhaps because of John's presence in the early chapters of Acts (e.g., 3:1-4, 11; 4:1, 19-23). In addition to Peter and John, only James appears again in the pages of Acts after this summary (12:2).

Although Luke identifies only one of the women by name, he does report their presence in Jerusalem as well. Some commentators deduce that these women are the wives of the apostles (a supposition fed by the fifth-century manuscript Bezae, which adds that children were present as well), but nowhere in Acts does Luke mention wives of the apostles. More telling is the fact that Luke's Gospel does draw attention to women who traveled with Jesus (8:1-3), who watched at the cross (23:49, 55-56), and to whom angelic figures announced his resurrection (24:1-11), which makes it quite likely that these women are indeed followers of Jesus rather than simply followers of their husbands.

Luke has not mentioned Mary by name since the end of the infancy narrative in Luke 2. Her reappearance here in Acts forges another link to the introduction to Luke's Gospel. More significantly, it signals that she does stand with the community of Jesus' followers, something that has remained unsettled since the final scene of the infancy narrative (see Luke 2:41-52; Gaventa 1995, 66-69). There, despite her earlier consent to Gabriel's annunciation, Mary does not understand Jesus' actions, and the remainder of the Gospel narrative leaves it tantalizingly unclear what her relationship is to Jesus and his mission (see, e.g., 8:19-21; 11:27-28). She appears only here in Acts, but Jesus' brother James emerges as spokesman in chapter 15 and again in 21:18 (see also 12:17).

Luke's terse description of the group's activity merits attention. Translated more literally than in the NRSV, the beginning of v. 14 reads "these all were persisting together." "Together" (*homothymadon*) is a word Luke uses often in these early chapters to emphasize the unity of the Jerusalem community (e.g., 2:46; 4:24; 5:12). That the gathering is not an end in itself becomes clear with the added words, "to prayer." Throughout Acts, believers engage in prayer together (e.g., Acts 1:24; 2:42; 6:6; 8:15; 13:3) just as Luke's Gospel regularly depicts Jesus in prayer (see, e.g., Luke 3:21; 6:12; 9:18; 22:45; Crump 1992).

Replacing Judas (1:15-26)

By sharp contrast with the presumably small group mentioned in vv. 12-14, v. 15 specifies that one hundred twenty people comprise the Jerusalem community. Various attempts have been made to identify the significance of this number. For example, some connect it with requirements at Qumran that one priest be available for each group of ten community members (1QS 6:3-4), and others identify it with a mishnaic text that specifies one hundred twenty as the minimum number of men required for a city to have a ruling council (*m. Sanh.* 1:6). These connections are slender, however; the number probably serves primarily to indicate that the community's strength already extends well beyond the small circle of the apostles and the women who had traveled with Jesus. During this period of prayerful waiting ("In those days," v. 15) Peter emerges as the spokesman, fulfilling Jesus' admonition in Luke 22:32. He will continue in this role through the conversion of Cornelius (10:1–11:18). Then a shift occurs. Although Peter does speak at the Jerusalem Council (15:7-12), it is James rather than Peter who takes the more prominent role. Following the Jerusalem Council, Peter vanishes from the narrative. By contemporary standards, Peter is a central character, even though in Acts Luke demonstrates little interest in depicting his human characters as individuals or as independent agents.

The speech that follows concerns the replacement of Judas. Although all the Gospels identify Judas as the betrayer of Jesus, only Matthew and Luke account for him after Jesus' arrest. The stories differ significantly, in that Matthew presents a repentant Judas who first returns his bribe money to the priests and then hangs himself in remorse (27:3-10). Acts, of course, makes no mention of repentance. Given the deaths of others who act in opposition to the word of God, Luke probably also views this death as divine retribution (see 5:1-11 and 12:20-23). Matthew and Luke both associate Judas with a piece of land, and they both identify it as "Field of Blood," although they account for it differently. Taken together, these traditions suggest that Judas met with an untimely and even gruesome death, but few histori-cal details can be wrung from them (see also Papias, *Catena in Acta i*, in Routh 1846-48, 1:9).

Whatever became of the historical Judas, the Lukan story con-tains several interesting features. First, it provides Luke with another occasion for connecting Jesus' death with scripture. Divine necessity includes not only Jesus' death and resurrection (Luke 24:26-27, 44-46; Acts 2:22-24), but even the fate of Judas and the need to identify his replacement. The quotations in v. 20 come from Pss 69:25 (LXX 68:26) and 109:8 (LXX 108:8) respectively. Among the minor changes introduced in the quotations is the change from plural to singular in the first line of Ps 69:25; where the psalm refers to "their" homestead, Peter speaks of "his" as better fitting the situation. Luke's emphasis on the role of the Holy Spirit emerges again here as he identifies the Spirit as the voice behind the psalms (v. 16; cf. 4:25). In addition, the story employs intriguing language concerning Judas and his place among the twelve. Peter initially recalls that Judas had a "share" (*klēros*) in the ministry, and the same word appears in v. 26 for the casting of lots and the lot (*klēros*) that falls on Matthias. By contrast with Luke's Gospel, where ministry (*diakonia*) includes the work of the women traveling with Jesus (Luke 8:3; see also Luke 22:26-27), here it designates the specific task of witnessing to Jesus' resurrec-tion and acquires the vocabulary of apostleship (v. 25).

Verse 25 also plays on the language of "place," as the vacancy among the Twelve has come about because Judas went to "his own place." This expression could refer to a place of final reward (as in LXX Isa 33:14; Tob 3:6; *1 Clem.* 5:4, 7; 44:5; Ign. *Magn.* 5:1; see also Pol. *Phil.* 9; *Barn.* 19:1). Yet Luke sets this place of Judas over against his former place among the twelve apostles. He also emphasizes the change of location with the expression "Judas turned aside to go to . . . ." Similar movement is reported in the Gospel, when "Satan entered into Judas called Iscariot" who then "went away" to consult the enemies of Jesus (Luke 22:3-4; see also 22:53). Judas's physical movement may mirror movement from one sphere of power to another, a move-ment we would term apostasy (Brown 1969, 82-84).

The selection process itself proves intriguing, both for the personnel involved and for the means employed. Two persons fit the requirements identified by Peter (on which see below). Neither of them has appeared earlier in Luke–Acts, and neither appears again, which indicates that the dynamic of the story has little to do with the etiology of the apostleship of Matthias.

By contrast with the crucifixion, which associates the casting of lots with the betrayal and humiliation of Jesus (Luke 23:34*b*), here the casting of lots functions to identify the replacement of the one who served as agent for that betrayal. As a means of decisionmaking, it appears in a variety of Jewish sources (e.g., Lev 16:8; 1QS 5:3; *m. Yoma* 4:1). Although people might cast lots in a number of settings and with varying understandings, v. 24 leaves no doubt that God is the one making the decision about where the "lot" would fall. Interpreters occasionaly highlight the fact that the community does not employ this method again after Pentecost and thereby suggest a denigration of it, but it needs to be noted that Acts depicts the communication of God's will to the community in a multitude of ways, no one of which appears to be normative.

Most important, the story defines the requirements for apostleship. The successor to Judas must be someone who was associated with Jesus throughout his ministry. The fact that Luke repeats this requirement (both "all the time that the Lord Jesus went in and out among us" and "from the baptism of John until the day when he was taken up from us") indicates its importance. The presence of women in the group does not mean that one of them may be chosen, since Peter's statement specifies that the new witness will be a male (*anēr*). The specification does not require the general exclusion of women from the tasks of witnessing, however. If it did, then Paul, Barnabas, and James would also have to be excluded, since none of them was present throughout Jesus' ministry.

This definition puts Luke's account in conflict with Paul's letters in two ways. First, Paul regularly identifies himself as an apostle of Christ (Rom 1:1; 1 Cor 1:1; 2 Cor 1:1; Gal 1:1). Despite his prominence in Acts, he does not meet the criteria for apostleship and remains a witness additional to that of the apostles (see 13:31-32). For Luke, the term "apostle" is virtually identified with the Twelve. Only in the most incidental way does Luke refer to Paul as *apostolos* (14:4, 14). Second, Paul does not hesitate to name Junia as an *apostolos* (Rom 16:7), a title Luke would apparently withhold from her.

◊   ◊   ◊   ◊

Although located just prior to the dramatic story of the outpouring of the Holy Spirit and the conversion of three thousand people, this scene contains dark undertones similar to those sounded in Luke 1–2 by Simeon's second oracle ("and a sword will pierce your own soul . . ." 2:35). The community has gathered in obedience to Jesus' instructions, they wait together for the anticipated gift of the Holy Spirit, but it is also clear that Satan is still at work. Satan filled Judas, Judas received a reward for his unrighteousness, and now Judas has gone to "his own place." Luke plays on the association between money and evil that emerges time and again in both his volumes.

Despite that somber reminder of the resistance to God's will, Matthias is selected to become a witness to the resurrection (v. 22). Theologically, this choice of words is revealing. Beginning with Peter's sermon at Pentecost, the testimony of the apostles has Jesus' resurrection as a primary focus, not his ministry nor his crucifixion (2:32). That feature remains a constant from Pentecost through Paul's final defense speech, in which he reiterates that the resurrection is what Israel has hoped for all along (26:6-8, 23).

Divine necessity drives this episode, as it does much of the action in Luke–Acts. Peter remarks that one of the appropriate men "must become a witness," again invoking the language of divine necessity ("must" translates the Greek *dei*, "it is necessary"). The completion of the twelve functions symbolically to represent the twelve tribes of Israel (Luke 22:28-30), of course, although it remains unclear exactly how the apostles stand in relationship to those tribes. Equally important, the fact that this is divine necessity means it is not a merely pragmatic decision that twelve apostles will be needed to achieve particular goals; rather, the number is determined by God's own plan.

The Holy Spirit and Its Aftermath (2:1-47)

With the ascension of Jesus, the gathering of believers in Jerusalem, and the identification of an apostle to replace Judas, the stage is now set for the outpouring of the Spirit, an event that has been promised again and again but one that still comes with startling force. As fascinating as the scene depicting the Spirit's arrival is (2:1-13), Luke does not dwell on the mechanics of the manifestation; instead, Pentecost serves largely to introduce the Spirit's work. On this occasion the Spirit empowers Peter to speak and enables amazing growth in the community's size and conduct. Peter's speech (2:14-40) occupies a pivotal place in Luke–Acts, because it interprets what has already happened in the death and resurrection of Jesus and because it offers essential clues for understanding what is about to unfold in Jerusalem and beyond. The speech consists of four distinct movements, the first three of which begin with direct address by Peter to the audience. The final movement also begins with direct address, this time from the audience to Peter and his colleagues:

v. 14	"Men of Judea and all who live in Jerusalem"
v. 22	"You that are Israelites"
v. 29	"Fellow Israelites" [lit. "Brothers"]
v. 37	"Brothers"

The aftermath of Peter's speech provides a summary report about the life of this emerging new community (vv. 41-47).

◊ ◊ ◊ ◊

The Coming of the Spirit (2:1-13)

Pentecost, the harvest festival identified in the Hebrew Bible as the Feast of Weeks (Exod 23:16; 34:22; Lev 23:15-21; Num

28:26-31; Deut 16:9-10), provides the setting for the arrival of the Spirit. At least since the time of Augustine, interpreters have attempted to find significance in an association of Pentecost with the giving of the Torah, and some Jewish texts roughly contemporary with Luke do appear to associate Pentecost and covenant renewal (*Jub.* 1:1; 6:17-19; 14:20; and cf. 1QS 1:8–2:25; Fitzmyer 1998, 233-37). Most Jewish texts connecting Pentecost with Torah are substantially later than Acts, however, and Calvin may have been closer to the mark when he observed that by specifying Pentecost Luke is explaining why Jerusalem would have been full of people, both residents and pilgrims (1965, 49; and cf. Acts 20:16). Alongside this temporal setting, it is equally important to notice Luke's assertion that "they were all together in one place" (v. 1), an assertion that cries out for attention. Luke does not say merely that they were together, or all were present, but instead "all together" *and* "in one place." Neither the number of persons present nor the place is specified. Because the immediately preceding verse refers to the apostles, Luke might have only the Twelve in mind. Yet the selection of Matthias occurs in the presence of the larger community (see 1:15), and the fact that the quotation from Joel includes daughters and female slaves makes it more likely that the outpouring of the Spirit encompasses the larger group (a view that was held at least as early as Chrysostom, *Homilies on Acts* 4 [NPNF 11:25-26]).

The extravagant production Luke describes in vv. 2-3 has all the hallmarks of the divine presence. Both wind and fire are regularly associated with theophanies (e.g., Exod 3:2; 13:21-22; 19:18; 1 Kgs 19:11-12; Isa 66:15; 4 Ezra 13:1-3, 8-11). Beyond understanding that these are traditional signs of the divine, it is futile to attempt to reconstruct the scene. What exactly "divided tongues" are or what it means that they rested on each person is quite unclear. What is clear is that the Holy Spirit pervades the gathered community so that all are in its grasp.

No private event, the arrival of the Spirit simultaneously involves a public venue and public accountability. In some unexplained way, the walls of the house dissolve and the community finds itself outdoors and in the presence of Jews "from every nation under heaven living in Jerusalem." The notion of Jews living in "every nation" might seem odd except that for centuries Jews had emigrated for a variety of reasons. By the first century, far more Jews lived outside Palestine than within it. Many Jews made the pilgrimage to Jerusalem for Passover and stayed through Pentecost; other diaspora Jews lived in Jerusalem for reasons of commerce or settled there late in life (note also 6:9).

The list of peoples in vv. 9-11 has counterparts elsewhere (Gen 10:2-31; *Syb. Or.* 3:156-95, 205-209; Philo, *Embassy* 281-83; *Flaccus* 45-46), as various writers testify to the presence of Jews and the adoption of Jewish practices in a wide range of places in the Roman world (see also Josephus, *Ag. Ap.* 2.282; *J.W.* 2.398). Luke's list does not so closely resemble any other such list as to suggest literary dependence, however, and this list serves less to emphasize the geographical spread of Judaism than to signal the imminent spread of the gospel. What appears to control the selection and ordering of the list is a grouping of locations around the four compass points, viewed through the assumption that Jerusalem is the center of the earth (cf. Ezek 5:5; *Jub.* 8:19; *1 En.* 26:1). The first group begins east of Jerusalem (Parthians, Medes, Elamites, Mesopotamians) and then moves back to Judea; the second group moves north from Jerusalem (Cappadocia, Pontus, Asia, Phrygia, and Pamphylia) and then back in the direction of Jerusalem; the third group moves west from Jerusalem to north Africa, Rome, and then again back to Jersualem by means of Crete; and the fourth compass point is represented by the collective "Arabs" (Bauckham 1995, 417-27). This observation helps to explain one of the most puzzling features of the list, the inclusion of Judea: Why refer to Judeans as if they were resident aliens?

Luke's understanding of Spirit-filled speech differs from that of Paul, the only other New Testament writer to refer to this phenomenon. First Corinthians uses the same word (*glōssa*), but the context makes it clear that Paul has in mind ecstatic speech that requires the presence of an interpreter (1 Cor 12:10, 28; 13:1, 8; 14:1-33, 37-40). For Luke, however, the speech is that of other languages. Neither does Paul nor anyone else speak of some originating gift of the Holy Spirit. Attempts to reconcile the two accounts are more passionate than persuasive; what Paul and Luke share is an awareness of the Spirit's power and its unpredictability.

This miraculous event prompts a divided response, as gospel proclamation will do later in Acts (e.g., 4:1-4; 17:32; 28:24). Some observers are "amazed and perplexed" at what it might mean, while others offer the more pedestrian interpretation that the believers are drunk. The latter view may not be merely cynical, since Plutarch reports that wine augments prophetic speech (*Oracles at Delphi* 406B; *Obsolescence of Oracles* 437E; cf. Mic 2:11).

Peter's Response (2:14-40)

The Prophecy of Joel (2:14-21): The charge of drunkenness impels Peter to speak. He begins with the conventions of oratory eliciting attention for what will follow (v. 14), denies the charge of drunkenness, and then interprets the Spirit's outpouring by means of a quotation from Joel (vv. 17-21). Peter identifies this event with Scripture but, more important, with God's own promise of the Spirit in the "last days."

Luke introduces several telling alterations into the quotation, which comes from the LXX of Joel 3:1-5 (NRSV 2:28-32). Unlike the original, which opens with "Then afterward," here the opening words are "In the last days" (v. 17), a change that clearly connects the event of Pentecost with the eschatological promise of Jesus' return. As in 1:6-11, where the promises of the Spirit, the witness, and the return of Jesus are interconnected, here also the Spirit's presence is connected with the eschaton.

Luke alters the LXX text to state God's role in the event even more sharply. "God declares" (v. 17) does not appear in Joel and serves to make explicit whose words these are. In addition, v. 18 adds "my" before the phrase "slaves, both men and women," so that the words no longer refer only to a socio-economic category but to those who are obedient to God (see Luke 1:38; 2:29; Acts 4:29; 16:17).

The quotation not only identifies the present outpouring of the Spirit with scriptural prophecy; it also underscores the prophecy that is to be expected from the new community. The words "and they shall prophesy" at the end of v. 18 do not appear in Joel, and their addition here emphasizes the prophetic character of this community. Despite the claim that both men and women are to prophesy, the story that follows never narrates the content of a woman's prophecy, although it does refer to female prophets (21:9; cf. Luke 2:36).

A final small alteration occurs in v. 19, where Luke adds the words "above," "signs," and "below," emphasizing the inescapability of these events (i.e., they happen everywhere) and also preparing for Peter's statement about Jesus in v. 22. The apocalyptic imagery of vv. 19-20 serves to underscore the eschatological context of the Pentecost event; for Luke the giving of the Holy Spirit secures the promise that "the Lord's great and glorious day" will indeed come.

The quotation culminates in the assurance of salvation for those who call on the Lord's name, an assurance that touches on central issues in Luke–Acts. From the birth narrative on, Luke has insisted that God is acting in Jesus for the salvation of women and men (Luke 1:69, 77; 2:30). This salvation is not a merely private and spiritual affair, but concerns Israel as a people and later the Gentiles also as God's people (e.g., Luke 1:69-71, 77; Acts 13:47; 28:28). In the context of Joel, the "name of the Lord" refers to God, but later in Acts it is the Lord Jesus' name that the apostles invoke (e.g., 3:16; 4:10), and a clear distinction between the two is difficult to support (see Introduction).

Jesus of Nazareth (2:22-28): Having solemnly declared the significance of this occasion, Peter turns to the proclamation of God's action in Jesus Christ. Phrases such as "attested to you by God" and "signs that God did" make it clear that the initiative comes from God, but English translations scarcely do justice to this feature of the speech. In the Greek, a single sentence begins in v. 22 with "Jesus of Nazareth" and extends through v. 24; "God raised" (v. 24) is the main subject and verb, so that the assertions preceding in vv. 22-23 are subordinated to this primary action.

The complex sentence makes three distinct claims, all of which have to do with actions taken by God. First, God acted through Jesus by means of powerful deeds (v. 22). This statement recalls the miracles of Jesus' ministry and anticipates those that the apostles will do in his name; both stem from God. Implied but not stated here is that this evidence, although known ("as you yourselves know") did not secure the response it merited. Second, Jesus died, both as a result of God's plan and by virtue of the action of those present. At first glance, this accusation stands in conflict with Luke's Gospel, since it is the rulers and not the people who plan Jesus' death (as in Luke 22:1-6; 23:1-12). Yet the people themselves do turn against Jesus, and it is their demand that finally persuades Pilate to act (23:13). That it happened through "those outside the law" or, more literally, "lawless ones," may refer to the fact that the Roman officials are Gentiles (i.e., outside the law's scope). It could also refer more pointedly, however, to Jesus' death as a lawless act brought about by Jews. Third, God raised Jesus from the dead. The repetitive formulation of this third claim indicates its central importance: (1) God raised Jesus, (2) God freed him from death (cf. Ps 18:4-5 [LXX 17:5-6]; 116:3 [LXX 114:3]), (3) death could not hold Jesus in its power.

This second part of the sermon culminates in the quotation from Psalm 16:8-11 (LXX 15:8-11), a psalm quoted in a parallel context in Paul's speech in 13:35 and nowhere else in the New Testament. The quotation serves as an important transition from this section of the speech (vv. 22-28) to the one that follows. It both expands on the claim of v. 24 that Jesus could not remain in the grip of death, and it anticipates the contrast between David and Jesus that begins in v. 29.

Lord and Messiah (2:29-36): The direct address, "Fellow Israelites" [lit., "Brothers"], opens the third part of the sermon, in which the topic of the resurrection and its consequences dominates. Having introduced the psalm of David, Peter now employs David in two ways. First, Peter contrasts Jesus with David, in that David remains buried and Jesus does not (see also v. 34). As evidence of David's death, all have the tradition of his burial place (Neh 3:16; Josephus, *J.W.* 1.61; *Ant.* 13.249). Second, David serves as a prophet of Jesus' resurrection, which Peter finds in Ps 16:10, although he alters the pronoun from second person to first, making it better fit the context.

With vv. 32-36, the sermon moves to its climactic moment. Not only has God raised Jesus from the dead, but Jesus now sits at God's right hand (see the quotation from Ps 16 in v. 25, in which David sees Jesus at his own right hand). The outpouring of the Spirit has come from God (see v. 17), but it comes through Jesus as God's agent. The final quotation in vv. 34-35, taken from LXX Ps 109:1 (NRSV 110:1), reinforces both Jesus' exaltation and the expectation of a future victory over God's enemies (cf. 1 Cor 15).

Several features of v. 36 enhance its solemn character. The phrase "let someone know" or "let it be known" draws attention to the statements that follow (see also 4:10). By identifying "the entire house of Israel" as those who need to know, Peter further emphasizes the significance of the occasion (see 4:10; 13:24). "With certainty" (*asphalēs*) recalls the prologue to the Gospel, where Luke asserts that he will narrate "the truth" (or, more literally, "the certainty"; Luke 1:4) about events. The content of the declaration falls into two parts, each of which begins by identifying Jesus as the object ("both Lord and Messiah," "this Jesus") and each of which ends by identifying the actor and action taken with respect to Jesus ("God has made," "you crucified"). The sharp juxtaposition of God's action with that of humanity underscores the blindness of those who crucified Jesus and prompts the audience to respond.

The Promise for All (2:37-40): Often in Acts, speeches come to an end when they are interrupted (e.g., 7:54; 10:44; 22:22). This inaugural speech works in a slightly different way, however; here the audience interrupts, but the interruption moves the sermon to its final appeal rather than stopping it entirely. The crowd asks, "Brothers, what should we do?", the same question asked by those who heard John the Baptist (see Luke 3:10). Peter's answer also echoes John's, by calling for repentance and baptism (Luke 3:3, 8; cf. Acts 10:47-48; 11:18). In the chapters that follow, baptism signals entry into the fellowship of believers (8:12, 16; 10:47-48; 16:15; 19:5).

Peter's comment in v. 38*b* about the Holy Spirit requires careful attention. A simple copulative conjunction (*kai,* "and") joins this statement to the one preceding it, which negates any attempt to understand the Spirit as the necessary result of baptism. Later episodes in Acts provide evidence of the Spirit's independence of any such formulaic interpretation (e.g., 8:16; 10:44-48). Neither does the gift of the Spirit express itself in a single manifestation, such as that of glossolalia, since Luke shows the Spirit at work in a variety of ways (4:8; 8:29, 39; 13:9; 16:6).

Verse 39 extends to the audience a promise. The content of this promise remains unspecified; although it includes the elements in v. 38, it surely also includes salvation (v. 21) and, more generally, incorporation into the community of those who are obedient to God and who wait for the return of Jesus and fulfillment of God's promises. If the content of the promise remains undefined, its range does not. It extends temporally to incorporate both those present and the generations that will follow, and it extends geographically to incorporate those who are "far away." Although Peter says nothing specific about the "far away" including Gentiles, this claim anticipates the extent of that promise to "the ends of the earth" (1:8). That it is God who calls powerfully reinforces the quotation of Joel at 2:17-21.

Luke rounds off Peter's speech in two ways. First, he indicates that Peter continues to speak (see Luke 3:18). His warning about "this corrupt generation" again recalls John the Baptist (Luke 3:7) and Old Testament passages as well (Deut 32:5; Ps 78:8). Although "save yourselves" is technically possible as a translation of the Greek, it would be better translated as "receive salvation"; in no sense does Luke understand that human beings are capable of self-salvation any more than they are able to baptize themselves (Barrett 1994, 156).

Daily Life in the Community (2:41-47)

The second conclusion to Peter's speech comes in the description of the response it arouses. Luke employs a number of similar statements that summarize the activity of the community and especially the work of God within it (e.g., 4:32-37; 5:12-16). Assessing the accuracy of the number reported either here or later (4:4) is impossible, although it is worth noticing that such reports soon disappear and a divided response to Christian preaching becomes the norm (e.g., 13:43-45; 17:32). At this early stage, however, growth is continuous (see v. 47).

Luke does not dwell on accounting but quickly turns to characterize the activity of the community, and it is a community, not merely an aggregation of autonomous individuals. Luke speaks of this in several ways, stressing their fellowship and worship (v. 42), underlining their being "together," and explaining their sharing of all things in common (vv. 44-45). Luke's details sound very much like descriptions from other philosophical and religious groups that stressed the importance of friendship. In descriptions of other philosophical and religious groups of the period, such claims serve to demonstrate the close friendship that obtains, and probably the same dynamic is at work here (see, e.g., Plato, *Republic* 449C; Plato, *Laws* 5.739C; Philo, *Abr.* 235; Seneca, *Epistles* 90.3; Strabo, *Geography* 7.3.9). Later stories reveal occasions when believers did not live up to this ideal (5:1-11; 6:1-6); nevertheless, Luke regularly contrasts the appropriate use of possessions with those who would exploit possessions or exploit the gospel in service of their own greed (e.g., 8:9-24; 16:16-19; 19:13-20).

Response to Pentecost comes also from those outside the community. "Everyone" stands in awe (v. 43), as the apostles now undertake the "wonders and signs" previously brought about through Jesus (v. 22). The community itself meets with approval, just as Jesus is said to encounter good will early in Luke's Gospel (Luke 2:52).

◊ ◊ ◊ ◊

Because Luke depicts the Holy Spirit's activity at Pentecost in such dramatic terms, students of Acts sometimes treat this passage in narrow isolation and forget that the Holy Spirit figures not only in Luke's two volumes but throughout the Old Testament as well (see, e.g., Judg 3:10; 11:29; 1 Sam 10:10; 19:23). The Spirit's action at Pentecost proves decisive because of its empowerment of the church for life and witness, but the Spirit that acts here is no different from the Spirit that brings about Mary's conception of Jesus (Luke 1:35) or the Spirit that descends at Jesus' baptism (Luke 3:22).

Although prompted by the Spirit's astonishing action, the bulk of Peter's speech concerns God's action in Jesus, particularly in his resurrection. According to the Pentecost speech, the crucifixion was a human mistake, which God corrected through the resurrection. This interpretation contrasts sharply with that of other New Testament texts; for example, Hebrews interprets the crucifixion through the lens of the sacrificial system, and Paul interprets it as itself a moment of revelation. Such elements are not entirely absent from Luke–Acts, but the emphasis falls on the resurrection. In the resurrection, God demonstrates conclusively that Jesus is God's agent, and because of the resurrection Jesus is at God's right hand (v. 33). The crucifixion can be said to be both an act for which human beings are culpable and part of God's plan.

Neither the Holy Spirit's outpouring nor the resurrection of Jesus exists without the activity of God. This chapter draws attention to God's speech (v. 17), God's action through Jesus' miracles (v. 22), God's foreknowledge of the crucifixion (v. 23), God's raising of Jesus from death (vv. 24, 32), God's exaltation (v. 33), God's promise (v. 33), and God's call to humanity (vv. 39, 47). In other words, nothing in this story happens apart from God's design and intent.

PART ONE

WITNESS AND RESISTANCE IN JERUSALEM (3:1–8:3)

The events of Pentecost not only fulfill the promise of the Spirit's empowerment but also inaugurate the witness to Jesus. This section of Acts provides ample indication of the witness of the apostles in Jerusalem (1:8). In response to that witness, many join the believers, and the community continues to generate awe. Alongside this reception of the gospel, however, grows a negative reaction that culminates in Stephen's death and the flight of believers in the face of persecution.

A Healing Prompts a Second Speech (3:1-26)

As at Pentecost, here also a miraculous event compels Peter to serve as a witness to the gospel. This time the event takes the form of a miracle that corresponds to the pattern of Jesus' miracles in the Synoptic Gospels (vv. 1-10). First, the afflicted individual appears on the scene, together with some indication of the severity of his or her condition (v. 2; e.g., Luke 5:18-19). Second, the healer intervenes, most often with little or no elaboration of the healing itself (vv. 3-7*a*; e.g., Luke 5:20-24). Third, the healed individual acts in some way that demonstrates the success of the healing (vv. 7*b*-8; e.g., Luke 5:25). Finally, bystanders respond with amazement (vv. 9-10; e.g., Luke 5:26).

Unlike most healing stories in the Synoptic Gospels, however, this one is followed by a speech of explanation. In general, this speech resembles the form of the Pentecost speech. It opens by connecting the healing to Jesus and returns to the charge that Jerusalem Jews were responsible for his death (vv. 12-16), then calls for repentance (vv. 17-21) and identifies Jesus as a prophet like Moses (vv. 22-26).

◊ ◊ ◊ ◊

A Healing in Jesus' Name (3:1-10)

Although the story begins abruptly, with little transition from chapter 2, important factors nevertheless tie it to the preceding description of community life. Confirming the report that believers spent "much time together in the temple" (2:46), Peter and John enter the temple precincts for prayer. The healing itself provides a vivid illustration of the "wonders and signs" ascribed to the apostles (2:43). Connections extend not only to the previous section of Acts, however, but further back into the early chapters of Luke's Gospel, where Jesus heals a paralytic and discusses with the scribes and Pharisees his authority to do so (Luke 5:17-26).

The story in Acts occurs at "three o'clock in the afternoon," in the vicinity of the "Beautiful Gate." According to Josephus, the daily sacrifices required by the Torah (see Exod 29:38-39; Lev 6:20) occurred early in the morning and at three o'clock in the afternoon (Josephus, *Ant.* 14.65-66; see also *Ant.* 3.237). Ancient sources make no mention of a "Beautiful Gate," but it may coincide with what the Mishnah identifies as the Nicanor Gate, which was constructed of bronze (see *m. Mid.* 1:4; 2:3; Josephus, *J.W.* 5.201).

Like most biblical healing stories, this one shows little interest in the individual who receives the healing. He is described simply as having been "lame from birth," a condition about which Luke demonstrates considerable concern (e.g., Luke 7:22; 14:13, 21; Acts 8:7; 14:8-10). Commentators sometimes argue from Lev 21:16-18 that his handicap would have prohibited him full access to temple worship (see also *m. Šabb.* 6:8; Witherington 1998, 173-74), but those restrictions apply only to priests who are offering sacrifices. More probably, the man's daily station at a temple gate offered him access to the considerable traffic into the temple area. Since the bestowing of alms is understood to reflect a virtuous life, both in Luke–Acts (e.g., Luke 11:41; 12:33; Acts 9:36; 10:2-4) and elsewhere (e.g., Tob 4:7-11; 12:8-9; Sir 3:30; 12:3; Matt 6:2-4; *Syb. Or.* 2:78-80; *Did.* 15:4; *2 Clem.* 16:4), his request is an honorable one.

Despite the pairing of Peter and John (as in 4:1, 13; 8:14, 17, 25; cf. Luke 8:51; 22:8), it is Peter alone who responds to the man's appeal. Peter's words evoke a dramatic contrast between the money the man seeks as a temporary respite and the healing available through Jesus' name. Because they are spoken in the shadow of the temple with its ornaments of silver and gold, there is also a contrast between the money Peter *does not* have and the faith that he *does* have. The contrast reinforces Luke's rhetoric about the peril of money (see, e.g., 8:20 [silver]; 16:16; 20:33 [silver and gold]).

The result of Peter's action comes "immediately," as is frequently the case with miraculous events in Luke–Acts (e.g., Luke 1:64; 4:39; 8:47; Acts 5:10; 12:23). Although miracle stories normally include some indication of the effectiveness of the healing, the demonstration here runs well beyond convention, as the man not only jumps up and walks but then enters the temple "walking and leaping and praising God." The exuberant physical response recalls Isa 35:6: "then the lame shall leap like a deer"; by going into the temple and praising God, the man indicates his awareness of the source of this miracle. This action also directly connects him with the actions of the believing community, which spends time in the temple and praising God (see 2:46-47).

The impact of the healing extends well beyond the individual himself. Since the term "people" (*laos*) in Luke–Acts most often refers to Israel (see, e.g., Luke 1:68; 2:32; 24:19; Acts 2:47), "all the people" includes, at least in a symbolic fashion, far more people than those actually present for the event (see 4:4). As 2:47 reports on the goodwill believers enjoyed among "all the people," here also the news of this event has spread well beyond those who happened to be in the vicinity of the Beautiful Gate at the time of this encounter.

Peter's Second Speech (3:11-26)

The Author of Life (3:11-16): The venue changes prior to the speech itself, for the crowd assembles in Solomon's Portico, a colonnade that may have run along the eastern wall of the temple enclosure (although the location is by no means certain). Similar to Pentecost, Peter begins his speech by addressing a misconception about the occasion (see 2:15). Contrary to the conclusion that might have been drawn from the healing, Peter and John make no claim for themselves. This is no mere rhetorical flourish, since later episodes will provoke similar confusion in response to the miraculous (14:8-18; 28:1-6). In addition, the story of Herod's death demonstrates God's judgment against those who refuse to acknowledge their humanity (12:23; but see also 28:6, where Paul does not correct those who mistake him for a god).

In vv. 13-15a, as in 2:22-24, Peter begins by sharply contrasting the actions of God with those of the inhabitants of Jerusalem; these verses once again drive home the culpability of Jerusalem's populace in the death of Jesus and the powerful counteracting deed of God in the resurrection. To begin with, the description of God as the "God of Abraham, the God of Isaac, and the God of Jacob, the God of our ancestors" invokes the theophany at Sinai by means of identifying the one who has overturned the rejecters of Jesus (see Exod 3:6, 15; Luke 20:37). Although Pilate is portrayed in other ancient sources in harsh terms (Josephus, *Ant.* 18.55-62, 85-88; Philo, *Embassy* 299-305), Luke's Gospel declares that he made a just decision (see Luke 23:13-25).

A series of escalating verbs draws attention to the injustice of the people's actions against Jesus. First, they "handed over" Jesus, then they "rejected" him before Pilate. Peter again charges them with rejecting Jesus, seeking the release of a murderer, and becoming murderers themselves in that they "killed" Jesus. The NRSV obscures the fact that the "you" in vv. 13-14 translates an emphatic pronoun (*hymeis*) that underscores the contrast between God and Israel ("you yourselves").

The language used here for Jesus draws attention to this contrast. He is God's "servant" (*pais*; see 4:27). He is also the "Holy and Righteous One," recalling especially the declaration of Jesus at the cross as righteous ("innocent" in the NRSV, Luke 23:47; see also Acts 22:14). He is also the "Author of life" (*archēgos tēs zōēs*). Luke uses this term again in 5:31, where it refers to Jesus as "Leader and Savior" (NRSV; see also Heb 2:10; 12:2). Although the exact connotation here, whether author or originator or leader, is unclear, the irony of charging the audience with killing the very originator of life is inescapable.

Perhaps because v. 16 makes several important assertions simultaneously, it reads awkwardly even in the NRSV, which has considerably smoothed out the inelegant syntax of the Greek. To begin with, v. 16 reminds the audience that they know this man and that they have seen his now "perfect health" (cf. v. 10). Also, it is faith that has brought about his restoration ("by faith in his name," and "the faith that is through Jesus"). In the Gospels, the faith that acts in a healing is usually that of the afflicted person (Mark 1:40-45; 10:46-52) or of someone who intercedes for the afflicted (Mark 5:22-43; 9:14-29). In this account, however, the faith that is active must be that of Peter and John, since the man himself shows no sign of expecting a healing. (On the contrary, he is explicitly said to be hoping for alms.) Yet Luke is not boasting in the faith of Peter and John, for v. 16 recalls Peter's earlier words of v. 6: it is the name of Jesus Christ of Nazareth that has brought about this restoration.

The Appointed Messiah (3:17-21): Having both addressed the question of how this miracle occurred and thereby introduced the gospel of Jesus, the speech moves quickly to call for repentance. Despite the harsh rhetoric of vv. 13-15, Peter concedes that the people and their rulers acted out of ignorance. He recalls again that this series of events fulfills God's plan, here with the extraordinary claim that "all the prophets" had said the Messiah would suffer.

The call for repentance in vv. 17-21 elaborates on the call in the Pentecost speech. On this occasion, the plea is not only that the audience should "repent," but also that it should "turn." The words "to God," added in the NRSV, do not appear in the Greek. "Turning to God" is an expression normally used of Gentile conversion (as in Acts 26:18; 1 Thess 1:9). Jews already know God through Israel's history (see v. 13), although they also have sins that require forgiveness (see especially v. 26).

The call for repentance significantly identifies both the benefits of repentance and, in v. 23, the consequences for those who will not repent. Repentance brings with it the "wiping out" of sins, a graphic image used also in Ps 51:1, 9 (LXX Ps 50:3, 11; see also Isa 43:25, Col 2:14). Beyond this essentially negative act, repentance also brings "times of refreshing," a phrase that has no counterpart elsewhere in Luke–Acts. Luke employs time designations in the plural for those events that lead up to some culminating event, and time designations in the singular for the event itself (e.g., Luke 17:22-31; Acts 2:17, 20), so "times of refreshing" probably refers to a period prior to the parousia itself (Carroll 1988, 143; Kurz 1977, 309-10), in all likelihood synonymous with the "refreshing" power of the Holy Spirit and the new community and its joyous common life (2:43-47).

Verse 21 extends the remarks about Jesus in an unusual way, with the claim, found nowhere else in the New Testament, that Jesus "must remain in heaven until the time of universal restoration." This assertion recalls not only the story of Jesus' ascension in Luke 24 and Acts 1, but also the relationship between that ascension and the promise of Jesus' return (1:11). A literal translation of "the time of universal restoration" would be "until the times of the restoration of all." Here again a plural reference to times precedes an event in the singular (as in v. 20, see above), so that, while the restoration times are not the equivalent of the return of Jesus, they anticipate it. Given that the apostles have already inquired about the "restoration" of the kingdom (a cognate verb rather than the same noun, 1:6), the "restoration of all" surely includes restoring the kingdom of Israel (see also Acts 1:6), but it may extend well beyond that promise to include other prophetic statements such as those of Mary (Luke 1:46-55), John the Baptist (Luke 3:4-8), and Jesus (Luke 24:46-47).

A Prophet Like Moses (3:22-26): With v. 22, Peter turns again to Scripture, as in the Pentecost speech. Here, instead of comparing Jesus with David, he quotes the promise of a "prophet like Moses." The quotation draws primarily from Deut 18:15-19 but contains also phrases from Lev 23:29. Evidence from other early Jewish and Christian texts indicates that there may well have been extensive eschatological expectation of this "prophet like Moses" (see, e.g., 7:37; John 1:21; 6:14; 7:40; 1QS 9:11; 4QTest 1-8). Peter appeals to the authority not only of Moses but of "all the prophets" who join in this expectation (Luke 24:27; Acts 3:18; 10:43; 26:22; 28:23).

Unlike the Pentecost speech, which contains little by way of threat for those who reject the witness (although see 2:40), this one carries an unequivocal threat for those who will not hear and obey (recall Simeon's prophecy of "falling and rising" in Luke 2:34). What is at stake here is nothing less than whether the audience will continue to be part of Israel (Juel 1992, 45-47). Yet vv. 24-25 reinforce the identity of the hearers as Israel even as they threaten, for these are the "descendants of the prophets," the children of "the covenant," the first to whom God sent "his servant" so that they might receive the blessing. Especially noteworthy here is the expression "descendants [lit. sons] of the prophets," a phrase that appears nowhere else in the New Testament and in the Old Testament refers to particular groups of prophets (e.g., 1 Kgs 20:35 [LXX 21:35]; 2 Kgs 2:3, 5, 7, 15; 4:1, 38; 5:22; 6:1; 9:1). The only exception is Tob 4:12, which appears to refer to all Israel as "descendants of the prophets." In view of the charge Stephen will soon make, that his own Jerusalem audience consists of the children of those who persecuted and murdered the prophets, this identification takes on an ironic coloration (7:51-52).

◊ ◊ ◊ ◊

Important features of Luke's Christology come to the fore in this passage. Here as elsewhere Luke uses a variety of titles for Jesus (servant, Holy and Righteous One, Author of life, Messiah, prophet), giving little indication what content any of those titles carries. More revealing is the narrative of human rejection, even murder, followed by God's resurrection and glorification. Luke's emphasis on the ascension of Jesus into heaven (1:11) comes to its most forceful expression with the claim that he "must remain in heaven." Yet if Jesus is absent, he is also powerfully present by means of his "name," which here brings about a miraculous healing and soon will bring about a conflict with religious authorities (MacRae 1973).

As in the Pentecost speech, Peter interprets the death and resurrection of Jesus as part of God's plan. By contrast with other important New Testament writings, Luke makes no claim about the saving efficacy of Jesus' death or resurrection. Luke does not interpret the death of Jesus as sacrificial (see especially Hebrews) or as revelatory (as in Paul's letters). For Luke, salvation comes through God's comprehensive plan for human salvation (see Introduction).

Consistent with 1:7, the speech makes no effort to predict when Jesus will return and offers no guidelines for those who might wish to venture such predictions. For Luke, eschatology has far less to do with chronology than it does with Christology, in the sense of understanding the identity of Jesus as God's Messiah, and with community, in the sense of the urgent need for the people of Israel to hear and respond. Even as this speech addresses an audience of Israel and does so in terms of their identity as God's people, however, it also anticipates the extension of the promise to "all the families of the earth" (v. 25).

Resistance and Response (4:1-31)

The response that follows Peter's Pentecost speech is overwhelmingly positive, with fabulous numbers of people added to the community and no mention of resistance to Christian proclamation. Following the speech of chapter 3, however, the religious leadership in Jerusalem sounds the first notes of resistance. The narrative transition at 4:1-4 introduces these leaders and their reaction to the activity of Peter and John. The brief custody itself

(vv. 5-22) Luke narrates in two distinct parts. First, a question addressed to Peter provides him with an opportunity to recapitulate his earlier speeches (4:5-12). Second, the authorities, realizing their own inability to take more severe measures, threaten and then release Peter and John (4:13-22). Peter and John subsequently return to their fellow believers and respond to this initial conflict with corporate prayer, a prayer that is apparently answered with gifts of emboldened speech and other signs of God's power (4:23-31).

◊ ◊ ◊ ◊

Peter and John in Triumphant Custody (4:1-22)

Luke's inclusion of the Sadducees in the group arresting Peter and John is striking, for they had no particular standing as authorities in the temple precincts, although they were the group within first-century Judaism most sympathetic with the priesthood and most protective of its prerogatives (see Josephus, *Ant.* 13.297-98; 18.16-17; *J.W.* 2.164-65). Because they also rejected belief in the resurrection of the dead, they become the ideal foils for the apostles and their preaching (see also 23:6-10).

Those who arrest Peter and John contrast not only with the apostles but also with the people of Jerusalem. Luke conveys this contrast by means of the double reference to the people (*laos*) in vv. 1 and 2, which prepares for the report that follows about the authorities' concern for the reaction of the populace (see vv. 16-17, 21). He also conveys the contrast with the notice in v. 4 that believers "numbered about five thousand." In order to render this large figure more credible, commentators, at least since the time of Calvin, have suggested that the 5,000 includes those baptized at Pentecost (Calvin 1965, 113). Yet even if the figure is a combined one (i.e., 3,000 at Pentecost and 2,000 following the first healing), the Greek at 4:4 says there were 5,000 "males" (*andres*), which would make Luke's estimate of the total number of believers even larger when women and children were included (see also Luke 9:14).

What provokes the authorities is that the apostles were "teaching the people" (cf. 5:25, 42; 11:26; 18:11; 21:28, and 28:31) and preaching "resurrection of the dead." The phrase Luke employs is ambiguous; it can refer either to the resurrection of Jesus himself (and only that) or to Jesus as the first proof that there is such a thing as resurrection. Peter's sermon speaks only of God's raising of Jesus (3:15; cf. 2:24, 31-32), but later passages in Acts do anticipate the general resurrection of the dead (e.g., 23:6-10; 24:10-21; 26:8). Whatever connotation applies here, the sermon does not dwell on resurrection, and it seems likely that this statement serves largely as a pretext for opposition and as evidence of the leaders' general resistance to proclamation of the gospel.

Luke's identification of the group that assembles to interrogate Peter and John raises some historical questions. Annas was removed as high priest in 15 CE, nearly two decades before this event could have taken place (see also Luke 3:2; John 18:13, 24). Caiaphas was high priest during the years 18–36 (cf. also Matt 26:3; Luke 3:2; John 11:49; 18:13-14; Josephus, *Ant.* 18.26-35). Neither John nor Alexander is known from other sources. Discerning whether Luke is simply mistaken in this list or whether he follows a custom of honoring former high priests with that title throughout their lifetimes is less significant than perceiving the intimidating scene evoked by this list, especially when contrasted with the "uneducated and ordinary" Peter and John. Luke specifies that they gather "in Jerusalem," which seems amusingly gratuitous except for the reference to Jerusalem in v. 27 ("this city") and the importance of Jerusalem throughout Luke–Acts. Jesus' own words echo here: "Jerusalem, Jerusalem, the city that kills the prophets and stones those who are sent to it!" (Luke 13:34*a*).

No single individual emerges as questioner; instead, with one voice the authorities ask through what "power" or "name" Peter and John accomplished this deed. The question appears artificial at first glance, one designed only to provide Peter with an opportunity to preach, particularly since the arrest initially occurs because of their teaching and preaching (v. 2), not because of the miracle itself. Yet the question is not entirely disingenuous; the

Gospels consistently show a populace that accepts the reality of powerful deeds but also knows that they can originate either with Satan (e.g., Luke 11:15) or with God (e.g., Matt 13:54; Luke 5:17; John 3:1). The "you" of the question is emphatic in the Greek, suggesting that the authorities question not only the origin of the miracle but also the apostles as its agents.

Empowered by the Holy Spirit (v. 8), Peter responds with considerable rhetorical flourish in the form of an address to the audience (v. 8), a restatement of the interrogators' question (v. 9), and the disclosure formula in v. 10 ("let it be known to all of you"). Even as Peter restates the question, he substantially transforms it. No longer the unspecified "this" act or deed, as in v. 7, Peter identifies it as a "good deed" and, more important, an act in which the man is healed (or, more literally, "saved"). The answer to the question consists of a summary of the speech of chapter 3, together with an allusion to Scripture and a dramatic claim about the "name" through which the healing has occurred.

Peter then introduces Ps 118:22, a verse cited also in Luke 20:17 (and see Matt 21:42; 1 Pet 2:4, 6-8). The Greek here differs from the LXX version used in Luke 20 in several respects, one of which is crucial for the context. Here it is "you, the builders" who reject the stone. As the footnote in the NRSV indicates, the Greek phrase may be translated either as "cornerstone" or "keystone." This is not a modern "cornerstone," however, the function of which is largely ceremonial and commemorative, but a stone that bears weight for the entire construction (Fitzmyer 1998, 301; BDAG 542). In this context the citation serves less to identify Jesus in some specific way than to indict the audience for its rejection of him.

Peter's speech culminates with the powerful assertion that there is "salvation in no one else." Having answered the interrogators' question positively with the name of Jesus, Peter now answers it negatively: the miracle came about through Jesus and could not have come about otherwise. The second half of v. 12 elaborates this claim by means of some phrases that add little content but considerable emphasis. "Under heaven" is the equivalent of "under the sun" or "on earth," and "given among mortals" probably refers simply to what God has "provided" (Barrett 1994, 232). In English the expression "by which we must be saved" sounds rather peculiar, but the Greek is again Luke's favored term *dei* ("it is necessary"), which regularly refers to events that take place as part of God's will (e.g., Luke 9:22; 13:33; 21:9; Acts 3:21; 9:6, 16; 19:21). In context, the emphasis falls on God's gift of salvation rather than on a negation of other religious practices. In addition, Peter again identifies the healing as an act of salvation. This is not merely a play on words, a pretext for a sermon on some other kind of salvation: physical healing is in itself salvific.

Irony dominates the aftermath of Peter's speech (vv. 13-22). The authorities have extensive power, but they dare not use it because public opinion prevents them (v. 21). They are further revealed as religious leaders who lack any concern for the content of Peter's speech or even for the miracle itself, the reality of which they acknowledge (v. 16). By contrast, Peter and John possess no power, but they do possess boldness (v. 13; see the commentary on boldness in vv. 23-31). Also, although they are outside of the religious power structure, they are the ones who seek to obey God (vv. 19-20) and through whom God is praised (v. 21).

Peter's climactic remark (vv. 19-20) to the authorities has antecedents at least as early as Plato (*Apology* 29D). Similar assertions in the face of resistance occur in the Maccabean literature, when Jews choose martyrdom rather than disobey the Mosaic law (2 Macc 7:2; 4 Macc 5:16-38; and see also Josephus, *Ant.* 17.158-59). Literarily, Peter's remark anticipates the next confrontation in chapter 5, in which the necessity of proclamation forces the authorities to make a judgment. Despite being in custody and severely outnumbered, Peter emerges as the one who is actually in charge of the situation!

The Community's Response to Resistance (4:23-31)

Peter and John return to "their friends" (lit. "their own"), a group that is left unspecified. Although the mass conversions in chapters 2 and 3 make it quite unlikely that Luke imagines all believers as gathered in a single space, neither does he give any indication that only the apostles are involved. When the apostles act as a distinct group, the text consistently makes that clear (e.g., 4:33; 6:1-6; 8:14; 15:6, 23). Probably Luke has in mind "the community 'as a whole,' but not necessarily the whole of it" (Barrett 1994, 243). That wholeness comes to expression with the characteristic Lukan word *homothymadon*, "together" (v. 24); so intent is Luke on displaying a united community that here we find the church praying both extemporaneously and in unison.

The prayer opens by addressing God as creator, using language that not only draws from Scripture (e.g., Exod 20:11; Neh 9:6; Ps 146:6 [LXX 145:6]) but also echoes through Luke–Acts (e.g., Acts 14:15; 17:24). The most instructive antecedent to this opening address appears in Isa 37:15-20 (and its parallel in 2 Kgs 19:15-19), another prayer regarding the enemies of God's people, in that case a prayer by King Hezekiah for the deliverance of Jerusalem from the threat of Sennacherib. There, as here in Acts 4, the prayer begins by addressing God as creator.

With v. 25, the prayer moves from the notion of God as creator to introduce a quotation from Ps 2:1-2. The introduction to v. 25, however, is a syntactical nightmare, although English translations routinely obscure that fact. Translated somewhat literally, v. 25 reads: "Who [i.e., God] spoke through the mouth of our father David your son through the Holy Spirit." As the textual variants and numerous suggestions for emendation demonstrate, the main problem is how to understand the relationship between God as speaker and the agency of both the Holy Spirit and of David. Nowhere else does Luke say that God speaks through the Holy Spirit (von Wahlde 1995, 265). Some scholars maintain that the problem arises from an Aramaic original, while others argue that v. 25 retains several early drafts or a later scribe's insertion. Such speculation has little ground in the manuscript tradition, and more seriously, it overlooks the significance in Luke–Acts of both David and the Spirit. Indeed, Acts 1:16 refers to a Scripture "which the Holy Spirit through David foretold." It is entirely possible, then, that Luke attributes this psalm both to David and to the Spirit without reflecting on the relationship between those two agencies (Gaventa 1986b, 78).

Whatever the intended introduction, the quotation in vv. 25b-26 conforms exactly to the LXX of Ps 2:12. Verse 27 echoes the phrases "gathered together" and "whom you anointed" from v. 26 (the Greek word is *christos* or "anointed one," rendered by NRSV as "Messiah"). Verse 27 also connects the psalm to recent events by adding the expressions "in fact," "in this city," and "against your holy servant Jesus." Luke uses "in fact" or more literally "truly" or "in truth" (*ep' alētheias*) elsewhere also for emphasis (Luke 4:25; 20:21; 22:59; Acts 10:34; cf. Isa 37:18). "In this city" makes the accusation concrete and specific. No longer does the psalm refer to a general threat but to those in Jerusalem who have acted with violence against Jesus. The description of Jesus identifies him both as the anointed one of the psalm and as a *pais* (child, servant) of God like David.

Verse 27 lists the specific persons and groups who acted against God's anointed. The "Gentiles" and "peoples" of the psalm reappear here. And Herod fulfills the role of the "kings" of the psalm, just as Pontius Pilate stands in place of the "rulers." This parallelism is somewhat forced, however, since in Luke's Gospel neither Herod nor Pontius Pilate actually seeks the death of Jesus (see Luke 23:1-25). Nevertheless, Luke's is the only passion narrative that includes a trial before Herod (Luke 23:6-12). Although "the peoples of Israel" in the form of their religious leaders sought Jesus' death (Luke 20:19; 22:52, 66; 23:13; 24:20), it is difficult to see how Gentiles as a group were involved in the death of Jesus.

Verse 28 employs several characteristically Lukan expressions to underscore the fact that God was in control even of those who executed Jesus. Within the New Testament the noun *boulē* (plan or counsel) and related words appear almost exclusively in Luke's writings, most often referring to God's plan (Luke 7:30; Acts 2:23, 5:38; 13:36; 20:27). The verb translated "predestined" (*proōrizein*) occurs only here in Acts, but Luke does employ a number of words with the prefix *pro*, referring to

God's prior will or plan (e.g., *proeipein* or "foretold" in 1:16; *prognōsis* or "foreknowledge" in 2:23; *prokēryssein* or already proclaimed in 13:24).

With vv. 29-30, the prayer turns from those who executed Jesus to the present situation. The move is grammatically difficult, since the "their" of v. 29 has its antecedent in v. 27 in the form of Herod and Pilate and the others, despite the fact that the text clearly refers to the present enemies of the church. This anomaly leads some to conclude that Luke is drawing on an earlier source, which he has not adequately covered over in his redaction (Haenchen 1971, 227). The identification of these events with one another is precisely Luke's point, however, in that the persecution of the apostles *corresponds* to the persecution of Jesus. The threats against Peter and John by the Jewish leaders are the equivalent of the threats against Jesus. Later on in Acts, a similar connection occurs between those who persecute the prophets and Paul's persecution of the church (7:51-53; 8:3).

"And now" at the beginning of v. 29 draws attention to what follows as it does elsewhere in Acts (17:30; 20:32; 27:22). Here the parallel between this prayer and that of Isa 37:15-20 breaks down, since Hezekiah prays for the deliverance of the people: "Save us from his [Sennacherib's] hand." Instead of asking for revenge on their oppressors or even simply for deliverance from persecution, the community prays first for "boldness" while God's hand performs "signs and wonders."

In Luke–Acts, "to speak your word" consistently refers to proclamation of the gospel (e.g., Acts 8:25; 11:19; 13:46; 14:25; 16:6, 32), but here Luke specifies that proclamation is to occur "with all boldness." The word "boldness" (*parrēsia*) he has already connected with apostolic witness in 4:13, when the Jewish leaders interrogate Peter and John and they see "the boldness of Peter and John." The prayer for bold or forthright speech thus refers to the preceding incident in which the apostles' boldness elicits consternation from the authorities. The second part of the petition similarly recalls the healings and other "signs and wonders" accomplished by Jesus in the Gospel and in his name already in Acts. Pentecost, with its display of ecstatic gifts, Peter interprets as a gift of God (2:14-21). He also explains the healing in chapter 3 as an act brought about through Jesus' name (3:12-16).

Verse 31 dramatically depicts God's response to this prayer. The place itself is shaken, and those who are present experience the Holy Spirit again, as at Pentecost, and speak God's word with boldness. That the place itself is shaken indicates the presence of God (see Exod 19:18; Isa 6:4; *4 Ezra* 6:15, 29; Josephus, *Ant.* 4.51), and the outpouring of the Holy Spirit enables them to proclaim "with boldness."

◊ ◊ ◊ ◊

"Salvation" is a difficult word, perhaps more readily described in terms of what one is saved "from" and "for" than in absolute terms. Often in Luke–Acts, as is the case here, salvation involves rescue from illness or some other debilitating condition (e.g., Luke 6:9; 8:36, 48, 50; 17:19; 18:42; Acts 7:25; 14:9). Moreover, it does not belong entirely to the future but occurs in the present time (Throckmorton 1973, 526). Other passages speak of salvation as "forgiveness of sins," or restoration to community, and Luke also anticipates a future for salvation (e.g., Luke 1:77; 7:50; 13:23; 18:26; 19:9-10; Acts 2:21). Yet salvation is not merely some future state of soulful bliss in Luke–Acts; it has a body and a present.

The community's prayer in vv. 23-31 makes a strong interpretive move, in which it identifies the plight of the present community with that of Jesus and both Jesus and the community with the plight of the "Lord" and "his Messiah" depicted in Ps 2. The later tradition's notion of the communion of saints finds a small antecedent in such identifications. If the story of the community runs through Israel's history, so does the story of resistance. Even if Luke does not invoke the name of Satan in this account, Calvin is nevertheless right when he claims that in this narrative "Satan sets himself in opposition to [the Gospel] by every means in his power, and uses every endeavor to crush it in its earliest beginnings" (Calvin 1965, 111). In Luke–Acts those who oppose Jesus and the proclamation about him are identified with Satan.

In this account, boldness emerges as a primary characteristic of the apostolic witness. Not only do Peter and John speak with boldness (4:13; cf. 2:29) but the church seeks boldness in response to intimidation and threat. The boldness granted here in response to prayer runs throughout Acts, even to its closing line (28:31; see also 9:27-28; 13:46; 14:3; 18:26; 19:8; 26:26). The attempt of the religious authorities to silence the apostles does not simply fail; it produces a mission of even greater urgency.

Satan Intrudes in God's Community (4:32–5:16)

The signs and wonders that connote God's presence in the community extend to the sharing of possessions. Yet God's powerful actions within the community are also challenged by the works of Satan (5:1-11).

The passage opens with a summary description of community life (vv. 32-35; cf. 2:41-47). No clear demarcation separates the summary of community life (vv. 32-35) from the scene prior to it, and it might well be regarded as continuing the community's response in vv. 23-31 (just as 2:43-47 follows on the Pentecost speech). Although Luke employs repetition as a literary device, however, he does not do so without also making use of variation. The vignette of Barnabas in vv. 36-37 follows seamlessly on vv. 32-35 and provides a crucial contrast for the story of Ananias and Sapphira, suggesting that the summary of 4:32-35 belongs more closely with chapter 5 than with chapter 4.

The summary introduces two illustrative scenes. The first concerns Barnabas, who enacts the oneness described in the summary (vv. 36-37). The more elaborate second scene consists of a miracle of retribution for the behavior of Ananias and Sapphira, who have been overtaken by Satan (5:1-11). A concluding summary demonstrates that even the work of Satan will serve to draw attention to God's actions in the community (5:12-16).

◊ ◊ ◊ ◊

The Unity of the Community (4:32-37)

The description of community life begins with the unity of believers "heart and soul," which revisits the theme of unity that has been prominent in this early section of Acts (e.g., 2:1, 44, 46). As a way of demonstrating this oneness, Luke refers to the sharing of goods in v. 32 and again in v. 34. Historical questions about this report abound, and the sources permit few answers. Yet a variety of sources demonstrate the conviction of early Christians that their fellowship included material goods, particularly the responsibility of wealthier believers to share with other believers who were in need (e.g., 2 Cor 8–9; James 2:1-7; *Did.* 4:5-8).

At first glance, v. 32 appears to be contradicted by what follows. If believers practice common ownership, then it is difficult to see how Barnabas would have a field to sell or how Ananias and Sapphira could have something to withhold (see 5:3-4). Yet v. 32 need not imply common ownership as such; instead, it may mean that those who did possess property did not *claim* it as such but thought of it as property to be shared with those in need. That interpretation is consistent both with Aristotle (*Politics* 2.5 [162B-163B]) and with the instruction of Deut 15:4. Verse 33 continues the characterization of the community. Not only is it unified by the sharing of possessions, but the apostles bear witness to Jesus' resurrection (see 1:22). The frequent reference to apostolic witness recalls the promises of the risen Lord in 1:8 and identifies the community with those promises. Despite the verse division, v. 33*b* and v. 34 belong together. The Greek conjunction *gar* ("for") connects the two and indicates that "great grace" comes on the community precisely because its members care for one another's needs (as in Deut 15:4). The text does not specify whose grace or favor they receive. Although God's grace or favor is elsewhere said to be with individuals in Luke–Acts (Luke 1:30; 2:40, 52; Acts 7:46), in those cases God is specifically mentioned. Here, as in 2:47, the favor granted to believers appears to be that of their neighbors in Jerusalem.

Even if vv. 34-37 do not necessarily contradict v. 32 (see

above), they do expand by explaining how it is that the needy received care. Those who had possessions sold them and placed the proceeds "at the apostles' feet" (v. 35). The repetition of the phrase in v. 37 and again in 5:2 (see also 5:10) surely merits notice. To place oneself or one's belongings at the feet of another is to be in submission to that person's authority or instruction (see Luke 8:41; 10:39; 17:16; Acts 10:25; 22:3; and also 1 Sam 25:24; Ps 8:6). Whether or not this action reflects submission to apostolic authority, it clearly does remove the goods from the control of their previous owners and subjects them to the control of the community.

The vignette concerning the example of Barnabas begins with considerable detail that has little bearing on the incident itself (vv. 36-37). Unlike the NRSV, the Greek begins with his name, Joseph. The name added by the apostles, Barnabas, is especially intriguing, since Luke explains that it means "son of encourage-ment," which it does not, and no one has offered a convincing explanation of the name's origin and meaning. Yet Barnabas does become an encourager when he reappears later on in the story, introducing Saul to the Jerusalem community (9:27) and encouraging the church at Antioch (11:19-26). The Holy Spirit commissions him along with Paul, and the two witness together until their quarrel following the Jerusalem Council. According to Old Testament law, Levites were not permitted to own land (Num 18:21-24; Deut 18:1-4; Josh 13:14; but see Num 35:1-8; Josh 14:4; 2 Chr 11:13-15), although the extent to which that law was followed in the first century is unclear. Barnabas's con-nection with Cyprus is interesting, given the importance of that island later in the narrative (11:19-20; 13:4; 21:16).

Ananias and Sapphira (5:1-11)

Luke supplies no introduction for Ananias and Sapphira. Nevertheless, the repetition Luke employs here and the drama he invests in this event suggest that he understands it to be impor-tant. Ananias and Sapphira come before Peter separately. Ananias places money at the apostles' feet, as have others before him (4:35, 37). Later Sapphira falls at Peter's feet when she dies. Several questions are of major importance in understanding the story: What exactly do Ananias and Sapphira do, and how does that action cohere with the earlier reports of the sharing of possessions? How does Peter interpret their action? What consequences does this event have for the developing portrait of the Jerusalem community?

Ananias and Sapphira (Luke indicates her complicity twice in the opening verses) sell some possession and present the proceeds "at the apostles' feet," but they retain a portion for themselves. In vv. 3-4 Peter claims that the property had been theirs prior to its sale, and the profit from the sale was also theirs. When he confronts Sapphira, he asks that she confirm the amount raised by the sale, and she does so. Taken together, these comments reflect an assumption that, once property has been sold and *declared to belong* to the community by presenting it to the apostles, then *all* of the proceeds are those of the community. The verb translated "kept back" in v. 2 reinforces this interpretation, since the Greek word *nosphizomai* frequently refers to misappropriation of funds belonging to others, even to theft (e.g., Josephus, *Ant.* 4.274; 14.164; Epictetus, *Discourses* 2.20.35; Plutarch, *Pompey* 4.1; Strabo, *Geography* 2.3.4; 2.3.5).

When Peter confronts Ananias and Sapphira, however, he interprets this misappropriation in theological terms. First, Peter asks, "Why has Satan filled your heart to lie to the Holy Spirit?" (v. 3). Later he insists, "You did not lie to us but to God!" (v. 4). To Sapphira, Peter asks, "How is it that you have agreed together to put the Spirit of the Lord to the test?" (v. 9). In other words, Ananias and Sapphira have acted not merely against their fellow-believers but against God. A similar identification comes in 9:5, when the risen Jesus confronts Paul, persecutor of the *church*, with the assertion: "I am Jesus, whom you are persecuting." References in these verses to lying to the Holy Spirit, lying to God, and testing the Lord's Spirit do not constitute three different actions but serve cumulatively to reinforce the severity of their deed.

Peter's first words remove Ananias and Sapphira's action from the realm of mere human resistance and interpret them as the result of Satan's interference. Like Judas, who was under Satan's power when he betrayed Jesus for money (Luke 22:3), Ananias and Sapphira also reflect the power of Satan, this time acting *within* the Jerusalem church. It is noteworthy how often in Acts Satan must be stopped as the witness of the church continues (Garrett, 1989), but only here is Satan's influence seen within the community itself.

Even if Luke does not say that these deaths resulted from divine judgment, the sudden deaths and the awe they inspire make that relationship clear. Peter does not cause the deaths of Ananias and Sapphira; rather, they come as a result of God's confrontation with Satan. And that confrontation makes itself known. Three times Luke narrates what happens when people hear of this confrontation. In v. *5a*, Ananias hears Peter's declaration of judgment and falls over dead. In v. *5b*, "great fear" overtakes "all" who hear of this encounter. And at the end of the story, great fear overtakes both the church itself *and* all who hear of the occurrence (v. 11). Similar to the outpouring of the Holy Spirit in chapter 2 or the healing in chapter 3, this event generates awe in the presence of God's power. Interestingly, this is also the first time Luke uses the term *ekklēsia* in Acts (it does not appear in the Third Gospel).

Numerous attempts have been made to explain the origin of this story, the most common of which is that Luke is reworking the story in Joshua 7 of the theft by Achan of property taken in the fall of Jericho and set aside for God. The two have in common the verb *nosphizomai* (LXX Josh 7:1) as well as the activity of God in punishing a wrongdoer. Yet there are more differences than similarities. Achan's secret action brings defeat on Israel, he immediately confesses when confronted, and all Israel takes part in the stoning of Achan and the destruction of his entire family and all his property. Less important than the question of the story's origin is its function, and that function becomes clear in vv. 12-16.

The Community Restored and Strengthened (5:12-16)

This transitional summary of the community's life provides further evidence of God's presence with the community. It also explains why the temple authorities take action against the apostles in the scene that follows.

The passage portrays the community not only restored following the crisis of Ananias and Sapphira but even strengthened. The opening statement of v. 12 recalls the "wonders and signs" of 2:43. The apostles gather in Solomon's Portico, the location of Peter's earlier speech (3:11). The awe generated by the apostles' deeds, especially the wondrous deaths of Ananias and Sapphira, prompts responses, and Luke's depiction of those responses is somewhat difficult to untangle. Verse 13 first says that "none of the rest dared to join them" and then that "the people held them in high esteem." Verse 14 further complicates matters with its report about increasing numbers of believers, and the Greek of v. 15 leaves unspecified who exactly carries the sick into the presence of the apostles for healing. The first step toward clarity here is to recognize that *kollaomai*, which the NRSV translates "join," need not mean full membership in the community but can mean simply drawing near to the apostles (notice the range of usage in Luke 10:11; 15:15; Acts 8:29; 9:26; 10:28). The healings accomplished through them inspire sufficient awe that those outside the circle of believers stay a safe distance away, and at the same time the people (*laos*) regard them highly. Verse 14 is then a parenthetical statement (BDF 243), which depicts the result of this high regard, and does so by referring explicitly to both men and women. Verse 15 follows logically on v. 13 (BDF 243); the general populace, not only believers, bring their sick for healing. The curious report that even Peter's shadow heals people may reflect folk traditions about the power attached to a person's shadow (van der Horst 1976), but it also reflects the conviction that the power that works through Peter is so effective that the usual strategies of healing are not necessary. Verse 16 increases the volume on this report even further, with people coming for healing from the entire region, all of whom receive assistance.

The story of Ananias and Sapphira, together with the transitional summaries that surround it, reintroduces an important character in the Lukan narrative. The powerful opposition of Satan in Luke's Gospel here re-emerges, as even those within the community of believers fall prey to Satan's influence. Without understanding that feature of the story, it is impossible to make sense of the fierce retribution that takes place here. Ananias and Sapphira receive not even an opportunity for repentance, since they serve at the behest of their master, Satan. Ironically, Satan's intrusion increases the stature of the believing community. The residents of Jerusalem, perceiving the awesome power of God in these deaths, rightly understand that the community is God's and that Peter and the other apostles act by means of God's power.

As with the report about the sharing of possessions in 2:4-5, this text also has generated considerable speculation about Luke's message to his audience. Does Luke offer these reports in order to instruct the wealthier members of his audience in the importance of sharing possessions with lower status Christians (Mitchell 1997)? Or does he depict the earliest Jerusalem community as an example of Christian values so that his own community can formulate an apology to outsiders (Sterling 1994)? Wringing a precise answer from these few lines is a precarious undertaking. When placed alongside the passages that either recall the beneficence of believers (e.g., 9:36-42; 16:11-15) *or* depict judgment against those who impede the gospel or employ it for financial advancement (e.g., 8:18-24; 19:23-41), however, it becomes clear that for Luke faithfulness to the gospel involves the wise and generous use of possessions.

Resistance Intensified (5:17-42)

Just as Peter's speech in chapter 3 prompted the authorities to arrest him and John, the increasing awe attached to the community's life in 5:12-16 prompts official resistance once more. This scene bears some resemblance to 4:1-31, in that both include an arrest, a confrontation between the authorities and Peter, a brief restatement of Christian preaching about Jesus, and an emphatic assertion of the need to obey God rather than human authorities. The similarities have led to speculation that 5:17-42 is a doublet of 4:1-31; that is, Luke found differing accounts of one event in two sources and mistook them for separate events. Whatever the origin and literary relationship of the two accounts, the second does not merely repeat the first, for here the apostles are released from custody by an angel and must be rearrested (vv. 19-21, 26). Perhaps more important, Gamaliel intervenes to prevent the deaths of the apostles (vv. 33-39). With these two features, Luke considerably enhances the drama in this arrest, showing the increasing resistance to Christian proclamation and preparing for the death of Stephen and arrival of Saul, himself the embodiment of resistance.

◊ ◊ ◊ ◊

Arrest and Deliverance (5:17-21a)

Verses 17-21a narrate the arrest and the miraculous delivery of the apostles with stunning economy (contrast 12:6-11). As in 4:1, Luke identifies the Sadducees as the circle associated with the temple priesthood and its power to arrest and confine. The NRSV states that the apostles are placed in "the public prison," but the phrase is better translated adverbially: "they put them in prison publicly." The latter translation is consistent with Luke's use of the Greek word *dēmosia* elsewhere in Acts (16:37; 18:28; 20:20), and it draws attention to the authorities' plan to impose their will on the apostles. By contrast, the angel of the Lord acts at night, when no audience is available, simply releasing the apostles and directing them to continue their teaching in the temple. The repetition of the word "temple" here underscores the conflict between the apostles and the authorities over who better perceives the will of the God of this same temple (vv. 20, 21, 24, 25, 42). Given the immediate rearrest of the apostles, the angelic release seems futile, but Calvin rightly observes that this deliverance demonstrates that the apostles are in God's hand and God's care (Calvin 1965, 143).

Second Arrest (5:21b-26)

The release also sets up the opportunity for the irony in vv. 21b-26, a scene over which Luke lingers. Verse 21b details those who are present, listing both the council and the "body of the elders," synonymous expressions that increase the sense of expectancy. The authorities come together to confront their captives only to find that the supposed captives are themselves teaching in the temple! Not only does the council look foolish because they do not know what is going on (v. 24), but they dare not fully exercise their authority because they fear the people (as in 4:21, and see Luke 20:19; 22:2). Luke specifies that the leaders fear stoning, a detail that interestingly anticipates the stoning of Stephen (7:54–8:1). Instead of the apostles being afraid of the powerful, the powerful are afraid of the apostles.

"We Must Obey God" (5:27-32)

When the apostles do arrive, the high priest reminds them in sharp terms of the previous prohibition (4:17-18, 21), and he carefully avoids uttering Jesus' name as he does so. (With the addition of a single Greek word in some manuscripts, the high priest's initial statement becomes a question, as the note in the NRSV indicates. Copyists may have introduced this minor alteration in order to render the high priest's words a question in conformity with words of v. 27, "the high priest questioned them.") Far from obeying the previous order, the apostles have "filled Jerusalem" with their teaching and wish to "bring this man's blood" on them, that is, hold the authorities responsible for his death.

The response tersely summarizes Peter's earlier speeches (2:14b-36; 3:12-26; 4:8-12), but several distinctive features merit attention. Peter is mentioned by name, but he speaks together with all the apostles (cf. 4:8), emphasizing their unity in the face of peril. Their response to the high priest in effect concedes his charges, since they have every intention of filling Jerusalem with Christian teaching and they do regard the leaders as culpable in Jesus' death. With the assertion, "We must obey God rather than any human authority," they succinctly restate 4:19-20 (here in a form close to that of Socrates in Plato's *Apology* 29D: "I shall obey the god rather than you."). Within the brief restatement of the kerygma, the speech specifies that the authorities killed Jesus "by hanging him on a tree," a phrase that has not appeared earlier in Acts (but see 10:39 and 13:29). A close parallel to this expression appears in Deut 21:22-23, in the context of prohibiting the exposure of the corpse of an executed criminal, but already at Qumran it was applied to death by crucifixion (4QpNah 3-4 i 6-8; 11QTemple 64:7-8) as it is here and in Gal 3:13 (Fitzmyer 1998, 337). The speech closes with the established assertion that the apostles are witnesses (2:32; 3:15), but here adds the claim that the Holy Spirit witnesses along with them.

Gamaliel Intercedes (5:33-42)

The enraged response of those present goes well beyond the amazement of 4:13. The scene that follows elicits considerable interest, both because it is the first time a nonbeliever has spoken at length (Fitzmyer 1998, 333) and because of the content of the speech. Gamaliel is Rabban Gamaliel I (Gamaliel the Elder) who is later said to have been Paul's teacher (22:3) and who is honored in the Mishnah (*m. Soṭah* 9:15), yet Luke does not assume that his audience will recognize the name. First, Luke specifies that Gamaliel is a Pharisee, and thus an apparent minority in this crowd of Sadducees. Pharisees have not appeared previously in Acts, but they play an ambiguous role in Luke's Gospel. Sometimes Pharisees are grouped together with scribes in their questioning of Jesus (e.g., Luke 5:21, 30; 6:7; 11:53), but they also invite Jesus to their homes (e.g., Luke 7:36-37; 11:37; 14:1) and even warn him about the threat of Herod (13:31). They are not identified among those who seek Jesus' death. Thus, in itself the labeling of Gamaliel as a Pharisee is neither positive nor negative. The additional note that Gamaliel is also "a teacher of the law, respected by all the people" (v. 34) suggests at least that the audience constituted by the council will attend to him, either because they respect his wisdom or because they must reckon with the opinion of the people (see v. 26).

Gamaliel introduces the figures of Theudas and Judas, both of whom led unsuccessful movements. First, he recalls Theudas as "claiming to be somebody." Since a similar expression in 8:9 describes the unambiguously negative character Simon Magus, Gamaliel's assessment of Theudas is clear (see also Gal 2:6). Theudas misled four hundred people, but he was killed and his movement dispersed. Then "after him" appeared Judas the Galilean, who persuaded people to follow him and perished along with his movement.

If the place of Theudas and Judas in Gamaliel's argument is clear, their place in Luke's history is sharply contested. The difficulty arises because the Jewish historian Josephus reports on both Theudas and Judas (Josephus, *Ant.* 20.97-98; 18.1-10; *J. W.* 2.117-18; 7.252-53). The broad strokes of his description of their movements generally coincide with that of Luke, but the chronology differs considerably. Judas's revolt at the time of the census puts it roughly in the first decade of the common era. Theudas, however, emerged during the procuratorship of Fadus (44–46 CE), which is not only *after* rather than before Judas, but after the time period during which this speech would have been given. The suggestion is sometimes made that Luke refers to an earlier Theudas on whom Josephus does not report, but it seems more likely that either Josephus or Luke is simply mistaken. Because such rebellions have particular importance for Josephus's interpretation of Israel's recent past, he may be more reliable than Luke in this instance.

Whatever the historical facts, Gamaliel's reasoning from them is clear. If the apostles represent only themselves, as was the case with Theudas and Judas, they will fail. If they are from God, they cannot be silenced and even the attempt to silence them is dangerous. Gamaliel's conclusion is surely right, from the narrator's point of view, but it is based on an extremely flawed comparison. The apostles are not giving themselves out to be someone, nor do they follow a leader of rebellion. In a sense, Gamaliel's statement resembles the ambiguous warning of Luke

13:31, for when Pharisees warn Jesus about Herod, they comprehend the threat of Herod but not the mission of Jesus (as Luke 13:32-35 makes clear).

Gamaliel's conclusion forms the high point not only of this scene, but of the entire story of resistance up to this point. However wrongheaded his comparison, Gamaliel speaks the theological truth: these men are from God and they cannot be silenced. The next verse will nevertheless make it clear that the effort to stop them will also continue, for the apostles are again beaten and ordered to desist. Luke closes the scene with a vivid depiction of their defiance. They rejoice *even as they leave* the presence of the council, but the rejoicing is not mere relief. As the community in 4:24-31 prays for God's power among believers rather than the overthrow of their persecutors, here the apostles rejoice in their connection to "the name" rather than in their own safety. Verse 42 shows the relentlessness of the apostles: "every day" their activity continues, both in the public space of the temple and in private homes.

However ambiguous the figure of Gamaliel in this story, and however faulty his comparison of the Jerusalem community with Judas and Theudas, his concluding words clearly voice Luke's conviction: The apostles are from God, they will not be silenced, and those who oppose them are in fact fighting God. Within the Lukan narrative world, as Luke retells the story of the earliest community, perhaps in order to strengthen his own beleaguered community, Gamaliel's statement functions importantly to recall that the gospel is God's story and that it cannot be stopped by human power. Taken out of context, this appears to be the triumphalism of which Luke is often accused. A more sustained consideration of v. 39 in its narrative context suggests otherwise. To say that the council will not be able to overthrow the apostles is not to say that the movement will proceed unchallenged and that ever larger numbers will be attracted to it. Stephen's violent death and the persecution that follows amply confirm that point, when the people desert the apostles and join the outraged council members (6:12). Gamaliel affirms that, if the movement is God's, it cannot be overpowered. Attempts to silence the movement are the equivalent of resisting God. The resistance to Stephen, whose face resembles the face of an angel (6:15), and the resistance of Saul to Jesus himself (9:5) serve as dramatic fulfillments of this warning.

Grumbling and Growing (6:1-7)

Commentators sometimes treat this scene and the following story of Stephen (6:8–8:3) in isolation from the preceding chapters. Reasons for that practice include the use of the term "disciples" for believers for the first time in Acts, reference to the apostles as "the twelve" (for the only time in Luke–Acts), the introduction of groups known as Hellenists and Hebrews, and the dominance of the new character Stephen throughout this section. Despite those distinctive features, however, this scene follows closely on chapter 5, since "during those days" connects it tightly to preceding events. The summary statement in v. 7 also recalls the earlier summaries of 2:43-47 and 4:32-34, although this one makes no reference to the sharing of possessions and includes the addition of priests to the community. Verses 6:1-7 continue the drama of proclamation and resistance in Jerusalem, demonstrating that the continuing growth in the community generates a problem in caring for the needy and that the community quickly takes action to rectify the situation.

Verse 1 plunges readers into a series of difficult questions, the most contested of which is the identity of the Hellenists and the Hebrews. The term "Hellenist" is rare, not found in writings earlier than Luke–Acts, although it is clearly derived from "Hellene" which refers to someone who is Greek or, more broadly, to any non-Jew (as in Acts 14:1; 18:4; 19:10; 20:21). This lexical connection has prompted the suggestion that the Hellenists in this passage are Gentile Christians (Cadbury 1932, 69), but that seems impossible given the care Luke lavishes on the inclusion of the Gentiles. If Gentiles were already present in the Jerusalem community, the Cornelius account in 10:1–11:18 and especially the ensuing controversy of chapter 15 would be difficult to understand. Luke tends to identify groups of people by the primary language they speak (e.g., 14:11; 21:37; 22:2; 26:14; see also Plato, *Charmides* 159a; Chrysostom, *Homilies on Acts* 3 [NPNF 11:21]), and Hellenist here probably refers to Greek speakers. Later at 9:29 he will use "Hellenist" to refer to Jews who are not Christians (see also 11:20, where there is a text critical complication). Nevertheless, the "Hellenists" are almost certainly Jewish Christians speaking Greek, and the "Hebrews" then would be Jewish Christians speaking Aramaic. Those differences in language usage may well correlate with other differences in culture, making conflict a genuine possibility. Some interpretations take these potential differences further than the evidence allows, postulating separate Christian parties, the liberal Hellenists who are critical of the temple and favorable to the inclusion of Gentiles and the conservative Hebrews who protect the temple and the law of Moses. Yet the story is remarkable for its portrait of the forthright solution to a serious problem, and it contains no hint of a protracted struggle about the temple or law-observance (Hill 1992, 19-40). (That is not to deny the historical likelihood that the early church experienced conflict and division, but deriving the contours of such division from Luke's account is exceedingly difficult since his interests lie elsewhere.)

The exegetical furor over the identification of Hellenists and Hebrews should not eclipse the problem that gives rise to the story in the first place—the neglect of "their widows." Because most women spent their lives first in households that belonged to their fathers and then their husbands, they controlled little property and had little economic opportunity. When widowed, which often happened at an early stage since women customarily married early and to husbands considerably older than themselves, women became all the more vulnerable economically and socially. (There are exceptions to this generalization, as we see in the figures of Tabitha and Lydia, who appear to operate independently and have access to property. Luke refers to these widows by name, reserving the designation "widow" for those who are in situations of need [Seim 1994, 243]). As early as the appearance of the prophet Anna in the infancy narrative, Luke has displayed interest in widows, referring to them more often than does any other Gospel writer (e.g., Luke 4:25-26; 7:12; 21:2-3; Acts 9:39, 41). Luke's concern recalls the Old Testament and the way in which Israel is commanded to care for the widow and the orphan (e.g., Exod 22:24; Deut 14:28-29; 24:17-21). Of special pertinence to Acts 6, Israel is also chastised sharply when its widows are neglected (e.g., Isa 10:1-2; Zech 7:10-12). That history makes the neglect of widows within this community a serious matter (Spencer 1997, 65). To claim that this community, in which "there was not a needy person" (4:34), neglects its widows is to offer a stinging indictment.

Commentators sometimes identify the complaining (*gongysmos*) of the Hellenists with Num 11:1, in part because the cognate verb appears in the LXX. The appearance of a single noun does not suffice to connect the two stories, however, and they otherwise have little in common. In Numbers, the Israelites complain unjustly against God because of the hardships of their life in the desert, and they incur God's wrath for doing so. In Acts 6, the grumbling is directed by one group to another group within the community rather than to God, and the treatment of the complaint suggests that it is entirely appropriate. The widows within this community must receive the care they need.

Neither here nor elsewhere does Luke provide details about the nature of this "daily distribution" ("of food" does not appear in the Greek). According to later Jewish writings, the poor were provided with meals on a daily basis and there was provision for other needs as well (*m. Pe'ah* 5:4; 8:7; *m. Demai* 3:1; *m. 'Abot* 5:9), and it may be that the earliest Christian community continued that practice just as it continued to worship in the temple.

The context in which neglect of this distribution has arisen is also important. Luke says nothing of a series of squabbles between Hellenists and Hebrews, but he does say that the number of believers is growing. The passage opens with that comment (6:1), and three other times the passage refers to multitudes and their growth (6:2, 5, 7). The NRSV obscures the fact that all four of these references have a common Greek root (*plēth*), which might be translated as "multiply" and "multitude." The neglect of Hellenist widows points to rapid growth that requires more attention than the twelve apostles can provide.

Confronted with this disruption to unity, the apostles respond by convening the entire community, stating their understanding of their own tasks, and finally proposing a solution to the problem. Their assertion that they should not "neglect the word of God in order to wait on tables" is susceptible of the interpretation that the task of proclamation is more significant than that of service to the needy. Such an interpretation puts the apostles' statement in clear conflict with the Lukan Gospel, however, in which Jesus identifies himself with just such service (Luke 22:26-27). Instead of denigrating service to the needy, the statement reminds the community (and the reader as well) that the fundamental apostolic task is that of witnessing to the resurrection of Jesus (as at 1:8; 2:32; 3:15; 4:33; 5:32). Moreover, the number of believers now exceeds the resources of these twelve men, and, for that reason, the story is comparable with that of Moses selecting judges to assist in adjudicating conflicts within Israel (Exod 18:13-27; see also Num 11:16-30).

The situation requires more workers. Unlike the selection of a replacement for Judas, these do not have to be people who witnessed the ministry of Jesus (Acts 1:21-22), but as in that story they do have to be male, as the gender specific term *anēr* is used here. Why the apostles propose the number seven is anyone's guess (Fitzmyer 1998, 349), although the Old Testament recounts several occasions on which seven leaders play a role (Josh 6:4; Esth 1:14; Jer 52:25). More puzzling than the number seven is the fact that these men who are appointed to table service are never seen serving tables. Perhaps we are to assume that they carry out those responsibilities but also that they enhance the larger witness of the Jerusalem community, so that it is natural that Stephen is found debating and that Philip evangelizes when he flees Jerusalem for Samaria.

About the seven themselves, Luke offers very little information. As in 1:13, where the prominent figures Peter and John appear first in the list of the apostles, Stephen and Philip appear first here. Stephen is described as "full of faith and the Holy Spirit" in v. 5, which anticipates his role in chapter 7. Philip returns in chapter 8 in the context of the Samaritan mission (see also 21:8-9). The details regarding Nicolaus may be significant. He is said to be a proselyte, which almost certainly means that the others are not, that they were born into Jewish families. In addition, Nicolaus is from Antioch, a city that figures prominently later in the mission (beginning in 11:19). That his non-Palestinian origin is specified here may mean that the others are indeed Palestinian.

Are the seven themselves Hellenists? The answer to that question is by no means obvious. "From among yourselves" in v. 3 does not narrow the candidates to Hellenists, since the apostles are addressing the entire gathering of believers. The names are Greek, which might place them among the Hellenists, although many Jews of the period bore Greek names.

The commissioning of these seven men involves not the apostles alone but the entire gathering of believers. The apostles take the initiative for addressing the problem (v. 2), but they call everyone together in order to do so. They propose a solution, to which the community gives its assent (v. 6). And, despite the NRSV's rendering of v. 6, it is not necessarily the apostles alone who pray and lay hands on the seven. The Greek is ambiguous. It may mean that "they [i.e., the apostles]" or that "they [i.e., the group addressed in v. 3] prayed and laid hands on them." Luke's very ambiguity at this point suggests his lack of interest in lines of human authority.

As in the Old Testament, prayer and the laying on of hands invokes God's blessing on the persons receiving the gesture (e.g., Num 27:18-23). Because laying on of hands carries formal connotations of ordination later in the church's history, it is important to notice that in Acts it serves more than one function. In 13:1-3, as here, the commissioning of witnesses is marked by prayer and the laying on of hands, but laying on of hands also is used for conveying the Holy Spirit (8:17-19; 19:6) and for healing (9:12, 17; 28:8; cf. Luke 13:13).

Verse 7 sums up the situation with the comment that the word of God continued to spread. Although Luke does use "word of God" to refer to the content of the gospel (8:14; 11:1; 13:5, 7), he also uses it here and elsewhere for the general flourishing of the community generated by that gospel (12:24; see also 19:20). The additional note regarding the obedience of many priests is intriguing. The gospel has now extended in a dangerous direction. As the apostles teach in the temple (5:42), they draw hearers not only from the general population but even from the ranks of those most closely identified with the temple, and presumably identified with the hostile chief priests of 4:5 and 5:17. That some priests are attracted is not only astonishing, given the Jerusalem leadership's resistance to Christian preaching, but may also explain the development that follows, since attraction of those who were thought to be in the high priest's camp could prove provocative.

◊ ◊ ◊ ◊

Far from merely introducing Stephen and Philip, this passage depicts a community that temporarily fails to care for its own and then takes action to rectify the problem. The appointment of the seven has provided warrant for an order of deacons, but it is noteworthy that Luke never uses the term "deacons" here. He employs instead the abstract noun "service" and the verb "serve," an activity rather than an office. Although the passage is also mined for Luke's understanding of ecclesiastical hierarchy, perhaps the most important ecclesial assumption in the passage is that the church adapts its ministry as situations change.

Stephen as Accused and Accuser (6:8–8:3)

The resistance to Christian preaching that begins in chapter 4 with the arrest of Peter and John and becomes violent in chapter 5 now erupts in the death of Stephen and the persecution of the Jerusalem church. The sheer length of this episode provides some hint of its importance. Luke's portrayal of Stephen's arrest and murder identifies him, and by extension other Christian witnesses, closely with Jesus. And Stephen's rendition of Israel's history locates Israel's present resistance to Christian proclamation solidly within the tradition of Israel's persistent rejection of God's messengers. The aftermath of Stephen's death should be disaster, but it is not.

Structurally, the long episode is straightforward. Stephen's arrest (6:8-15) and the account of his death and its aftermath (7:54–8:3) stand as bookends for his lengthy speech. The speech itself narrates Israel's history in four stages: God's dealings with Abraham (7:2-8), the vindication of Joseph (7:9-16), the rejection of the prophet Moses (7:17-43), and the construction of the temple, which introduces Stephen's accusation against his hearers (7:44-51). (See below on the speech's sources and its relationship to the accusations against Stephen.)

◊ ◊ ◊ ◊

The Arrest of Stephen (6:8-15)

Stephen, who has been commissioned as one of the seven to oversee the distribution of food in 6:1-7, never appears explicitly in that role, although nothing excludes service from the category of "great wonders and signs" performed by Stephen. The description of Stephen in v. 8 signals that readers are to understand Stephen in continuity with others who accomplish "wonders and signs," including Moses (7:36), Jesus (2:22), and the apostles (2:43; 5:12; see also 2:19). Despite various interpreters' attempts to distinguish the theology of Stephen from that of Peter and the remainder of the Jerusalem church, Luke's introduction places Stephen firmly within their circle.

Resistance to Stephen comes, not from the Sadducees or the ruling council as earlier in 4:1 and 5:17, but from a new source. The Greek here is somewhat ambiguous, making it unclear whether there is one synagogue composed of Freedmen (former slaves or the descendants of former slaves) from four different places, five synagogues (one composed of Freedmen *and* four made up of people from four other locations), or possibly two synagogues (the Freedmen from Cyrene and Alexandria and another synagogue composed of Cilicians and Asians). Whatever the alliances within the group that takes action against Stephen, they appear all to be Diaspora Jews. Many reconstructions identify Stephen himself with the Diaspora and see in this episode a conflict among Hellenists, but it is far from certain that Stephen is a Hellenist (see commentary on vv. 1-6). Although Diaspora Jews have been among believers since Pentecost (assuming that some of those mentioned in 2:7-11 are among the 3,000 baptized), they only now are identified among the opposition—indicating the broadening of resistance to Christian preaching.

Not only do these Diaspora Jews take the initiative in arguing with Stephen, but they take steps that bring about his death. Finding that they cannot defeat him in debate, because he speaks with more wisdom and spirit than they (just as Jesus promised, see Luke 21:15), they provoke others to bring charges against him. Luke infuses this prelude to Stephen's speech with a sense of danger. First, the opponents do not themselves bring the charges, but they suborn others to do so. Verse 11 characterizes these initial charges as "blasphemous words against Moses and God." Second, the opponents of Stephen incite not only the leaders but the people (*laos*), who have previously been favorably disposed to the Christian community and whose goodwill afforded them protection in 4:21 and 5:26 (Tannehill 1990, 84). Third, when Stephen stands before the council, the opponents bring false witnesses who expand on the charges of v. 11. The vague phrase "against Moses and God" now becomes more specific: Stephen "never stops saying things against this holy place and the law."

The false witnesses introduce yet another charge; that Stephen claims that "Jesus of Nazareth will destroy this place and will change the customs that Moses handed on to us." Although Matthew and Mark place the accusation about threatening to destroy the temple within the trial of Jesus (Matt 26:59-61; Mark 14:55-58; and cf. John 2:19-21), Luke places it here instead, where it intensifies the danger to Stephen by associating him with Jesus, who has already been perceived as a threat. The charge reinforces the thoroughly corrupt nature of the trial, but it also focuses the conflict between believers and their opponents on the question of which side can rightfully claim for itself the temple and the law of Moses. Since the beginning of Acts, believers have gathered at the temple (2:46; 3:1; 5:12, 20, 25, 42; note also the emphasis on the temple in Luke 1–2), but resistance to the word of God has also come from those identified with the temple. Now the question emerges: Which group rightly identifies itself with the temple and its traditions?

The fury created by these charges comes to expression in v. 15, as all stare at Stephen, just as those present stared at Jesus in Luke 4:20. What they see, the face of an angel, indicates God's presence with Stephen, a presence to which the council seems immune.

Stephen's Speech for the Prosecution (7:1-53)

Contemporary readers who anticipate a traditional defense speech, in which a defendant or an attorney itemizes charges and rebuts them in explicit detail, necessarily find Stephen's speech puzzling, to say the least. This disparity has led some scholars to conclude that the speech itself is independent of its narrative context, since it does not respond to the charges of speaking against the law and the temple (e.g., Haenchen 1971, 286-89; Conzelmann 1987, 57). They suggest that Luke has adapted another source or sources, and the disparity results from poor editing. Theories about Luke's use of sources for Acts are generally unpersuasive, however, since no parallel accounts exist that would permit the sort of comparison possible for the Synoptic Gospels (see Introduction). And some of the elements of the speech that scholars have identified as secondary may well be integral to the story (e.g., v. 35, which is pivotal to the connections Luke makes between past rejection of Moses, recent rejection of Jesus, and present rejection of Stephen).

The question of the speech's relationship to the charges against Stephen is complex. Stephen does not directly respond to individual charges, but he does speak about the law and the temple, and his response to the charges may be teased out from those remarks. For example, Stephen is accused of speaking against Moses, but he claims that it is Israel who actually rejected Moses. Moreover, Luke is not writing a biography of Stephen, such that he must give an account of his death. Luke is narrating God's actions for Israel and the world in Jesus Christ, and that larger story is always in view. Thus, the speech has a greater purpose than merely to respond to charges against Stephen.

Stephen's speech also stands out from earlier speeches in Acts in that the earlier speeches do not provide an extensive recital of Israel's past, and Stephen does not proclaim Jesus as Messiah (at least not overtly). Yet Peter appeals extensively to Israel's history (2:25-31; 3:13, 22-25), as Paul will do in 13:16b-25 (Tannehill 1990, 85-86). And the rhetorical movement of this speech does resemble others in Acts, for Stephen begins on mutually held territory with apparently innocuous points and moves from there to claims that are less acceptable and then to claims that openly incite the audience (see also 17:22b-31; 22:3-21).

The recitation of Israel's history has parallels in many Old Testament passages (e.g., Josh 24:2-15; Neh 9:6-37; Pss 78; 105; Ezek 20). Such rehearsals vary from one another considerably in their detail, content, and purpose. Joshua 24:2-15, for example, marks the covenant ceremony at Shechem; Neh 9:6-37 recounts Israel's disobedience as a prelude to repentance and renewal; and the recital of God's history with Israel in Ps 78 serves a didactic function (see v. 4). A major question regarding Stephen's speech, then, is how it functions in its own context. The answer to that question is not singular, and interpretations that so argue fail to do justice to the multiple ways in which Luke's story works. This speech does at least three things. First, it addresses the Diaspora Jews who are in the *narrative audience* (i.e., those within the story itself who bring charges against Stephen), implicitly condemning their false interpretation of the temple (Fitzmyer 1998, 367). They come to Jerusalem to worship, but they do not understand that no handmade building can contain the living

God. Second, the speech addresses the Jewish leaders in the *narrative audience* (within the story itself), repeating the claim that they are liable for the death of Jesus and connecting that death with the rejection of Moses and all his prophetic successors. Third, it addresses the *authorial audience* (those who are hearing or reading Luke's account), teaching Israel's story to a group that may have known very little about this history, and especially connecting Moses to Jesus, Stephen, and soon Paul.

God's Dealings with Abraham (7:1-8): Stephen introduces his speech by recalling the patriarch Abraham, but the focus is less on Abraham than on God, whose initiative is central to every point Stephen makes. God appears and commands (vv. 2 and 3), God instructs Abraham to move again (v. 4), God promises (v. 5), God speaks about the captivity in Egypt (vv. 6-7), God gives the covenant of circumcision (v. 8). In this review of Abraham's life, he acts only in response to God's instructions.

Several details in v. 2 merit attention. Stephen begins the narration by invoking the "God of glory." This way of referring to God is rare, appearing only in Ps 29:3 (LXX 28:3), but it is especially appropriate given Stephen's vision of God's glory following the speech itself (7:55-56). Stephen also speaks of Abraham as "our ancestor" (literally, "our father") using the first-person plural that connects Stephen with the audience. This connection persists throughout the speech (e.g., vv. 11, 12, 15, 19, 38, 45), changing only when Stephen takes up the explicit attack against his hearers in v. 51.

Stephen's recital does not fit snugly with a careful reading of Genesis, since Stephen recalls that God appears to Abraham in Mesopotamia before the move to Haran, but according to Genesis 12 God only appears to Abraham (Abram) when he is already living in Haran (although see Gen 15:7; Neh 9:7). Also, Stephen says that the move from Haran took place *after* the death of Abraham's father, Terah, but the Genesis account indicates otherwise. That Terah is still alive at the time of Abraham's call is far from obvious in Genesis, however, and requires particular attention to narrative detail (note Gen 11:26, 32; 12:4; and cf. Philo, *Migration* 177).

Not surprisingly, Stephen draws his comments on Abraham largely from Genesis 11 and 12. The promises of vv. 6-7, however, draw upon the LXX of Gen 15:13-14 and perhaps also Exod 2:22. The very last phrase ("[they shall] worship me in this place") appears in neither Old Testament passage. It may be based loosely on Exod 3:12, which anticipates Israel's worship of God on Mount Sinai, something not mentioned in either Gen 15:13-14 nor Exod 2:22. That reference to the place of worship, particularly formulated as "this place," in the context of Stephen's speech, anticipates the questions of worship that figure prominently later in the speech (especially vv. 39-50; cf. Luke 1:73-74).

What is not said is also significant. Stephen makes no reference whatsoever to Sarah. And the entire story of Isaac and Jacob is compressed into v. 8. Stephen instead moves quickly to Joseph, and with him the topic of rejecting God's chosen one enters the speech.

The Vindication of Joseph (7:9-16): Stephen introduces the second section of the speech on a strikingly different note from the introduction to the first. Abraham enters on the high note of God's appearance to him, but the first word regarding Joseph is that the patriarchs were jealous of him and "sold him into Egypt" (v. 9). Genesis does recount the resentment of Joseph's brothers (Gen 37:4, 5, 11), and contemporaries of Luke draw attention to that feature of the story (Josephus, *Ant.* 2.9-10; Philo, *Joseph* 5-6), but introducing Joseph in this way recalls the jealousy of the high priest and Sadducees against the apostles (5:17).

"God was with him" stands as an apt summary for all of v. 10 and continues the parallel between Joseph and the Christian community, which also experiences God's protecting presence (see 10:38). As God called Abraham and made promises to him, God protected Joseph. First, God delivered Joseph from "his afflictions," presumably referring to the false accusations of

Potiphar's wife as well as to Joseph's subsequent imprisonment (Gen 39–40). Second, God gave him "favor and wisdom before Pharaoh, king of Egypt" (AT). This phrase tersely recalls Gen 41:1-45 and continues the parallel with believers, who have experienced the favor of the people (2:47; see also Luke 2:52). Stephen himself is said to possess wisdom such as his opponents cannot resist (6:10). God makes Joseph ruler over Egypt and all of Pharaoh's house. Although the NRSV identifies Pharaoh as the one appointing Joseph, in the Greek there is no change of subject. Just as God delivered Joseph and granted him favor with wisdom, God also made him ruler over Egypt. God remains the agent in charge, befitting Luke's insistence on God's guidance of events.

Verses 12-15 concisely paraphrase Gen 42–47, the convoluted saga of the restoration of Joseph to his father and brothers and their safe arrival in Egypt. Commentators sometimes make much of the reference in v. 13 to the "second visit," seeing in this comment some parallel to a second appearance of Jesus through the apostles as his messengers. Yet it is difficult to imagine a parallel that would identify Jesus and his apostles with the plotting brothers of Joseph. And the frequent reference to the brothers of Joseph as "our ancestors" forges an identification elsewhere: the brothers' jealousy of Joseph in the past parallels the resistance of those to whom Stephen is speaking. Stephen's distinction of first from second visits more likely assists the audience in keeping their place during this long and complex story.

Given the length of the Joseph cycle in Gen 37, 39–50, and the multitude of details that might have found their way into this brief retelling, it seems peculiar that Stephen lingers over the death and burial of Jacob and his sons (vv. 15-16). To complicate matters further, the details of Stephen's report conflate two Old Testament texts. According to Genesis, Jacob is buried in a plot Abraham purchased from Ephron the Hittite in Hebron (see Gen 23; 49:29-33; 50:7-14). And according to Joshua, Joseph is buried at Shechem in a burial plot purchased by Jacob from Hamor (Gen 33:18-20; Josh 24:32). Luke combines the two, placing Jacob and all the ancestors at Shechem. The reference to

Shechem, the center of Samaritan territory, may anticipate the Samaritan mission in Acts 8. Beyond these details and their confusion is the sheer fact of the burial of Jacob and his sons. Luke has already drawn attention to the death and burial of David (2:29; see also 13:36-37). Like David, Jacob and his sons all died and were buried and their burial places were known, by contrast with Jesus who did not remain buried.

Understanding Joseph as a "type" of Stephen, or even of Jesus himself, may overstate the matter. Nothing in the speech explicitly connects Stephen with later figures. Yet the parallels between past and present abound in the jealous opponents, the wisdom and favor of God's agents past and present, and the vindicating acts of God. If Stephen does not yet spring the rhetorical trap on his audience, he does—like every able narrator—tell the story in a highly selective way that serves the purpose of his final indictment in vv. 51-53. Indeed, the attention given Joseph in this recital of Israel's history is in itself intriguing, since comparable recitals in the Old Testament and Apocrypha seldom refer to him (see, e.g., Josh 24:2-15; Neh 9:6-37; Ps 78; Ezek 20; Sir 44-50; Jdt 5:6-21; with Ps 105 as an exception).

The Rejection of Moses (7:17-43): The speech's treatment of Moses falls into five distinct sections: vv. 17-22 introduce the situation of the Israelites in Egypt and the arrival of Moses; vv. 23-29 concern the conflict between Moses and fellow Israelites that causes him to flee Egypt; vv. 30-34 recall the theophany at Sinai; vv. 35-38 compress events of the flight and wandering, emphasizing Israel's rejection of Moses; and vv. 39-43 concern the dire consequences for Israel of its rejection of Moses.

The critique of Israel hinted at in v. 9 emerges with blunt force in the recital of Moses' life. Stephen begins by recalling the promise to Abraham (see e.g., Gen 12:2-3; 13:14-17; 15:18-21). Unlike Paul, who interprets the promise to Abraham in terms of offspring (see Gal 3:8, 16), the promise here is understood largely as a promise of land, and even of deliverance from Egypt. The situation of Israel in Egypt Stephen recalls with brevity, presumably in order to set the stage for Moses' entrance. The very language of vv. 17-20 draws heavily on the LXX, with v. 18 quoting directly from Exod 1:8. One modification in the LXX is noteworthy; where the LXX refers to the increase of "the sons of Israel," Stephen refers to "the people" (*laos*), using Luke's characteristic word for Israel (e.g., Luke 1:10; 2:32; Acts 2:47; 13:17; 28:17).

Stephen retells the Exodus story of Moses' early life, structuring it by means of a conventional formula employed in biographies: birth, nurture, and education (e.g., Acts 22:3; Philo, *Moses* 2.1; van Unnik 1973). Moses' beauty "before God" recalls Luke's comments about the growth and grace of Jesus (Luke 2:40, 52), although Josephus also weaves an elaborate legend about the beauty and size of the young Moses (Josephus, *Ant.* 2.230-32). The comments of v. 22 stand out, since Exodus says nothing about either Moses' education or his power in "words and deeds." That Moses is "powerful in words and deeds," of course, connects him with Stephen (6:8, 10) and with Jesus himself (2:22; Luke 24:19). Other legends about Moses emphasize his great intelligence (Philo, *Moses* 1:20-24; Josephus, *Ant.* 2.229), yet Stephen does not speak of Moses' own intellect but his instruction in the wisdom of the Egyptians. This comment may reflect contemporary regard for the learning of Egypt (see Strabo, *Geography* 1.395).

With the retelling of the conflict that leads to Moses' flight from Egypt, we see a clear and likely intentional shaping of the story. At the age of 40 (apparently Luke took Deut 34:7 as a guide and divided Moses' life into thirds accordingly), Moses kills an Egyptian who is mistreating an Israelite. Stephen diplomatically omits the fact that Moses surveyed the surroundings for possible witnesses before killing the Egyptian, a fact that might imply cowardice (see Exod 2:12). More important, Luke adds an interpretation of this event (v. 25), an interpretation that assumes not only that this individual Israelite but all of them ("his kinsfolk") should have known about Moses' mission. Of course, in Exodus, even Moses does not know his calling, but Stephen's comment introduces the motif of Israel's failure to receive Moses and recalls Peter's earlier claim about the ignorance of Israel regarding Jesus (Acts 3:17). The NRSV obscures the connection somewhat, because it translates "rescuing" where the Greek text reads "salvation" (*sōtēria*), a word Luke uses, along with its cognates, for the multiple blessings conveyed by God's actions in Jesus Christ (Luke 1:69; 6:9; 19:9; Acts 2:21; 4:9, 12; Green 1998, 83-106). The verses that conclude the scene reinforce both Moses' role and the Israelites' lack of understanding. Moses is the figure who attempts to reconcile the quarreling Israelites (v. 26); although omitted in the NRSV, the Greek includes the word "peace" as the goal of Moses's intervention (see Luke 1:79; 2:14, 29; Acts 10:36). And the Israelites respond with words taken directly from Exod 2:14. According to Stephen, Moses flees because of their comments, not out of fear of Pharaoh (see Exod 2:15; and cf. *Jub.* 47:12).

The third section in Stephen's recital of Moses' life, God's appearance to Moses at Sinai, again draws heavily on the language of Exodus. Stephen changes the order of events slightly, by reversing God's command that Moses remove his sandals (Exod 3:5) and God's own self-disclosure as the God of the patriarchs (Exod 3:6). Stephen also omits some of the details of the Exodus account regarding the oppression of the Israelites, thus drawing more attention to God's directive to Moses. Most telling, Stephen completely omits the lengthy treatment of Moses' resistance to God's call (Exod 3:13–4:17). Including that reluctance would create a direct conflict with Stephen's earlier comments about Moses' powerful words and deeds. It would also create problems for Luke's parallel between Moses and Jesus, if the forerunner were found to be stammering and timid.

With the final section about Moses, the rhetoric of the speech shifts markedly. Rather than continue the narrative of Moses' life, vv. 35-38 consist of a chain of statements about him, each of which begins with a demonstrative pronoun. The NRSV obscures this feature, but vv. *35a, 35b* ("whom God now sent"), 36, 37, and 38 all begin with a demonstrative pronoun referring to Moses:

v. 35*a*:   "As for this Moses. . . ."
v. 35*b*:   "This one God sent. . . ."
v. 36:   "This one led them out. . . ."
v. 37:   "This is Moses, who said to the children of
              Israel. . . ."
v. 38:   "This is the one who was in the congregation.
              . . ." (AT)

This repetition forcefully draws attention to the content of these verses. Verse 35 returns to Moses' rejection by the quarreling Israelites, but contrasts their denial with God's appointment; although they would not have Moses as "a ruler and a judge," God now sent him as "both ruler and liberator." Both the style and the content of this verse recall Peter's similar claim about Jesus in 2:22-24. Verse 36 characterizes Moses' actions as "wonders and signs," like those performed by Stephen (6:8), the apostles (5:12), and Jesus himself (2:22). Verse 37 leaps all the way to Deut 18:15 to recall Moses' promise of the prophet whom God would send after him, surely understanding that prophet as Jesus rather than Joshua (as in Acts 3:22). And v. 38 concludes the chain with a reminder of Moses' experience at Sinai and his role as receiver of "living oracles."

Although a relative pronoun connects v. 39 to v. 38 grammatically, the chain of references to Moses ends with v. 38. Verse 39 turns to a pointed attack on the disobedience of Israel, still referred to as *"our* ancestors." The various instances of grumbling in the wilderness Stephen distills into one large act of disobedience, after which he moves to the ultimate disobedience, that of idolatry. As the ancestors turned to Egypt, so God turned from them (v. 42) and "handed them over" to false worship. The language recalls that of Rom 1:18-32, in that both texts declare that God "hands over" those who refuse to recognize God to the consequences of their refusal (cf. Wis 13–15). Verses 42-43 quote Amos 5:25-27, so that the consequences of the rejection of Moses reach all the way to the Exile. With the change of the LXX's "Damascus" to "Babylon," Stephen identifies as one event the Israelites' rejection of Moses and the idolatry that brought about the sixth-century exile (Spencer 1997, 77).

The Construction of the Temple (7:44-53): The final section of Stephen's speech begins with an apparent change of focus. Each prior section has taken an individual (Abraham, Joseph, Moses) as the beginning point for recalling God's actions. This one has as its starting point not an individual but a place—the tent of testimony—and the relationship between that place and God. The harshness of the transition should not be overemphasized, however, since here also Luke attends to God's actions, which Stephen contrasts with Israel's resistance, a theme that begins with the Joseph section, intensifies in the Moses section, and here erupts in the attack of vv. 51-53.

Another feature that connects vv. 44-53 with the preceding discussion is the reference to the work of human hands. The Greek words *poieō* (to make or build something) and *cheir* (hand) run through the recital of Israel's idolatry (vv. 40, 41, 43), since one persistent charge about the absurdity of idolatry is that people make their gods with their own hands and then worship them (17:24; 19:26; Ps 115:4; Isa 40:18-20; Jer 1:16). The same language appears in vv. 48-50, where Stephen identifies as futile the notion of humans making a house for God. (*poieō* also appears in v. 44, but there the tent of testimony is carefully identified as a work ordered by God.)

The section begins in v. 44 by recalling the "tent of testimony," which the ancestors had with them in the wilderness. By contrast with the tent of Moloch (v. 43), God directed that this tabernacle be built, and God dictated its design (Exod 25:1–31:18). Verse 45 passes over the generations following Moses with the comment that they had the tabernacle with them *and* that God acted on their behalf as they took the land (as promised to Abraham, vv. 5-7). The age of David and Solomon also receives scant attention, especially by contrast with its importance for Israel's history. Stephen says both that David found favor with God and that David wanted to "find a dwelling place for the house of Jacob." The first part of that statement surely negates any attempt to view David's request as an act of bad faith or flawed judgment, since Luke reserves reference to God's favor for figures like Jesus and Mary (Luke 1:30; 2:40, 52; Acts 6:8). The second part of the statement contains a text-critical problem, as the footnote in the NRSV indicates. Some ancient manuscripts read "house of Jacob," while others read "God of Jacob." The earlier and more important manuscripts favor the reading "house of Jacob," but some interpreters argue that "God of Jacob" is more appropriate to the context (Johnson 1992, 132-33). Overturning early evidence should not be done casually, however, and "house of Jacob" is understandable: the temple means that Jacob's descendants (his "house") have a place for worship (Barrett 1994, 372). Verse 47 tersely recalls the fact that David did not receive what he sought, but his son did build the temple.

Assessing the role of v. 48 in the argument is exceedingly difficult. Following the recollection of Solomon's temple, and introduced by a strong adversative particle (*alla*, "but"), it may strike out at Solomon himself. Yet such a sharp reading is neither necessary nor persuasive. The verses that follow, taken together with the criticism of idolatry in vv. 39-43, suggest that the problem is not the temple *per se* but Israel's false perception that the temple somehow renders God manageable. The Israelites are recalled for celebrating "the works of their hands" (v. 41) in the wilderness. Similarly, Stephen claims that they took the temple as an occasion for reveling in their own creation rather than recognizing that God is greater than any house humans can imagine and build. When read in light of vv. 49-51 (which draw on LXX Isa 66:1), Stephen seems to be saying only what is found also in Jer 7:1-4: the temple is not a possession to be taken for granted (see also Mic 3:9-12; Josephus, *Ant.* 8.106-21).

Stephen moves to direct attack in v. 51, although his object is not the temple but his audience, those who falsely see themselves as the temple's protectors. In this direct assault, the audience becomes "you" rather than "we" for the first time in the speech. With the opening of v. 51, the language of "stiff-necked" and "uncircumcised in heart and ears" characterizes them as the polar opposite of Abraham, who was obedient (not "stiff-necked"), and who received the covenant of circumcision (vv. 2-8; see also Exod 33:3, 5; Jer 6:10). The second part of the verse brings to the surface a fundamental element of the speech. In the Greek, it reads even more emphatically than in the NRSV: *"You always resist the Holy Spirit, as your fathers also you"* (AT, emphasis added). This identification of actions past and present is elaborated in vv. 52-53. The assertions of v. 51 are hyperbolic: that the prophets were consistently persecuted is simply untrue, yet the charges of this verse are rhetorically effective, since they move from the prophets as a general category to those specific prophets who proclaimed Jesus' coming (see Luke 24:25-27) to Jesus himself.

Designating the audience as Jesus' "betrayers and murderers" is Luke's strongest formulation of the charge regarding Jesus' death. Earlier speeches make the charge, but they consistently add that this death was part of God's plan and they seek the audience's repentance (see 2:23; 3:13, 18). The charge is all the more powerful, given that Stephen himself is killed almost immediately and persecution erupts in the aftermath. With the final statement in the speech (v. 53), Stephen returns to the false charges brought against him. That those who received the law and who accuse him of speaking against it do not themselves keep it serves as his final accusation. (On the characterization of the law as "ordained by angels," see Deut 33:2; *Jub.* 1:26–2:1; Josephus, *Ant.* 15.136; Gal 3:19; Heb 2:2).

The Death of Stephen and Its Consequences (7:54–8:3)

Luke describes Stephen's death with a series of sharp contrasts between the crowd and Stephen, confirming that Stephen is the innocent witness to God's will and the people in the crowd are the faithless heirs of Israel's past. Like the council in 5:33, the audience is enraged; grinding of the teeth frequently characterizes the enemies of God or God's people in the Old Testament (e.g., Job 16:9; Pss 35:16; 37:12; 112:10; and see also Luke 13:28). With Stephen's claim to christophany in v. 56, the rage erupts into violence, as they drag Stephen outside the city and stone him (see Lev 24:10-23; Num 15:32-36).

Here the account poses a number of historical problems. The Stephen story opens in a way that suggests a judicial proceeding, with witnesses giving testimony (however unreliable), the council sitting in judgment, and the high priest presiding. Now all appearance of a legal proceeding vanishes, and mob action takes its place. To complicate matters, it is exceedingly difficult to discern what steps were open at this particular time for Jewish authorities under Roman law (Brown 1994, 1:363-72; Fitzmyer 1998, 390-91). Even an answer to that question does not mean that Luke knew the legal situation in Jerusalem in this particular period. Whatever the historical context, the Lukan story seems clear: resistance to Christian proclamation has not only reached the level of violence, but it has now burst out of the council and into mob action.

Stephen's innocence is multiply confirmed. First, the narrator describes Stephen once again as "filled with the Holy Spirit" (6:3, 5, 10), contrasting him with the audience he has just accused of consistently opposing the Spirit (v. 51). Then the narrator reports Stephen's vision. Finally, lest the point be missed, Stephen speaks, describing the vision himself. Stephen's vision of God's own glory serves to reinforce his speech: God is not to be found in the temple but in heaven. And the fact that Jesus stands at the right hand as Son of Man confirms not only Stephen's innocence but the rightness of Christian preaching.

Stephen's identification of Jesus as "the Son of Man standing at the right hand of God" is noteworthy for several reasons. This is the only time the expression "Son of Man" appears in the New Testament outside the Gospels. In this context, it connects Stephen's death with that of the Lukan Jesus, who anticipates the Son of Man's enthronement at God's right hand (Luke 22:69). Nowhere else is the Son of Man said to stand rather than sit; that unique feature of the passage has given rise to considerable speculation (e.g., he stands to welcome Stephen into his presence, he stands to vindicate the witness of Stephen, he stands alongside Stephen as advocate, he stands in judgment against Stephen's killers). The reasons for this anomaly are probably less important than the general impact of the christophany that serves as Stephen's final vindication.

Stephen's final words not only complete the parallel with Jesus but also display a generosity of spirit that grates sharply against the crowd's violence. As Jesus commended his spirit to God (Luke 23:46; see also Ps 31:5 [LXX 30:6]), so Stephen prays that Jesus himself will accept his spirit. As Jesus had prayed for the forgiveness of those who did not know their own actions, so Stephen prays for his accusers and assailants that this act might not be held against them (Luke 23:34; although note that many early manuscripts do not include this verse).

Tantalizingly, Luke selects this occasion to introduce Saul. Although it is tempting to read into this introduction facts that Luke reveals only later (e.g., that Saul/Paul is a Pharisee who studied with Gamaliel), Luke reveals almost nothing at this point. First, Saul is simply a "young man" at the periphery, keeping coats so that others can do wickedness without impediment. Then, in 8:1, he is said to approve of Stephen's death. Finally, in 8:3, he emerges as the only individual named as a persecutor. Having introduced him so compellingly, Luke is content to leave his story aside and turn to the Samaritan mission (cf. the introduction of Barnabas at 4:36-37).

The character and extent of this "severe persecution" are unknown, and discovering the exact nature of it is impossible. Since Luke indicates that the apostles remain in Jerusalem, some have argued that only the Hellenists were driven out. Yet it is of theological importance for Luke that the apostles remain in Jerusalem (Haenchen 1971, 293), and that makes it perilous to deduce historical developments from Luke's narrative. More important is the irony that lies just beneath the surface of 8:1: the resistance to the gospel has reached its peak, it appears to triumph in the scattering, but the names "Judea and Samaria" already recall 1:8 and the promise of the risen Lord. Soon, even this devastation will prove to be part of the growth of the gospel (9:31). The contrast of vv. 2-3 brings the long cycle to its end: the devout bury Stephen and grieve for him, but Saul engages in persecution.

◊ ◊ ◊ ◊

Students of Luke struggle with the question whether Stephen's speech reflects a Lukan polemic against the Jerusalem temple. Elsewhere, Luke seems favorably disposed toward the temple (e.g., Luke 1:8-23; 2:22-40; Acts 2:46; 21:17-26). Solving the difficulty by distinguishing *Luke's* attitude from that of *Stephen* himself does not suffice, since Luke's vocabulary and perspective permeate the speech. It also seems unlikely that Luke would have given such prominence to a speech with which he disagreed (Stanton 1978, 350-51). Luke's attitude appears to be complex, and one factor in that complexity may be that the temple itself no longer exists by the time Luke writes (see Introduction). On the one hand, the temple is an appropriate location for certain important features of Luke's story, since the temple symbolizes God's continuing care for Israel. On the other hand, the temple is also a potent way for Luke to identify Israel's disobedience and misunderstanding. Just at the point in Stephen's speech where he might have attacked the temple itself (v. 51), he instead sharply attacks those present. All of God's actions on their behalf, beginning with Abraham and continuing through the building of the temple and the arrival of the Righteous One, met with the same response.

Here Luke's understanding of Israel's history with God emerges clearly. Again in this scene, as in the community's prayer in 4:24-30, the times run together. Israel's distant past, in which Joseph is betrayed, Moses is rejected, and God replaced with idols, replays itself in the immediate past of Jesus' crucifixion and the imminent future of Stephen's martyrdom. God's vindication of Joseph, Moses, Jesus, and Stephen is equally prominent here, especially in Stephen's dying christophany. The themes of resistance and persistence continue in the persecution of the church and the scattering of its faithful.

Stephen's speech also introduces a polemical note regarding idolatry, a note that is by no means surprising in a recital of Israel's history, but one that serves little function in the present context. Later on, however, Luke will sound this note again in

Gentile settings—first in Lystra, then in Athens and again in Ephesus. The decision of the Jerusalem Council also contains a note of concern about idolatry. The God of Israel's history is also God of all the nations.

"For All Who Are Far Away" (8:4–11:18)

This section begins in Jerusalem, with the persecution that follows the death of Stephen, and ends in Jerusalem, with the church's own amazement at God's inclusion of Cornelius and his household. In between Luke shows the increasing scope of the gospel among those "who are far away" (2:39). First Philip goes to the Samaritans who live outside the limits of acceptable Judaism (8:4-24; and see 1:8), then he finds himself witnessing to an Ethiopian eunuch who is both outside Judaism and from the end of the world as Luke knows it (8:25-40). The story of Saul concerns a Jew, but one who is as far away from the gospel as a Jew can get (9:1-30). Two brief vignettes show the healing power of Jesus and the faithful life of believers in Lydda and Joppa (9:31-43), and then finally comes the elaborate story of the centurion Cornelius and the church's conversion (10:1–11:18). Although the unit both begins and ends among believers in Jerusalem, much changes in between.

The Samaritans and Simon (8:4-24)

The violence that follows Stephen's death does not long dominate Luke's account. Immediately after the dire picture of Saul's relentless attack on believers in 8:3, 8:4 finds those who have fled Jerusalem engaged in preaching in Samaria. Literarily, the unit is complex, which has prompted suggestions that Luke combines two preexisting traditions, one about Philip and one about Peter and John (Barrett 1994, 395), but the shift of evangelizing personnel is a concern of latter-day readers preoccupied with matters of authority. Luke is less interested in questions of *who* enters Samaria than he is in the reception accorded the gospel there.

Luke depicts the first witness outside Jerusalem with two sharply contrasting events. In one, the Samaritan crowds receive the gospel gladly, first in response to Philip's preaching (vv. 4-8), and then through the visitation of Peter and John (vv. 14-17). The other story concerns the powerful magician Simon, whose power falls away in the gospel's presence (vv. 9-13, 18-24). By placing the two stories together, Luke shows not only the foolishness of the persecution in Jerusalem, but also the powerlessness of magic, as well as its author Satan, in the face of Jesus Christ.

◊ ◊ ◊ ◊

Philip Preaches in Samaria (8:4-8)

The passage opens with a transitional description of the flight from Jerusalem and then moves to the single figure, Philip, whom Luke has already placed among the seven (see 6:5; 21:8-9). Nothing indicates that Philip plans or decides to engage in mission; instead, his proclamation seems inevitable. Philip cannot *not* preach (see 4:19-20). Here stereotypical language sketches both the Christian witness and the appropriate response to that witness. The phrases "proclaiming the word" and "proclaimed the Messiah" (see also v. 12) stand as summaries for the lengthy speeches previously delivered by Peter. The Samaritans respond by paying attention to Philip, by hearing and seeing signs accomplished by him, and by the great rejoicing that will later characterize the Ethiopian's reception of the gospel (8:39; cf. 13:48; 15:31). Luke even describes the Samaritans as "with one accord," as he has earlier described the believers in Jerusalem (1:14; 2:46; 4:24; 5:12; in all cases NRSV obscures the Greek).

If the language here is stereotypical of the Christian witness, the setting is not. Having fled the Jewish center of Jerusalem, Philip finds himself among the despised Samaritans. Although Samaritans traced their ancestry to Abraham, they had long been in conflict with Jews (Josephus, *Ant.* 11.306-12; 13.275-83; 18.29-30) so that traveling through Samaria was regarded as dangerous for Jews (Josephus, *Ant.* 20.118; *J.W.* 2.232). In addition, Jews considered Samaritans as outsiders, even as Gentiles (Matt 10:5; John 4:9; Josephus, *Ant.* 11.340-41). Luke's Gospel includes stories that place Samaritans in a positive light (10:30-37; 17:11-19), however, and Acts 1:8, taken together with those stories, makes the response of the Samaritans more understandable.

Philip's exact location is disputed. As the note in the NRSV indicates, some manuscripts read "a city" and some "the city" of Samaria—a tiny discrepancy that creates exegetical problems. The difficulty with "the city," which has the stronger basis in the manuscript tradition, is that, by the first century, the leading city of Samaria is a largely Gentile city renamed "Sebaste" rather than the earlier "Samaria." It is possible that Luke is simply misinformed (Conzelmann 1987, 62), although it may well be that the earlier name persisted in common practice (as in Josephus, *Ant.* 17.289; Hemer 1989, 225-26), and that Luke prefers "Samaria" over "Sebaste" because "Samaria" brings to the surface the promise of 1:8 (Jervell 1998, 259).

Among the signs Luke connects with Philip's activity in Samaria is exorcism, as in the ministry of Jesus as well as in the Jerusalem ministry of the apostles (e.g., Luke 4:33, 36; 6:18; 8:29; 9:42; Acts 5:16). The NRSV smooths out the awkward Greek of v. 7, in which Luke indicates both that the unclean spirits came out of people *and* that they cried out as they did so. The awkwardness may reflect the emphasis Luke draws to this feature of Philip's work, since the battle with unclean spirits reflects the battle between Jesus' agents and Satan. More than simply providing relief for human suffering, exorcism also signals God's power over Satan's realm and prepares for the conflict with Satan implicit in the Simon story (see also Luke 10:17-20).

Even Simon Is Amazed (8:9-13)

Having briefly depicted the gospel's powerful arrival among the crowds in Samaria, Luke turns to an individual whose response to the gospel is far more complicated. With virtually every phrase of vv. 9-11, Luke's portrait of Simon grows increasingly negative. First, he establishes that Simon has been in the city for some time, so that it might be regarded as his "territory." That he is a practitioner of magic means that Luke wishes readers to recognize him as a charlatan, but the label "magician" reaches well beyond that of mere tricksterism. Jews are strictly prohibited from any involvement in magical practices (Deut 18:9-14), not just because it is deceptive but because it is associated with idolatry and with the demonic (Garrett 1989, 13-17, 65-69). Making things worse, Simon has been preaching himself, an act that recalls provocatively the devil's temptation of Jesus (Luke 4:6-7; see Garrett 1989, 67). The result of such perfidy is seen in the populace's response; "from the least to the greatest," they speak of him blasphemously (which is consistent with the negative stereotype of Samaritans as idolaters). Verse 11 sums up the fascination with which the Samaritans have attended to Simon—a fascination that vanishes with Philip's arrival.

Verse 13 completes the reversal: Simon is no longer the one who amazes. He is himself amazed. As early as the patristic period, interpreters debated the sincerity of Simon's actions. Does Simon truly believe Philip's proclamation? If so, what happens to that faith later? Verse 13, in particular, has been combed for any slight hint that perhaps Simon is less than sincere. Yet that approach misconstrues the force of the story. Luke is not concerned about Simon's interior life, he is concerned about Simon's connection with Satan. As with Ananias and Sapphira, this is not a story about the degree of an individual's conviction, but about a conflict of powers—as soon becomes evident.

Jerusalem and Samaria Joined (8:14-17)

Verses 14-17 leave Simon aside and return to the witness among the Samaritans. By sending Peter and John, the Jerusalem community responds to the report that "Samaria had accepted the word of God," and acts to connect Samaria with Jerusalem. Given the rancor between Jews and Samaritans, this in itself is an amazing act. The laying on of hands by representatives of the

Jerusalem church signals this joining of the two. Because Peter and John serve as official envoys from Jerusalem in a region where Philip has been working, some have drawn conclusions about church order and the establishment of an institutional church, inferring that Philip's work requires the approval of the apostles as represented by Peter and John (Fitzmyer 1998, 400-401), but that approach reads Peter and John's journey as an inspection, about which Luke says not a word. Any notion that Peter and John themselves *decide* who receives the Spirit is sharply overturned by v. 20 (not to mention 10:1–11:18, which follows shortly).

The Powerlessness of Simon (8:18-24)

With the completion of the Samaritans' inclusion, Luke returns to the story of Simon (vv. 18-24), and the crowds of Samaritans disappear once again. Witnessing the laying on of hands, Simon offers to pay Peter and John to bestow such power upon him. Simon's brief statement in v. 19 reveals a trinity of profound errors. First, the request reinforces Simon's amazement in v. 13—however great his magic, he has no power of the order of the Holy Spirit. (It is noteworthy that Luke manages to show this without even a hint of how it is that Simon sees the Holy Spirit.) Second, Simon has concluded that Peter and John have the Holy Spirit at their own disposal. Third, Simon regards bribery as the way to achieve the Spirit's power.

Understanding the extent of Simon's error, and especially his association with Satan, makes the apparent harshness of Peter's response understandable. Peter first makes explicit Simon's conviction that he could purchase what only God can give (v. 20). Then Peter declares Simon "without part or share," the same language used of Judas in 1:17, and probably referring to the Spirit's activity rather than the community as such. Declaring that Simon's "heart is not right before God," and that he exists in the "gall of bitterness" and the "chains of wickedness" dramatically signals Simon's opposition to all that God is doing.

The story concludes with v. 24, in which Simon seeks prayer.

As with the earlier claim about Simon's faith, it is futile to ask whether this is genuine repentance or what readers are to imagine becomes of Simon. Instead, what Luke puts on display is the utter powerlessness of the man once declared to be "the power of God that is called Great" (v. 10). Simon cannot even pray for himself, but is reduced to seeking mediation from Peter (Spencer 1997, 89).

Not content with Luke's silence about Simon's fate, later tradition elaborates. Stories include his partner Helen, a miracle contest between Simon and Peter that takes place in Rome, and Simon's own claim to be the Christ (Justin, *1 Apol.* 1; *Trypho* 120; *Acts of Peter* II.4.8-10; *Pseudo-Clementine Homilies* 2.22.3; Stoops 1992).

◊ ◊ ◊ ◊

Flight from persecution in Jerusalem leads both to proclamation and to confrontation. By contrast with those residents of Jerusalem who kill Stephen and reject Christian preaching, and with those Samaritans who would not hear Jesus (Luke 9:51-56), the Samaritans in Acts 8 respond with joy. Now crowds believe and are baptized—both men and women. Samaria is joined together with the faithful in Jerusalem.

By distinguishing baptism in Jesus' name from the reception of the Holy Spirit, Luke appears to contradict Peter's Pentecost sermon, which places repentance, baptism, forgiveness of sins, and the gift of the Holy Spirit in an orderly sequence (2:38). That Luke does not understand that sequence to be universal and rigid becomes apparent not only here but in the Cornelius account as well (10:34-44). The Spirit is not subject to human control, either by purchasing it or by dispensing it liturgically.

If the Samaritan mission displays a warm reception for the gospel, it also acknowledges that resistance to the gospel will extend well beyond Jerusalem. Here that resistance comes in the person of Satan's agent Simon, who seeks to reduce the gospel to a commodity that can be traded for personal gain. The dazzling and powerful Simon is rendered dazzled and powerless in the face of the gospel, however. Finally, he acknowledges the greater power of the Spirit and pleads for intercession.

An Ethiopian Eunuch (8:25-40)

The story of the Ethiopian eunuch initiates a series of conversion narratives, culminating in the conversion of Cornelius (and, along with him, Peter and the Jerusalem church). The Ethiopian's is a dramatic and unusual story, marked by a peculiar setting, multiple directions from divine agents, and a visitor from an exotic homeland whose questions provide the framework for the encounter with Philip (vv. 31, 34, 36).

Structurally, the story is simple. Following a transition statement (v. 25), two human characters come together through divine intervention (vv. 26-28). They enter into a conversation that culminates in the Ethiopian's baptism (vv. 29-38). They go their separate ways (vv. 39-40). It is the detail lavished on the description of the Ethiopian, the conversation between Philip and the Ethiopian, and the introduction of a passage from Isaiah, that renders the story both elusive and instructive.

The story is largely self-contained (Conzelmann 1987, 67). Acts affords the Ethiopian eunuch no further role. Apart from the transitional statement in v. 25, which would seem to return the audience's attention to Jerusalem, the scene could be excised from the book without any logistical difficulties. That sense of its narrative independence, however, has to do with its function as anticipatory event. The Ethiopian is proleptic of all those who will be reached for God through the witness to the gospel (see below).

A Wondrous Traveler (8:25-28)

The story opens, as did 8:4-24, with a summary statement about the witness in Samaria. Although the NRSV identifies "Peter and John" as the ones preaching in Samaria, the Greek has the indefinite "they," which could well include Philip (as in "now those who were scattered," 8:4). With the opening of v. 26, then, readers might expect to see an individual singled out, as Philip is singled out in 8:5. Instead of a human agent, however, Luke provides an unexpected agent, "an angel of the Lord." And the angel directs Philip, not to make a timely visit to another city, but to make a trip at noon to a deserted place. As the note in the NRSV indicates, the phrase "toward the south" may also be translated "at noon." Many interpreters prefer "toward the south," since the midday heat makes travel difficult, even dangerous, in the Middle East. Yet Luke refers to travel at noon elsewhere in Acts (22:6; 26:13; see also Gen 18:1; Jer 6:4), and the sheer unlikeliness of such travel serves the story. Only God could construct such a scenario.

A second improbability occurs in the location to which Philip is directed. He is to go to "the road that goes down from Jerusalem to Gaza. (This is a wilderness road.)" Philip, who has just completed a great work of preaching in Samaria to crowds of people (8:6), now finds himself directed to a deserted place at a time when no sensible person would be present. The force of the command lies in its very absurdity, since God commands what is unexpected, even what is ridiculous (see also, e.g., 5:20; 9:11-12; 10:9-16; Gaventa 1986a, 101-102). Philip does as he is told without question or complaint (contrast Ananias in 9:13-14 and Peter in 10:10-16).

The word "behold" (*idou*; NRSV: Now), as often in biblical narrative, commands attention for what follows (e.g., 1:10; 5:9; 7:56). Precisely here Luke introduces a dramatic figure he identifies as "an Ethiopian male, a eunuch, treasurer of the Candace, queen of the Ethiopians, who was over all her treasury" (AT). The fact that this man is identified as an Ethiopian indicates that he comes from regions south of Egypt and has dark skin. The description importantly plays on well-established interest in Ethiopians. Homer speaks of the "far-off Ethiopians . . . the farthermost of men" (*Odyssey* 1.22-23), and Herodotus describes them as the tallest and most handsome of all the peoples (3.20). Strabo remarks that Ethiopians come from the extremities of the inhabited world (*Geography* 17.2.1; see also Diodorus Siculus

3.1-37; Pliny, *Natural History* 6.35; Dio Cassius 54.5.4). Old Testament and patristic texts also portray Ethiopia as the border of the known world (e.g., Esth 1:1; 8:9; Ezek 29:10; Zeph 3:10; see Snowden, 1970, 1983).

The Ethiopian is also a eunuch. Interpreters have customarily given considerable attention to this fact, because of Old Testament texts that exclude eunuchs from full inclusion in Israel (Deut 23:1; Lev 21:20; Josephus, *Ant.* 4.290-91; but cf. Isa 56:3-5; Wis 3:14). Castrated males often carried major responsibilities in courts of the Near East, however, and the remainder of the description emphasizes this man's importance rather than his impairment. The significance of his work is spelled out in terms of his oversight of the queen's treasury.

The Ethiopian serves "the Candace, the queen of the Ethiopians." He comes from Meroe, a kingdom established and powerful since before the time of Alexander the Great, and one whose queens conventionally bore the title "Candace." Recent events would have placed Meroe in the spotlight, since Augustus's general Gaius Petronius had led a military campaign against the Candace's army when Ethiopians pushed into Elephantine. Scientific expeditions into Meroe were conducted under Nero around 62 CE, and he had also planned, though never executed, a military campaign against Meroe (Dio Cassius 54.5.4; Strabo, *Geography* 17.1.54; Pliny, *Natural History* 6.35; Dinkler 1975, 91).

Luke comments at the end of v. 27 that the eunuch had come to Jerusalem in order to worship. Although the remark has prompted some interpreters to conclude that he must be a proselyte to Judaism, Gentiles were permitted entrance to the outer court of the Jerusalem temple (Josephus, *J.W.* 2.409-16; Schürer 1979, 2:309-13; Sanders 1992, 72-76). In addition, the popular mind seems to have viewed both Ethiopians and eunuchs as especially sensitive to religious matters. Thus, worshiping in Jerusalem indicates the receptivity of this particular individual, but it does not necessarily imply his conversion to Judaism.

Having been to Jerusalem, the Ethiopian now returns and is reading aloud along the way, as was customary for travelers (Hock 1980, 28). What is at first perplexing here is that the eunuch has in his possession and is reading a scroll that contains a passage from Isaiah. Although some have concluded from this detail that the eunuch must have been a proselyte, that does not necessarily follow. It suffices to notice that he is a person of means or at least access to wealth (he has a scroll and rides in a chariot), and he has an interest in reading Jewish scripture. The fact that he reads from the scroll provides Philip (or the Spirit) with an opportunity for approaching the eunuch.

One area of debate over this passage is whether Luke understands the Ethiopian to be a proselyte to Judaism (or perhaps a "God-fearer") or a Gentile. Because of his worship in Jerusalem, and especially because Luke clearly marks the conversion of Cornelius as the first occasion for the inclusion of Gentiles, commentators often insist that the Ethiopian is a Jew (either by birth or conversion; see, e.g., Fitzmyer 1998, 412). That is unlikely, however, because of the exclusion of eunuchs noted earlier in Old Testament texts. He is a Gentile, which contributes to Luke's portrait of him as an unlikely but eager recipient of the gospel.

The Ethiopian and Philip (8:29-38)

The detailed introduction of the Ethiopian now completed, the Spirit speaks to Philip and directs him to the chariot. Earlier, an angel instructs Philip (v. 26), and now the Spirit; each scene is choreographed by divine agents. As Philip complies with this new instruction, he hears the man reading from Isaiah, something the narrator has already mentioned in v. 28. The repetition underscores the importance of this text and its discussion in the verses that follow.

Philip and the Ethiopian exchange questions. Literarily, the exchange prompts Philip to join the Ethiopian in the chariot and introduces the remarks that follow. Theologically, the exchange coheres with Luke's understanding of Scripture in an important way, for Scripture requires interpretation. Earlier, the risen Jesus himself discloses the meaning of Scripture for his followers (Luke 24:44-47), and here Philip interprets Scripture through the events of the gospel.

The passage to which Luke draws attention is Isa 53:7-8. Both in the Hebrew and in the LXX translation that Luke quotes, the passage abounds with unclarity. Among the major difficulties is v. 33, which can be translated in almost contradictory ways. Verse 33*a* can be read as the NRSV does, "justice was denied him," or "his condemnation was taken away." The exact implication of v. 33*b* is also unclear, since the connotation of "generation" might refer to his family history or to his own generation. Verse 33*c* can mean either that his life "is taken away" (NRSV) or perhaps that he is "taken up" in the sense of resurrection. By contrast with these considerable problems, the eunuch's question is precise, namely, about whom does the prophet speak (a question that has consistently plagued interpreters of the Isaiah passage).

From the vantage point of Luke, of course, there is no debate on this question, and Philip "begins with this scripture" to proclaim Jesus. Another important feature of Luke's understanding of Scripture appears here, since, for Luke, all of Scripture has to do with Jesus. Exactly what this passage may say about Jesus, Luke does not specify. At the very least, it concerns the death of one who is innocent. It may also be significant that the passage the Ethiopian reads does not refer to Israel's ancestors (cf. 2:29; 3:13), since that lineage does not include the Ethiopian as it does the Jewish audience in Jerusalem.

Luke reports nothing more of the conversation or its content, moving immediately in v. 36 to the Ethiopian's request for baptism, introduced with "Behold!" (*idou*; NRSV: Look). Again here, the eunuch's eagerness emerges as he takes the initiative, asks the question about baptism, and commands that the chariot halt. Perhaps it is discomfort with the haste of the narration, which includes not even a profession of faith, that prompted an early scribe to insert v. 37, but the verse does not appear in early or significant manuscripts.

"On His Way Rejoicing" (8:39-40)

The conclusion of this story is no less amazing than its beginning. As Luke describes it, the Spirit grasps Philip almost as the two leave the baptismal water. With no explanation of how Philip's transport is accomplished, Luke notes only that he "found himself" in Azotus, a city on the coast some twenty-two miles north of Gaza. He continues to preach in the cities between Azotus and Caesarea, which apparently is (or becomes) his home. Much later, Paul will stay with Philip in Caesarea and meet his four prophesying daughters (21:8-9).

Luke's only comment about the Ethiopian eunuch is that he "went on his way rejoicing" (v. 39). That remark bristles with significance, since it later becomes a hallmark of the response of Gentiles to the gospel (13:48; 15:31). Later church tradition reports that the Ethiopian returns home as a proclaimer of the gospel (Irenaeus, *Adv. Haer.* 3.12.8), a trajectory that extends beyond Luke's story but one he would surely have appreciated.

◊ ◊ ◊ ◊

Discerning the theological importance of this story requires that readers take seriously its fantastic character. The timing in the heat of noonday, the location in the wilderness, the exotic description of the Ethiopian, the citation of a bewildering passage of Scripture, and the divine direction all contribute to the impact of the story—to say nothing of the Spirit's unusual mode of transportation. Luke offers a story suffused with the unexpected, and in so doing he presents the Ethiopian as the ideal convert, one who is already seeking God, who hears and responds, and who rejoices in the gift of the gospel. That this particular convert comes from the boundary of the experience of Luke and his audience—an Ethiopian, a eunuch, a powerful official in a court from the end of Luke's world—suggests that he anticipates all those from "the ends of the earth" who will rejoice in the good news of Jesus Christ. In a sense, the Ethiopian's story stands above the developing plot, inviting the audience to understand that "the ends of the earth" includes all; the story of the Ethiopian does not conflict with but anticipates the story of Cornelius and the church (Gaventa 1986a, 106-107).

Receptive as the Ethiopian is, he is not the initiator of this wondrous event. Nor does the church take the lead here; Jerusalem and its representative Peter are nowhere in view. The initiative comes entirely from God's agents—the angel who sends Philip on his way, the Spirit who nudges Philip toward the chariot, and the Spirit who whisks Philip away following the baptism. Throughout the story, Philip does what he is told, but very little else (Haenchen 1971, 316).

The familiarity of the Isaianic text employed in this story tempts readers to discern here distinctive features of Luke's Christology. That Luke does not quote the preceding verses from Isaiah 53:4-6 with their language about vicarious suffering, has often been emphasized as indicating that Luke downplays the atonement. Particularly given the difficulty of translating v. 33, it may suffice to note that the figure in the quotation, like the Lukan Jesus, dies wrongfully. Luke is less intent on developing specific elements of this passage from Isaiah than he is on the sheer fact that it provides a beginning point for proclamation of Jesus.

From Persecutor to Proclaimer (9:1-30)

Among Luke's finest stories is this account of God's transformation of the persecutor Saul into an ardent proclaimer of the gospel. The drama unfolds in five scenes: (1) the persecution of Christians that Saul exports from Jerusalem to Damascus (vv. 1-2), (2) the encounter between Saul and the risen Jesus (vv. 3-9), (3) the commission of Ananias and his resistance to that commission (vv. 10-16), (4) the action of Ananias and its resultant healing of Saul (vv. 17-19a), and (5) the emergence of Saul as one persecuted on behalf of the gospel (vv. 19b-30). Along with its several echoes of Old Testament narratives, its use of a double vision is an important literary feature of the drama. The vision in which God directs Ananias to Saul contains within it Saul's own vision of Ananias coming to him (vv. 11-12). The two reinforce each other and serve a single narrative purpose (Lohfink 1976, 73-77).

Luke will return to this event two more times (22:3-21; 26:2-

23), and scholars have often attributed the complex similarities and differences among the three versions to Luke's use of multiple sources (Hirsch 1929, 305-12). Contemporary scholars generally agree, however, that Luke made use of a single account and modified it in ways appropriate for three distinct narrative contexts. In the present context, following the conversion of the Ethiopian eunuch, emphasis falls on the extension of the Christian witness beyond Jerusalem and its inhabitants. Fulfilling Jesus' promise in 1:8, the gospel first moves into Samaria (8:5-24), then encounters the wondrous Ethiopian eunuch who seeks after God (8:25-40), and finally overcomes the raging enemy Saul in chapter 9. All of these steps anticipate the story of Cornelius in chapter 10 (Gaventa 1986a, 123-25).

The question of how to reconcile Luke's accounts with the scanty comments in Paul's letters is also complicated (1 Cor 9:1; 15:8-10; Gal 1:11-17; Phil 3:2-11). Historical assessments range from arguments in favor of Luke's general accuracy (e.g., Wenham 1993) to the classification of Luke's story as legend (Conzelmann 1987, 72-73), with little prospect of a consensus emerging. The differences between Luke's accounts and Paul's remarks are so extensive that the similarities emerge sharply. The accounts agree that Paul persecuted Christians, although it is unclear that Paul refers to officially sanctioned, physical persecution. They further agree in their insistence that the conversion was God's own doing. Both connect the revelation to a call to proclaim the gospel, and both comment on the amazement of believers at the emergence of Paul as witness for Jesus (Gal 1:23; Gaventa 1978, 196-245).

◊ ◊ ◊ ◊

Persecution Beyond Jerusalem (9:1-2)

Scene 1 reintroduces Saul with clear references back to his initial appearance at Stephen's death (7:58; 8:1, 3). Luke explains that Saul is "still breathing threats and murder," thereby fulfilling Stephen's words in 7:52 (see also the "threats" of 3 Macc

2:24; 5:18, 37; 4 Macc 4:8). The objects of his wrath are the "disciples of the Lord." Although the noun "disciple" (*mathētēs*) appears seven times in this chapter and twenty-eight times in Acts as a whole, this is the only time the word bears the qualification "of the Lord." The earlier contrast between Saul and Stephen now becomes a contrast between Saul and the Lord's disciples. Saul's fearsome breath takes specific form in v. 2, when he seeks from the high priest official authorization to find believers in Damascus. This movement outside Jerusalem escalates Saul's persecution yet again: If the preaching of the disciples is no longer confined to Jerusalem (8:4-40), the same is true of their persecution. Questions about how Christians came to be in Damascus (refugees from persecution in Jerusalem? an unreported mission there? returning pilgrims from Pentecost?), how Saul knows of them, and why he selected that city all fall by the wayside as Luke focuses on the story of the persecutor Saul.

"I Am Jesus, Whom You Are Persecuting" (9:3-9)

Scene 2 opens as Saul, the church's enemy, sets out for Damascus. Verse *3b* describes an abrupt interruption in Saul's journey, in response to which he falls to the ground. The heavenly light signals divine intervention; it also coheres with the larger Lukan motif of the gospel as an occasion for the giving of light (see Luke 2:32; Acts 26:18; Tannehill 1990, 121). The language used recalls descriptions of hearing God's voice in the Old Testament (e.g., Num 7:89; Isa 6:8). What Saul hears begins with the double vocative ("Saul, Saul") familiar from Old Testament narratives (e.g., Gen 22:11; 46:2; Exod 3:4; 1 Sam 3:4, 10). Following the double vocative comes the question that epitomizes Saul's activity to date: "Why do you persecute me?" The verb "persecute" (*diōkō*) seldom occurs in Luke–Acts apart from its connection with Saul (Acts 22:4, 7, 8; 26:11, 14, 15; see also Luke 11:49; 17:23; 21:12; Acts 7:52). Saul is, for Luke, the one who deserves the title "Persecutor."

Saul responds with a question that enhances the drama of this scene. The question necessitates the explicit identification of the speaker and permits repeating the accusation against Saul. It also introduces a note of irony. Saul addresses the speaker as *kyrios*, which may signify either the worshipful "lord" or simply the polite "sir." Because the question itself indicates that Saul does not know the identity of the one who has spoken, it seems that the latter definition is implied. Saul will soon, however, regard this speaker as "lord," and Luke's introduction of *kyrios* here anticipates that time.

The response to Saul's question is emphatic: "I am Jesus whom you are persecuting" (v. 5*b*). Both pronouns are emphatic, heightening the distance between Jesus and Saul, and underscoring the importance of this statement, which recalls Luke 10:16, "Whoever rejects you, rejects me" (Haenchen 1971, 322). At this point, Saul's role remains unchanged; he still figures entirely as the persecutor. What is new here is the identification of Jesus as the object of Saul's persecution. All that Saul has been involved in now acquires its proper title: persecutor of Jesus.

A simple command follows: "But get up and enter the city, and you will be told what you are to do" (v. 6). In the single word "but" stands the disjuncture between Saul the enemy and the new figure who emerges from this event. "Get up and enter" reflects once more the language of the Septuagint, where *anistēmi* frequently introduces divine commissions (e.g., Gen 21:18; 31:13; 1 Kgs 17:9; Jonah 1:2). Verse 6*b* announces that a commission will follow, although not yet what it will be. Here Luke again uses *dei* ("it is necessary"; obscured in the NRSV's "what you are to do"), a word he associates with the fulfillment of the divine plan (as in, e.g., Luke 21:9; 22:37; 24:26; Acts 1:16; 17:3; 19:21; 23:11).

With the announcement that Saul will be told what he must do, the encounter closes. This scene, which identifies Saul's activity and brings it to an abrupt halt, forms a major turning point in the narrative of Acts. The crescendo of Luke's portrait of Saul the enemy has stopped. Verses 7-9 have a transitional function. They look back to the encounter with Jesus and emphasize its results, but they also prepare for Ananias's role by describing Saul's blindness.

Verse 7 mentions Saul's companions for the first time: they

"stood speechless, because they heard the voice but saw no one" (cf. Acts 22:9; 26:14). The companions stand in contrast to Saul and underscore the importance of the encounter because their own experience of it differs. When Luke says that they do not see anyone, he uses the verb *theōreō*, frequently employed for seeing some manifestation of God's activity (e.g., Luke 10:18; 24:37, 39; Acts 3:16; 7:56) or for understanding the import of an event (Acts 4:13; 17:22; 21:20; 27:10). That the companions do not see may imply that they are unmoved by what has occurred. Certainly they do not figure elsewhere in this account as witnesses to the reality of Saul's experience.

If v. 7 presents Saul's companions as unaffected by the event, vv. 8-9 convey quite the opposite regarding Saul himself. The encounter renders him helpless and Luke's repetition makes the point inescapable: although he opens his eyes, Saul cannot see (*blepō*, not *theōreō* as in v. 7). Unable to follow the Lord's order on his own, he must be led into Damascus by the hand. Finally, in addition to the fact that he remains blind for three days, he neither eats nor drinks.

Because Luke says that Saul did not eat or drink, interpreters sometimes contend that this is a period of penance (Haenchen 1971, 323). The text does not describe this period as penance, however, and evidence elsewhere in Luke–Acts does not support that conclusion (cf. Luke 4:2; 7:33; Acts 23:12; see also Exod 34:28; 1 Sam 20:34; LXX Tob 10:7). Indeed, this report parallels the very first reference to Saul in 7:58, where the witnesses to Stephen's death place their cloaks at the feet of a bystander. In both passages, Saul is passive, and each text introduces him. In addition to their function of closing off the encounter scene, vv. 8-9 also introduce the new Saul. As before, he is at first passive; his real identity emerges only gradually.

Ananias Resists the Lord (9:10-16)

Verse 10 introduces a new character, Ananias, who is a disciple in Damascus. Ananias receives instructions regarding an unexpected turn of events, and he receives the instructions by means of a vision, as happens often in Acts (e.g., 10:3, 17, 19; 11:5; 16:9, 10; 18:9; cf. 2:17). When Ananias hears his name, he responds with the stereotypical formula, "Here I am" (see Gen 22:1; 1 Sam 3:6, 8; Isa 6:8). The first stage in the instructions Ananias receives is straightforward. He is to go to a particular place and seek a particular individual. The *idou gar* ("for behold," omitted in the NRSV) at the end of v. 11 announces that something surprising follows, something worthy of note (e.g., Luke 1:44, 48; 2:10; 17:21; van Unnik 1973a, 330-31). In this instance two developments account for the *idou gar*: (1) Saul is praying, and (2) in a vision, Saul sees Ananias come so that he might be healed.

That Saul is praying signals that he has moved beyond the immobility described in vv. 8-9. Whether his prayer implies faith is more difficult to say. The prayer may parallel Saul's earlier approval of the murder of Stephen (8:1); he consents, but he does not yet actively participate. The fact that Saul sees Ananias stands as the final part of Ananias's commission, and the commission itself is not explicitly stated. Because Ananias understands the description of Saul's vision as a commission for himself, he begins to object. What he says in vv. 13-14 recapitulates information about Saul from 8:3 and 9:1-2, but it does so in an emphatic way. Ananias has heard about Saul "from many"; he did evil things to "your saints," and here he has authority against "all who invoke your name." In other words, Ananias says, "But this one is the enemy."

The response of the Lord in vv. 15-16 also centers on the identity of Saul. For the Lord, however, he is not enemy or persecutor, but "an instrument whom I have chosen." In addition, like Ananias's description, the response emphasizes the relationship between Saul and the Lord: "to bring my name . . . I will show him . . . suffer on behalf of my name." In the new description of Saul, emphasis rests on the phrase *skeuos eklogēs* (lit., chosen instrument), which stands at the beginning in the Greek text. This is the only instance of the noun *eklogē* in Luke–Acts, but a related verb occurs in connection with the choosing of someone for a particular role (see Acts 1:2, 24-25; 6:5). Saul's calling is not simply that which belongs to any believer; instead, he is chosen for a particular role.

The remainder of v. 15 reinforces that conclusion. Saul is "to bring my name before Gentiles and kings and before the children of Israel." Nowhere else does Luke employ this exact expression, but he frequently refers to the power of "the name" and belief "in the name" (e.g., Luke 24:47; Acts 2:38; 3:6; 4:10; 5:28). One of the ironies in this scene involves the contrast between Saul as the one who persecutes those who "invoke the name" (v. 14) and Saul as the one who himself bears the name (vv. 15, 16). The order in which the groups appear (Gentiles, kings, children of Israel) has caused some consternation because it does not represent the order in which Paul actually preaches. It is not obviously programmatic as is Acts 1:8, which anticipates the movement of the church's preaching, but it does look ahead to the time when Paul will witness before Gentiles (Acts 13:44–28:32), kings (Acts 26), and the children of Israel (Acts 22) (Schubert 1968a, 7).

Verse 16 completes the new description of Saul by reference to the suffering that will eventually be a part of his identity. The verse exactly reverses Ananias's words in vv. 13-14 (Haenchen 1971, 325). The one who did *hosa kaka* ("how much evil") to those "who invoke your name" will now suffer *hosa* "for the sake of my name." This verse also recalls v. 6, in which Saul hears that he will be told what it is necessary for him to do. Now at least part of that divine necessity has been revealed, in that Saul will bear the name and "he must suffer" (lit., "it is necessary"; *dei*).

Brother Saul (9:17-19a)

Scene 4 opens with Ananias fulfilling the vision of Saul exactly as v. 12 had originally anticipated—he enters the house and lays hands upon Saul. With his first words to Saul, Ananias enacts the changed identity of Saul. He speaks no longer about "this man" (v. 13), but to "Brother Saul." Ananias then explains that "the Lord Jesus who appeared to you" has sent him as well. One additional phrase refers back to Saul's encounter. "On your way here" recalls both Saul's interrupted journey and the "Way" of v. 2.

Ananias's final words explain that he has come so that Saul may "regain your sight and be filled with the Holy Spirit." Immediately after these words, "something like scales" fall from Saul's eyes, he regains his sight, is baptized, and is strengthened with food (vv. 18-19*a*). At first glance, there seems to be some difficulty with this report. Ananias says that he has come so that Saul may see and receive the Spirit. In what follows, however, no mention is made of receiving the Spirit. Instead, Saul is baptized. This tiny anomaly should not prompt the conclusion that Luke believed Saul never received the Spirit or that some earlier text has been edited. Instead, Ananias's words together with Saul's actions comprise the whole event.

This fourth scene bears considerable resemblance to a miracle story. The subject's illness and the intensity of the illness are not described, having already been introduced in vv. 7-9. The healing itself is tersely stated, followed by a demonstration of the cure (vv. 18-19). The next scene offers further evidence of the cure (v. 20) and the (delayed) amazement of the bystanders (v. 21). Unlike most healings, however, the focus here is on the subject of the healing rather than on the healer. The agent of the healing, Ananias, has completely disappeared from view by the end of this scene, and the healed Saul remains at the center of the drama. No longer reduced to inactivity or in the consensual stage of prayer, Saul becomes active once again. He sees again, he rises to be baptized, and he is strengthened by food. The parallel to his emerging activity as persecutor in 7:58, 8:1-3, and 9:1-2 is complete.

The Proclaimer Persecuted (9:19b-30)

Scene 5 describes the aftermath of the conversion and introduces certain themes that are significant throughout Luke's portrayal of Saul. Crucial both for what precedes and what follows are vv. 20-21. Saul's "immediate" action is to preach that Jesus is the Son of God. The declaration is remarkable, since v. 20 is the only time the title "Son of God" appears in Acts (although see Luke 1:32, 35; 3:22; 4:3, 9, 41; 22:70). As had Ananias before them, those who hear Saul's preaching respond with the old identification of Saul as the persecutor. Such a response only serves to increase the intensity of Saul's preaching (v. 22).

With v. 23, the prophecy that Saul would suffer on behalf of the name begins to be fulfilled, as some who hear Saul concoct a plot to kill him, something that happens often later in the narrative (see especially 20:3, 19; 23:12-23; 25:1-5). Just as Luke has given no motivation for Saul's own persecution of Christians, so here no motive accounts for the actions of this group. For the first time, Luke distinguishes "the Jews" from Saul and his fellow-believers. Although Saul will later adamantly identify himself as a Jew (22:3), the phrase "the Jews" in Acts frequently signals those who actively oppose the gospel (e.g., 13:45, 50; 14:2, 5; 17:5, 13; 18:12; 20:3, 19). Saul's escape through the wall (see Josh 2:15; 2 Cor 11:32-33) is facilitated by "his" disciples. Only here does Acts speak of the disciples of anyone except Jesus, and it is not surprising that some ancient manuscripts read "the disciples" instead of "his" disciples. In the context of this story, the phrase "his disciples" emphasizes the reversal, since the one who earlier went to Damascus to hunt down "the disciples of the Lord" now has the Lord's disciples, in some limited sense, also as his own.

Escaping from danger in Damascus, Saul finds that his "way" is not an easy one even in Jerusalem, because Jesus' followers do not believe that he is a disciple (v. 26). Here Barnabas returns to the story, and the faulty etymology Luke gave for his name in 4:36 is proved an accurate description as Barnabas becomes the encourager of the community. He defends Saul and thereby repeats once again the story of Saul's encounter with the risen Jesus. As a result of Barnabas's intervention, Saul preaches "boldly" (see 4:13, 29-31; 18:26; 28:31) in Jerusalem and finds himself in conflict with "the Hellenists." The term here apparently refers to Greek-speaking Jews who have not become believers, although it was earlier used for Greek-speaking Jews among Jesus' followers (6:1). Yet another threat to Saul's life prompts his exile to Tarsus, and he remains out of sight until 11:25. The cycle is complete: the persecutor has become the persecuted.

◊ ◊ ◊ ◊

Resistance to God's will takes many forms in Acts, but perhaps this story of the reversal of the enemy Saul is the most vivid and developed instance, involving not only Saul's resistance to God but believers' resistance to Saul. From his very first appearance in Acts 7:58 until he departs for Tarsus in 9:30, the story deals with Saul as the enemy. He is first the active persecutor of disciples, then the immobilized persecutor, and finally the preacher whose former persecution arouses suspicion. By means of the increasing activity of Saul, first as persecutor and then as believer, Luke has underscored the reversal aspect of the narrative. In this sense, then, it is entirely appropriate to identify this story as one of conversion, because the persecutor has been converted into a proclaimer.

Saul is not the only resister in the narrative, of course. Ananias resists God's demand that he go to Saul. Christians in both Damascus and Jerusalem resist Saul's initial preaching, clinging to their perception of him as the community's enemy (Marguerat 1995, 147). And some Jews in both cities act out their resistance in a plot to kill him.

Precisely as a story about the overthrow of an enemy and the necessity of overruling even disciples, Acts 9:1-30 contributes to one of Luke's major themes, the power of God. Throughout his two-volume work, Luke relentlessly shows God as the author of events. One of the ways in which God's authorship of events is depicted is when the church finds itself in adverse situations: those who oppose the will of God find themselves thwarted.

Although this is primarily a narrative of the reversal of an enemy, it also contains a call or commissioning. The call comes to expression explicitly in v. 6 and vv. 15-16, as well as in Saul's actions in vv. 19b-30, his initial fulfillment of that call. Conversion and call here are one event, since the reversal of Saul has to do with the task he is to undertake. This is not a story of salvation by conversion but of conversion to a particular mission (see also Gal 1:16).

Lydda and Joppa Turn to the Lord (9:31-43)

The summary description of the church that opens this unit recalls others Luke provides at a number of transitions (v. 31; see also 2:41-47; 4:32-37; 5:12-16; 6:7). Although the statement in some sense points backward, especially to developments in Judea and Samaria, it is connected with v. 32 grammatically. The NRSV obscures the fact that v. 31 opens with "on the one hand" (*men*), and v. 32 with "on the other hand" (*de*; for similar constructions, see e.g., 1:6-7; 2:41-42; 8:4-5, 25-26). In substance also, v. 31 belongs with vv. 32-43, since these stories of healing and conversion give specificity to the assertions of the summary statement about the growth and well-being of the church.

Two healing stories comprise the remainder of the unit. Verses 32-35 narrate the healing of Aeneas, and vv. 36-43 narrate the more elaborate account of the healing of Tabitha. Both stories follow the conventional form for healings—introduction of the individual with some indication of the severity of the condition, the healing itself, a demonstration of the effect of the healing, and response to the healing—except that in both stories the stereotypical amazement includes turning to or believing in the Lord.

Some features of these stories recall the miraculous healings of Elijah, Elisha, and Jesus, including prayer in an upper room (1 Kgs 17:17-24), healing of a man suffering from paralysis (Luke 5:17-26), and the restoration to life of one who has died (1 Kgs 17:17-24; 2 Kgs 4:18-37; Luke 7:11-17; 8:49-56). Later on Paul also will heal a man who cannot walk (14:8-12) and will restore the life of Eutychus (20:7-12).

This unit reintroduces Peter, who has not appeared in the narrative since his return to Jerusalem from Samaria (8:25) and who will figure importantly in 10:1–11:18. The miraculous healings and the responses to those healings prepare for the remarkable events of Cornelius's conversion. Preparation for the Cornelius episode is not the sole function of this passage, however, since it demonstrates the Lord's healing power as well as evidencing the mutual support and care in one believing community.

◊ ◊ ◊ ◊

In Greek, the summary statement that opens the unit consists of one lengthy statement, rather than the two sentences of the NRSV. Verse 31 characterizes the church as increasing while "having peace," "being built up," and "walking in the fear of the Lord and by the comfort of the Holy Spirit." Tempting as it is to wonder whether there is some correlation between peace in the church and sending Paul away to distant Tarsus, Luke early on identifies peace as among the signs of the salvation brought by Jesus (Luke 1:79; 2:14, 29; 7:50; Acts 10:36). Similarly, references to the strengthening of the church and the presence of the Holy Spirit have appeared in the narrative since Pentecost as indications of the church's existence in God's favor. Luke has not previously characterized the church itself with the phrase "fear of the Lord," the awe that is an appropriate response to the divine (although see 2:43), but it may be especially important here, as one of the first things said about Cornelius is that he fears God (10:2).

Several other details in the summary merit notice. Because Luke elsewhere employs the singular noun "church" to refer to a group of Christians in a particular location (e.g., 8:1; 13:1; 20:7), its appearance here with regard to believers in the whole of Judea and Galilee and Samaria is noteworthy. It is also exceptional to find the locations listed in that particular order, since geographically one moves north from Judea through Samaria to Galilee, not from Judea to Galilee and then Samaria (see also Luke 17:11). More significant than the ordering of place names is the fact that Galilee has not been mentioned since the reference to the apostles as "Men of Galilee" in 1:11. The lack of reference to Galilee as a venue for Christian mission may mean that the Christian community in Galilee was never strong (Barrett 1994, 473; Davies 1974, 421-44).

The Healing of Aeneas and the Conversion of Lydda (9:32-35)

The story opens with scant detail. Without a word about Peter's activities since returning to Jerusalem in 8:25, the narrator begins with his travels, expressed in general terms. It remains unclear what motivates his journey, and none of the traditional language for preaching or teaching amplifies the description (cf. 8:4, 40). He arrives in Lydda, a town at the southern end of the coastal plain of Sharon.

Once in Lydda, Peter goes to the "saints" who live there. The reference to Paul as persecuting the "saints" in 9:13 and 26:10 surely means that the "saints" in Lydda are believers rather than the Jewish population in general. Again, however, Luke has said nothing about believers in Lydda, leaving it quite uncertain whether there has been a mission there (perhaps carried out by Philip as he traveled to Caesarea; see 8:40) or whether believers arrived there as they fled the persecution in Jerusalem (8:1). Luke's attention to the movement from Jerusalem to Judea and Samaria (1:8) does not make this narrative into a detailed chronicle itemizing the arrival of the gospel in various individual locations.

Aeneas, the man who will be healed, also receives no introduction beyond his name and his condition. Luke does not even identify him as a believer. Since he enters the story immediately following the introduction of the "saints" of Lydda, it seems likely that he is among them, but that point is perhaps irrelevant to the story, which turns on Jesus' healing power rather than on Aeneas's character or even his faith.

The story proceeds with remarkable economy, as Luke explains that Aeneas has been paralyzed for eight years. Peter speaks directly: "Aeneas, Jesus Christ heals you. Get up and make your bed." By contrast with the healing in chapter 3, in which Peter's declaration contains an elaborate introduction that attributes healing to Jesus' name, here the statement directly identifies Jesus as the healer. (See also 26:23, where Paul describes Jesus as the preacher of light.)

With brevity of expression consistent with the remainder of the story, the result unfolds. Aeneas arises, and "all the residents of Lydda and Sharon saw [the now restored Aeneas] and turned to the Lord." Luke often uses the language of "turning" for repentance and conversion (e.g., 3:19; 11:21), especially in the case of Gentile believers (14:15; 15:19; 26:20). The hyperbole of the claim that "all" turned to the Lord recalls Luke's description of the response to John the Baptist (see Luke 3:7, 15, 21) as well as the multitudes baptized in Jerusalem (2:41; 4:4).

The Raising of Tabitha and the Conversion of Joppa (9:36-43)

Luke frequently presents pairs of scenes, one of which involves a male character and the other a female character (e.g., Luke 1:11-20//26-38; 2:25-35//36-38; 24:12//1-11), so it is not surprising, at this point, to find a story involving a female character. What is unusual in this instance is that the story of Aeneas is told with such brevity and that of Tabitha in considerable detail (contrast this pair, e.g., with Simeon and Anna in Luke 2:25-38 or Ananias and Sapphira in Acts 5:1-11). Another unusual feature of the story is that healings generally involve individuals about whom little information is revealed, but here substantial information emerges about Tabitha.

After a brief introductory phrase shifts the location to Joppa, the story introduces Tabitha as a disciple. Unlike Aeneas, whose stance toward the gospel Luke never specifies, the first thing revealed about Tabitha is that she is a believer. This is the only time the feminine noun *mathētria* ([female] disciple) appears in the New Testament. Next Luke provides for her both an Aramaic name, Tabitha, and its Greek translation, Dorcas, or gazelle. Tabitha is further described as devoted to good works and acts of charity. Luke does not specify what those activities are, although sewing clothing for widows is certainly to be included among them (v. 39). The reference to "acts of charity" anticipates the parallel description of the generosity of powerful Cornelius in 10:2 (the Greek word is *eleēmosynē* in both texts). In addition, this description of her conforms to Luke's implicit association of faithful believers with the responsible use of possessions (see, e.g., 4:36-37; 16:15; 20:33-35).

Verse 37 briefly reports Tabitha's death and, in another slight departure from the conventional healing story, reports the washing of her body and the placing of it in a room upstairs (see 1 Kgs 17:17-24; and also Acts 1:13; 20:8). Although washing a corpse is a common custom in antiquity, no mention of it elsewhere makes its way into biblical narrative. The inclusion of this intimate detail here provides one of several indications of Tabitha's significance to this community of believers.

Further evidence of care for Tabitha emerges in v. 38 as the disciples of Joppa learn about Peter's presence in nearby Lydda and send an urgent request that he come to Joppa. As often in Luke–Acts, two messengers make the trip (e.g., Acts 1:10; 10:7; 19:22; 23:23). Luke does not explain how news of Peter's presence in Lydda reaches Joppa; nor does he bother reporting the exchange between these envoys and Peter.

Details do return to the story in v. 39*b*, with the entrance of "the widows" who have gathered to mourn and who show Peter the clothing made for them by Tabitha. Earlier, Luke narrated a critical moment in Jerusalem, when certain widows found themselves neglected by the community that was said to allow no one to be in need (6:1-6). In Joppa, the fact that the widows have been cared for by Tabitha's own labor exemplified her "good works," but it should not be assumed that sewing for others is the extent of her labor (Reimer 1995, 61). The exhibition of the clothing Tabitha provided reveals something specific in her activity, but it also concretizes the bond between her and the widows. Their loss is severe.

Luke recounts the restoration of Tabitha's life simply, but still again with more detail than is provided concerning the healing of Aeneas. Peter dismisses others from the room, kneels for prayer, and then addresses her directly: "Tabitha, get up." Following the miracle itself, Peter shows her to "the saints and widows," perhaps distinguishing the widows again because of their concrete needs and the responsibility of the community to care for them. Luke does not provide the anticipated comment here about the amazement of these witnesses (see, e.g., Luke 5:26; 7:16-17; Acts 3:10), and it may be that the point of this reunion is less to confirm the miracle than to restore Dorcas to her community and her continued service.

The story concludes with two brief reports, one in v. 42 about the faith-generating character of this event, and the other in v. 43 about Peter's continued stay in Joppa.

◊ ◊ ◊ ◊

Because Luke provides a more extensive presentation of Tabitha than of other persons who receive healing, and because she is female, this story has figured in scholarly discussions about Luke's treatment of female characters (see Introduction). The question is a complicated one and ought not be reduced to the question whether Luke is "favorable" or "unfavorable" in his characterizations. Neither here nor elsewhere does Luke show women in the act of prophesying or preaching (despite 2:17-18 and 21:9). Yet Tabitha's actions evidently play an important role among believers in Joppa, for whom her death constitutes a crisis.

Perhaps there is a slender connection between the significance of Tabitha's actions and the faith-generating power of the healings. The notion that miracles of this sort would cause whole populations to "turn to the Lord" raises concerns about "cheap faith" that will fade as quickly as Peter sets out for Caesarea. Luke, however, does not seem compelled to include a report of preaching and teaching in Lydda and Joppa, because the healings themselves constitute a witness to Jesus. Perhaps Tabitha's actions constitute the same sort of witness, in that her actions are a form of proclamation.

Luke carefully distinguishes between Peter's presence in these events and any ascription of healing power to Peter himself. He directly announces to Aeneas that it is Jesus Christ who sends healing, and his prayer in v. 40 signals that the raising of Tabitha is also not his own doing. In fact, nothing in the passage draws attention to Peter; apart from his name, nothing in the text identifies him or qualifies him, so that it is misleading to refer to these incidents as demonstrations of Peter's authority or power.

Scholars sometimes comment on the absence of Jesus from the Acts of the Apostles, and it is certainly correct to observe that the ascension depicts him graphically removed from the disciples' presence (and see 3:21). Yet there are important indications that Luke understands Jesus as very much present and active in the work of the apostles, and this passage provides one of those indications. It is not Peter who heals Aeneas and restores Tabitha, but Jesus Christ himself.

Lord of All . . . Even All the Gentiles (10:1–11:18)

This elaborately narrated unit constitutes the climactic moment of the first half of Acts. Luke signaled it with the promise of the risen Lord in 1:8 ("You will be my witnesses in Jerusalem, in all Judea and Samaria, and to the ends of the earth"). The stories of the witness in Samaria, the marvelous conversion of the Ethiopian eunuch, and the reversal of the enemy Saul have further extended the gospel's scope and anticipated fulfillment of the promise that Jesus would be a "light for revelation to the Gentiles" (Luke 2:32; see also 3:6; Acts 2:39). Here Luke narrates both the revelation of the light to a Gentile household and the church's own resistance to that development. Immediately following the Cornelius narrative comes the formation of a Gentile Christian community at Antioch (11:19-26). With the beginning of the mission of Paul and Barnabas begins also the pattern of divided response, in which many Gentiles turn to God (13:44-52). Finally in Acts 15 it becomes necessary for the Jerusalem church to address directly the consequences of this event.

Analyses of the Cornelius account have often attempted to identify an earlier and "simpler" conversion story to which Luke has made additions (e.g., the vision of Peter in vv. 9-16, Peter's sermon in vv. 34-43; Dibelius 1956, 109-122). In the absence of other versions of the Cornelius story that would establish a basis for comparison, separating Luke's source from his own modifications is highly speculative. More important, the elements some would identify as later additions contribute significantly to the shape and dramatic import of this event (Gaventa 1986a, 107-112). Read as a continuous whole, the narrative of Cornelius consists of a series of parallel scenes, as follows:

Visions	Scene 1	Cornelius	10:1-8
	Scene 2	Peter	10:9-16
Journey and Welcome	Scene 3	Cornelius	10:17-23a
	Scene 4	Peter	10:23b-29
Speech	Scene 5	Cornelius	10:30-33
	Scene 6	Peter	10:34-43
Confirmation	Scene 7	Holy Spirit	10:44-48
	Scene 8	Community	11:1-18

First, Cornelius sees the divine messenger, and then Peter experiences his ecstatic vision. Each receives instructions without explanation. Second, Cornelius's delegation arrives at Peter's lodging and is welcomed. Likewise, Peter and his colleagues journey to Caesarea and are welcomed at Cornelius's home. Third, Cornelius makes a brief speech in which he explains why he sent for Peter. Peter then makes a speech in which he summarizes the Christian kerygma. Finally, the Holy Spirit confirms the rightness of this event by inspiring Cornelius and his household to speak in tongues. Peter then must defend his actions in Jerusalem, where the community also confirms the rightness of the event.

Alongside the visions, journeys, and speeches that contribute to the effectiveness of this account, Luke makes extensive use of repetition. For example, Peter's vision is repeated three times, the men sent by Cornelius repeat the description of him already given by the narrator, Cornelius repeats for Peter his encounter with the angel, and the Jerusalem inquiry replays the entire episode yet again. This feature suggests, not the heavy hand of an intrusive editor of earlier sources, but Luke's insistence that his audience pay particular attention to this story.

◊ ◊ ◊ ◊

The Vision of Cornelius (10:1-8)

Scene 1 begins with a relatively full introduction of Cornelius. He is a "centurion of the Italian cohort"; that is, he is the leader of a Roman army unit consisting of one hundred men. Like the earlier centurion in Luke 7, this one is described in favorable terms, making it clear that he is far from abusing the power and wealth available to him (by contrast with Felix, see 24:24-27). The giving of alms and the faithfulness in prayer appear together elsewhere as indications of faithfulness (Tob 12:8; Matt 6:2-6; 1 Pet 4:7-11; Did. 15:4; 2 Clem. 16:4), but here they serve to distinguish someone who is not only faithful but also Gentile. Luke further specifies that his alms go "to the people," namely, Israel (see, e.g., 2:47; 3:9; 6:8; and notice the building of the synagogue in Luke 7:5).

Luke also identifies Cornelius as "a devout man who feared God with all his household," introducing an expression that he uses elsewhere of Gentiles who worship Israel's God and who are often associated with synagogue observance without having been circumcised or otherwise having completed the steps toward full conversion (see 13:16, 26, and also the "devout," as in 13:50; and also "a worshiper of God" as in 16:14). Whether "God-fearer" serves in this period as a technical term for such Gentiles remains a hotly contested point (e.g., Kraabel 1981; Murphy-O'Connor 1992; Levinskaya 1996; Fitzmyer 1998, 449-50). The evidence suggests that there were such persons, certainly in Luke's narrative world and probably beyond as well, quite apart from whether there is fixed technical vocabulary with which to refer to them.

Like the stories of the Ethiopian eunuch and of Saul, this one also features instruction by a heavenly agent when an angel of God appears to Cornelius. When taken together with the angel's declaration that Cornelius's piety has been remembered by God (see Tob 12:12), this event in itself further signals the worthiness of Cornelius, as he is the only Gentile in Luke–Acts to be the recipient of an angelic visitation.

The instruction Cornelius receives is, in one sense, quite full. He learns where to send his men, which Simon to seek, which Simon is host, and where his house is located. In another sense, however, the directive is extraordinarily brief. The angel says not a single word that indicates what Cornelius or his agents should expect once they have found Simon Peter, leaving the goal of this intervention to be revealed later (see Acts 8:26 for a similarly unexplained directive).

Peter's Vision (10:9-16)

The time reference at the beginning of Scene 2 tightly connects it with the parallel vision in Scene 1. While Peter is engaged in prayer, he becomes hungry and falls into a trance. He sees a container in which are "all kinds of four-footed creatures and reptiles and birds of the air" (v. 12; see Gen 1:24; 6:20; Lev 11:46-47). The animals involved in this vision and the relationship between the vision and the larger development of the narrative have elicited considerable discussion. The container Peter sees lowered from heaven, which offers both clean and unclean animals, and the fact that they all appear in the same container does not alter the distinction between them, which means that Peter could select something acceptable for lunch. Peter's response seems therefore highly artificial, since the container offers items he could have chosen without violating Mosaic law.

Attention has also focused on what some see as a disjuncture between the animals of the dream and the people in the story (which in turn fuels theories that the Petrine vision is a Lukan addition to an earlier account). The question is why the dream concerns items of food when the larger story concerns human beings. In a fundamental sense, such objections are misplaced because they ignore the character of Peter's experience. The function of the vision is to be suggestive, as is evident in v. 17; like dreams or visions in some Old Testament narratives, its meaning is not immediately obvious (e.g., Gen 41; Dan 2:31-45; 4:1-27; 5:1-28; Gaventa 1986a, 110). The implications of the vision emerge as the narrative develops. As that happens, it becomes clear that Peter's rejection of the animals parallels his rejection of Gentiles. Also, the dietary question in the dream is especially important because food laws were a major impediment to social relations between Gentiles and Jews (as emerges in 11:3, when Jerusalem Christians respond critically to news that Peter had eaten with Gentiles).

The actions that take place within the vision are also important. First, Peter sees heaven opened, which clearly implies some revelation from God or the presence of God (e.g., Ps 78:23; Isa 24:18; 64:1; Ezek 1:1; Matt 3:16; Rev 19:11). Peter then hears a voice instruct him to "Get up," as in the preceding story he instructed Aeneas and Tabitha to get up (9:34, 40; Spencer 1997, 110). Instead of obeying the divine demand, however, Peter rejects the command emphatically, just as he would have assumed was right and proper (as in, e.g., Dan 1:8; Tob 1:10-11; Jdt 10:5; 12:2; 2 Macc 5:27; 6:18-31). He thereby recalls Ananias's objection to being sent to Saul (9:10-16); both men assume that they know more than God. In response, however, the heavenly voice does not praise Peter's faithfulness. Instead, the voice says, "What God has made clean, you must not call profane." This pronouncement retrieves the final words of Peter's own refusal, converts them to the appropriate verb forms, and reverses their order:

Peter: profane (*koinon*) or unclean (*akathartos*)
Voice: What God has made clean (*katharizō*), you must not call common (*koinoō*)

Enhancing the contrast is the use of the emphatic pronoun "you" by the heavenly voice, so as to contrast God's action with Peter's action. What is at issue between Peter and the heavenly voice is not Peter's luncheon menu but the way he applies the terms "profane" and "unclean." The subject is not his practice, but his assumption that he knows what is clean and what is unclean. In this sense, the vision may apply to both food and people, as it does in the story that follows.

Journey and Welcome I (10:17-23a)

The content of Scene 3 might have been presented in a sentence, but Luke extends the drama by elaborating it. It opens with Peter's confusion about the vision, which is stated in v. 17 and repeated in v. 19. The narrator announces in v. 17 that the agents of Cornelius have arrived and are seeking Peter, and then again in v. 19 the Spirit directly informs Peter of their arrival. The Spirit then commands Peter to go with the men, and this time in no uncertain terms: "for I have sent them." Luke underscores the drama of this moment by the use of an intensive form of several key terms: "greatly puzzled" (*diaporeō*), "asking" (*dierōtaō*), "thinking" (*dienthumeō*), and "hesitation" (*diakrinomai*) all bear the same intensive prefix (*dia*).

When Peter obeys the directive of the Spirit, he learns that these men have been sent to summon him to the house of Cornelius. The men describe Cornelius in language that largely repeats his introduction in vv. 1-2, although this time with the notable hyperbole that "the whole Jewish nation" speaks well of Cornelius. As the men summarize the angel's words to Cornelius, they add a detail that did not appear in the initial account, that Cornelius is to "hear words from you" (AT; see also v. 33 and 28:28). The scene closes as Peter invites the men in and becomes their host (v. 23; cf. 21:16).

Journey and Welcome II (10:23b-29)

The arrival of Peter and fellow-believers Luke presents in an elaborate form that parallels the attention lavished on the arrival of Cornelius's representatives in Joppa. When Peter and colleagues arrive at Joppa they find Cornelius waiting for them, along with his family and friends. Cornelius responds to Peter's arrival by falling at his feet to worship him (v. 25). Although this response is mistaken, and Peter moves quickly to correct it, it does not necessarily signal a profound misunderstanding on Cornelius's part (Stenschke 1999, 151-52). Cornelius may have confused Peter with the angel of v. 2, but he does not engage in the egregious behavior of the Lystrans (see 14:8-18). Peter raises Cornelius to his feet, and they enter together and find many who have come, so that Luke twice comments on the entry. As in the preceding scene, Luke uses these elaborations to draw attention to the coming together of Peter and the Gentiles. That they are together Luke underscores not only with Peter's remarks but also with the repeated use of the Greek prefix *syn* ("with" or "together") in this scene (rendered in the NRSV as "accompanied," "called together," "relatives," "met," and "talked with").

Peter's initial comment (vv. 28-29) serves the same function as the report of Cornelius's representatives in v. 22. It introduces the situation in which he finds himself. On the one hand, he regards association with these Gentiles as unthinkable; on the other hand, God has shown him that he must not call anyone profane or unclean. Here Peter offers his first interpretation of the vision, and it is a minimalist interpretation. To declare that he may not call anyone profane or unclean is to connect the dream with the situation; it is God who decides what and who is clean. Peter does not yet proclaim the gospel (as he will do shortly), declare Gentiles eligible for baptism (v. 47; 11:16-17), or declare that God has included them in salvation (11:18). At this point in the narrative, all Peter indicates is that he has understood the dream well enough to obey the Spirit's order to attend to Cornelius. He transfers responsibility for the visit from himself to God (Soards 1994, 71), and now he wishes to hear why he has been summoned.

The NRSV's rendering of v. 28 is problematic. Peter declares that it is *athemitos* for Jews to associate with non-Jews, translated "unlawful" in the NRSV. The word may be translated in that fashion, but here it has a nuance of being irregular or unconventional rather than strictly illegal (BDAG, 24). It was not contrary to Torah for Jews to associate with Gentiles. In this period, as for centuries prior to it, many Jews had lived in largely Gentile areas and had conducted business and otherwise maintained relations with Gentiles. Careful observance of food laws made many forms of association awkward, however, not only because of Jewish dietary restrictions but also because of the possibility of eating food that had been sacrificed to idols (e.g., Lev 11; Dan 1:8-17; Jdt 10:5; 12:1-2; Tob 1:10-13; *Let. Arist.* 139, 142; *Jub.* 22:16; see also Tacitus, *History* 5.5; Juvenal, *Satire* 14:96-106; Schürer 1979, 2:83-84; Sanders 1990).

Cornelius's Speech (10:30-33)

Cornelius's response to Peter's question constitutes Scene 5. The bulk of his response merely restates his original vision. This time, however, Cornelius specifies that he was praying when the messenger appeared and that the messenger wore "dazzling clothes" (Luke 24:4; Acts 1:10). The messenger's words vary only slightly from their form in Scene 1. Cornelius concludes by announcing solemnly that all are gathered "to listen to all that the Lord has commanded you to say" (v. 33; cf. v. 22). The final statement of Cornelius is especially important, since it solemnly places the assembly before God (Soards 1994, 71). In addition, Cornelius's assurance that the assembled company will listen to "all that the Lord has commanded you to say" anticipates the final Lukan claim that the Gentiles will listen to the gospel (28:28). Cornelius's brief speech largely serves to introduce Peter's speech, but its recital of his own earlier vision makes an important point: God has initiated this moment through both the apostle Peter *and* through Cornelius.

Peter's Speech (10:34-43)

Peter's speech contains much that is familiar from his earlier speeches (2:14-36 and 3:12-16; see also Paul's speech in 13:16*b*-41), but the opening announcement of vv. 34-35 clearly reflects the present narrative situation. The claim that there is no partiality with God is found also in the Old Testament, but there it has a far more limited function. Deuteronomy 10:17, for example, asserts that God is not partial to the rich or powerful, and demands that Israel care for the powerless follow from this assertion about God (Lev 19:15; 2 Chr 9:17; Ps 82:2; Sir 35:15-16). In that setting, however, impartiality concerns Israel and its treatment of those dwelling within Israel (Bassler 1982, 7-45). Here, as in other early Christian literature, impartiality becomes a fundamental theological claim (as also in Rom 2:11).

This pronouncement constitutes Peter's third statement concerning unfolding events, and here for the first time he seems to have grasped the significance of his summons to Caesarea. When

Cornelius's messengers arrived at Joppa (vv. 17-18), Peter responded in an uncommitted manner: "I am the one you are looking for" (v. 21). Arriving at Cornelius's home, Peter said that such dealings with Gentiles were reprehensible, yet he acknowledged that God had demonstrated that he "should not call anyone profane or unclean" (v. 28). Following Cornelius's explanation of why he sent for Peter, Peter recognizes that even more has been established: there is no partiality with God. The full implications of this insight for the Christian community have yet to be worked out, but here God's decision is at least acknowledged.

Verse 36 is exceedingly difficult to translate, in part because a small but difficult text critical problem makes it unclear whether v. 36 is to be understood as an expansion further explaining vv. 34-35 (Riesenfeld 1979; Neirynck 1984), whether it stands alone as an anacoluthon, i.e., a grammatical inconsistency (Burchard 1985, 292-93), or whether it is closely connected with v. 37 (as the NRSV suggests when it uses "message" at the beginning of both verses, but translating two different Greek words). No proposed solution to this problem is entirely satisfying, but two details of the verse warrant special attention. First, Peter says that God is "preaching peace." It is tempting to read this reference in a limited sense as referring to peace between Jew and Gentile, but Luke's use of the term elsewhere (Luke 1:79; 2:14; Acts 9:31) as well as the remainder of the speech suggests otherwise. Peace here surely includes peace between these ethnic groups—at the human level—but it also includes a cosmic dimension in the defeat of the devil's power (v. 38). Second, v. 36 concludes with the strong assertion that "he is Lord of all." Grammatical problems sometimes prompt translations that place this statement in parentheses, as if it were a subsidiary point in the speech. Yet the claim that Jesus is Lord of all summarizes what has been said in vv. 34-35. It is precisely because Jesus is Lord of all that there can be no partiality with God (see 2:39).

The phrase "Lord of all" carries important associations of several sorts. Although this exact phrase does not appear elsewhere, closely related expressions in the LXX refer to God as "Lord of all the earth" (Josh 3:11, 13; Ps 97:5; Zech 6:5; Wis 6:7; 8:3; see also Josephus, *Ant.* 20.90), and elsewhere to other gods (Pindar, *Isthmian Odes* 5.35; Plutarch, *Isis and Osiris* 355E). Human beings can also be said to be "lord of all" in the sense of their ownership of property (e.g., Plato, *Laws* 922D; Gal 4:1), but there are also political connotations, as when Epictetus refers to the Emperor as "lord of all" (Epictetus, *Discourses* 4.1.12). In the home of a Roman army officer, the claim that someone other than the Emperor is "lord of all" surely carries both political and religious implications (to use a distinction that would have been foreign to Luke's world).

Verse 37 returns to the ministry of Jesus and offers a concise summary of the gospel, although with some interesting features. Peter announces that God "anointed" Jesus with the Holy Spirit, a description the Gospels do not give to Jesus' baptism by John (Fitzmyer 1998, 465). Peter goes into some detail regarding the healings done by Jesus and characterizes those as victories over the devil (cf. 2:22). One detail seems especially appropriate to the Cornelius episode. In v. 41, Peter specifies that the witnesses include those whom God chose, those "who ate and drank with him after he rose from the dead." Although the sharing of food may be implied by Acts 1:4, none of the other speeches in Acts refers to this qualification of the witnesses, but it is especially appropriate for a story that concerns itself with hospitality for Gentiles, one in which the sharing of food plays an important role (see especially 11:3). Peter's sermon moves toward its customary conclusion by announcing that all who believe in Jesus will receive forgiveness of sins (cf. 2:38-39; 3:19-20). He does not, however, promise the gift of the Holy Spirit, and Peter himself is about to be interrupted by the Spirit.

The Spirit's Intervention (10:44-48)

Earlier responses to Christian preaching might prompt readers to imagine Cornelius and his household responding, "What should we do?" (2:37) or "What is to prevent me from being baptized?" (8:37). No response is forthcoming, however, and

Peter does not seek one. Instead, even while Peter is speaking, the Holy Spirit falls on all (v. 44). Nowhere else does Luke narrate an event in which the gift of the Holy Spirit comes prior to baptism. Such an unprecedented gift causes the circumcised believers who are with Peter to respond with the amazement that normally accompanies a miracle. Peter himself responds that these Gentiles cannot be denied baptism and, subsequently, he orders that baptism. Although commentators sometimes dwell on Peter's action as an indication of his apostolic authority, something else is at work here. Just as Peter has been the one throughout the narrative who announced the importance of events (vv. 28, 34-35), so also now he announces their full implication. Gentiles cannot be denied baptism because God has overtly and unmistakably included them.

The closing remark in this scene deserves comment. Luke adds this notice: "Then they invited him to stay for several days" (v. 48b). Consistent with the entire narrative, this request suggests that the inclusion of Gentiles does not have to do only with a grudging admission to the circle of the baptized. Including Gentiles means receiving them, entering their homes, and accepting hospitality—even meals—in those homes.

Jerusalem Questions (11:1-18)

As the scene opens, believers in Jerusalem hear that the Gentiles have received the word of God (11:1; see 8:14), but nothing indicates that this announcement was experienced as good news in Jerusalem (cf. 15:3). Those of the circumcision party respond critically to Peter, charging him with going to uncircumcised people and eating with them (11:2). Here Luke uses a verb he had earlier applied to Peter; the Jerusalem believers criticize or debate him (*diakrinomai*) as the Spirit expressly prohibited Peter from debating or hesitating following his vision (*diakrinomai*, 10:20; Johnson 1992, 197).

Prompted by the accusation, Peter reviews the events leading up to his disputed table-fellowship. Although Peter relates the story from his perspective (thus beginning with his own vision rather than with that of Cornelius) and in first person, much of what he says repeats Acts 10. The major change within the review of events occurs in v. 14. Earlier versions report that Cornelius's visitor merely directs him to summon Peter (10:5-6, 32). Now, however, Cornelius expects Peter to present a message of salvation for Cornelius and his household (11:14).

Peter declares to his challengers that the coming of the Spirit to these Gentiles reminded him of Jesus' promise of a baptism by the Holy Spirit. Since the Gentiles have received the same gift as other believers, Peter asks in v. 17*b*, "Who was I that I could hinder God?" Peter's question forces the issue. His challengers are silenced. The final scene and the larger narrative conclude with their response. They glorify God because God has granted "repentance that leads to life" (v. 18*b*) even to the Gentiles. Importantly, no qualifier limits the group to Cornelius and company or even to those Gentiles who already lead exemplary lives (Barrett 1994, 543). In addition, v. 18 suggests that God gives the Gentiles not simply the possibility of repentance, but repentance itself (see also 5:31; Calvin 1965, 326-27; Stenschke 1999, 156-64).

◊ ◊ ◊ ◊

Although it is conventional to speak of this as the story of the conversion of Cornelius, or the story of Peter and Cornelius, such shorthand expressions threaten to eclipse the primary actor in the story—namely, God. It is God whose angelic agent prompts Cornelius to send for Peter, God whose vision Peter initially resists, and God whose Spirit directs Peter to go to Cornelius and finally baptizes the Gentiles themselves. God thoroughly directs the action, insisting that the church itself finally conclude that "God has given even to the Gentiles the repentance that leads to life" (v. 18).

Not only is God the major actor in this drama, but it reveals God to be "impartial." Since contemporary English usage sometimes understands "impartial" to mean "indifferent," the ancient Israelite roots of the claim are important. To say that God is "impartial" meant, not that God was unconcerned, but that God's concern encompassed all within Israel. God's concern specifically meant that Israel could not neglect the widow and orphan in the midst of the people. Here, however, the claim emerges in a way that encompasses not Israel alone but all humanity. That is why the end of 10:36 may be the most important line in the drama: "He is Lord of all" means not only that there is no other Lord but that no one can be excluded from that lordship.

Here, as elsewhere in Acts, careful delineation of the work of God from that of Jesus is nearly impossible. Peter's speech moves without distinction from declaring God's acceptance of all to declaring Jesus' lordship over all. Jesus is able to heal those "oppressed by the devil" (10:38) because God is with him. Luke does not parse out the responsibilities, but he does make clear that the activity of Jesus aligns him with God and over against God's enemies, including the devil (see Introduction).

The role played by the Holy Spirit in this episode is remarkable, since it is the Spirit who finally forces Peter to move toward baptism for Cornelius and his household. Theological efforts to restrict the Spirit's role to something predictable stumble over this passage, in which Cornelius makes no profession of faith or repentance and Peter does not convey the Spirit through the laying on of hands. The Spirit indeed blows where it wishes (see John 3:8).

God is not the only actor in the story, of course. Luke introduces Cornelius in such a way as to make it clear that he is an exceptional Gentile, leading some to conclude that only those Gentiles who are already associated with the synagogue may apply for admission to the church (Bassler 1985). Again, the details of the story are revealing. Cornelius is indeed introduced as a pious Gentile, and he certainly cooperates with God by following the orders he is given. At no point, however, does Luke indicate that Cornelius believes the gospel or that Cornelius repents. God's action is unilateral.

To take that point a step further, some interpreters have placed significant weight on what they perceive to be the specification of 10:35 that limits God's favor to "anyone who fears him and does what is right." Such a reading fails to see that the primary subject matter here is God and only secondarily human beings. When the Spirit acts, it acts not only on the carefully described Cornelius but on all the assembly. Even if that group includes his household, it also includes "friends" whose loyalties Luke makes no attempt to describe. Also, in his report to the Jerusalem faithful, Peter does not include a character reference for Cornelius or his household. And most important, 11:18 declares that God has determined that salvation is for "Gentiles," with no qualification as to their faith or their behavior. That does not mean that Luke is indifferent to moral questions, but it does mean that the church does not consist only of those whose behavior qualified them for admission (a notion that would seem to preclude the conversion of Saul).

Luke describes Cornelius's devotion to the God of Israel with care, not as a way of setting minimal requirements for conversion, but as a way of further dissociating Gentile converts from idolatry. Up to this point, Luke's concern with idolatry has surfaced only in Stephen's speech (see 7:40-43, 48-59), but that concern will emerge more forthrightly with the extension of the gospel to Gentiles (as in 14:8-18; 17:22-31). It would be difficult if this important story of the first Gentile believer lauded someone who worshiped idols.

Because Acts is so often read with regard to questions of church "leadership," it is important to notice the role of Peter and other believers in this account. In no sense would it be accurate to claim that Peter or the Jerusalem church *decides* to include Gentiles. The programmatic statement of the risen Jesus in 1:8 functions as a promise fulfilled by events, not as a commandment the apostles set out to obey. Here, in particular, Peter calls for baptism of Cornelius and others, but he does so only after the Holy Spirit has dramatically indicated that the decision has been made elsewhere. In fact, for a time both Peter and the Jerusalem community join forces with those who would resist God, Peter by insisting that he does know what (and who) is clean and what is not, and the remainder of the church by its grumbling reception of the news.

TO THE GENTILES: BUT HOW? (11:19–15:35)

The extension of the witness beyond Jerusalem—to Samaritans, an Ethiopian, the persecutor Saul—has reached its culmination in the praise of Jerusalem believers: "Then God has given even to the Gentiles the repentance that leads to life" (11:18). But nothing in the Cornelius account indicates how that divine gift is to be offered elsewhere and on what basis. This section of the book works out those implications. Response to Christian preaching in Antioch brings Barnabas and then Saul back into the narrative as a church emerges there (11:19-30). The story of Herod's violence and God's response evidences the relentless nature of the resistance to Christian witness (12:1-25). The Holy Spirit determines that Barnabas and Saul should set out on their own witness, first in Cyprus (13:4-12), then in Pisidian Antioch (13:13-52), and later in Iconium, Lystra, and Derbe (14:1-28). The relationship of the Gentile believers in these locations to their Jerusalem sisters and brothers presses again at the Jerusalem Council, where yet again God's inclusion of the Gentiles is recognized, as is their need to remain separate from practices of idolatry (15:1-35).

An *Ekklēsia* Also in Antioch (11:19-30)

Two reports about the gospel's arrival in Antioch comprise this passage. Both are highly compressed summaries of actions (as distinct from dramatic scenes). The first (vv. 19-26) begins with language that closely parallels the introduction to the Samaritan witness in chapter 8:

8:4	Now those who were scattered went out proclaiming the word (AT)
11:19	Now those who were scattered . . . went out . . . preaching the word (AT)

11:19 differs from 8:4 in ways entirely appropriate to the context: it adds the persecution that prompted the flight from

Jerusalem, the itinerary of those fleeing Jerusalem (cf. 8:5), and the restriction of the witness to Jews alone. In other ways also, the report of the gospel's arrival in Antioch resembles that of the witness in Samaria: both Philip and the unnamed proclaimers meet with a generous reception; in both cases the report about a favorable response causes the Jerusalem church to send representatives; in both cases there is joy (among the Samaritans in chapter 8, and on the part of Barnabas in chapter 11). The second report, vv. 27-30, has only a slight literary connection to vv. 19-26. It also has no counterpart in chapter 8, apart from the fact that the Spirit is at work in both stories.

◊   ◊   ◊   ◊

Christians at Antioch (11:19-26)

The relationship of this passage to the Cornelius incident is puzzling. Nothing in the Antioch account refers back to the conversion of Cornelius, so that the stories appear to be quite independent of one another, and events in Caesarea do not offer precedent for the mission in Antioch. On the other hand, nothing in this incident suggests the sort of resistance to the conversion of Gentiles that might be expected if this development took place independently of the events narrated in 10:1–11:18. Part of the difficulty is that modern readers expect clear lines of accountability, so that the mission in Antioch would refer explicitly to its precedent in Caesarea, and Barnabas would appeal directly to Peter's experience. Luke, however, is far less concerned with individual witnesses than are contemporary readers. In this case, he does not describe the preachers in Antioch beyond their regional identities. More important for Luke is that the geographical and ethnic boundaries of the gospel are extended. In other words, the theological outcome of the Cornelius account is the formation of an *ekklēsia* outside of Jerusalem and among non-Jews.

The unnamed persons who have fled Jerusalem venture northward through the coastal region of Phoenicia, to the island of Cyprus, and then to Antioch. The third largest city in the Roman world (surpassed in size only by Rome and Alexandria), Antioch was the center of a large Jewish population (See Josephus, *J.W.* 3.29; 7.41-62). Luke does not bother distinguishing this Antioch from the several others in existence (all named for the Seleucid king Antiochus), probably because its size and importance would bring it to mind immediately. (Note that at 13:14, he does specify that Barnabas and Paul arrive in another Antioch, this time Antioch of Pisidia.)

The church at Antioch plays an important role in Luke's emerging story, as it commissions Barnabas and Saul on the instructions of the Holy Spirit (13:1-3), serves as the center of their work (14:26), and is generally identified with Gentile believers (15:22, 23, 30, 35). The multiplication of the city's name in this otherwise brief account hints at its significance for the story that lies ahead (11:19, 20, 22, 26, 27). Scholars have often argued that one of Luke's sources is an Antioch source, consisting perhaps of 6:1–8:4, 11:19-30, and 12:25–15:35, and have sometimes drawn conclusions about Luke's historicity on the basis of these sources (Barrett 1994, 54-56). Since no independent evidence for such a source exists, and since even proponents of source theories acknowledge that these very passages bear marks of Lukan style, it seems better to conclude that, whatever Luke's sources may have been, they are no longer available (see Introduction).

Just as 8:5 distinguishes Philip's activity from the group named in 8:4, 11:20 distinguishes the activity of the Cyrenians and Cypriots from the generalized "they" of 11:19. The Cypriots and Cyrenians speak not only with Jews, but also with "Hellenists." The note in the NRSV reveals a thorny problem here. Some early manuscripts do read "Hellenists," but others read "Greeks." The difference between the two is a matter of the presence or absence of three Greek letters. The rare word "Hellenists" Luke has used twice, in both instances referring to Greek-speaking Jews (see commentary on 6:1; 9:29). In this context, however, the audience is being differentiated from the Jews of v. 19, so that many scholars prefer the less well-attested "Greeks" (i.e., non-Jews, as in 18:4; 19:10). "Hellenists" appears in early manuscripts, however, and it is easy to see why a scribe would have changed "Hellenists" to "Greeks," but difficult to imagine reasons for the opposite move. And even if the earliest reading was "Hellenists," the connotation of the word here certainly includes Gentiles (Tannehill 1990, 146).

However the text-critical question is resolved, the context makes it clear that this is a different audience than the one in Jerusalem (and even than the Samaritans). Here, there is no reference to preaching "the Messiah," a term with currency only for Jews (cf. 2:36; 5:42; 8:5; 9:22). Instead, the evangelizers proclaim "the Lord Jesus" or "Jesus as Lord." In addition, the citizens of Antioch "turned to the Lord," an expression more closely associated with Gentile conversion than with the conviction of Jews that Jesus is Messiah (e.g., 14:15; 15:19; 26:18, 20; 1 Thess 1:9; but see Luke 1:16; Acts 9:35). Jews must repent and believe in Jesus as Messiah, but Gentiles must first turn to the true or living God from the worship of false gods.

Luke attributes the eager reception of the gospel in Antioch to "the hand of the Lord" (v. 21). This phrase conventionally refers to God's own power (e.g., 4:30; 13:11; Luke 1:66; Exod 9:3; 1 Sam 5:3; Isa 59:1). The proximity of this phrase to the phrases "turned to the Lord" and to "the Lord Jesus" in v. 20 exemplifies Luke's close association of Jesus and God (see Introduction).

Recalling Philip's mission in Samaria, news of the welcome of the gospel in Antioch reaches Jerusalem, and the church sends Barnabas. His reappearance is consistent with Luke's pattern of introducing a character, allowing that character to disappear without comment, and then reintroducing the character when she or he is again needed (cf. Mary's reappearance in Acts 1:14). In his earlier intervention on behalf of Saul, Barnabas has already enacted Luke's interpretation of his name as "son of encouragement," and now he takes that role again. Seeing the evidence of God's grace (*charis*), he responds with joy (*chairō*) and admonishes the Gentile believers. The description of Barnabas in v. 24 connects him with proclaimers who have preceded him (6:3, 5, 10; 7:55); for all of them, faith and being filled with the Holy Spirit are not traits of an individual personality but signs of God's presence. Barnabas does not rejoice over Antioch because he possesses an optimistic disposition, but because of God's grace (Haenchen 1971, 267).

The reappearance of Saul in v. 25 raises a host of questions about Barnabas's reasons for seeking him out, the nature of Saul's stay in Tarsus, as well as the relationship between this report and Paul's comments in Galatians 1–2. None of those does Luke answer, intent instead on reporting their joint work in Antioch over a period of time.

Two aspects of v. 26 again signal the importance of the growing response in Antioch. First, Luke refers to the believers in Antioch as an *ekklēsia*, a term he has not yet used for believers outside of Palestine. Second, Luke explains that it is in Antioch that disciples are first called "Christians," meaning people associated with Christ (as, e.g., "Herodians" are those identified with Herod, Mark 3:6; 12:13). Luke does not say who first used the name, and the Greek can mean either that they took the term for themselves or that outsiders gave them the name (perhaps derisively; see 26:28; 1 Pet 4:16). However the name came about, it is revealing that a new name is needed, given the presence of Gentiles alongside Jews. Luke's refrain of "bearing the name" now takes on a new dimension in Antioch (see 9:15-16; Fitzmyer 1998, 474).

Antioch Assists Judea (11:27-30)

The brief vignette in vv. 27-30 indicates that the connection between Jerusalem and Antioch is not a unilateral motion from Jerusalem to Antioch, but also involves Antioch in concern for Jerusalem. Christians at Antioch learn of a famine through the prophecy of Agabus, who is unknown apart from another brief appearance in 21:10-14. Although Luke has not mentioned the Spirit falling on new believers in Antioch, he does mention the Spirit's activity here (and in v. 24). Through the Spirit, Agabus predicts "a severe famine all over the world." There is evidence of food shortage and famine during the reign of Claudius (41–54 CE; see also 18:2), although not of a worldwide famine

(Suetonius, *Claudius* 18-19; Tacitus, *Annals* 12.43; Josephus, *Ant.* 3.320-21; 20.101; see Winter, 1994). Probably the *oikoumenē* (NRSV: all over the world) here means the world of the empire; otherwise, it is sheer hyperbole.

Barnabas's role as deliveryman for the Antioch church nicely recalls his introduction in 4:36-37, where the first thing he does is sell a field and contribute the proceeds to the community. The collection for Jerusalem figures importantly in the letters of Paul, so that it seems reasonable to find him associated with the delivery of funds for Jerusalem. Far more perplexing is the attempt to coordinate this reference with those in Galatians about trips to Jerusalem and Antioch (1:18–2:14) and those in several letters about the collection (Gal 2:10; 1 Cor 16:1-4; 2 Cor 8–9; Rom 15:25-29). Luke's account makes such endeavors difficult, but it amply portrays the life of the church in Antioch. Just as the first *ekklēsia* acts for its poor, the new *ekklēsia* in Antioch acts on behalf of fellow-believers in Judea. In neither place is beneficence practiced only by the wealthy, but characterizes the community as a whole.

◊ ◊ ◊ ◊

Theologically, the fact that Luke describes no cause-and-effect relationship between the mission in Antioch and the conversion of Cornelius is important. Those who preach in Antioch do so, not because the Jerusalem leaders had devised a mission strategy, but because they have fled Jerusalem during persecution (Tannehill 1990, 146). Once they arrive in Antioch and begin to preach, God's activity brings about the emergence of a church there as well. In other words, the emergence of a church in Antioch is God's doing through the Holy Spirit, not that of any individual or group.

Luke's concise description of the activities of believers in Antioch justifies his applying the word "church" to them. Their initial reception of the gospel warms the heart of Barnabas. They welcome Barnabas and Saul to continue teaching them and others. And they instantiate the connection among believers, Jew and Gentile, by the relief they send to the needy in Jerusalem. No less than the early community in Jerusalem are they "of one heart and soul" (4:32).

Herod's Demise and Peter's Deliverance (12:1-25)

The story that opens in 12:1 appears quite self-contained. A reader who accidentally skipped from 11:30 to 12:25 would scarcely perceive a gap in the narrative; Barnabas and Saul set out for Jerusalem with famine relief (11:30), and then they return to Antioch to rejoin believers there (12:25). Although the story is therefore detachable in a sense (Barrett 1994, 568), it also richly echoes not only the earlier release of the apostles in Jerusalem but also Israel's rescue from Pharaoh's Egypt as well as God's deliverance of Jesus from death.

Structurally, the chapter dramatically contrasts Herod's actions and their outcome with the power of God to overcome God's enemies (12:24). Herod's murderous self-aggrandizement and its consequences (vv. 1-5, 20-23) form an inclusion around the miracle of Peter's deliverance (vv. 6-19). The miracle itself comprises two units, the first of which concerns the deliverance (vv. 6-11), and the second the believers' fumbling response to that miracle (vv. 12-19). A summary statement in vv. 24-25 concludes the unit and forms the transition to the Antioch community in chapter 13.

The Violence of Herod (12:1-5)

Luke's opening description of Herod's actions replays the earlier arrests of the apostles (4:13; 5:17-18), but here in a sharply escalated form. First, the agent is "King Herod." Only Luke so refers to Herod Agrippa I, grandson of Herod the Great (see Josephus, *Ant.* 18.126). This is now the second member of Herod's family to have entered Luke's story (see Luke 3:1; 9:7; 23:6-12), and Luke ties them together with the common designation "Herod." The signal to readers is that an enemy is at hand (see especially 4:27, and contrast the reference to yet another member of the Herodian family in Acts 25:13 as Agrippa [Herod Agrippa II], that figure being presented more sympathetically).

So intent is Luke on identifying Herod as the agent of resistance to believers that he words vv. 1-2 as if Herod himself had seized Christians and killed James (contrast the NRSV's indirect translation: "had James . . . killed"). Unlike the religious authorities who have earlier arrested apostles (cf. 4:2; 5:17), no motive explains Herod's initial action in killing James, the brother of John (see Luke 5:10; 9:54). Herod then arrests Peter "after he saw that it pleased the Jews" (v. 3). This chilling detail conveys the depth of Herod's evil: the religious leaders of chapters 4 and 5 are profoundly wrong in their stance toward the apostles, but they do not act solely for public approbation. In addition, v. 3 indicates that public opinion has shifted once again; those who earlier prevented the apostles' deaths (4:21; 5:26) and later were incited by Stephen's enemies (6:12) have now become the pretext for murder.

Luke twice connects the time of this violence with the season of Passover (vv. 3, 4). Mere chronology is not the point, as should be clear from the vague reference in 12:1 to "about that time." Instead, this double reference identifies Herod's murder of James and anticipated murder of Peter with the death of Jesus around Passover (Luke 22:1). And the Passover reference in turn recalls Israel's situation before Pharaoh. As in the prayer of 4:24-30, Luke posits a profound connection between past and present resisters of God's will.

The details of Peter's confinement in v. 4 starkly escalate this imprisonment over Peter's earlier detention. The bare requirement of the plot is that Peter be arrested and confined, as is established by v. 3, but v. 4 intensifies the situation by reference to the prison (as in 4:3; 5:18) and the four squads of soldiers who stand guard, one for each watch of the night. Verse 5 reiterates that Peter is in prison, but now adds the church's response: the church prays. Prayer is characteristic of gathered believers (2:42; 4:24-30), but here the modifier "fervently" and the redundant "to God" (cf. Luke 6:12) indicate the intensity with which the community importunes God on Peter's behalf.

Peter's Deliverance (12:6-11)

Verses 6-11 narrate the miracle of Peter's release, but the introduction to that release takes the form of yet another reminder of the danger to Peter. Herod is about to bring Peter out to his certain death (again Luke mentions no agents, as if Herod himself would escort Peter from his confinement), and Peter waits under severe guard. Divine intervention begins with the arrival of the angel and the presence of light, often associated with epiphanies (e.g., Acts 9:3; 22:6, 9, 11; 26:13). Curiously, neither the angel's presence nor the light is sufficient to rouse Peter from sleep. In his extreme confinement, he is close to death (Garrett 1990, 670-77).

The angel takes charge, striking Peter on the shoulder and giving orders. Peter complies with five abrupt commands by the angel and soon realizes that this is no "vision": his deliverance is accomplished. God's most recent instruction to Peter came through a "vision," one he neither understood nor eagerly obeyed (10:17); here he complies even before he understands. Verses 10-11 detail the second stage of Peter's deliverance, escalating both the difficulty of it and Peter's response. Verse 10 finds the angel and Peter passing two guards and then standing before an iron gate, which opens automatically. Shortly the angel himself disappears.

Having been delivered from these multiple guarantees of imprisonment, Peter now announces formally what has occurred: "Now I am sure that the Lord has sent his angel and rescued me from the hands of Herod and from all that the Jewish people were expecting." As delicious as the details of this miracle are, Peter's declaration places it in another category. Peter's deliverance signals once again that God will thwart the plans and actions of those who resist the gospel. The wording of the announcement recalls the Exodus, with its rescue of Israel from the hands of another tyrant:

"And I have come down to rescue them from the hand of the Egyptians. . . ." (Exod 3:8 LXX, AT)

"The God of my father is my helper and he rescued me from the hand of Pharaoh." (Exod 18:4 LXX, AT; see also Exod 18:8-10)

The Believers' Response (12:12-19)

Verses 12-19 find Peter no longer a prisoner in Herod's charge, but instead standing in front of a house where believers have gathered to pray. That Luke describes it as Mary's house perhaps means that she is a widow, since it would otherwise be identified by her husband's name. Identifying her by reference to John Mark may signal that he is better known than his father, but it is also consistent with Luke's pattern of introducing people briefly and then returning to them later (e.g., Barnabas in 4:36-37; Saul in 7:58-8:3).

Developments at Mary's house smack of slapstick humor. Although an iron gate has not kept Peter in prison, the gate to the house that should provide him with welcome keeps him out (Spencer 1997, 126). Rhoda recognizes Peter's voice but does not open the door, then tells the faithful who refuse to believe her. They are praying for Peter's deliverance, but they apparently do not expect to see him (Tannehill 1990, 155). Instead, they tell Rhoda that it is Peter's angel (see, e.g., Ps 91:11; Tob 5:22; Matt 18:10; Heb 1:14). Meanwhile Peter stands outside knocking!

Luke makes use of some stock features of ancient narrative in this account (Pervo 1987, 21-22; Harrill 2000), but alongside the entertainment value of the episode is a connection between this account and the Lukan story of Jesus' death and resurrection. In Luke 22:54-62, an earlier maid confronted Peter during Jesus' arrest (*paidiskē* in both texts). It is sheer joy that prevents Rhoda from opening the door, like the joy of those who recognize the risen Jesus (Luke 24:41). As with the women who report the resurrection, Rhoda also is not believed (Luke 24:11).

The resistance to the truth of God's return of Peter from certain death ends in the astonishment of recognition: Rhoda was right, after all. The statements that follow in v. 17 are no mere aftermath but reinforce the significance of this event. Peter makes the gesture for silence that elsewhere announces the beginning of a speech (13:16; 21:40; 26:1). He then describes how the Lord has once again delivered his agent, recalling for readers both the deliverance of Israel from Egypt and the resurrection of Jesus.

The final statements of v. 17 have generated much discussion but little clarity. Peter's command that news should be conveyed to James and the brothers has little or nothing to do with a transition in authority figures, as is sometimes suggested (Wall 1991). In the context of the story, it is an instruction that the good news of this deliverance be conveyed to James and the others. (Indeed, it corresponds to the instruction in Mark 16:7 that Jesus' resurrection be proclaimed.) The closing notice about Peter's departure recalls the peril from Herod and conveys Peter out of Herod's sight. The brief notice in vv. 18-19 demonstrates the urgent need for Peter to escape. Following Roman law (*Code of Justinian* 9.4.4), Herod has the soldiers executed for their supposed failure to comply with orders. Then Herod (not Peter, see the footnote in the NRSV) departs for Caesarea.

Herod's Demise (12:20-25)

Verse 20 opens the second Herod scene with the report that Herod was angry with the people of Tyre and Sidon. Given events just prior to this scene, this is an ominous note indeed. These populations take the prudent course, however, engaging the services of an otherwise unknown Blastus so that they may have peace as well as food. The outcome of this event and the end of Herod Luke narrates with amazing leanness: Herod dresses, sits on the throne, and speaks. The citizenry responds, "The voice of a God and not a man" (AT). Immediately the angel of the Lord "strikes" Herod; the same Greek verb describes both the angel's awakening touch of Peter in v. 7 and the afflicting touch of Herod in v. 23. Luke expends few words over Herod's demise: "he was eaten by worms and died."

An account of Herod's death appears also in Josephus, although in a much expanded fashion (*Ant.* 19.343-52).

According to Josephus, Herod wore a garment of silver, and the sun's reflection inspired flatterers to address him as a god. He remained silent, tacitly accepting the glorification, and then an omen indicated his imminent death. Nothing in Josephus's account connects Herod with any threat to the nascent Christian community, of course, although the motif of an agonizing death as appropriate for one who scorns God or who is guilty of some other heinous act is widespread (Isa 66:24; Jdt 16:17; 2 Macc 9:5-12; Josephus, *Ant.* 17.168-70; Herodotus, *Histories* 4.205; Pausanias, *Description of Greece* 9.7.2-3; see also Allen 1997, 29-74).

By contrast with Josephus's account, which closes with a brief recapitulation of the reign of Herod Agrippa I and the intrigues that swiftly followed his death, Luke's story immediately returns to its primary concern. With piercing irony, v. 24 contrasts Herod's end with the progress of God's word (see also 6:7; 19:20). Verse 25 completes the transition by returning to Barnabas and Saul, together with the newcomer John Mark. As the note in the NRSV indicates, some important early manuscripts of v. 25 have Barnabas and Saul returning *to* Jerusalem, which creates logical confusion, since 11:30 has Barnabas and Saul setting out from Antioch *for* Jerusalem. A possible solution to the problem is to translate, "Barnabas and Saul returned [to Antioch], having completed their mission. . . ."

Numerous details make this story a delight, yet much is at stake theologically. Because of the climactic events of Peter's deliverance and Herod's demise, it might appear at first that Acts 12 is an account of conflict between the adversaries Peter and Herod (Haenchen 1971, 388). That way of reading the account profoundly misconstrues the theocentric character of Luke's story, however, since Peter is God's agent and Herod is God's resister. The allusions to the Exodus, in which God delivers Israel from the hands of Pharaoh, and the resurrection, in which God triumphs over a host of enemies, confirm that the "hero" here is God.

If the story is overwhelmingly about God's action in the face of human resistance to the gospel, it also engages the Lukan dynamic of recognition. Peter does not initially understand that the angel has indeed released him (vv. 9, 11). The gathered believers are not prepared to recognize Rhoda's word as reliable, and they apparently do not expect God to do anything (v. 15). Further recognition of God's work is anticipated by the instruction of Peter that James and the others be informed (v. 17). As with Jesus' resurrection, recognition is the appropriate human response to God's deliverance (Luke 24:31).

Many scholars associate this passage with the succession of leadership in the nascent church. After this point, Peter virtually departs the Lukan story; his name appears again only in 15:7 (and cf. 15:14), where he briefly speaks at the Jerusalem Council. The fact that Peter sends a message to James, who emerges in chapter 15 as spokesman for the Jerusalem church, reinforces the view that this chapter marks a shift in leadership. Those features of the text scarcely amount to a succession narrative, however, and Luke had ample models for such successions in Scripture. Given his use of Moses traditions elsewhere (e.g., 3:22-23; 7:20-44), Luke could easily have drawn on the commissioning of Joshua (Josh 1:1-9). In fact, matters of ecclesiastical personnel, in the sense of who has decision-making power, seem alien to Luke. Although he names human individuals here, it is obvious that none of these individuals is in charge of events, certainly not King Herod, in spite of his power and pretension, and not even the apostle Peter.

The Spirit Commissions and Bar-Jesus Obstructs (13:1-12)

Following the deliverance of Peter from certain death and the destruction of King Herod in chapter 12, Luke returns to the church in Antioch and the dramatic beginning of the Spirit-commissioned labors of Barnabas and Saul. The journey that begins here ends when the two return to Antioch (14:21-28), just before the crisis that produces the Jerusalem Council.

Two scenes comprise this passage. The first explains the

Spirit's requisition of Barnabas and Saul (vv. 1-3), setting the stage for their proclamation of the gospel in 13:4–14:28. The second scene (vv. 4-12) inaugurates that journey with a confrontation with Bar-Jesus, a figure who recalls Simon Magus and continues the Lukan theme of the conflict between God and Satan. In form, this story resembles a miracle story, although the miracle in this instance is not one of healing but of inflicting blindness on Bar-Jesus. Like healing stories in the Synoptic Gospels (e.g., Luke 5:18-26; 7:12-17), it contains a description of the illness (the address to Bar-Jesus in v. 10), a brief indication of the healing itself ("the hand of the Lord is against you," v. 11), some demonstration of the healing's effectiveness (v. 11*b*), and the response of bystanders (v. 12).

◊   ◊   ◊   ◊

The Holy Spirit Commissions Barnabas and Saul (13:1-3)

The first scene is less scene than summary. Verses 1 and 3 summarize the presence of prophets and teachers and their response to the Spirit's direction. By placing v. 2 in the form of direct address and locating it between the two summaries, Luke draws attention to the fact that the initiative for this movement is God's rather than the church's. Verse 1 begins by stating simply that there were "prophets and teachers" in Antioch. Except for Barnabas, who initially traveled to Antioch at the instigation of the Jerusalem church (11:22), nothing in this description implies that the prophets and teachers in Antioch are appointed by Jerusalem.

Unlike the list of the apostles in 1:13, which begins with Peter and John, who appear together at several points in the early stages of the Jerusalem witness (3:1, 3, 11; 4:1), this list divides Barnabas from Saul, the pair who will shortly be sent out by the Holy Spirit. Why Saul's name appears last is unclear, although at this point in the story Saul is still a secondary character. For the remaining three names, Luke provides frustratingly slender identifications. First comes Simeon "who was called Niger." The use

of a double-name introduced by "who was called" or "also
known as" is common (Horsley 1992). "Niger" transcribes the
Latin word *niger*, or black, and may indicate that Simeon is also
African. Certainly Lucius "of Cyrene" is African, Cyrene being
the capital of Cyrenaica in northern Africa (see 11:19-20). No
location identifies Manaen, but Luke describes him as a *syn-
trophos* of the tetrarch Herod (NRSV: Herod the ruler), which
can mean that he was brought up with Herod or more generally
that he was a "member of the court" (NRSV). This identification
of a Christian leader as an intimate of the Herodian family may
provide an ironic reminder of the fall of King Herod in chapter
12 (Spencer 1997, 137). Taken together, the names on the list
signal the gospel's early reach well beyond Jerusalem. Apart from
Barnabas and Saul, it is unclear how these men came to be in
Antioch.

This group (and perhaps others?) is described as "worshiping
the Lord and fasting" when the Holy Spirit speaks. *Leitourgeō*
(NRSV: worshiping) and its cognate noun often refer to the service carried out by religious leaders (e.g., LXX Exod 28:35; Sir
4:14; Heb 10:11), so that it may refer specifically to the functions of these apostles and teachers, although other Lukan
descriptions of the common life of believers suggest that the setting here is the church's worship rather than official duties of the
few (2:46-47; 4:23-31). Fasting appears here for the first time in
Acts, but it is associated with prophecy and the activity of John's
disciples in the Gospel (Luke 2:37; 5:33-35; Acts 14:23). In the
context of the church's devotion, the Spirit speaks, ordering that
Barnabas and Saul be set apart. The importance of this instruction is clear from the fact that the Spirit nowhere else in Acts
directly orders the church to take a particular action (as distinct
from an individual; see 8:29; 10:19-20; 21:22; 28:25-27).
Despite the manifold ways in which Luke conveys the work of
the Spirit and the divine will as guiding events, this is the only
time the Spirit issues a direct command to the church.

The wording of the Spirit's demand further enhances its significance. Although untranslated by the NRSV, the tiny particle *dē*
signals that the matter is an urgent one (cf. Luke 2:15; Acts

15:36, where the same word appears for heightened emphasis). The exact nature of the work (see 14:26; 15:38) for which Barnabas and Saul are set apart is left unspecified, although Paul's vocation has been announced in 9:15-16. In response to this demand, the community fasts and prays and sends the two away with the laying on of hands. That this commissioning continues to be God's rather than the church's is clear in that the laying on of hands comes in the context of invoking God's presence and will through fasting and prayer (cf. 6:6).

Paul Confronts Bar-Jesus (13:4-12)

Lest the community's role be misunderstood, v. 4 provides further evidence that the initiative for this journey lies with God, since it is the Holy Spirit that sends the pair on its way. Travel by sea is implied earlier in the narrative, when the unnamed group that flees Jerusalem goes as far as Cyprus (11:19), but it is here for the first time that Luke draws attention to the fact that Barnabas and Saul depart by sea. They first go to Seleucia, the port city of Antioch, and from there they sail for Cyprus. Travel by sea figures prominently in Greek narrative, of course, and will play an even more significant role later as Luke demonstrates God's power over the sea (see on Acts 27; Alexander 1995).

Barnabas and Saul do not travel alone. The tiny introduction of John in v. 5 as assistant to Saul and Barnabas has given rise to curiosity disproportionate to the text itself. Almost certainly this John is the John Mark introduced in 12:12. Because tradition later identifies John Mark with the author of the second Gospel and the cousin of Barnabas mentioned in Col 4:10, interpreters have offered all manner of conjecture about his situation. The reference to John here is further complicated by the designation of John as assistant, since Luke employs the Greek word *hypēretēs* sometimes for servants of the word in the sense of witnesses (Luke 1:2; Acts 26:16) and sometimes for figures offering routine assistance (the synagogue attendant in Luke 4:20; the temple "police" in Acts 5:22, 26). Without drawing on considerations external to this text, however, a reasonable reading of

13:5 is that John Mark of Jerusalem went along, not as someone "officially" set apart for the task of proclaiming the word of God, but as a helper to those who were so designated (Black 2001, 99-102).

Readers who recall that believers earlier reached Cyprus (11:19) may expect to learn that Barnabas and Saul seek out Christians who are already there, but Luke leaps past such questions. A sentence summarizes the activity in Salamis as "proclaimed the word of God in the synagogues" (v. 5). The story to which Luke quickly moves begins in earnest in v. 6 when Barnabas and Saul have made their way across the island to the western city of Paphos, an important religious center with a famous temple to Aphrodite (Nobbs 1994, 280-81). There Barnabas and Saul encounter two characters, Bar-Jesus and Sergius Paulus.

As with Luke's introduction of the Ethiopian eunuch in 8:27, Luke's introduction of the first character is a dramatic treat. Rendered somewhat woodenly, v. 6 reads: "they found a certain man, a magician, a false prophet, a Jew by the name of Bar-Jesus" (AT). With the word "magician," Luke signals that this character is associated with evil (see on 8:4-24). That he is a "false prophet" only compounds matters. Although Luke does not indicate the content of any such prophecy here, both his attempt to dissuade Sergius Paulus from the gospel and the charge of v. 10 (making "crooked the straight paths of the Lord") reinforce the claim. The next word in the description complicates matters immeasurably, for this particular magician is a Jew, one who is expected to know the prohibition of Deut 18:9-14 and whose association with magic and false prophecy makes him reprehensible. Given this story's concern with names, the fact that Luke identifies him as "Bar-Jesus" can only anticipate his resistance to "the word of God."

The second man Luke describes is the proconsul Sergius Paulus, the head of the government in this Roman province. Numerous attempts to identify him further have proved inconclusive (Nobbs 1994, 282-87). For Luke's purposes, the most relevant element in the identification comes next: Sergius Paulus is a wise man. Evidence of that wisdom comes to expression in the final element of the introduction, when Sergius Paulus summons Barnabas and Saul because he is eager to hear the word of God. If Bar-Jesus recalls Simon Magus, Sergius Paulus may recall the earlier Ethiopian, who was similarly eager to hear Philip interpret Isaiah (8:31, 34).

Despite Sergius Paulus's importance in Paphos, he is not central to the conflict in this story, and Luke returns quickly to Bar-Jesus. Now, however, he is called "Elymas." What exactly Luke means with the phrase "for that is the translation of his name" remains mysterious, since it is not clear whether Luke means that Elymas translates Bar-Jesus (which it does not) or that Elymas translates "magician" (which it also does not). Bar-Jesus/Elymas may have more designations than interpreters can manage, but his evil is unmistakable, evidenced by his attempt to turn the proconsul away from the faith.

Luke has consistently named Barnabas and Saul together until this point, but here it is Saul, now named Paul, who speaks. Any confusion about the nature of this conflict disappears as Luke specifies that Paul is "filled with the Holy Spirit" and confronts one who is "full of all deceit and villainy" (vv. 9-10). Here the agent of God confronts and overpowers the agent of Satan (cf. 5:3; 8:22-23). The names Bar-Jesus and Elymas both disappear as Paul pronounces this final name: "son of the devil." Not only the devil's child, this man is "enemy of all righteousness," "full of all deceit and villainy." Paul's fierce rhetorical question recalls v. 8, since the same verb appears in both places; Bar-Jesus/Elymas attempts to turn aside (*diastrephō*; v. 8) Sergius Paulus, which is to make crooked (*diastrephō*; v. 10) the Lord's straight paths. He is the literal opposite of the Isaianic language applied to John the Baptist, who prepared to make the crooked straight and the rough paths smooth (Luke 3:5).

The punishment miracle follows directly. First, Paul announces that "the hand of the Lord" will bring blindness on Bar-Jesus/Elymas, and the result is immediate. The language Luke employs effectively conveys the result: blind, not seeing even the sun, mist and darkness, groping about for a guiding hand. Taken on its own, the depiction is chilling. Read in context both of Saul's earlier blindness (9:8) and of Luke's use of sight/light and blindness/darkness metaphorically for perceiving or not perceiving God's work, the depiction becomes far more powerful (e.g., Luke 2:29-32; 24:31; Acts 13:47; 26:18). The blindness into which Satan's agent is plunged conveys his utter powerlessness and the defeat of his master (Garrett 1989, 79-87).

The proconsul has not been forgotten; Luke explains that the proconsul believed when he saw what had happened, having been astonished "at the teaching of the Lord." Interpreters are often made nervous by the conclusion to this story (v. 12), with its close association between a punishment miracle and faith. Some clasp the omission of reference to baptism as evidence that Sergius Paulus's conviction is something less than complete. Yet Luke does not write accounts of faith development, with attention to the maturation of Christian conviction. His attention here, as elsewhere, is fixed upon God's action and its impact. Here, seeing the agent of God render the agent of Satan utterly helpless, the proconsul recognizes "the teaching about the Lord" as genuine.

Luke mentions in v. 9 that Saul is "also known as Paul," the designation that remains constant throughout the remainder of Acts. As noted concerning Simeon in v. 1, such double names were common, but the change here from the Grecized form of the Hebrew name Saul to the Roman Paul reflects a changed context for Saul/Paul's work and his emergence as the central figure through whom Luke narrates his story of God's activity. With this change of nomenclature, the conversion of the Roman official Sergius Paulus, and the blinding of the enemy Bar-Jesus/Elymas, Luke dramatizes rather than announces that the inclusion of the Gentiles now enters a new phase.

◊ ◊ ◊ ◊

Students of Luke–Acts often refer to this scene as the beginning of the mission of the church of Antioch or the place at which Paul emerges as the central hero in Luke's story. Such designations accurately identify changes in the story, since Antioch is "home base" for Barnabas and Saul, and since Paul does here confront and confound Bar-Jesus/Elymas. Yet to think of this as the story of the Antiochene mission or the beginning of Paul's missionary journeys is fundamentally to misunderstand Luke's perspective. The Holy Spirit is the one who demands that Barnabas and Saul be set aside, and the Holy Spirit sends them on their way. The "hand of the Lord" blinds Bar-Jesus/Elymas. In Paul's action Sergius Paulus recognizes nothing less than "teaching about the Lord." The Antioch church, Barnabas, and Saul/Paul are agents of what is fundamentally God's mission, now moving across the sea and coming into contact with Jews as well as Gentiles in every place.

The names in this account have given rise to many technical questions, but they also touch on a theological feature of Luke–Acts, in that Luke frequently pits God's naming of people over against the identifications they bear elsewhere. In this instance, the elusive names Bar-Jesus and Elymas give way to the name "son of the devil." Earlier, Ananias names Saul as enemy of believers, but God names him "an instrument whom I have chosen" (9:13-15). Earlier still, the woman identified as "crippled" and "bent over" is renamed as "daughter of Abraham" (Luke 13:10-17), and the chief tax-collector and rich man Zacchaeus is renamed as "son of Abraham" (Luke 19:1-10). In each case, the renaming serves a slightly different narrative function, but in all cases the power to name resides with God.

As in the conflict with Simon Magus in Samaria (8:4-24), this new stage in the mission finds an agent of Satan standing in the way. This time it is not the misplaced attempt to control the Spirit that reveals Satan's presence. And Elymas does not practice magic here, even if he is said to be a magician. Instead, Satan reveals himself in Elymas's attempt to dissuade Sergius Paulus from hearing the gospel. As colorful as Luke's descriptions of human characters may be and as interesting as his stories of their actions are, this narrative reflects a larger drama in which God's gospel battles the power of Satan. Having defeated Satan's agent in Paphos, Paul and his companions are now able to move on to Pisidian Antioch.

Conflicted Response in Pisidian Antioch (13:13-52)

This stage of the journey of Paul and Barnabas finds them in a synagogue in Pisidian Antioch, where Paul addresses both Jews and "others who fear God" (v. 16). The speech, which is the first occasion on which Luke reports the content of Paul's proclamation rather than the mere fact of it (see 9:20, 27-28; 11:26; 13:5), dominates the unit. The speech comprises three distinct sections, each introduced by direct address:

"You Israelites, and others who fear God," v. 16.
"My brothers, you descendants of Abraham's family, and others who fear God," v. 26.
"Let it be known to you therefore, my brothers," v. 38.

The opening section sketches Israel's history, beginning with Israel's sojourn in Egypt and moving through the reign of David to the arrival of Jesus (vv. 16-25). The middle of the speech concerns the recent history of Israel, in which Jerusalem crucified Jesus and God raised Jesus from the dead (vv. 26-37). The brief peroration offers forgiveness for those who believe in Jesus and warnings for those who do not (vv. 38-41).

In terms of its literary context, the speech recalls the inaugural sermon of Jesus at Nazareth (Luke 4:18-27). That sermon followed a struggle with Satan (Luke 4:1-13), took place in a synagogue (Luke 4:16), and precipitated a harsh response (Luke 4:28-29), as will this one. In terms of its content, the speech resembles the earlier speeches of Peter and Stephen in that it places the proclamation of Jesus within the context of Israel's history (see below for details).

Unlike other speeches in Acts, Paul appears to complete his sermon without interruption (e.g., 7:54; 22:22; 26:24). The response that does ensue takes place in two stages. The initial response seems overwhelmingly positive, but a second stage introduces the motif of Jews who not only refuse to hear the gospel themselves but who interfere with the proclamation of the gospel to others (vv. 44-52). In that sense, they come perilously close to the activity of Elymas/Bar-Jesus, who interferes with Sergius Paulus's desire to hear the gospel (13:8).

◊ ◊ ◊ ◊

Arrival in the Synagogue of Pisidian Antioch (13:13-16a)

With a lean description, Luke narrates the movement of Paul and "his companions" northwest from Cyprus to Perga on the mainland and then further inland to Pisidian Antioch. The reference to the gospel's agents as "Paul and his companions" reflects the place of Paul in the previous story and his function here as spokesperson. Once again, Luke mentions the name of John [Mark], whose departure for Jerusalem frustrates readers for its lack of explanation. Because the term translated "left them" (*apochōreō*) can connote withdrawal or retreat in a negative sense (e.g., 3 Macc 2:33; Josephus, *Ant.* 15.149), the implication could be that there is a dispute about the mission, but the nature of that dispute is unspecified (Black 2001, 102-105).

Neither the location nor the personnel detains Luke's narration, which moves so quickly that readers might conclude Paul and his colleagues landed at Perga and marched directly from there to the synagogue of Pisidian Antioch (Haenchen 1971, 407). Luke does not specify the texts read on this occasion (contrast Luke 4:18-19), but he does depict an official invitation to speak (on such synagogue instruction see Philo, *Spec. Laws* 2.62). A "word of exhortation" may be a technical term for a sermon (e.g., Heb 13:22; Black, 2001, 115-33). Perhaps more important in this context, "exhortation" (*paraklēsis*) both begins and ends the sermon, since Paul and Barnabas are urged or exhorted (*parakaleō*) by their hearers to return on the next Sabbath. The synagogue officials specifically seek a message for the people (*laos*), Luke's term for the people of Israel.

197

Paul's Synagogue Speech (13:16b-41)

God's Deeds for Israel (13:16b-25): Paul addresses himself
both to Israelites and "others who fear God." At several points,
the speech and its aftermath refer to people who are not part of
Israel by birth but who are part of the synagogue service, presumably on a regular basis (vv. 26, 43; see also vv. 46-48). As
noted earlier, the question of the category "God-fearers" is heavily disputed (see above on Cornelius), and the various designations for non-Jews in this chapter complicate matters even
further. However readers resolve that question, at this juncture,
the narrative audience clearly consists of Jews as well as non-
Jews who have associated themselves with Judaism in some way.

The speech begins as a narrative of certain prominent
moments in Israel's history. In that sense it resembles Stephen's
speech, although Stephen begins with the call of Abraham (7:2),
and Paul begins with only the briefest reference to the creation of
a people ("God . . . chose our ancestors") and then moves to the
Exodus, the wilderness wanderings, the possession of the land,
the period of the judges, the prophet Samuel, the kings Saul and
David, and then the promised Savior Jesus.

Two things distinguish this section of the speech. First, it
relentlessly presents Israel's history *as* the history of God's activity. From v. 17 through v. 23, almost every verb has God as its
subject; for example, God "chose . . . made the people great . . .
led them out . . . gave them judges . . . made David their king."
The two exceptions to this recital are also telling. First, Paul
recalls that Israel "asked for a king" (v. 21), a request that
1 Samuel equates with a rejection of God's own rule (1 Sam 8:4-
22). Israel's rebellion in that early instance prefigures its rejection
of God's Messiah, Jesus. Second, drawing on 1 Sam 13:14, Paul
recalls God describing David as "a man after my heart, who will
carry out all my wishes." Jesus is David's heir not only by physical descent, but by virtue of his obedience to God's will. (On
Jesus' Davidic descent, see also Matt 1:1; Luke 3:31; Rom 1:3;
2 Tim 2:8.)

A second distinguishing feature of this section of the speech is the way in which it highlights the role of John the Baptist. Paul introduces God's sending of Jesus as the promised Savior, the heir of David, but then dwells on John the Baptist. John has appeared in Acts in very brief notices (1:5, 22; 10:37; 11:16), but here his announcement of a "baptism of repentance" and his deliberate distinction of himself from Jesus (see Luke 3:16) become a part of the subject matter of Christian proclamation.

The Death, Resurrection, and Witness of Jesus (13:26-37): The second section of the speech, marked again by direct address to the audience, identifies the topic as the "message of this salvation." Paul now replays some themes of Peter's early speeches in Jerusalem, although there are also revealing differences. First, he recalls the crucifixion of Jesus, portraying it starkly in terms of the responsibility of "the residents of Jerusalem." The context requires that Paul identify those responsible for Jesus' death in the third person ("they") rather than in the second person ("you") as Peter does earlier (2:22-24; 3:13-15; 5:30). Perhaps playing on the Sabbath setting of this speech and the reading of Scripture that precedes it, Paul identifies the actions of the Jerusalemites with their failure to understand Scripture (v. 27), a move not made in earlier speeches. Verses 28 and 29 serve only to underscore the guilt of the Jerusalemites, since they find no fault with Jesus but nevertheless ask for his death. Verse 29 is especially telling, for it presents the Jerusalemites themselves as taking Jesus down from the tree and placing him in a tomb. This claim conflicts with Luke 23:50-56, which ascribes that action to Joseph of Arimathea, but it serves the speech's rhetorical purpose of highlighting the offense of Jerusalem in Jesus' death.

Unlike earlier speeches, which also interpret the death of Jesus as part of God's will (2:23; 3:18), this one moves directly to the actions of God, contrasting God's raising of Jesus with Jerusalem's killing and burying. Paul first asserts the resurrection (v. 30) and then amplifies that assertion by references to the witnesses (vv. 31-32) and with an extended proof from Scripture (vv. 33-37). Verse 31 takes readers back to the opening of Acts and the instruction of the apostles by the risen Lord; it also recalls their witness in Jerusalem, which has itself become part of Christian preaching (cf. 2:32; 3:15). Verse 32 extends the activity of the witnesses to include the moment of the speech itself. The pronouns "we" and "you" in v. 32 are emphatic, drawing both the evangelists and their hearers into the circle of the promise.

Verses 33-37 then identify the fulfillment by appeal to Scripture. First, Paul quotes Ps 2:7, a text Christians early on identified with Jesus (4:25-26; Heb 1:5; 5:5). Associating the "today" of the psalm with the resurrection could mean that Luke understands Jesus to become Messiah only at his resurrection, and there are other indications of that view in Acts (2:32-36; perhaps also 17:31). The fact that the same verse appears at Jesus' baptism in Luke's Gospel stands in tension with that conclusion, however, and probably means that Luke is less concerned about locating Jesus' Messiahship in chronological time than he is about locating it in Scripture.

The exegetical claims about Jesus' resurrection continue, as Paul contrasts Jesus' resurrection with the corruption experienced by David (see 2:36). This passage has generated considerable debate, but it appears that the argument proceeds by *gezerah shewa*, the association of two texts by means of a catchword. First, Paul draws upon LXX Isa 55:3:

"I will give you the holy decrees pertaining to David." (AT)

Then he adds a quotation from LXX 15:10:

"You will not permit [lit. give] your holy one to see corruption." (AT)

The catchwords at work here are "give" and "holy." The first quotation both recalls the promises to David and identifies Jesus as the "you" who receives those promises. The second quotation serves to distinguish Jesus rather than David as the "Holy One." The thrust of this exegesis becomes quite clear in vv. 37-38: David served God, died, was buried, and decayed. The Holy One whom God raised did not decay, even though he also had been buried (note v. 29; cf. 2:29-31).

The identification of Jesus as son of God recalls numerous important passages in Luke's Gospel, including the annunciation of Gabriel (1:35), the heavenly voice at Jesus' baptism (3:22), and the voice at Jesus' transfiguration (9:35; see also 4:3, 9; 41; 8:28; 10:22; 22:70). In Acts, however, the expression is used only here and in 9:20, both times by Paul.

A Concluding Warning (13:38-41): The peroration begins with a disclosure formula ("let it be known to you," see, e.g., 2:14, 36) designed to underscore the solemn importance of what follows. "Forgiveness of sins" has appeared earlier in the apostolic witness (2:38; 3:19; 5:31), but the assertion of v. 39 is both new and difficult to understand. It is unclear whether Paul refers to some particular sins for which the law is ineffective or whether he intends a reference to the general impotence of the law; the Greek can be read either way. Given that the speech is associated with Paul, whose letters demonstrate struggles among early Christians over the implications of the gospel for the law of Moses, especially in relation to Gentiles, commentators have often labored to reconcile v. 39 with Paul's letters *or* to depict v. 39 as a Lukan misunderstanding of Paul.

Another possibility lies within Acts itself. If Stephen's speech does not indict the law of Moses, it surely indicts some of the law's supposed interpreters (see commentary on 7:2-53). Later on, Peter discovers that even the law cannot prevent God from including the Gentiles within the new community (10:1–11:18). Now, there is at least a hint that the law has not done all that was needed (Spencer 1997, 146). Paul begins his speech after the reading of "the law and the prophets." He ends it with warnings about failing to hear the prophets (v. 41; and see v. 27); perhaps the addition of a question about the law's power belongs within this Lukan context after all.

Paul concludes with a quotation from Hab 1:5 (LXX). He introduces it as a warning about the urgency of the message, but the quotation also anticipates the rejection that follows. The citizens of

Pisidian Antioch are about to repeat the actions of the Jerusalemites, who read the prophets every Sabbath but did not recognize Jesus as God's Messiah (v. 27). The quotation well serves Luke's purpose, since the word "work" (*ergon*) refers often in Acts to the work of God or the labors of the witnesses on behalf of the gospel (5:38; 13:2; 14:26; 15:38).

A Divided Response (13:42-52)

As with the early activity of the apostles in Jerusalem, Paul's speech also meets with a divided response. Initially, the response is receptive, even enthusiastic. Those present at the synagogue urge Paul and Barnabas to return (v. 42). Verse 43 supplements that general picture with Jews and proselytes following Paul and Barnabas, who appear to continue their exhortation even as they leave the gathering. Verse 44 takes the response to the level of hyperbole, with "almost the whole city" gathering to hear the witnesses.

This outpouring of enthusiasm gives rise to a new round of resistance. As earlier, when the Jerusalem authorities acted on their jealousy (5:17), here a vague group designated "the Jews" looks upon Paul and Barnabas with jealousy. In response to their resistance, Paul and Barnabas speak *together* and boldly about the word of God, giving what follows solemn importance. They insist that the word of God was sent first to Jews, who now "reject it" and "judge" themselves unworthy (v. 46). As elsewhere in Acts, independent decisions or actions by human beings bring disaster, for the Jewish residents of Pisidian Antioch have made this decision on their own. Paul and Barnabas further announce that they are "turning to the Gentiles." The move does not result from their own planning, but from the Lord's instruction. Here they quote LXX Isa 49:6, echoing the canticle of Simeon in Luke 2:32 and anticipating Paul's final defense in Acts 26:18: "I have set you to be a light for the Gentiles, so that you may bring salvation to the ends of the earth."

Luke repeats the theme of the divided response again in vv. 48-50. The Gentiles "were glad and praised the word of the

Lord," recalling the response of the Ethiopian eunuch (8:39). Although Luke does not tarry over the numbers or the details, some of them become believers and their calling itself spreads "the word of the Lord" (v. 49). In response to this growth, some Jews act again, this time inciting both women and men. The reference to "the devout women of high standing" may well mean Gentile women who were attracted to Judaism (cf. Josephus, *Ant.* 20.34-35, 38). That persecution does not have the last word becomes clear in v. 51; the evangelists shake "the dust off their feet" in protest against the city (see Luke 9:5; 10:11) and travel on to Iconium, filled "with joy and the Holy Spirit."

Students of Luke–Acts have lavished attention on this passage, particularly on what it may yield regarding the difficult question of Luke's stance toward Israel and especially the continuing mission among Jews. On the one hand, Paul and Barnabas together announce that, although the gospel had to be proclaimed first to Jews, they have now rejected it and the gospel will instead go to the Gentiles. The word of judgment here seems clear. On the other hand, Paul's speech places Jesus squarely within Israel's history, and Paul and Barnabas continue immediately to another Jewish synagogue (14:1). In effect, the word of judgment is limited to Pisidian Antioch.

Addressing this question clearly requires another framework. Rather than categorizing this passage as "Jewish rejection" versus "Gentile receptivity," readers need to look at the question of divine versus human initiative and how that initiative is received. Verse 46*b* connects the priority of Israel with all of the ways in which God has acted for Israel, ably recalled in the speech itself. Just as God called Israel and sent prophets and kings, God has now sent Jesus as Messiah, and sent him first to Jews. Verse 46*b* identifies these particular Jews in Pisidian Antioch with those in Jerusalem who did not recognize Jesus and condemned him (v. 27), as well as with the Israelites who asked for their own king (v. 21). In every case, the people acted of their own will and against the will of God. By taking the initiative in seeking a king, in condemning Jesus, in stirring up trouble against the witnesses, the people have brought disaster upon themselves: "You reject [the word of God] and judge yourselves to be unworthy of eternal life." Ironically, the Gentiles now resemble David, who "will carry out all [God's] wishes" (v. 22). They not only rejoice, but the ones who are called by God become believers (v. 48). In other words, the story Luke tells may have less to do with the standing of Jews *per se* than it does with obedience to or rejection of God's plan. As elsewhere in Luke–Acts, those who reject the gospel do so by virtue of their own schemes and plans.

Witnessing in Iconium, Lystra, and Derbe (Acts 14:1-28)

This chapter traces the movement of the witnesses to the gospel through various new cities, in each of which they encounter reception as well as resistance, and concludes with their return to the starting point of Antioch. The audiences continue to consist of both Jews and Gentiles, but the central section's emphasis on Gentiles is especially important, as is confirmed by the concluding statement that God "had opened a door of faith for the Gentiles" (v. 27). The Lystra episode dramatizes the arrival of the gospel among those Gentiles who are, unlike Cornelius, not already worshipers of the God of Israel.

Verses 1-7 summarize rather than narrate the group's witness in Iconium, where again the bold witness generates a divided response. Verses 8-20 narrate a dramatic encounter in Lystra, as the healing of a lame man prompts a severe misunderstanding, which then requires an explanation in the form of a missionary speech. Although the nature of the misunderstanding is striking, the pattern resembles early scenes in the Jerusalem ministry, where the outpouring of the Spirit or the healing at the temple gate must be explained in response to misunderstanding (see especially 2:12-16; 3:12; 4:7). The report of the healing resembles the one in 3:1-10 in several respects (see below).

Verses 21-28 again summarize, this time tracing the witnesses' return to previously visited cities and the activities there. With the arrival of Paul and Barnabas in Antioch, the cycle begun by the Spirit in 13:1-3 concludes, and the stage is set for the question raised in chapter 15: How are these Gentiles to come through the door that God has opened for them?

◊ ◊ ◊ ◊

Division in Iconium (14:1-7)

As in the journeys of chapter 13, Paul and Barnabas arrive in Iconium and begin speaking in the synagogue. That location undermines any interpretation of 13:46-47 as terminating the witness among Jews. As at Pisidian Antioch, this synagogue includes both Jews and "Greeks," either proselytes to Judaism or Gentiles who have associated themselves with the synagogue (see on 10:1-8; 13:16b-25).

Verse 3 constitutes a miniature portrait of authentic Christian witness. First, the witnesses "remained for a long time." Second, they speak "boldly for the Lord," a hallmark of Christian witness (e.g., 4:13, 29, 31); apostles and other witnesses do not back away in the face of resistance. Here, interestingly, Luke describes the Lord himself as witnessing (NRSV: testified) to "the word of his grace" through signs and wonders. The gifts sought by the church's prayer in the context of persecution in Jerusalem (4:23-31) also mark the activity of Paul and Barnabas in Iconium.

Troubles nevertheless persist, since "unbelieving Jews" provoke Gentiles and "poisoned their minds against the brothers" (v. 2). Resistance to the gospel comes from both Jews and Gentiles, but Luke ascribes special responsibility to those Jews in synagogues who take an active role in dissuading Gentiles (v. 2). Spilling out beyond the synagogue, division infects the city itself (v. 4) and erupts into the violent plan that sends the witnesses on their way—still proclaiming the gospel (vv. 5-7).

Interpreters puzzle over the appearance of the term "apostles" in 14:4 and 14 (the NRSV supplies it in v. 6, although it does not occur in the Greek), since nowhere else in Acts are people other than the Twelve called "apostles," and the stipulation Peter makes prior to the selection of Judas' replacement would appear to disqualify Paul and probably Barnabas as well (see 1:21-22). Scholars who attempt to identify sources behind Acts sometimes contend that here Luke has simply not carefully edited his source to bring it into conformity with his views (Haenchen 1971, 420; Conzelmann 1987, 108), but the passage is otherwise consistent with Luke's vocabulary and style. And, however Luke imagines the qualifications for apostleship or the number of apostles, clearly Paul and Barnabas do engage in the primary apostolic task of witnessing to the resurrection of Jesus (1:22).

Healing and Confusion in Lystra (14:8-20)

The cultural identity of Lystra plays a part in the story in vv. 8-20, just as the cultural identity of Athens does in Acts 17 and that of Ephesus in Acts 19. As residents of a cultural backwater, Lystrans were frequently characterized as largely rustic and uncivilized. Their gullibility in this story plays on the stereotype, just as the disdainful sophistication of the philosophers in Acts 17 plays on the stereotype of Athenians (Bechard 2000).

The beginning of the story in vv. 8-20 is abrupt, with no attention to where or how Paul encountered the man crippled from birth. Three separate phrases depict the man's disability ("could not use his feet," "had never walked," "crippled from birth," v. 8) so that the healing that follows becomes the more impressive. Where v. 8 elaborates the presenting situation, v. 9 condenses the exchange between Paul and the unnamed man. The man listens to Paul, and Paul sees "that he had faith to be healed." The healing follows immediately, confirmed by the man's ability to walk (v. 10).

Several features of the story replay the earlier healing in Jerusalem in Acts 3. Both men are described as "lame from birth" (3:3; 14:8). Both Peter and Paul look intently (3:4; 14:9). In both cases, the demonstration of the healing's efficacy involves leaping up (3:8; 14:10). And both connect the healing itself with faith (3:16; 14:9). In addition, both healings precipitate a response from local religious leaders, the temple authorities in Jerusalem (4:1-4), and the priest of Zeus in Lystra (14:13), although the responses differ dramatically.

Miracle stories routinely conclude with some stereotypical word about the response of bystanders (e.g., Luke 5:26; 8:25; 9:43), but in this instance that stereotyped feature becomes dramatic confrontation. First, crowds respond in Lycaonian, presumably unintelligible to Paul and Barnabas, declaring them to be gods in human form. Stories in which people confuse human beings with divine visitors are a stock feature of ancient narrative (Dan 2:46; Josephus, *Ant.* 10.211-12; Chariton, *Chaereas and Callirhoe* 1.1.16; 1.14.1; 3.2.15-17; Xenophon, *Ephesian Tale* 1.12.1), and a well-known variation involves Phrygia itself, tying the confusion here to a bit of local color. According to Ovid, two gods visit an unrighteous village in the region, where they are treated hospitably by a couple who eventually recognize them as divine; when the village is destroyed, the home of the couple is not only spared but turned into a beautiful temple *(Metamorphoses* 8.574-698).

In the Lukan variation, the local priest of Zeus prepares to offer sacrifice, compounding the error of the populace rather than correcting it. This response by the residents and their priest prompts an equally dramatic response by Barnabas and Paul, who tear their clothing as a sign of grief (e.g., Gen 37:29, 34; 2 Sam 1:2, 11; Jdt 14:16, 19; 1 Macc 2:14) and then announce the truth: "We are mortals just like you." By striking contrast with King Herod, who dies for his failure to acknowledge his humanity when faced with a similar error (12:23; but cf. 28:6), Barnabas and Paul aggressively resist this misunderstanding of the healing.

The speech begins by confronting the erroneous conclusion of the Lystrans, but it quickly turns to proclamation of "good news." Since the context makes it impossible to begin with Jesus or even the history of Israel, Paul and Barnabas begin by contrasting the "worthless things," worship of gods such as Zeus and Hermes, with the living God. This beginning point of contrast reflects conventional Jewish treatments of idolatry (e.g., Isa

44:9-20; Wis 13-15; 1 Thess 1:9-10; Philo, *Decalogue* 66-81; *Jos. Asen.*). Although this polemic has not appeared earlier in Acts, it does recall 4:24 with its invocation of the God of creation (see also Exod 20:11; Ps 146:6; Isa 37:6), and it anticipates Paul's sermon in Athens (17:24; see also 7:39-43, 47-50). From this traditional beginning point, Paul and Barnabas move on to introduce, in an indirect way, the claim that Gentiles *should* have known all along about the existence of the God of creation. God has previously "allowed all the nations to follow their own ways," yet they had a witness to God in the gifts of nature (cf. Rom 1:19-20; see also Pss 145:15-16; 147:8-9; Jer 5:24).

The response of the crowd to these words appears to function in several ways. Luke cannot approve of the Lystrans' desire to offer sacrifice to Paul and Barnabas as if they were divine, but certainly he approves their enthusiastic welcome of the witness. Later references to believers in Lystra indicate that some of the residents were persuaded by Christian proclamation (14:21-22; 16:2). The enthusiasm of many, however, proves ephemeral, as is evident in the very next verse.

The stay in Lystra culminates in further resistance, since Jews from Antioch and Iconium succeed in stirring up the Lystrans against the witnesses. As in Jerusalem, where the resistance led to the stoning of Stephen outside the city (7:58), here it prompts the stoning of Paul and removing him from the city, abandoning him as a corpse. Luke is more concerned with demonstrating the intensity of persecution and the concern of Paul's fellow-believers than he is with verisimilitude, and a number of details drop by the wayside. For example, how is it the disciples know that Paul is alive and the crowd does not? How does the apparently dead Paul rise and reenter the city without precipitating further persecution? And how is he capable of traveling on the following day?

Returning to Syrian Antioch (14:21-28)

Instead of supplying such detail, Luke resumes summary mode as the team returns to visit disciples in various cities, finally arriving back in Syrian Antioch itself (vv. 21-28). As with the summary in 14:1-7, this one also identifies important features of the work of witnesses. They nurture disciples (v. 22); they also identify leaders, handing them over to the Lord's care (v. 23). Upon their arrival in Antioch, they call believers together and narrate their own activity, so that their witness to the Gentiles also becomes part of the gospel to be told and retold.

Two statements in this summary merit attention. In translation, v. 22 might be understood as identifying persecution as a requirement for entry into the kingdom, except that Luke uses here the word *dei* ("it is necessary"), which the NRSV translates "we must." Elsewhere in Luke–Acts, *dei* signals something that is part of the divine plan, such as the suffering and death of Jesus (Luke 9:22; 17:25; 24:7, 26; and note also Acts 9:16). The implication seems to be that the persecution of believers is to be understood as consistent with God's plan, not that it is an entrance requirement that believers must meet by virtue of their own conscious choice.

Verse 27 offers the final comment on this section and serves to interpret everything that has happened in the story since at least 13:1. When Paul and Barnabas give their report, what they report on is *God's* work with them, that is, what God has done through the apostles. They further identify this work as God's opening "a door of faith for the Gentiles," so that the focus is less on Jewish resistance than it is on God's persistent openness.

◊ ◊ ◊ ◊

Because of the dramatic conclusion to the witness in Pisidian Antioch, with Paul's pronouncement about turning to the Gentiles, it is tempting to read the events in Iconium and Lystra with attention fixed on the differing responses of Jews and Gentiles. Yet the story does not generalize easily, since *both* Jews and Gentiles continue to respond with *both* faith and resistance. Luke's comments at the end of the chapter return readers to the larger perspective of what God is doing rather than how humans respond.

Luke also provides here some important indications of what

evangelism involves. The witnesses are engaged in preaching and teaching, but their work also involves staying on the scene for a period of time (vv. 3, 28), encouraging believers (v. 22), and providing for the oversight of local gatherings of believers (v. 23). Not even in a brief report about the early witness does Luke imagine that evangelism consists entirely of preaching. As often in Acts, he takes note of the spending of time in a particular location (e.g., 9:43; 10:48; 11:26; 15:33, 35; 16:12; 18:11, 18, 23; 19:8, 10, 22; 20:3, 31; 21:10).

Although the setting and the response are different from that surrounding the healing of 3:1-10, both stories raise the question of whose power is at work. In Jerusalem the question is asked explicitly and the answer the apostles give is rejected by the authorities (4:7, 18; and see 3:12). In Lystra the question is answered implicitly when the crowd—including even the priest of Zeus—greets Paul and Barnabas as if they were divine. The beginning of preaching to those Gentiles who have no association with the synagogue consists of affirming that there is only one such power, that of Israel's God.

A Conference in Jerusalem (15:1-35)

At the end of chapter 14, Paul and Barnabas return to Antioch where they report on God's activities and remain for "some time" in what seems to be a joyous reunion. That productive and harmonious tone shatters when unidentified persons arrive from Judea and make demands (15:1), thereby setting in motion the developments that lead to what is customarily referred to as the Jerusalem Council. Verses 1-5 introduce the problem and provide the necessary transition, so that the Antioch delegation makes its way to Jerusalem.

Verses 6-21 present the discussion in Jerusalem, which comprises three addresses, that of Peter (vv. 7-11), that of the collective voice of Barnabas and Paul (summarized rather than reported [v. 12]), and that of James (vv. 13-21). Despite Luke's assertion that there is "much debate" (v. 7), none of the arguments of the group demanding circumcision make their way into the account of the debate. Neither do Gentile believers from the Antioch church speak. Instead, the debate culminates with James's proposal in v. 20.

The response of those gathered in Jerusalem comes in vv. 22-29, and it coheres with the speeches and with James's proposal in particular. The bulk of the response consists of a letter that conforms to Greco-Roman letter writing practices as evidenced elsewhere both within and outside the New Testament (vv. 23-29; Aune 1987, 128, 158-82). The final scene completes the story by depicting the response of believers in Antioch and the continued work there of Paul and Barnabas (vv. 30-35).

Identifying the constituent elements in this passage is relatively simple, but understanding its place in Luke's larger narrative is far more difficult. Students of Acts frequently employ terms such as "centerpiece," "turning-point," and "watershed" to convey their sense of its importance (e.g., Haenchen 1971, 461; Conzelmann 1987, 115, 121; Johnson 1992, 268; Witherington 1998, 439; Barrett 1998, 709), and it does occupy the literary center of the volume, standing at the end of the first half of the book. It is not clear, however, that the Council is the dramatic turning-point of the book; even some of those who refer to the Council as central note that the problem addressed here would seem to have been settled in the story of Cornelius (10:1–11:18; Wilson 1983, 71; Barrett 1998, 700; Fitzmyer 1998, 546). There not only does Peter acknowledge God's decision (10:34-35, 47; 11:17), but he and his companions stay in Cornelius's home, evidently sharing meals with Gentiles (10:48; 11:3). The questions emerge: What relationship exists between the Cornelius story and the Jerusalem Council? And what does that relationship reveal about the place of the Jerusalem Council in the larger framework of Acts?

As indicated earlier (see Introduction and above on 10:1–11:18), the story of the conversions of Cornelius and Peter is the climactic event in the first half of Acts. From perhaps as early as 1:8 (see also 2:39; 8:26-40; not to mention Luke's Gospel, as in Luke 2:32; 3:38), the narrative anticipates that God intends the gospel for all people, Gentiles as well as Jews.

However reluctant Peter is to recognize God's action, 10:47 makes it clear that he understands God has made an irrevocable decision about the Gentiles, and 11:1-18 shows the Jerusalem community consenting to that decision. From 11:19 through the end of chapter 14, no voice is lifted against those who proclaim the gospel among the Gentiles, and no one raises the question of law observance by the Gentiles. That narrative development strongly suggests that the Jerusalem Council is not so much narrative climax as narrative denouement; along with the journey of Barnabas and Paul in 11:19–14:28, it works out the implications of 10:1–11:18 but does not represent a new stage in the church's story. It works out those implications by underscoring once more God's intention to grant repentance and salvation to Gentiles.

Literarily, then, 15:1-35 concludes the denouement for Part I of Acts. Indeed, the summary in v. 35 resembles the end of chapter 28. Both 15:35 and 28:30-31 refer to an extended stay, and both summarize the activity involved as teaching and preaching.

Even a casual reading of Acts and the letters of Paul prompts many historical questions about the events narrated in this passage. Among the more obvious are: How are the demands for observance of Mosaic law related to the response of the Jerusalem community in 11:1-18? How is this account to be reconciled with Paul's comments in Galatians 1–2? How should the three visits to Jerusalem in Acts be correlated with references in the letters of Paul? Why do Paul's letters make no reference to the stipulations agreed to here (the so-called apostolic decree)? The fact that both Luke and Paul write about the conflict over Gentiles and law observance strongly suggests that there was such a dispute in the early decades of the church's existence. Beyond that, historical reconstruction becomes exceedingly difficult. A number of studies explore the questions in great detail, but there is very little consensus and an endless variety of hypotheses (Achtemeier 1987; Cousar 1992). Consistent with the approach identified in the Introduction, the attempt here will be to understand Lukan theology by means of the story and to leave aside most historical questions.

A Dispute in Antioch Leads to Jerusalem (15:1-5)

In Antioch, some people arrive announcing to Gentiles that they must undergo circumcision in order to be saved (v. 1). Luke does not elaborate on their identity or their motives, except to indicate that these new arrivals are "from Judea" (see vv. 5, 24). Curiously, Luke reports that they are also instructing "the brothers," which in the context surely means fellow-believers or Christians, yet the demand they make implies that these Judeans would not recognize the Gentile believers in Antioch as their "brothers" (Barrett 1998, 688). The appellation "brothers" reveals Luke's disposition on the matter, a disposition that is never in question throughout the story.

Curiously, the Judeans refer to circumcision as "according to the custom of Moses," which creates another small difficulty, since circumcision derives from God's demand of Abraham rather than from Mosaic law (see 7:8; Gen 17:9-14; and cf. John 7:22). Ascribing the practice to Moses perhaps recalls the charge that Stephen speaks against Moses (6:11, 14) and anticipates later accusations against Paul (21:21, 28). Derivation aside, circumcision was understood both by Jews and by non-Jews as a crucial identity-marker for Jews. Jewish males were to be circumcised, and Jewish females were to marry only circumcised men. Interpretations of circumcision vary in this period, but the practice itself was scarcely questioned (Barclay 1996, 411-12, 438-39).

The demand of the unnamed Judeans provokes significant dispute with Paul and Barnabas ("no small" being an instance of *litotes*, a rhetorical device using understatement for emphasis, which employs a negative statement of the contrary; see also 26:26). Gentile believers themselves do not appear to have a voice in the dispute; they are spoken about both in Antioch and in Jerusalem (Jervell 1998, 389). The church's decision is to send Paul, Barnabas, and others to Jerusalem (v. 2). Although it is God's Spirit and not the Jerusalem community that has directed the mission that began in Antioch and will direct Paul's witness in chapters that follow, Jerusalem nevertheless plays an important role in Luke–Acts, and the judgment of the "apostles and the elders" weighs heavily.

Luke spares few words for describing the discussion in Antioch, but he does linger over the interactions of the Antioch delegation as they travel to and arrive in Jerusalem. First, they pass through Phoenicia and Samaria. The reference to Samaria recalls the story of the early witness in Samaria in Acts 8, but Phoenicia has not previously entered the story, suggesting again that Luke has no plan for a comprehensive chronicle of church foundings. In Samaria, however, Paul and Barnabas announce the conversion of the Gentiles. Luke's language here is telling, since the verb he employs (*ekdiēgeomai*; NRSV: reported) is related to the noun Luke 1:1 uses for earlier gospel narratives (*diēgēsis*; NRSV: account). Already the preaching of the witnesses has included the witness itself within the narrative of God's accomplishments, and this verse confirms that association (10:39, 42; 13:31-32), the more so because this account brings "great joy" to believers. Elsewhere in Acts, "joy" and "rejoicing" follow in the wake of the gospel's proclamation (8:8, 39; 11:23; 13:48, 52).

Verse 4 narrates the arrival of the group from Antioch somewhat abruptly, as if they had walked into the city and immediately entered a meeting with the "apostles and the elders." Their report consists of "all that God had done with them," and the content of that "all" surely includes the Gentile mission (as in the reports of 14:27 and 15:3). Unlike the believers of Phoenicia and Samaria, who respond to this report with joy, a group of Pharisees responds by repeating the demand made in Antioch, this time in a more extensive form that explicitly includes both circumcision *and* obedience to Mosaic law. The demand here is emphatic, opening as it does with the Greek word *dei* (NRSV: it is necessary), a word Luke elsewhere uses to refer to elements of God's plan for salvation (e.g., Luke 2:49; 4:43; 24:44; Acts 1:16; 4:12). Christian Pharisees apparently understand themselves to be speaking about a theological necessity. Such a forceful assertion of the demand requires a response.

Deliberation in Jerusalem (15:6-21)

With the group gathered and the volume turned up on the demand that Gentile believers adhere to Jewish law, the scene is prepared for the deliberation of vv. 6-21. Luke specifies that the "apostles and the elders" gathered, suggesting that they are the ones whose judgment will decide the matter, but v. 4 indicates that it is "the church and the apostles and the elders" who welcome the group from Antioch, and the fact of intense debate might indicate a more diverse group than that consisting of "the apostles and the elders" alone. As elsewhere, Luke does not seem especially interested in precision about the persons gathered, suggesting that questions of personnel are less important to him than either the subject under discussion or the underlying conviction that it is God who decides.

Peter's Recapitulation and Reinterpretation (15:7-11): The first speaker is Peter, who begins by appealing for the attention of those assembled with the conventional "my brothers," followed by an emphatic pronoun that is difficult to capture in English translation but has the effect of underscoring and complimenting the audience's knowledge (something like, "*You* already know" or "*You* surely know"). What follows in vv. 7-9 recapitulates the conversion of Cornelius (10:1–11:18), but it does so with unrelenting focus on God's activity and omits any attention to Peter's earlier resistance or that of the Jerusalem community (Tannehill 1990, 184-85). The emphasis on God's initiative in v. 7 is more pronounced in the Greek than in the NRSV, since a more literal translation would be, "God chose through my mouth the Gentiles to hear the word of the gospel and believe." God's selection has here a double object in that God chooses the mouth of Peter and *also* chooses that the Gentiles hear the gospel. The verb translated "made a choice" is revealing, because it is used elsewhere for the choosing of Israel or the choosing of the disciples (1:2, 24; 13:17; Luke 6:13). Verses 8-9 continue the emphasis on God's role: God knows human hearts (cf. 1:24), God testified to them, God gave them the Holy Spirit, God did not distinguish them from Jewish believers, and God cleansed their hearts. In this last statement there is a wonderful irony with the Cornelius account, in which Peter claims not to eat anything that is common or unclean (10:9-16).

Having displayed God's actions in the case of Cornelius and household, Peter turns in vv. 10-11 to the assembly. The statements in vv. 10-11 require some attention, for both are ambiguous, but the introduction to them is far from ambiguous: "Why are you putting God to the test?" The demands of vv. 1 and 5 that Gentiles must adhere to Mosaic law Peter interprets as willful resistance to God's own actions, and the language Peter uses recalls important moments of Israel's rebellion against God (LXX Exod 15:22-27; 17:2, 7; Num 14:22; Deut 6:16; Isa 7:12; Wis 1:2; Luke 4:12; Acts 5:9). The difficulty with the remainder of v. 10 comes with understanding whether the emphasis falls at the beginning of the statement or at the end: Is the problem inherent in the law itself, which is too great a weight for either Gentile or Jew to carry? Or does the difficulty lie in the inability of Israel to live in accordance with the law? The former interpretation is the one most frequently adopted, but it contains several problems: elsewhere, the image of the yoke functions positively (see, e.g., Sir 51:26; *1 Clem.* 16:17; *m. 'Abot* 3.5; *m. Ber.* 2.2, 5; but cf. Gal 5:1; 1 Tim 6:1), and Luke generally portrays observance of the law in a positive fashion (e.g., Luke 2:22-24; Acts 21:17-26). Peter himself in 10:9-16 celebrates the law as something to which he has gladly submitted. Although less frequently adopted by translators and commentators, the second option is more compelling; in significant ways Israel has failed to keep the law (Nolland 1980; Jervell 1998, 392-93). This rendering preserves the positive sense of the law as a yoke and recalls Stephen's stinging indictment in 7:53 (not to mention the indictments uttered by the prophets, John the Baptist, and Jesus).

Verse 11 also prompts considerable confusion. In the NRSV's rendering, it sounds more like the letters of Paul than the narrative of Luke (Gal 2:16; 3:2; Rom 3:28). The word order Peter employs also seems odd, since one would expect the order to be "they will be saved . . . just as we will." The problem here again is one of translation, because the ambiguity of the Greek falls away in English translations. Rendered somewhat literally, v. 11 reads: "On the contrary, through the grace of the Lord Jesus we believe to be saved just as also they." The implication could be that both groups believe *in order to be saved* or that both believe it to be the case *that they will be saved*. Both cases can be made grammatically, and both can be argued from Luke, who closely links faith and salvation. Yet neither approach is satisfying in this context, where the emphasis appears to lie more on the commonality of salvation by the action of the Lord Jesus than on any human means to that salvation, especially in view of the earlier emphasis on God's intervention. Having indicted the crowd for resisting God's will, recalled the history of Israel's faithlessness, and underscored the role of God and the grace of Jesus in all salvation, Peter stops. No words of conclusion are necessary, since further speeches will provide the conclusion.

Barnabas and Paul (15:12): Luke's notice that the assembly was silent lends itself to much speculation about the meaning of the silence, but little evidence supports any interpretation, and it is entirely possible that the silence simply serves the narrative end of making the transition from Peter's speech to the ones that follow. "Barnabas and Paul" speak, and here the order of the names is that of the early association of these two (11:30; 12:25; 13:7; contrast 13:43, 46). Luke summarizes their speech, perhaps because the events it recalls are so recently a part of the narrative that an extended report is unnecessary (Dibelius 1956, 96). The wording of the summary is significant, for it describes not the work of Paul and Barnabas but God's own "signs and wonders." The actor here is not Barnabas or Paul or the Gentiles, but God.

James's Interpretation and Conclusion (15:13-21): After Barnabas and Paul are silent (*sigaō* in both v. 12 and v. 13, but obscured by NRSV), James speaks. No description gives him special authority or even introduces him, which could mean that the narrator assumes the audience knows him or recalls him from 12:17 (Tannehill 1990, 186), but it may also mean that the

speakers are nearly interchangeable for Luke, who is less interested in personnel matters than are contemporary readers.

In v. 14, James recapitulates earlier remarks and offers a pithy
theological summary of their importance. The name "Simeon"
here has puzzled interpreters, since Luke refers to Peter as Simon
(e.g., Luke 4:38; 24:34; Acts 10:5) but never elsewhere as
Simeon, which is the Grecized form of the Hebrew name Simon.
The early interpreter Chrysostom thought it a reference to the
Simeon of Luke 2 (*Homilies on Acts* 33 [NPNF 11:205-206]; see
also Fowl 1998, 111), who announces that Jesus will be a light
to the Gentiles, yet it could also be that Luke deliberately shows
James selecting the form of Peter's name most congenial to the
gathered audience of Jewish believers (Lake and Cadbury 1933,
175; and see 1 Macc 2:65, where the Maccabean leader Simon is
referred to by his father as "Simeon").

Verse 14 begins in a way that recalls the opening to Peter's
speech, in that both refer to the time of God's action ("in the
early days," v. 7; "first," v. 14), and both refer to God's choice of
the Gentiles (Conzelmann 1987, 117). The remarkable turn of v.
14 comes at the end, when James announces that God has visited
the Gentiles "to take from among them a people for his name."
Luke has routinely used the noun "people" (*laos*) for Israel,
either for Israel as a whole or for a particular group of Jews (e.g.,
2:47; 6:8; 13:17; Luke 24:19), and the notion that a people
could be drawn from among the Gentiles is paradoxical and
exceedingly powerful (Conzelmann 1987, 117; Tannehill 1990,
187). Just as God made Israel God's people, God has now made
a people from among the Gentiles (Dahl 1958, 326).

By way of reinforcing this dramatic conclusion, James turns to
the prophets, where he finds the same motif of God's building
and rebuilding. Introducing the citation, he says, "the words of
the prophets agree with this" (AT), not "this agrees with the
words of the prophets," as the NRSV puts it, suggesting that he
makes the bold move of looking for scriptural language with
which to express the church's experience of God's action. James
finds those words in a slightly altered citation of Amos 9:11-12,
although other prophetic texts may influence this citation as well

(Jer 12:15; Isa 45:21; Bauckham 1995, 452-62). The language James employs is that of the LXX, which seems incongruous in the narrative setting of Jewish believers gathered in Jerusalem: however, not only does Luke regularly draw on the LXX, but in this particular instance the Hebrew would undermine his argument, because the Hebrew of Amos 9:11-12 anticipates the defeat of the nations rather than their inclusion.

The importance of James's citation emerges when it is read both in the context of the developing Lukan story and with attention to the differences between the citation and the LXX passage. (Admittedly, the differences between the citation and the LXX could derive from a text of Amos no longer extant.) Verse 16 concerns "the dwelling of David" and its renewal. Some interpreters argue that Luke's James sees in this rebuilding a reference to the resurrection of Jesus (e.g., Haenchen 1971, 448; Talbert 1997, 140), but that seems unlikely, especially since Acts 15:16 employs the verb *anoikodomēsō* ("rebuild") rather than the verb *anastēsō* ("raise up") that appears both in LXX Amos 9:11 and in Acts for the resurrection of Jesus (e.g., 2:24, 32; 3:26; 13:33, 34). Instead of the resurrection of Jesus, the language of rebuilding refers to God's restoration of Israel (as in Luke 1:32-33 and Acts 1:6; Jervell 1998, 395). No longer is it Israel who attempts to build a house for God (7:47, 49), but God alone is the builder of a house for all people (Richard 1984, 195). Interestingly, among the words Luke omits as he quotes Amos 9:11-12 is the phrase "just as in days of old," perhaps because Israel is not so much to be restored to some former glory as to be rebuilt.

The result of that rebuilding, and the real point of the citation, comes in vv. 17-18, which follows LXX Amos 9:12 closely. Luke adds "the Lord" following "so that all other peoples may seek," and omits "God" at the end of the phrase, "Thus says the Lord." Luke also adds "known from long ago" in v. 18, so that the point is that these things are part of God's plan. Taken together, the second half of the citation reinforces the claim that the Gentiles also belong to God's name and that God has always intended to bring about their inclusion. The language of seeking after God also recalls the Ethiopian who wants instruction (8:26-40), as well as Cornelius's unquestioning obedience (10:1-8; Richard 1984, 200).

In its Lukan context, then, vv. 16-18 interpret all three speeches, and indeed everything back to and including the conversion of Cornelius, as consistent with God's plan. Not only is God capable of making a "people" out of Gentiles, but the creation of a people is itself part of the divine plan. The way is clear, then, for the proposal James makes in vv. 19-21.

James introduces what has come to be called the "apostolic decree" with words whose nuance is ambiguous. "I have reached the decision" could designate what follows as a formal verdict which James understands himself to have the authority to make (13:46; 21:25; 25:25; see Lake and Cadbury 1933, 177; Johnson 1992, 264, 266) or it may be simply his own judgment (16:15; 25:25; Fitzmyer 1998, 556). Since the language can be understood either way, the context needs to be the ruling factor, and references later on to the larger body of believers (vv. 22-23) suggest that James is here formulating a proposal he understands to be consistent with his speech as well as those of Peter and Barnabas and Paul.

The difficulties of understanding v. 20 are considerable. First, the decree appears three times in Acts, and in three slightly different forms:

15:20	... to abstain only from things polluted by idols (pl.) and from sexual immorality and from whatever has been strangled (sg.) and from blood. (AT)
15:29	... abstain from things sacrificed to idols and from blood and from things strangled and from sexual immorality. (AT)
21:25	... keep away from what has been sacrificed to idols (sg.) and from blood and from what is strangled (sg.) and from sexual immorality. (AT)

Second, early manuscripts of Acts differ as to the exact wording of v. 20; some of those differences reflect attempts to harmonize the three passages in Acts, and others appear to be clarifications of difficulties. The most distinctive of these variants appears in some manuscripts that add at the end of the verse the words, "Do not do whatever you wish not to be done to yourself" (cf. Luke 6:31; Matt 7:12). Third, some of the terms in the decree are obscure or ambiguous, as discussed below. The combination of these factors, together with the absence of explanation on the part of Luke, makes interpretation here especially treacherous.

The first of the four things from which Gentiles are to abstain is "things polluted by idols." The Greek noun translated as "things polluted" (*alisgēma*) is quite rare, attested nowhere in the LXX or in other Jewish writings of the period, but the cognate verb *alisgeō* means to pollute; hence the translation "things polluted by idols." Religious traditions of both Greece and Rome had long-established practices associated with the reverencing of many gods, and Jews had a long tradition of attacking the reverencing of many gods. "Things polluted by idols" could refer to a whole range of things, but perhaps especially to food and drink that had been dedicated to the gods (e.g., Dan 1:8, Mal 1:7, 12; Sir 40:29 [obscured in NRSV]; 1 Cor 8-10).

The second item in the list is *porneia*, "sexual immorality." Elsewhere in the New Testament, *porneia* refers to any form of sexual misconduct and often reflects Jewish notions about the indiscriminate sexual behavior of Gentiles (e.g., Rom 1:18-32; cf. Wis 14:12, 24). There is also a close association in Jewish tradition between sexual immorality and idolatry (Hos 5:3-4; Ezek 16:15-46; Jer 3:1-10; Wis 14:12, 24; *Syb. Or.* 4:1-39; *Jub.* 22:16-23; 1 Cor 10:7-8; Rev 2:14, 20).

The third and fourth items on the list are the most difficult. "That which is strangled" is so puzzling that some manuscripts of Acts simply omit it. The phrase translates a Greek word not found in the LXX or other Jewish writings, but in other ancient writings it refers to food preparations that involve baking or steaming (Wilson 1983, 91-92; BDAG 838). Probably it refers in Acts 15 to a method of preparation that did not drain the blood from the animal to be eaten, which would mean that the third and fourth items belong together. "Blood" could also refer to the blood of murder, but the fact that the other items in the list concern things of which the Gentiles are regarded as guilty almost by definition suggests that this one probably does too. That is, the third and fourth items either belong together or reinforce one another; to abstain from one of them is to abstain from both, since something that has been strangled and then eaten still contains the blood. Abhorrence of the eating of blood is so firm in the Old Testament that it would not be surprising to find it referred to here, even redundantly (e.g., Lev 3:17; 17:10-14; Deut 12:16, 23; 15:23; 1 Sam 14:31-35). And, importantly in this context, the practice of consuming blood is also connected with idolatry (Wis 12:2-5).

Where do these four items lead? Some scholars have argued that they derive from Lev 17–18, which identifies specific regulations that pertain to non-Israelites who reside within Israel. The fit is inexact, however, because Lev 17–18 treats requirements for Israelites and only occasionally refers to what is expected of resident aliens (17:8-9, 10-13). Moreover, the Gentile believers of Acts 15 do not reside within an otherwise Jewish territory. Other interpreters would suggest that these are the minimum requirements on the basis of which Jewish and Gentile believers could eat together, but it is worth noting that the possibility of sharing in meals does not enter the conversation here (by contrast with Gal 2:11-13); it appears that Gentile and Jewish believers have been eating together since the conversion of Cornelius in chapter 10.

The decree functions, not to make it less offensive for Jews to eat with Gentiles, but to guard Gentile believers from the ever-present threat of idolatry. All elements of the decree (whether there are three or four) are associated with idolatry, either directly or indirectly. That association becomes especially interesting when located among the number of other ways in which Luke reflects concern about idolatry, including Stephen's pointed recollection of the golden calf (7:40-41), Paul's sermons in Lystra and Athens (14:15-17; 17:22b-31), and the fearsome conflict in

Ephesus (19:23-41). These elements of the narrative serve not only to show the religious traditions from which Gentile converts emerge, but to *reinforce the danger of polytheism even for Gentile believers.* Separating oneself from the gods and their service was not a simple achievement in an environment where the overriding religious atmosphere assumed that piety required adherence to as many gods as possible. Later evidence makes it clear that this problem perdured for centuries in the church's life (Rev 2:14, 20; *Did.* 6; Justin, *Trypho*, 34.8; Minucius Felix 30.6; Eusebius, *Church History* V 1.26; Tertullian, *Apologia* 9.13; MacMullen 1984). These strictures against anything that might reek of the gods in the context of the church's earliest community offer a powerful reminder of the need for distinguishing God from the gods.

If the primary function of the decree, as recounted in Acts, is to guard Gentile believers from lapsing into polytheism, then the otherwise perplexing silence about circumcision becomes understandable. After the initial demands of the circumcision party in vv. 1 and 5, the subject is referred to again only in the most oblique fashion (vv. 19, 24, 28). No one explicitly concludes that Gentiles need not be circumcised. The demand for circumcision serves to introduce the question of Gentile behavior, but response to the demand does not play a significant role in the discussion itself or in the decree.

Verse 21 constitutes yet another difficulty. The problem arises, not from the statement itself, for other writers of the period make similar claims (Josephus, *Ant.* 16.43; *Ag. Ap.* 2.175; Philo, *Spec. Laws* 2.61-64), but with the "for" at the beginning of the verse. That conjunction indicates that v. 21 somehow explains v. 20, and yet the relationship between the two is left unstated. Some scholars take it as meaning that the law is so well known to Jews—even to Jews living in the Diaspora—that they will not tolerate the presence of Gentiles who do not conform with the law. Since nothing else in any of these speeches in chapter 15 reflects concern about the opinions of other Jews, it seems more likely that the claim is that the law of Moses, and perhaps the first commandment of the

Decalogue, is so widely recognized that even Gentiles should know better than to do these things.

Response of Believers in Jerusalem (15:22-29)

James's proposal meets with the approval of the whole community, since Luke indicates that "the apostles and elders together with the whole church" (AT) send a letter to Antioch by means of Judas Barsabbas and Silas along with Paul and Barnabas. Luke makes no other reference to Judas Barsabbas after this passage; Silas travels with Paul (15:40–18:5) and is probably the person the epistles identify as Silvanus (1 Thess 1:1; 2 Thess 1:1; 2 Cor 1:19). Here Luke describes them in the way most appropriate for the story: they are chosen (see 1:2, 24; 6:5; 13:17; Luke 6:13; 9:35) for this task and are leaders in the community.

The letter carried by the delegation opens with a conventional salutation, identifying the recipients of the letter as the *Gentile believers* in Antioch, Syria, and Cilicia. The letter addresses those whose conduct, indeed whose salvation (15:1), has been questioned and defended before the Council. The letter apparently does *not* concern Jewish believers whose observance of the law is unaltered, and that distinction is consistent with the conclusion that the decree has to do with preserving Gentiles from the worship of idols rather than making Gentiles safe for common meals.

Verse 24 returns for the third time (vv. 1, 5) to the people who precipitated this conflict, here describing them in pejorative terms; they are from Jerusalem but they acted without instructions, and their claims were troubling to Gentiles. As before, they are unnamed. By contrast, the four who bring the letter are named, they are unanimously chosen and delegated, and they will encourage and strengthen believers in Antioch (v. 32). The narrator having already described Judas and Silas as "leaders" (v. 22), the letter refers to Barnabas and Paul as "our beloved," and as people who have "given themselves over" for the Lord's name (v. 26 AT; the NRSV's "risked their lives" is one possible implication of this phrase, but as a translation it is misleading).

The relatively long introduction of the problem and the delegation seems to divert attention from the decree itself (Haenchen
1971, 453), but it underscores the unity of the community that
stands behind the letter.

The community stands behind the letter, but the decision is
first of all characterized as that which "seemed good to the Holy
Spirit." Through its reflection on events and Scripture, the community has perceived the Spirit's guidance and come to a decision. The desire is not to "burden" Gentiles beyond the things
that are "essential." The wording of the decree differs slightly
from that in v. 20, but the direction seems to be consistent:
Gentiles must keep themselves from the things that Jews associate with polytheism, which includes sexual immorality and the
eating of food associated with idol worship.

Response in Antioch (15:30-35)

Verses 30-35 bring the entire episode to a close by returning to
Antioch, where the dispute began. Paul and Barnabas return
there, together with Judas and Silas. The exhortation generates
joy, comparable to the joy brought by the gospel itself. This may
be another indication that the exhortation has to do with warnings about false gods, since it is the one real God whose gospel
generates joy elsewhere in Acts (8:8, 39; 11:23; 13:48, 52). Judas
and Silas continue to instruct the believers at Antioch, and then
they return to Jerusalem. Paul and Barnabas remain in Antioch,
where "they taught and proclaimed the word of the Lord." As
will be the case in 28:31, this summarizing line brings the first
half of the book to a conclusion by epitomizing the activity of
the witnesses—they are to teach and preach the Lord.

James's words in v. 14 are pivotal for understanding not only
the Jerusalem Council but much of the first half of Acts: "God . . .
looked favorably on the Gentiles, to take from among them a
people for his name." However unlikely God's choice may seem
to those who know the history of Israel, and perhaps especially

to those who know Gentiles, God has called even the Gentiles. Both the actions of God through the witnesses (vv. 7-9, 12) and the words of the prophets (vv. 16-18) confirm this choice.

The question that dominates much recent discussion of this assertion is how to understand the relationship between God's Gentile *laos* and the *laos* Israel. Do the Gentiles actually displace the *laos* Israel (Sanders 1988), so that Luke advocates the position later identified as supersessionism? Does God's action create a new entity, consisting of restored Israel and Gentile believers together (Jervell 1988)? These positions and others have their advocates, but it is important to pay attention to the fact that Luke does not address the question of the relative standing of these two groups. It may seem that the emphasis on Jerusalem and the Jerusalem community does give that community a kind of priority, but following this scene nothing in Acts suggests that Gentile believers owe loyalty to the views of human beings in the Jerusalem church. Luke's focus lies elsewhere, on God's actions, and he appears to be unaware of the question the church's later history will raise about relationships between Jewish and Gentiles believers.

More important to Luke is the primary assertion that God has taken a people from among the Gentiles. And the corollary to that assertion is equally clear. *The Gentiles are God's people in the sense that they do not belong to themselves or to the polytheistic practices with which they have most surely been associated.* As noted above, the ongoing pull of polytheism, whether in the time about which Luke writes or in Luke's own community, should not be underestimated. Luke's story constitutes a forceful assertion that the Gentiles, as God's *laos*, must not engage in those behaviors that have about them the slightest trace of idolatry. Luke's second volume narrates in a multitude of ways the folly of worshiping things that are not God, but here the essentials come to the foreground. Things that are associated with idolatry, whether sexual immorality, service of the gods, or the eating of food connected in some way with the gods, must not be continued. This concern with polytheism may also explain the decision not to require circumcision, since the narrative connects

Gentiles with the God of Israel, but does not necessarily make Gentiles into Jews.

This denouement to the conversion of the church and the inclusion of Cornelius and his household massively reinforces God's prerogative to claim the Gentiles as a people, and its polemic against idolatry underscores the exclusive nature of the relationship between this new people and God. The decision is not that of the church, but of God, yet the story does show the church discerning God's will (Johnson 1992, 279). The Jerusalem community attends to the voices of the dissenters (those who would require circumcision). It also hears from those who have witnessed God's actions among the Gentiles. Interestingly, Luke says nothing about the intensity of the Gentiles' convictions or the level of their commitment; what carries weight is God's intervention rather than human response. The community also attends to Scripture itself, not by sorting and weighing all the passages that concern the standing of Gentiles but by boldly reinterpreting Scripture in light of God's actions in the present. An individual leader proposes the decree, to which the community at large—both in Jerusalem and in Antioch—gives consent. The delivery of the decree offers an occasion for joy and hospitality, as well as further instruction. The church's role here is enormously active, but it is active because of its empowerment by God.

PART TWO

"ALL PEOPLE EVERYWHERE" (15:36–19:41)

Although the second half of Acts begins with Paul and Silas visiting believers in the cities where Paul had already witnessed, the journey eventually takes Paul into Philippi, then Thessalonica, Beroea, Athens, Corinth, and Ephesus. If "all people everywhere" (17:30) do not repent, the witness in these varied locations does find a hearing, and it also finds opposition. Toward the end of the section comes the first indication of Paul's impending journey to Jerusalem, and then to Rome (19:21). Early encounters with Roman officials as well as charges of anti-Roman behavior also hint that difficulties lie ahead (16:21; 18:12-17; but see also 16:37-39).

A Renewed Beginning (15:36–16:10)

The second half of Acts begins with a substantial transitional passage. As at the beginning of the book, here Luke recalls earlier events (15:36, 38, 40; 16:4-5; cf. 1:1-5, 16-17, 21-22), identifies the personnel of the mission (15:40; 16:1-3; cf. 1:12-14, 15-26), and defines the role of the witnesses (16:10; cf. 1:8, 21-22). Perhaps most important, both halves begin with the insistence that neither Peter nor Paul is the proper focus of attention or director of the action, but God alone. Here God's role comes to expression first through the Spirit, which frustrates the plans of Paul and his companions, and then through a vision that directs the witnesses to Macedonia (16:6-10; cf. 1:7; 2:1-4, 22-24).

Three distinct units comprise the transition. The first introduces

Paul's determination to visit believers in the cities in which he and Barnabas had previously preached and taught (13:4-14:28), a determination that produces the dissolution of that partnership (15:36-41). The second unit briefly recounts the visitation of Paul and Silas to Derbe and Lystra and adds the name of Timothy to the roster of witnesses (16:1-5). With personnel determined and previously established churches visited, the third unit recounts in an unusual way God's sending of the witnesses to Macedonia (16:6-10).

Another new "character" joins Paul, Silas, and Timothy at 16:10, the narrator "we." For the first time in Acts, the story as a whole (as distinct from a speech by a character within the story) proceeds in first person plural. Four times in the remainder of Acts, narration changes from third person to first person plural (16:10-17; 20:5-15; 21:1-18; 27:1-28:16), and with no explanation provided. In the history of interpretation, many theories regarding the "we" passages have emerged, falling into two general types: either Luke is indicating that he was himself an eyewitness of events or Luke employs a source written in the first person. Neither approach is satisfying, however, since the style and vocabulary of these passages are otherwise consistent with the remainder of the book, making it difficult to sustain the theory of a distinctive "we" source. In addition, recent study of ancient historiography reveals that shifts in narration from third to first person are not unusual (Campbell, 2000). It may well be that Luke's introduction of "we" in these passages has little to do with sources or eyewitnesses and more to do with enhancing the reader's sense of the urgency of events. That explanation certainly works well in 16:10, where "we" enters just after the directive to Macedonia.

◊ ◊ ◊ ◊

"Strengthening the Churches" (15:36-41)

The quarrel between Paul and Barnabas ought not cause readers to miss the opening statement of vv. 36-41: Paul proposes that he and Barnabas return to all the cities in which they had earlier preached, for the purpose of learning "how they are doing." This agenda overarches the story through 16:5. Just as Paul and Barnabas earlier lingered with communities and retraced their steps in order to ascertain their health (14:21-23), so here the initial reason for leaving Antioch is to learn how these fledgling communities fare.

Paul proposes the journey to Barnabas, assuming that the two of them will travel together as before. Barnabas in turn proposes that they take along John Mark. Luke gives no reason for Barnabas's wish, but this may be yet another instance in which Barnabas acts out Luke's explanation of his name by being an encourager (see on 4:32-36). By contrast with the silence of Luke regarding Barnabas's reasons, Paul's objections are stated rather sharply. Although not apparent in English translation, the vocabulary and order of the Greek of v. 38 both draw attention to Mark's earlier decision to return to Jerusalem. His reasons for withdrawing appear neither in 13:13 nor here, but the vehemence of Paul in this passage could suggest that Mark resists the Gentile mission (cf. Gal 2:11-14; and see Black 2001, 105-111). Luke 9:62 may imply, however, that Paul's adamancy is not so much about resistance to the Gentile mission as it is about any departure from the work of witnessing; the very fact that John Mark returned to Jerusalem generates Paul's scorn. Ultimately, the reasons for the separation remain unknown.

The quarrel produces a rupture between Barnabas and Paul, so that Barnabas and Mark travel to Cyprus (Barnabas's home, see 4:36), and Paul and Silas to Syria and Cilicia. Luke does not narrate the division neutrally, however. He gives no purpose for Barnabas's trip, as if Barnabas had merely retreated. Neither does Luke indicate that the Antioch church commends Barnabas and Mark to God, as it does with Paul and Silas. These two factors, together with the earlier silence about Barnabas's reasons for wanting to take Mark, indicate that Luke favors Paul's position in the dispute.

Barnabas and Mark now disappear from the pages of Acts. As with Luke's treatment of Peter and other characters who serve the story and then fade from view, Luke does not explain what happens to them. In the same way, Paul now selects Silas, who was introduced only briefly earlier in this chapter (vv. 22, 27, 32-33); indeed, earlier in the chapter Silas goes to Jerusalem (15:33), and Luke gives no account of his return to Antioch. (As the note in the NRSV indicates, one manuscript tradition remedies this difficulty by inserting v. 34.) Luke seems unconcerned with closely accounting for such comings and goings (cf. 13:13 and 15:37).

A Disciple Named Timothy (16:1-5)

Luke's story of Paul's return to cities visited earlier continues in Derbe and Lystra (16:1-5), where he introduces Timothy (see also 1 Thess 1:1; 3:2, 6; Phil 1:1; 2:19; 1 Cor 4:17; 16:10; 2 Cor 1:1, 19; Phlm 1; and cf. 1 Tim 1:2, 18; 6:20 and 2 Tim 1:2, which may well be post-Pauline). Timothy is "the son of a Jewish woman who was a believer; but his father was a Greek" (v. 1). Although the Greek is more ambiguous than the NRSV, it appears that Timothy's mother is a Jewish Christian (to employ an anachronism) and that his father was neither a Jew nor a Christian. Timothy enjoys a good reputation among local believers, but Paul fears that Timothy will not be received elsewhere among Jews, and so he circumcises him.

Several difficult and interrelated questions complicate interpretation of this brief story, one of which is whether Jews would have regarded Timothy as a Jew, by virtue of his mother, or a Gentile, by virtue of his father. Later Jewish law traces a child's lineage through the mother (*m. Qidd.* 3:12), but it is unclear whether or how widely these laws obtained in the first century, and the fact that early exegetes understand Timothy to be a Gentile has led some scholars to conclude that he is not legally Jewish (Cohen 1986). Whatever the legal situation, Luke understands Timothy to be someone other Jews would regard as Jewish or as subject to Mosaic law, and perhaps even the fact that he mentions Timothy's mother first secures that reading. In any case, Luke's account dwells less on the legal identity of

Timothy than on the fact that Jews in the region knew that his father was Gentile, intermarriage being stigmatized in Jewish tradition (Exod 34:15-16; Deut 7:3; Josh 23:12-13; Neh 13:23-27; Ezra 9:1-10:44; *Jub.* 30:7-17).

The fact that Paul circumcises Timothy in the immediate aftermath of the Jerusalem Council raises the question of his motivation for this action. The Council concludes that circumcision is not required for Gentiles, but it says nothing either negatively or positively about the circumcision of Jews. Some commentators conclude that the Timothy story shows that Luke affirms not only the ongoing importance of circumcision for Jewish males but even the reconstitution of Israel itself (Jervell 1998, 412-13), yet Luke's wording makes such large conclusions unwise. Luke does not say that Paul circumcised Timothy in accordance with the law (cf. 7:8; 15:5), or that he affirmed the importance of the covenant, but that he did it "because of the Jews who were in those places, for they all knew that his father was a Greek" (v. 3). Paul acts in order to secure the possibility of a reception for the gospel. His deed also anticipates the charge in 21:21 that he undermines the law of Moses; even at this point he is revealed to be innocent.

The two statements of vv. 4-5 succinctly characterize the visitation of Paul and his colleagues to believers. Verse 4 indicates that they offer instruction about the decree, and v. 5 depicts the flourishing of the churches. The summary statement of v. 5 has parallels at several points in Acts (e.g., 5:14; 6:7; 12:24), but it also appears to be connected with the preceding statement about the decree. That connection in turn reinforces the notion that the decree functions to consolidate the faith of Gentile believers specifically and to protect them from idolatry (see above on 15:13-21).

"Come Over to Macedonia" (16:6-10)

With no explanation, v. 6 shows Paul and his companions moving into regions where they had not previously preached. The place names of Asia, Mysia, Bithynia, Troas, and Macedonia

prompt readers to consult maps of the Roman world and reconstruct the journey westward, but the peculiarity of these verses
calls for a different sort of attention. Normally, Luke includes
only the places in which the witnesses preach and teach, but here
he provides an itinerary of places that they bypass (Ramsay
1925, 197). Not only do they bypass Asia and Bithynia, but they
do so because the Spirit so commands them, first identified as the
Holy Spirit (v. 6) and then as the Spirit of Jesus (v. 7). (Only here
does Luke use the expression "Spirit of Jesus," although see Rom
8:9, Gal 4:6; Phil 1:19; 1 Pet 1:11.) Verse 6 at least implies that
they wish to preach in Asia, and v. 7 indicates that they try to
enter Bithynia, so that their plans are simply rejected. In this
vignette, the Spirit is less an empowering (as in 2:1-3) than an
impeding force, in the sense that the witnesses are not allowed to
chart their own course (Tannehill 1990, 195).

These prohibitions of human plans enhance the commission of
vv. 9-10. As often in Luke–Acts, a vision prompts action (e.g.,
9:10, 12; 10:3). Here Paul sees a Macedonian who urges him to
come to Macedonia and "help us." Rationalizing questions
about how Paul knows the man is Macedonian overlook the
extent to which similar recognitions take place elsewhere in
Luke–Acts and are simply part of the revelation itself. Although
the vision comes to Paul, it is no mere private experience, since v.
10 depicts the response of the entire company: all were "convinced that God had called us to proclaim the good news to
them."

Theologically, the first two units of this transitional passage
(15:36-41; 16:1-5) underscore the place of continuing pastoral
oversight in Luke's understanding of evangelism. To the extent
that the expression "Paul's missionary journeys" conjures up
notions of traveling from place to place in rapid succession,
preaching and then leaving town, Luke's frequent references to
lingering for a period of time and strengthening churches offer
an important corrective. Being witnesses "to the ends of the

earth" also involves continuing care for those who receive the witness.

This transitional passage also draws attention to God as the one who directs Paul and his colleagues toward the new area of Macedonia. That direction comes in an unexpected way, since elsewhere Luke does not show the witnesses being prohibited from specific places. These prohibitions serve to reinforce one of Luke's major themes, that God and God alone directs this mission. When Paul and his colleagues attempt to steer the course, they are corrected. It is almost as if they wander around Asia Minor until God grants them a direction.

Stories of Philippi: Merchant, Slave, and Jailer (16:11-40)

By contrast with the meandering itinerary of 16:6-8, this section finds Paul and his colleagues heading directly for Philippi. Events in Philippi involve several intriguing characters, whose stories flow almost seamlessly into and out of one another. Lydia and the female slave make for a fascinating contrast, while the story of the slave in turn introduces the wrath of her owners and the imprisonment of Paul and Silas. From that imprisonment, there is the now customary rescue, but with a new twist.

Despite this literary unification, five scenes may be distinguished. The first, vv. 11-15, begins the story of the Philippian mission with the woman Lydia and her household. A second woman follows in vv. 16-18, a slave whose story takes the form customary for an exorcism, but her inhabiting spirit is specifically associated with the powerful oracle at Delphi. Unlike the conventional exorcism, however, the aftermath of this particular exorcism develops into a separate unit in which the owners of the slave incite action against Paul and Silas that leads to their being taken into custody (vv. 19-24). As earlier in Acts (5:19-21; 12:6-11), divine activity interrupts the imprisonment of Paul and Silas, but that interruption also prompts the conversion of their jailer (vv. 25-34). The final scene depicts the release of Paul and Silas, who not only receive implicit vindication but set the terms for their own release (vv. 35-40). The return to Lydia's household in v. 40 and the subsequent departure from Philippi round out the story.

◊   ◊   ◊   ◊

Lydia and Her Household (16:11-15)

Paul and his companions sail first to the island Samothrace, then to Neapolis to travel inland to Philippi. The NRSV's description of Philippi as "a leading city of the district of Macedonia" conceals a complex text-critical problem, only partially clarified by the footnote indicating that some ancient authorities read "a city of the first district." What exactly Luke conveys by "leading" or "first" city is unclear, since Thessalonica rather than Philippi was the capital of Macedonia. Although elsewhere Acts involves travel to other Roman colonies (Pisidian Antioch, Lystra, Troas, and Corinth), only here does Luke point out the fact. Noticing that detail prepares for the role Roman customs and citizenship play in events that will occur in Philippi (vv. 21, 37-38).

Whatever the exact wording of v. 12, it also emphasizes that the witnesses are now in Macedonia, the location to which the vision of 16:9-10 had called them. John Calvin noted a delicious incongruity in this account that has escaped most modern interpreters of Acts: the vision creates the expectation that the whole of Macedonia awaits Paul and his colleagues, but when they arrive they encounter no men (v. 9 specifically identifies the Macedonian in the vision as male), but a group of women, and the one woman who is converted is not Macedonian (Calvin 1966, 70-71).

By contrast with their practice elsewhere, Paul and his colleagues do not begin by going directly to a synagogue (see 13:5; 14:1), since Luke explains that they were in Philippi for "some days," after which they went searching for "a place of prayer" on the sabbath. In this context, *proseuchē* (NRSV: place of prayer) can refer to a synagogue building or to an informal gathering place (BDAG 878-89). Because Luke does not mention men among those gathered, commentators have often assumed that this was not a synagogue proper, but that argument is flawed. In the first place, it is not clear that the presence of men was universally required for synagogue service (Reimer 1995, 90-92), and in the second, the fact that men are not mentioned does not mean they were not present.

Among the women, Luke singles out Lydia and identifies her as "a certain woman by the name Lydia, a merchant of purple cloth, from the city of Thyatira, a worshiper of God" (v. 14 AT). Like Cornelius, she is a good Gentile, a "worshiper of God." Although Jews of course worshiped God, Luke employs the phrase for those Gentiles who associated themselves with the synagogue (Acts 13:43, 50; 17:4, 17; 18:7 [often rendered "devout" in NRSV]; and see Josephus, *Ant.* 14.110). Probably she is either divorced or widowed, as she is said to have a household (v. 15), an expression not normally attached to a married woman's name (*NewDocs* 4.93; Barrett 1998, 784). Although it is tempting to conclude from her association with purple cloth, a luxury good (e.g., Luke 16:19), that she is wealthy, the question is complicated. Various forms of purple dye were used, ranging significantly in price, and nothing in the text indicates how Lydia is involved in the business. At the very least, she has a house and the resources to entertain Paul and his company.

Although it is customary to refer to "Paul's conversion of Lydia," Paul nearly disappears from the story. Instead, God "opened her heart" (see Luke 24:32-35), so that she listens and is baptized, together with the household (see 10:24, 44-48; 11:14; 16:31-34). She also insists on offering hospitality to the witnesses. In some respects, Lydia inhabits the margins, since she is female, perhaps a freedwoman (i.e., a former slave), apparently operating without a male protector, and her story begins outside the margins of the city (Spencer 1997, 164). Yet Luke does present her as having control over her own household and as responding appropriately to God's "opening" of her heart; in these ways, she offers a striking contrast to the woman whose story follows.

A Slave and a Spirit of Divination (16:16-18)

The story of vv. 16-18 again takes place as the witnesses journey to the "place of prayer." This time they meet another woman, whom Luke describes as "a slave girl who had a spirit of divination and brought her owners a great deal of money by fortune-telling." Unlike Lydia, this woman is in control of nothing. She is a slave. Like Lydia, she earns money, but it belongs to someone else. She makes money by virtue of the fact that she has a "spirit of divination"; translated more literally, she has "a spirit of the Python," the serpent associated with the famous oracle at Delphi (Plutarch, *Obsolescence of Oracles* 414E). Under the control of this spirit, the slave could tell futures and thereby generate revenue for her keepers.

Encountering Paul and his colleagues, the slave announces, "These men are slaves of the Most High God, who proclaim to you a way of salvation" (v. 17). The announcement is wonderfully ambiguous, since the pagan bystanders of the narrative audience could understand it to claim priority for a particular god over other gods, while Luke and his Christian audience would see it as an unwitting announcement of the only God's salvation for all people (Luke 1:32, 35; Acts 7:48). Even though she has the facts right, Paul responds, not as if to a new companion in the witness, but as if to an enemy. Annoyed by the slave's persistence, he casts out the spirit "in the name of Jesus Christ," the first such exorcism in Acts.

From the vantage point of contemporary interest in female characters, the treatment of the woman is disturbing, for she disappears from view entirely at this point, and it is far from clear what the future holds for her. If the narrative treats her like a prop, that is no different from others who are healed in Luke–Acts (e.g., Luke 7:1-10; 14:1-6; Acts 3:1-10). The story is not *about* her any more than it is *about* Paul; instead it concerns the power of the "name of Jesus Christ" to expel this spirit of divination. Perhaps that is still to underinterpret the event, since here the famous spirit that empowers the Delphic oracle is unmasked as just another demon, moreover, one easily overpowered by the name of Jesus Christ.

Accusation and Violence (16:19-24)

The exorcism has yet another dimension, a corrupt understanding of money (vv. 19-24). Exorcisms normally conclude with some response of bystanders (Luke 4:36-37; 8:34-39), and this one is no exception. The response to the spirit's departure is that the slave's owners recognize that their revenue stream has abruptly halted. Interestingly, Luke provides no information about the owners, whether they are a husband and wife team (Lake and Cadbury 1933, 194) or a small syndicate; what matters is not their identity but their action. They drag Paul and Silas before the local Roman authorities and accuse them of causing an uproar, being Jews, and teaching customs that are alien to Romans (vv. 20-21). Readers search in vain for some connection between these charges and the lines that precede them. The owners report nothing of the real source of their outrage, but instead take one true statement (Paul and Silas *are* Jews) and weave it into a dangerous charge: Paul and Silas are outsiders who agitate against "real" Romans.

Response to the charges comes with immediacy and violence. Without a word of inquiry, bystanders join with the owners in physical action; the magistrates legitimate the persecution by making it official. Verses 23-24 cap off the violence with imprisonment. As with the earlier story of Peter's imprisonment, the jailer makes certain that Paul and Silas cannot possibly escape. The vindictiveness of the owners has reached a terrible conclusion.

Not Escape but Rescue (16:25-34)

Again this rapidly shifting story changes, now directing the reader's attention less to those carrying out the violence than to Paul and Silas in prison. Having followed Luke's story, readers will surely expect yet another miraculous escape, but this time it is the jailer as well as the prisoners who are delivered.

Paul and Silas are "praying and singing hymns to God," recalling the action of the Jerusalem community during Peter's imprisonment (12:5, 12). Other prisoners listen. Their imprisonment is interrupted, this time by an earthquake rather than by an angel. Questions of verisimilitude are many: How could an earthquake release all the prisoners, harm no one, and pass without the notice of the local authorities (Barrett 1998, 776)? Luke addresses none of these questions, but presses forward with his narrative to the situation of the jailer, who is about to commit suicide rather than face the dishonor of having allowed the prisoners to escape (recall Herod's slaying of the keepers of Peter in 12:19). As he will later do in the sea voyage of chapter 27, Paul intercedes to prevent the jailer from this action.

Unlike the earlier prison escapes, this jailer is not the oppressor but is himself in need of rescue. Whether or not he understands his own actions and query, the jailer asks the question appropriate to Luke's story, "What must I do to be saved?" (2:37; Luke 3:10). Paul and Silas answer the question directly, presenting "the word of the Lord," the gospel itself.

Verses 33-34 round out the story in an interesting way, since the jailer first tends to the wounds of Paul and Silas, and then he and his family are baptized. As elsewhere in Acts, baptism of the household reflects a culture in which the head (Cornelius, Lydia, the jailer) decides on behalf of all, and that all includes not only the immediate family but the extended family, as well as slaves and their families. The jailer then tends to other needs, in particular the need for food, which reflects the formation of community (see 2:42) and which extends the earlier motif of hospitality between believing Jews and Gentiles (10:48). The rejoicing with which this episode concludes is characteristic of the response to the gospel, especially among Gentiles (see 2:46; 8:39; 13:48; 15:31).

Paul as Roman Citizen (16:35-40)

The exchange that concludes this story returns to the question of Rome raised by the outraged owners of the slave (v. 22).

Unlike earlier imprisonments, the Roman officials anticipate no further action against Paul and Silas and order their release. The jailer takes this to be welcome news, relaying it to the prisoners with the joyous conclusion, "Go in peace." Paul then turns the incident upside down by interpreting it, not as a just action of authorities who understand themselves to be protecting Roman custom, but as an unjust action against Roman citizens who had not been charged legitimately. Underscoring Paul's accusation is the claim that the authorities earlier acted in public but now wish Paul and Silas to disappear privately.

Whether the historical Paul was in fact a Roman citizen occupies considerable space in the discussion of this passage, since Paul's letters make no such claim. Whatever the facts, Luke asserts such for Paul here and elsewhere (and seemingly includes Silas). The effect in the story is devastating. Knowing that such treatment of Roman citizens was illegal (see Cicero, *In Defense of Rabirius* 12; Cicero, *Against Verres* 2.5.66; Cicero, *Republic* 2.31.54; Livy, *History* 10.9.3-6), the officials now come themselves, apologize, and ask the witnesses to leave. The question of who in fact reflects the ideal of Roman citizenship here receives an ironic answer.

Paul and Silas comply with the request of the officials, although not before going to Lydia's home, which apparently now serves as the gathering place for believers in Philippi. The return to Lydia also returns this sequence of events to its literary starting place.

The important Lukan theme of resistance to the gospel emerges here again in a new form, that of the charge that Paul and Silas are disseminating values and practices that conflict with Rome (v. 21). Paul and Silas do not answer that charge, but the narrative itself reveals it to be utterly false. Ironically, it is those who beat Paul who acted in an "unRomanlike" fashion, since they took action without proper legal proceedings and against Romans citizens at that.

What Paul and Silas in fact did that prompted the resistance was to disrupt the income of the slave's owners. The owners form a sharp contrast with Lydia, who at least has a home at her disposal and who puts it to use on behalf of the gospel by offering hospitality to Paul and Silas. The owners not only fail to rejoice in the release of their slave from the power of a spirit, but falsely accuse those who served as agents of the release. Their preoccupation with money anticipates the reaction Paul will encounter at Ephesus, where the gospel threatens trade on a larger scale (19:23-40).

Calvin's observation about the disjuncture between the Macedonian vision and the first converts in Macedonia remains important and can be pressed even further. The two Philippian households whose baptisms are narrated in chapter 16 both exist on the margins of society. As a woman and as a Gentile attracted to Judaism (note again v. 20), Lydia stands somewhat outside acceptable society, so it is appropriate that Paul and Silas meet her outside the city. The unnamed jailer inhabits another sort of margin, the one between those in power and those prisoners utterly divorced from control over their lives. Luke's portrait of Gentile converts includes not only the powerful and well-placed Cornelius, but those whose power and place are far from clear.

"Turning the World Upside Down" (17:1-15)

Two brief scenes separate the important series of events in Philippi from Paul's confrontation with the philosophical elite in Athens. In a manner similar to the two brief scenes that stand between Paul's conversion and the conversion of Cornelius (9:32-35, 36-43), the episodes of 17:1-15 are variations on already established concerns. They display the ongoing commitment to carrying the gospel to the synagogue, the receptivity of both Jews and Gentiles, and the bringing of false charges before governing authorities.

The first scene, vv. 1-9, takes place in Thessalonica. Conforming to the pattern established in Jerusalem and elsewhere, Paul teaches (vv. 2-3; cf. 13:16b-41; 14:1), many are persuaded (v. 4; cf. 5:14; 13:43; 14:1), and then jealousy prompts sharp resistance (vv. 5-7; cf. 5:17; 13:45; 14:2). The scene concludes with the release of those accused (v. 8). The shorter second scene, vv. 10-15, replays the pattern in Beroea. Paul and Silas go to the synagogue, presumably to teach (v. 10), their message is well received (vv. 11-12), resistance arrives from Thessalonica (vv. 13-14), and Paul departs for Athens, leaving Silas and Timothy behind (vv. 14-15).

◊ ◊ ◊ ◊

Persuasian and Jealousy in Thessalonica (17:1-9)

Departing from Philippi, Paul and Silas travel west on the Via Egnatia, the main east-west road through Macedonia, until they arrive in Thessalonica, capital of the province of Macedonia. First Thessalonians, which may well be Paul's earliest letter, contains comments about Paul's work in Thessalonica that both agree and disagree with Luke's account. Paul refers to previous difficulties in Philippi (1 Thess 2:2) and to his later stay in Athens (3:1) in ways that cohere with Acts. Although the letter does indicate opposition faced at Thessalonica (2:2, 14-16), it presupposes that the church in Thessalonica consists of Gentile believers (1 Thess 1:9), which puts Paul at odds with Acts on that point.

Paul conforms to "his custom" by going to the synagogue and arguing from Scripture. Earlier in the Gospel and in Acts, Luke refers simply to the "synagogue," but he has employed the phrase "synagogue of the Jews" with some frequency now that the witness has moved outside of Judea (13:5; 14:1; 17:10). Luke's terse summary of Paul's argument contains two points: the divine necessity of the suffering, death and resurrection of the Messiah, and the identification of Jesus as that same Messiah. For those gathered in the synagogue of Thessalonica, this bare outline would scarcely make sense, but for Luke's readers and hearers these claims epitomize claims that extend back not only to Peter's proclamation in Jerusalem (2:22-24; 3:18), but to the appearance of the risen Jesus (Luke 24:26, 46).

The NRSV of v. 4 neglects the fact that the verb "joined" is actually in the passive voice in Greek. Presumably the divine passive is intended here, in that it is God who joins these Thessalonians to faith (Johnson 1991, 306). Those who are so persuaded include Jews but also, as elsewhere, "many" Gentile adherents of the synagogue ("Greeks"). "Not a few of the leading women" is another instance of *litotes*, meaning "a great many." Despite their number and status, these women apparently lack the kind of power that would enable them to stop the persecution of believers that soon erupts (Haenchen 1971, 507).

Luke makes no reference to counterarguments on the part of those who are not persuaded (Spencer 1997, 170). Like the authorities in Jerusalem (5:17) and other Jews in Pisidian Antioch (13:45), jealousy motivates the resistance, and the resistance takes the form of attack instead of argument. The action of these jealous Jews Luke describes in some detail. First, like those who set out to destroy Stephen, they obtain the help of others (see 6:11-12), in this case people whom Luke characterizes as "ruffians in the marketplaces." The action escalates when the opposition and their thugs together form a mob and stir up the city, and again when they search for Paul and Silas and, apparently in frustration, attack the house of Jason.

Luke does not bother identifying Jason, not even to the extent of indicating whether he is a Gentile or a Jew, or whether he in fact sympathizes with the Christians. (That the accusers so claim does not constitute evidence.) Luke provides no information, but that should not be especially surprising, since he wastes little time on such matters of human interest. And now, when the story so vividly depicts storm clouds gathering over the believers, identifying footnotes or parentheses would lessen the dramatic impact.

Verses 6-7 find the mob surging, Jason in tow, to the civil authorities in Thessalonica. The accusations they shout have nothing whatever to do with the teaching of Paul and Silas. They represent an enhanced version of the charges at Philippi, but instead of claiming that Paul and Silas are teaching non-Roman customs, the agitators claim that they "have been turning the world upside down," they have been "acting contrary to the decrees of the emperor, saying that there is another king named Jesus" (vv. 6-7; cf. Luke 23:2). The inflammatory and political nature of these charges can scarcely be overstated, particularly since "the world" here is the *oikoumenē*, the Roman Empire (BDAG 699; Josephus, *Ant.* 19.292). Again, as in chapter 16, those who bring the charge of disturbing the peace are the very ones who are in fact disturbing the peace. While the charges are false, they are in another, ironic and more profound, sense also true (see below).

Despite the mob's action, the outcome in Thessalonica does not duplicate that in Philippi. The authorities are "disturbed," they take security from Jason to ensure that there will be no further action, but they do release Jason and the others, and Paul and Silas leave the city immediately but without further difficulty.

Division Also in Beroea (17:10-15)

The slight differences between the scene in Beroea (vv. 10-15) and that in Thessalonica merit attention. First, Luke describes the residents as not simply "more receptive" than those in Thessalonica, but he explains what that means in terms of their attention to Scripture: they "examined the Scriptures every day to see whether these things were so." Second, he again specifies that those who believed included Jews (vv. 11-12) as well as both male and female Gentiles ("Greeks"), but this time he names the women first. The close connection between v. 11 and v. 12 ("therefore") suggests that the Gentiles, both women and men, are among those who search the Scripture in response to the teaching of Paul and Silas. Easy assumptions about the participation of males and nonparticipation of females founder here. Third, the resistance that inevitably forms comes from Thessalonica rather than from within Beroea, perhaps further indication of the warm welcome in Beroea.

Verses 14-15 bring both stories to a close, leaving Silas and Timothy in Beroea and transporting Paul to Athens, where he again confronts the problem of idolatry.

◊ ◊ ◊ ◊

Much in this interlude serves to underscore earlier Lukan concerns, especially the necessity of the Messiah's death and resurrection, the division created by Christian preaching, and the growing resistance to that preaching. What emerges sharply is the deep irony in the charges brought against believers. Nothing in the text suggests that Paul or anyone else set out to undermine the Roman Empire or to replace Caesar with Jesus. At the same time, fundamental to the gospel are the assumptions that the only genuine kingdom is the kingdom of the God revealed first to Israel and now to all people (Acts 1:6-8; 17:24-31) and that the appointed agent and heir of that kingdom is Jesus of Nazareth (Luke 1:32-33; Acts 2:33-36). To claim that "he is Lord of all" (10:36) is indeed to turn the world upside down.

God and the Gods in Athens (17:16-34)

Of the many memorable stories Luke narrates, Paul's stay in Athens is among the most familiar, and that for good reason. Luke's vivid depiction of Athens and its curiosity-seekers creates a highly dramatic context in which Paul attempts to translate the gospel into language the locals can understand.

Verses 16-21 provide the narrative introduction, sketching Paul's activity in the city as well as his initial perceptions of the Athenians. The speech extends from v. 22 through v. 31, and comprises three sections: first, Paul characterizes the Athenians as very religious people (vv. 22-23a); second, he issues a carefully worded critique of idol-worship (vv. 23b-29); third, he calls for repentance, declares that there will be a time of judgment, and connects that judgment with God's raising "a man" from the dead (vv. 30-31). The scene concludes with a brief narrative of the responses generated by the speech (vv. 32-34).

This simple structure belies many contested issues, particularly issues regarding the relationship between this speech and earlier speeches in Acts. By contrast with them, the Areopagus speech makes no reference to the history of Israel (e.g., 2:29; 7:2-47;

13:17-25), contains no direct quotation from Scripture (e.g., 2:17-21, 25-28; 3:22-23; 4:11; 13:33), and makes only indirect reference to Jesus (e.g., 2:32; 3:15; 4:10; 13:30, 37). In addition, the speech draws on language at home in the philosophical schools (see below), creating the impression that it is something of a foreign body in Acts.

That impression fades on closer examination, however, when it becomes clear that much in the speech coheres well with the remainder of Luke–Acts (Schubert 1968b). The assertion that God is creator (v. 24) is not only a fundamental presupposition of Luke–Acts but appears prominently in the community prayer of 4:24-30 (see also 14:15). Stephen has already asserted that God does not live in "houses made with human hands" (7:48 and cf. 19:26). God's control over the seasons (the "times of their existence," v. 26) echoes the words of the risen Jesus in 1:7. The call for repentance also figures prominently in earlier sermons (e.g., 2:38-40; 3:19; 11:18). In addition, the speech's assertions of the universal scope of God's work and God's claims have antecedents at least as early as the Pentecost speech (e.g., 2:39; 3:21; 10:34; 14:15-17). These similarities suggest that the speech is a "translation" of earlier Lukan themes into the local idiom, rather than an intrusion into the remainder of the book.

Another debated issue regarding this speech concerns its coherence with the letters of Paul. Particularly because Paul portrays himself as "apostle to the Gentiles," this speech to cultured Gentiles looms importantly in the debate about the historicity of Luke's depiction of Paul. That highly complex question generates conflicting answers that cannot be assessed adequately here. It must suffice to notice that both Acts 17 and Rom 1:18-32 address idolatry and God's judgment, but the contexts differ significantly. Here idolatry is condemned, but it is nevertheless imagined as a pale imitation of true worship, an indication of the impulse to seek God. By contrast, Rom 1:18-32 identifies idolatry with human rejection of God. Probably the resemblances reflect the shared tradition of Jewish resistance to idolatry (e.g., Wis 13–14) rather than Luke's use of an account of Paul's activity or Lukan access to Paul's letters.

◊ ◊ ◊ ◊

"Something New" in Athens (17:16-21)

Luke's narrative introduction immediately identifies the problem: Paul is distressed that Athens is "full of idols." Although Athens would scarcely have been Paul's initial encounter with polytheism, the association of the city with idols does find confirmation in other writers of the period (see, e.g., Livy, *History* 45.27.11; Pausanias, *Description of Greece* 1.17.1; Strabo, *Geography* 9.1.16). The Jewish monotheism that pervades Luke–Acts is equally evident here, both in the choice of words ("idol" is already a derogatory term) and in the identification of Athens exclusively with its idols.

The NRSV's "so" at the outset of v. 17 misleadingly suggests that Paul goes to the synagogue in reaction to Athenian idolatry. According to Luke, this is his regular habit, and he converses there with Jews and "devout persons," Gentiles attracted to the synagogue (see 13:50; 16:14; 17:4). Repetition of this common practice momentarily distracts from the focus on idolatry, but the end of the verse returns Paul to a public setting, for he is "every day" in the marketplace. This general audience consists of any who happen to be present, but it narrows in focus in v. 18 when the Epicureans and Stoics join the debate.

The Epicureans and Stoics were prominent among the philosophical schools of Athens. Particularly important in this context is the Epicurean emphasis on freeing humanity from the fear of the gods and the fear of death. Epicureans believed that the gods are utterly removed from human existence, and therefore the Epicureans ridiculed religious piety. The Stoics emphasized the cultivation of human virtue as the means to achieving one's goals and achieving independence from the control of the passions.

The initial responses take two forms, both of which significantly misconstrue Paul's activity. Some characterize Paul as *houtos spermologos* (NRSV: this babbler), "someone who picks up seeds," in this instance a disparaging characterization of a person who hangs around in public places gathering scraps

(BDAG 937; Demosthenes, *De Corona* 127; Dionysius of Halicarnassus, *Roman Antiquities* 19.5.3; Philo, *Embassy* 203). The demonstrative pronoun "this" compounds the insult (Croy 1997, 23). Luke distinguishes the second response (v. 18) in a way that elsewhere separates two different groups ("Some said . . . Others said . . ."; cf. 13:48, 50; 14:4). This response scarcely constitutes a warm welcome, but it does portray Paul as a legitimate proclaimer rather than a purveyor of "the second-rate at second hand" (Lake and Cadbury 1933, 211).

The conclusion that Paul offers "foreign divinities" comes about because he is said to be preaching "about Jesus and the resurrection." English translations have difficulty capturing the ambiguity of the Greek. Since *anastasis* (NRSV: resurrection) is a feminine noun, it can be construed as the name of a female god, companion to the male god named "Jesus." Because the charge of teaching new religions closely resembles the accusation against Socrates, it could mean that Paul is in serious danger (Plato, *Apology* 24B-C; *Euthyphro* 3B). In the case of Socrates, the charge was sedition, but the context here nowhere suggests that Paul is in danger. Instead, the respondents seem to be merely curious (see Strabo, *Geography* 10.3.18), as is confirmed by v. 21.

Whether disparaging Paul as a charlatan or a curiosity, both these initial responses conflict profoundly with Luke's presentation of Paul and the gospel. A "babbler" would be directed by little or nothing beyond self-aggrandizement, something clearly contradicted by Luke's presentation of Paul's mission (see especially 9:15-16). And Paul proclaims the only God who exists, not new imports to enhance the local shrines.

The responses prompt some people to take Paul to the Areopagus, which can refer either to a place (the Hill of Ares) or to an official governing body that met in that location. The wording of v. 22 (literally, "in the middle of the Areopagus") suggests a group rather than a place, but the narrative does not otherwise convey a judicial proceeding. Neither the questions asked in vv. 19-20 nor the responses in vv. 32-33 indicate that Paul is in any danger. Instead, he is being invited to make his case before a cultured, sophisticated audience.

Verse 21 rounds out the scene by characterizing the residents of Athens as obsessed with "telling or hearing something new." Again Luke's description coincides with that of others (Thucydides, *History* 3.38.5; Demosthenes, *First Philippic* 10). Not only does the statement play on stereotypes about Athens, but it further undermines any notion that this is a formal procedure (Haenchen 1971, 520). On the contrary, the setting is so dominated by curiosity that it gives the impression that little at all is at stake.

Paul's Speech (17:22-31)

The speech opens with the conventional direct address to the audience ("Athenians," see also 2:14; 3:12; 22:1) and introduction: "I see how extremely religious you are in every way." Given the critique of idolatry that follows and the fact that *deisidaimōn* (NRSV: extremely religious) can refer to superstition rather than genuine piety, it is tempting to read this statement as sarcastic. Yet, given the practice of introducing speeches with some praise of the audience (e.g., 26:2-3), and evidence elsewhere that Athenians were perceived to be religious (Sophocles, *Oedipus Coloneus* 260; Pausanias, *Description of Greece* 1.17.1; Josephus, *Ag. Ap.* 2.130; Strabo, *Geography* 9.1.16; Livy, *History* 45.27.11), the statement should be taken at face value. Verse 23a gives evidence of the religiosity, this time in nonderogatory terms (by contrast with "full of idols" in v. 16); it also introduces the phrase "an unknown god."

Verse 23b formally announces the topic Paul will address: the "unknown god" is what he will proclaim. What follows in vv. 24-29 carefully criticizes idolatry, and it does so in terms that would have been congenial to a gathering dominated by Stoics and Epicureans. Paul begins with an argument from creation; since God created the world and everything in it, it is impossible to imagine that God lives in buildings of human construction or requires assistance from human beings (vv. 24-25). These assertions appear elsewhere in Acts (4:24; 7:48), as well as in Scripture (e.g., 1 Kgs 8:27; Isa 57:15), but they also are congenial to the philosophically curious audience (by contrast with the audience in Ephesus, see 19:23-41; and see also Plutarch, *Stoic Self-Contradiction* 1034B; Seneca, *Epistles* 95.47; Lucian, *Charon* 12).

Verses 26-28 do not leave behind the assumption of God as creator (v. 26 begins as does v. 24, with the assertion that God "made"), but they move from the general act of the creation of all things to the specific creation of all humanity. Verse 26 is somewhat ambiguous, since it literally reads that God "made from one" supplying neither "ancestor" (as does the NRSV) nor "blood" (as does one early manuscript tradition). The strong appeal to the creation story that underlies this speech inclines many interpreters to think that the "one" is a reference to Gen 1:27-28 and the creation of humankind from Adam. The precise connotations of "the times of their existence" and "the boundaries of the places where they would live" are uncertain, but the larger point is clear: God not only created humankind but determined the parameters of human existence.

The point toward which this portion of the speech drives emerges in vv. 27-28. Humankind exists to seek after God, yet God is not far away "from each one of us" (see Josephus, *Ant.* 8.108; Dio Chrysostom, *Discourses* 12, 28). At this juncture, where the speech asserts that the intention behind creation is that humanity should seek God in spite of the inescapability of God's presence, Paul shifts into the use of first person plural (by contrast with the direct address of vv. 22-23). Verse 28*a* further underscores the inescapability of God, but the NRSV, following the KJV and the RSV, introduces problems here by translating the first quotation in a way that exaggerates its ontological implications. A far preferable translation is "For by him we live and move and are" (Johnson 1992, 312), which simply epitomizes all that has been said previously regarding God as the creator and sustainer of human life. With the line "For we too are his offspring," Paul alludes, although in unbiblical idiom, to the creation of humanity in God's image (Gen 1:27).

"As even some of your own poets have said" may refer to both quotations. If the first part of v. 28 is in fact a quotation

(Greek employs no quotation marks as such), the source is unknown. The second part is a quotation from Aratus (*Phaenomena* 5), one widely employed and perhaps known by Paul or Luke as a common expression (the equivalent of the pervasive contemporary knowledge of the "Freudian slip," which knowledge does not require the reading of Freud).

Verse 29 returns to the final indictment of idolatry. Since human beings are from God's own family, and are God's creations, it is simply impossible to imagine that God resembles objects created by human hands. In this argument, the speech reflects much in Jewish tradition that finds the notion of idolatry abhorrent (see, e.g., Pss. 115:4-8 [LXX 113:12-16]; 135:15-18 [LXX 134:15-18]; Isa 40:18-23; Hab 2:18-19; Wis 13-15; *Let. Aris.* 134-37; Philo, *Decalogue* 66-81; *Contemp. Life* 7; *Spec. Laws* 1.21-22; Josephus, *Ag. Ap.* 2.65-67; *Ant.* 19.290; *m. 'Abod. Zar.*). The same argument appears in pagan writers, however (as in Seneca, *Epistles* 31.11).

Up through this point (v. 29), Paul says little that would be uncongenial to his audience, the philosophically curious residents of Athens. With the final section of the speech, however, Paul moves to elements of the gospel with which his audience will disagree. Verse 30 begins by announcing that God has previously overlooked human ignorance (recalling the "unknown god" at the beginning of the speech). Given the preceding elements of the speech, that ignorance would seem to focus on pagans and their idolatry. This is not an unprecedented move, since Luke also characterized as ignorance the actions of Jerusalem Jews against Jesus (3:17; 13:27). The urgency of the present time Paul indicates with the "now" that marks the call for repentance. In other words, something has changed in the human situation "now," something the Lukan narrative has already identified as God's action in Jesus Christ, although the assembled Athenians can scarcely understand, since they had not received any basis for understanding.

"All people everywhere" are commanded to repent. Emphatic language here retrieves the numerous references to "all" in the preceding section of the speech:

v. 24   "The God who made the world and everything [Greek: *panta*] in it . . ."

v. 25   ". . . he himself gives to all [Greek: *pasi*] mortals life and breath and all things [Greek: *panta*] . . ."

v. 26   "From one ancestor he made all [Greek: *pan*] nations to inhabit the whole [Greek: *pantos*] earth . . ."

The unity of humankind consists not only in its common creator and common ancestor, but in its common need for repentance.

Verse 31 brings the urgency of the call for repentance into focus: God will judge the world "by a man whom he has appointed." Only here does the fact of Jesus come into the speech, and no name identifies him (although see v. 18). Focus continues to be on God's actions: as God has created, so God will judge. The final step in the speech comes with the introduction of the language of resurrection. Unlike earlier speeches, in which the resurrection proves that Jesus is in fact the Messiah of Israel (2:24, 32; 3:15; 13:30-39), in this one the resurrection proves that God will judge through "a man," Jesus. What the two appeals have in common is that the resurrection serves to validate God's own plan, whether the plan of the Messiah or the plan of judgment.

A Divided Response (17:32-34)

Verse 32 leaves no doubt that it is the resurrection that prompts a negative response by some of those gathered. Although Stoic teaching on the afterlife is ambiguous, that of the Epicureans is uniformly negative (Croy 1997). Luke does not, however, indicate that the crowd consists only of Stoics and Epicureans or that they divided along clear party lines. "We will hear you again about this," to be sure, pales by comparison with earlier scenes in which multitudes believe (e.g., 2:41; 4:4), but the contrast between the first and second parts of the verse follows an earlier pattern and does imply that the latter group is at least positively inclined. Verse 34 makes that clear, with its report about the believing response of the otherwise unknown Dionysius the Areopagite, Damaris, and unspecified others.

◊ ◊ ◊ ◊

The colorful details of this story and the quest to identify the various influences upon it should not distract readers from the theological issues at work. Beginning from the fundamental assertion that God is creator of all that exists, Paul argues that nothing that is crafted by the creature can be regarded as ultimate. The religious inclination of the Athenians is genuine, but they stand with all humankind in need of repentance before God's impending judgment. What Paul's sermon does, then, is to take basic presuppositions of the Christian gospel and translate them into language available to the narrative audience (Gaventa 2001).

Although it is customary to emphasize the uniqueness of this story, there are important continuities between the Athens scene and those that have preceded it. Just as the slave owners of Philippi accused Paul and Silas of being "unRoman," when it is the accusers who were "unRoman" (16:19-23), and the Thessalonian Jews who caused an uproar while accusing Paul and Silas of being troublemakers (17:1-8), here the Athenians accuse Paul of dabbling in new teachings, when it is they who merely dabble. That feature of the story may have been especially important for Luke's audience by further discrediting idolatry, in that idolatry here keeps company with people who themselves are merely curious and are seriously committed to nothing.

Conflict and Endurance in Corinth (18:1-17)

Although Luke stipulates that Paul remains in Corinth for eighteen months, the narration of his sojourn there is relatively compact, consisting of four brief scenes. The first depicts the arrival of Paul in Corinth and his initial association with Aquila and Priscilla (vv. 1-3). Next comes the conventional description of Paul's witnessing in Corinth followed by sharply divided responses to that activity (vv. 4-8). Verses 9-11 narrate a divine vision instructing Paul and his obedient response to the vision. The final scene concerns Paul's appearance before the Roman official Gallio as a result of Jewish resistance to his preaching of the gospel (vv. 12-17). In some respects the sequence in this passage resembles that in chapter 16, where Paul first encounters his new coworker Timothy (16:1-5), receives instruction by means of a vision (16:6-10), and then his witness generates divided response in Philippi (16:11-40).

◊   ◊   ◊   ◊

Aquila and Priscilla (18:1-3)

However limited the response to Paul's preaching in Athens, for once he is able to leave a city without a hostile mob at his heels. He travels west to the important port city of Corinth, the capital of Achaia. Luke does not linger over the city or its concerns (cf. 17:16-21), but gives attention to Paul's encounter with Aquila and Priscilla. Luke identifies Aquila as "a Jew," which might mean that he is not a Christian (as, e.g., at 13:45; 17:5, 11, 13), although here it serves to explain why the couple had to leave Rome (Conzelmann 1987, 151). Certainly the later appearances of this couple in Acts presuppose that they are believers (18:18, 26; and see Rom 16:3; 1 Cor 16:19; 2 Tim 4:19).

Of Priscilla, Luke indicates only that she is married to Aquila and has come with him from Italy. Both Luke and Paul's letters consistently refer to the two together, although Paul employs the name "Prisca," of which "Priscilla" is the diminutive form. In both writers, her name most often appears before that of Aquila (18:18, 26; Rom 16:3; cf. 2 Tim 4:19; although see 1 Cor 16:19). Because placing a woman's name before that of her husband is not customary in the ancient world, doing so may well indicate that she is of higher status than he; perhaps Priscilla is freeborn, for example, and Aquila only recently manumitted. The order could also reflect her prominence in Christian circles.

Although Paul did not arrive in Corinth as a refugee, Aquila and Priscilla did: "Claudius had ordered all Jews to leave Rome." Writing in the second century, the biographer Suetonius reports that Claudius expelled Jews from Rome because of "Chrestus" (*Claudius* 25.4), which almost certainly refers to "Christ." Probably early Christian activity in Rome created a disturbance among Jews, as a result of which Jewish Christians and perhaps other Jews were forced to leave the city. The edict is usually dated to 49 CE, and it would have lapsed at Claudius's death in 54.

Disputes persist about the exact nature of the labor Luke identifies as *skēnopoioi* (NRSV: tentmakers), whether it refers to leather work, the actual construction of tents, weaving, or even the construction of theatrical sets (Hock 1980, 20-21; BDAG 928-29). Paul's letters refer to his labor, but not to a specific trade (1 Cor 4:12). Similarly, interpreters differ in their estimates of the income and status attached to this labor. That Aquila and Priscilla are able to accommodate Paul at least suggests that they do not operate at a mere subsistence level, but that fact scarcely places them among the elite. In addition, nothing in the syntax permits identifying Aquila and Paul, but not Priscilla, as laborers (Reimer 1995, 195-226).

Attention to these historical questions should not eclipse the narrative role of this small paragraph. Aquila and Priscilla join the ranks of those who display discipleship by offering hospitality to Christian witnesses (e.g., 10:48; 16:15; 17:7). In addition, Paul's own labor reinforces Luke's emphasis on the responsible use of possessions. Later, he will recall for the Ephesian elders that he defrauded no one (20:33-35), which distinguishes him sharply from figures such as Ananias and Sapphira, Simon Magus, and the slave owners in Philippi.

In and Out of the Synagogue (18:4-8)

Paul's synagogue activity begins in v. 4, when Luke provides the customary report about his attempts to persuade both Jews and "Greeks," those Gentiles who were associated with the synagogue (as at 14:1; 17:1-4). That activity intensifies in v. 5, following the arrival of Silas and Timothy. Some scholars suggest that they bring funds with them from Macedonia that permit Paul to give up his work with Priscilla and Aquila (Haenchen 1971, 534; Bruce 1990, 392), but Luke's lack of attention to Paul's funding (except to indicate that he provided his own, as in 20:33-35; 28:30) argues against an economic reading of v. 5. Instead, the arrival of Silas and Timothy simply offers another opportunity for reinforcing the nature of Paul's activity. Verse 5 states this in strong terms: Paul is consumed with the word, he is testifying, and his testimony identifies the Messiah as Jesus.

This intensive description yields in v. 6 to a negative response from some in the synagogue, which in turn prompts a dramatic response from Paul. He first shakes out his clothing, recalling for readers his similar action in Pisidian Antioch (13:51) and the instructions of Jesus (Luke 10:1-12). He then announces "your blood be on your own heads," a sign that, like the watchman of Ezek 33:1-9, he has issued his warning and is not responsible for the people's reply (Tannehill 1990, 223; see also 2 Sam 1:16; Neh 5:13 [LXX 2 Esd 15:13]). He then announces "from now on I will go to the Gentiles." As in 13:46, however, this announcement clearly pertains only to Corinth; upon subsequently arriving in Ephesus Paul again heads straight for the synagogue (18:19).

Unlike Pisidian Antioch, however, or other locations in which Paul encounters conflict, here he does not leave town. Instead, he goes to the house of Titius Justus, a God-fearer. Although some interpreters understand this to be a reference to Paul's lodging (i.e., he is no longer with Priscilla and Aquila, but now with Titius Justus), the sequence of events implies that this is the place in which Paul engages in witnessing. Lydia's house served as the gathering place of believers in Philippi (16:15, 40), but here the house explicitly replaces the synagogue as the venue for Paul's work. That the protests of some Jews do not reflect the whole becomes quite clear in v. 8, where Luke refers to the faith of Crispus, "the official of the synagogue" and his whole household (see 1 Cor 1:14). With the possible exception of Gamaliel

(5:34-39), temple and synagogue leaders throughout Acts have doggedly opposed the gospel, yet Crispus becomes a believer (Spencer 1997, 179).

This scene concludes with the report that many Corinthians "became believers and were baptized." Presumably the many include both Jews and Gentiles, since Paul is now teaching in the house of the Gentile Titius Justus, and a synagogue leader is among those convinced. Although the NRSV specifies that the Corinthians who "heard Paul and became believers," the Greek does not supply Paul's name, leaving it ambiguous whether they respond to Paul's preaching or to the faith of Crispus (cf. 1 Thess 1:6-10; Rom 1:8). The very fact that Luke does not specify may reflect his indifference to the question of person: whether people believe because of Paul's preaching or because of Crispus's own faith is insignificant.

"Do Not Be Afraid" (18:9-11)

Previous experiences indicate that the situation confronting Paul is dangerous (13:50-51; 14:1-6, 19; 17:5-9, 13-15). Already he has encountered resistance in the local synagogue, and "many" have been baptized, including a leader of the synagogue; such receptivity is often followed by increased resistance. The vision of the Lord opens in such a way as to reinforce the sense of impending danger: "Do not be afraid, but speak and do not be silent." Admonitions against fear frequently appear in theophanies, since an appropriate response to the presence of the divine is awe (as in Luke 1:12-13, 29-30), but here the statements about Paul's fear may reflect his witnessing situation. "Speak and do not be silent" recalls the Lukan theme of bold speech (4:13, 29, 31; 9:27-28; 13:46; 28:31); one major feature of apostolic speech in Acts is that it persists despite adversity.

Verse 10 underscores the grounds for Paul's speech. No one can harm Paul, for the Lord is with him, as the Lord was with Abraham, Moses, Jeremiah, and others (see Gen 21:22; 26:3; 31:3, 5; Exod 3:12; 4:10-12; Josh 1:9; Isa 41:10; Jer 1:4-10). The scene that follows tests this claim, but Paul is not actually harmed. Similar divine reassurances appear later in the book, having to do with Paul's captivity and journey to Rome (23:11; 27:23-26). As in those later instances, the vision continues by explaining what *will* happen: "there are many in this city who are my people." The Greek word *laos* (NRSV: people), a term Luke has consistently used of the people of Israel, now includes Gentiles as well as Jews (as in 15:14).

Earlier Luke has indicated that Paul and others remained in a place for a considerable time (e.g., 11:26; 14:28; 15:33, 35), but he seldom specifies a period of time and this is the longest stay to this point in the narrative. Probably the specificity serves to underscore the fact that Paul is obedient to the vision and continues to teach in Corinth. And, of course, it is striking that the extent of time comes in the face of resistance and after the divine instruction.

"Before the Tribunal" (18:12-17)

The reference to Gallio is important for attempts to construct a chronology of Paul's labors, since an inscription at Delphi permits dating his proconsulate to circa 51–52 CE (Barrett 1987, 51-52). The text does not specify that Paul's opponents haul him before Gallio toward the beginning of his proconsulate, but that seems a reasonable inference, and it would allow dating Paul's work in Corinth just prior to and including 51 CE. In its narrative context, the notice functions less to mark chronology than to indicate that the resistance to Paul's labor has now increased. No longer simply resisted within the synagogue, the Jews "together" (NRSV: united) take Paul before the tribunal, the judicial bench.

The accusation in v. 13, rendered somewhat literally, reads as follows: "Against the law this one persuades people to worship God." Placing "against the law" at the beginning of the statement creates the impression that Paul constitutes a threat to Roman law (see 16:20-21; 17:6-7). Only at the end of the accusation does it become clear that the law being considered has to do with the worship of God. Debates about which religions were sanctioned are not in view here, as Gallio's response makes clear. Not even permitting Paul to speak, he dismisses the accusers; this is an internal Jewish dispute (v. 15), as is reinforced by his address "to the Jews" and "you Jews" (cf. John 18:31; 19:6). In deciding that there is no serious wrongdoing, of course, Gallio makes a mistake, since there is wrongdoing—that of the accusers (as at 16:19-24 and 17:5-9). He then sends the accusers away.

What ensues in v. 17 brings the story to a close on a note of perplexity. Someone grabs and beats a previously unknown Sosthenes, a synagogue official. Since Paul refers to a companion named Sosthenes in 1 Cor 1:1, it is tempting to connect the two, although Luke does not identify Sosthenes as a believer and Paul does not identify Sosthenes as a Corinthian. He remains an obscure character, not unlike Jason (17:6) and later Alexander (19:33). Perhaps because the early manuscripts of Acts do not name the tormenters of Sosthenes, later manuscripts attempt to "correct" the problem; some supply "the Greeks," and a few others "the Jews." The logic of the story dictates that the tormenters are not the Jews, since Gallio has just sent them away from the bench and this action takes place "in front of the tribunal" (v. 17). That location, together with Gallio's response of indifference, argues in favor of interpreting the action as an outbreak of Gentile anti-Judaism (as in 18:2 and 19:33-34; Tannehill 1990, 228-29).

While less dramatic than Paul's entry into Philippi after the vision of the man from Macedonia, this scene also depicts a transition in the work of Paul. Here he is accompanied in the witness not only by Silas and Timothy, but by Priscilla and Aquila. The latter pair will travel with him when he leaves Corinth, and will soon be joined by Apollos as well. In other words, the circle of witnesses is expanding. In addition, this scene anticipates Paul's suffering (v. 10), a motif that grows more prominent from this point on in the narrative (e.g., 18:21; 19:21; 20:23; 21:10-14). Already the vision in Corinth reinforces the perception that Paul will not be alone, that he must persist in his efforts, and that he will continue to meet with resistance.

The resistance of Jews in this scene raises again the question of Luke's attitude toward Israel. That question cannot be answered based on a single scene, and it may be that the concerns of modern readers cause it to be prominent in Acts in a way contrary to Luke's own interests (see Introduction). In this particular scene, however, it is important to notice that Jews are among those who respond favorably to Paul's preaching. More important, whatever is intended by "I will go to the Gentiles," it does not preclude going also to Jews, as Paul will do immediately upon his arrival in Ephesus in the following scene (18:19).

The small role Gallio plays in this scene also underscores the fact that Paul and others look to God, not to human compassion, for their protection. Gallio happens to rule in Paul's favor, but his indifference to Jewish complaints renders him equally indifferent to the abuse of a Jewish synagogue leader. The vision itself provides the interpretive framework for understanding what happens to Paul: it is God who ensures that no harm comes to Paul in Corinth.

The Word of the Lord Prevails in Ephesus (18:18–19:22)

This section of Acts opens with Paul in Corinth, but the focus of attention quickly shifts to Ephesus, remains there throughout this unit, and extends through the turmoil in 19:23-41. The attention given to Ephesus suggests that it occupies a place of significance in the church's developing witness, especially when considered together with Paul's farewell speech to Ephesian elders (20:17-38). That is not surprising, given the importance of the city in Luke's day. Ephesus was the fourth largest city of the Roman Empire, the capital of the province Asia, and a thriving commercial center (Strabo, *Geography* 14.1.21-22). In addition, Ephesus is also the location of the famous temple of Artemis, and this fact becomes crucial for understanding the scene at the end of chapter 19.

This lengthy section begins and ends with matters of travel. It opens with Paul first at Corinth, then traveling to Ephesus with Priscilla and Aquila, then going on to Jerusalem and Antioch, and finally returning to visit earlier churches (18:18-23). It closes with the anticipation of Paul's eventful journey to Rome, following his return to Jerusalem via Macedonia and Achaia (19:21-22).

Between these travel notices, Luke includes four distinct reports about the witness in Ephesus. The first, 18:24-28, concerns Apollos, his teaching, and how he was instructed by Priscilla and Aquila. The second, 19:1-7, portrays Paul's instruction of a group of unnamed disciples. The third, 19:8-10, summarizes Paul's preaching in Ephesus, first in the synagogue and then in the lecture hall of Tyrannus. The final and most developed scene, 19:11-20, sharply contrasts the miracles God accomplishes through Paul with the powerlessness of the ostensibly powerful Jewish exorcists.

Several elements are familiar features of Luke's account, including the concern about believers in areas already visited (18:23; also 14:22; 15:32, 41; 16:5), preaching in synagogues and conflict there (18:19; 19:8-10; see also 13:45; 17:5); miracles (19:11-12; see also 3:1-10; 5:15-16), and confrontation with magic (19:13-20; see also 8:9-24; 13:4-12). New elements also enliven this segment, including the introduction of Apollos, the role of Priscilla and Aquila as teachers who work without any reference to Paul, and disciples who know only the baptism of John. This combination of familiar and less familiar elements reinforces the importance of events in Ephesus that cause "all the residents of Asia, both Jews and Greeks" to hear the gospel.

Travels of Paul (18:18-23)

Verses 18-23 mark the transition from the work of Paul in Corinth to the initiation of the work in Ephesus. Paul, Priscilla, and Aquila leave Corinth, departing from the port city of Cenchreae. The vow referred to in v. 18 has elicited much controversy but little agreement. Most often scholars relate it to the Nazirite vows established in Num 6:1-21, although numerous questions arise about how this vow relates to those regulations. The fact that Luke stresses the vow so little probably indicates that what is important for Luke concerns Paul's faithfulness to a vow rather than the details surrounding the practice. The incident may well also anticipate 21:21-26, where Jerusalem Jews accuse Paul of instruction against the law.

A certain awkwardness enters the narration at vv. 19-21, since the threesome arrives in the city, then Paul is said to leave Priscilla and Aquila there, and then he goes into the Ephesian synagogue for discussion. The impression given is that Paul has left the two behind and enters the synagogue as something of an afterthought. The NRSV smooths out the logical awkwardness by introducing "first" in v. 19*b*, but the Greek contains no such clarification. Instead, the need to signal the arrival of the witness in Ephesus appears to dominate the transition at this point. By contrast with the resistance that will come later (19:9), here Ephesian Jews urge Paul to stay. His promise to return "if God wills" employs conventional language (James 4:15; 1 Cor 4:19; 16:7; Heb 6:3; Epictetus, *Discourses* 1.1.17; Plato, *Alcibiades* 1.135D); it also coheres with the larger motif of God's direction of important endeavors in Ephesus.

Verses 22-23 find Paul arriving at Caesarea, traveling "up" (almost certainly to Jerusalem, although the Greek text does not include the city name), and then to Antioch. These lines have been carefully scrutinized for the construction of a Pauline itinerary, yet their primary contribution is to demonstrate the continuing identity of Paul's witness with that of Jerusalem and of Antioch. Paul does not work as a solitary entrepreneur but plays a role in the one witness that God began in Jerusalem and effectively continued from Antioch (Tannehill 1990, 230). Verse 23 depicts the nurturing of believers that necessarily follows an initial witness (e.g., 14:22; 15:32, 41; 16:5).

Priscilla and Aquila Instruct Apollos (18:24-28)

Verses 24-28 introduce Apollos, and the scene generates many questions. As with the introduction of Priscilla and Aquila in 18:2, the term "Jew" here does not distinguish Apollos from those who would later be called Christians (as it does in 19:13-14); these are not mutually exclusive categories for Luke. Probably the designation serves clarity (as in 18:2); since Apollos bears a name derived from that of the Greek god Apollo, readers and listeners might well assume him to be a Gentile. In addition, the narrative will soon introduce other Jews who differ sharply from the receptivity of Apollos, making for a dramatic contrast. Apollos is a native of Alexandria, a city known both for its strong Jewish presence and also for its learning and culture (Pearson 1992), so that the eloquence attributed to him in v. 24 befits his city of origin. Apollos's eloquence takes on specificity in the language of v. 25, each phrase of which requires attention. First, Luke reports that Apollos had been instructed in "the way of the Lord"; the fact that he has been taught appears to be more important for Luke than questions of who taught him and where. Second, Apollos "spoke burning in the Spirit" (AT). The NRSV translates this phrase "with burning enthusiasm," probably because Apollos knows "only the baptism of John," but the role of the Spirit elsewhere in Luke–Acts (especially 10:44-48; 11:15-18) suggests that baptism is not a rigid prerequisite for the gift of the Holy Spirit (despite 2:38). The Holy Spirit's role finds further confirmation in the description of Apollos's activity; he "taught accurately the things concerning Jesus," and "he began to speak boldly in the synagogue," activities elsewhere associated with the apostles themselves (4:13, 31; 9:27-28; 13:46; 28:31).

Students of Acts have made much of the fact that Apollos requires instruction, presumably instruction concerning baptism. Taken together with the scene that follows, the attention to baptism has led some scholars to conclude that Luke is here correcting some who continue to follow John the Baptist (Johnson 1992, 338); others suggest that Priscilla and Aquila unite believers of various communities under the single shelter of the Pauline church (Fitzmyer 1998, 637). The problems with all of these proposals are considerable, since Apollos does not appear to be identified exclusively with John the Baptist, and since he also knows "the Way of the Lord" and teaches accurately about Jesus. The instruction he receives remains unspecified, and readers deduce its connection with baptism from the end of v. 25. In other words, the content of the instruction Priscilla and Aquila give him appears less important than the fact that they give it and he receives it without resistance. Apollos is apparently strengthened by the instruction, as vv. 27-28 depict him leaving to teach in Achaia and with the encouragement of the Ephesian believers (see 1 Cor 3:4-6).

Luke identifies Apollos's teachers as "Priscilla and Aquila," naming her first (as at 18:18), and showing no reluctance about including Priscilla among the church's teachers. Although some interpreters suggest that she gives her instruction at home (Calvin 1966, 145; Seim 1994, 129-30), the narrator's comment that Priscilla and Aquila "took him aside" (v. 26) implies only that they did not publicly confront him in the synagogue and does not require the conclusion that her teaching was confined to the domestic arena.

Paul Baptizes Disciples (19:1-7)

The second scene in Ephesus again concerns instruction for believers, but this time the instruction of a group rather than an individual, and the instruction is carried out by Paul (19:1-7). Arriving in Ephesus, Paul encounters "disciples." The narrator does not specify whose disciples they are, but the context as well as usage throughout Acts (e.g., 6:1; 9:1; 13:52) strongly argues in favor of their being disciples of Jesus (however inadequate their instruction). How there came to be disciples in Ephesus Luke does not say; neither does Luke indicate what prompts Paul to ask the question of v. 2. The disciples' response, that they "have not even heard that there is a Holy Spirit," strains credulity, since both John the Baptist and Israel's Scriptures testify to the work of the Spirit (Barrett 1998, 894). However odd their response may appear, it paves the way for the second question and answer in v. 3, allowing Paul again to recall the role of John's proclamation (see 1:22; 10:37; 13:24-25). Verses 5-7 complete the scene with the disciples' baptism, the laying on of hands, and the evidence of the Holy Spirit. The scene certainly implies the superiority of Jesus over John, but it also emphasizes the efficacy of Paul's teaching and the receptivity of the audience. As Apollos was subject to correction even in spite of his eloquence, these unnamed disciples also submit to further instruction.

Leaving the Synagogue (19:8-10)

Following these two initial scenes that display eager receptivity for further instruction, vv. 8-10 summarize Paul's synagogue proclamation and the ensuing conflict in familiar terms. The intensity of the description of Paul's work in v. 8 gives the impression that Paul is continually talking in the synagogue for three months, without even an interruption. Verse 9 depicts the disagreement in sharp terms as well, prompting Paul not only to leave but to take the disciples with him, language not used earlier of Paul's departures from the synagogue. Now Paul goes, not to a house next door as in Corinth (18:7), but to a public place, the hall of Tyrannus. The conflict does not silence Paul, since v. 10 confirms the extent of the hearing. Not only the residents of Ephesus, but "all the residents of Asia," both Jews and Greeks, heard the word of the Lord. (This large hearing in turn sets the stage for the eruption of vv. 23-41, when response to the gospel prompts deadly envy.)

Defeating the Sons of Sceva (19:11-20)

As earlier in Acts, this major witness is marked not only by proclamation, by instruction, and by hearing, but by encounter with human intractability, and also by conflict with the representatives of Satan. Verses 11-12 depict that conflict in one of the more unusual episodes in Acts. Initially, the story reports on miracles done by God through Paul. These are, of course, parallel to earlier healings accomplished by the fringe of Jesus' garment (Luke 8:44) and the shadow of Peter (Acts 5:15). They demonstrate God's power, but they also set up the dramatic contrast that follows in vv. 13-20.

Verse 13 introduces a group, "some itinerant Jewish exorcists." In itself, that designation is probably not a negative one, as evidenced by reports about the exorcistic abilities attributed to Jews (Luke 11:19; Josephus, *Ant.* 8.42-49; *PGM* 4:3019-3085). The description that follows renders a neutral reading of this group impossible, however, since they invoke the name of Jesus to perform their exorcisms (v. 13), and they are identified as "seven sons of a Jewish high priest named Sceva." That no such high priest appears in other records is scarcely surprising, given that the name itself is Latin in origin. The seven have a false relationship to the high priesthood, just as they fraudulently call on the name of Jesus. The seemingly humorous response of the evil spirit in v. 15 turns serious with v. 16: not only are the exorcists unable to perform their professional duty, but they themselves fall victim to the man with the evil spirit.

This event generates awe among "all residents of Ephesus," an appropriate response to the presence of God. In this particular instance, a number of narrative contrasts enhance the reader's own sense of awe. Although Apollos spoke accurately and was instructed to speak more accurately still, these seven fraudulently speak the name of Jesus (Spencer 1997, 185). The Jew Apollos and the (presumably) Jewish disciples in 19:1-10 receive instruction with evident eagerness, but these seven Jews persist in their errors. Most striking, God performs miracles through even the rags that have touched the individual Paul, but this group of seven professional exorcists is defeated by a single demon.

The residents of Ephesus are not only "awestruck," but many come forward as believers and "disclose" their practices. What that means becomes clear in v. 19: some have been engaged in magic, and they bring their books of formulae forward to be burned. The narrator's report on the value of these books is no mere aside. It demonstrates the financial gain previously available to those whose practices have been defeated by the gospel, and it also coheres with Luke's portrait of the church's witness as responsible in its use of possessions (e.g., 2:44-45; 11:27-30; 20:33-35). The summary of v. 20 recalls earlier notices about the growth of the word of the Lord, but with an ironic twist; only here is the word of the Lord said to prevail (*ischuō*), repeating the verb used in v. 16 of the overpowering of the seven exorcists.

Paul Will Go to Rome (19:21-22)

Although this lengthy section concludes with Paul in Ephesus, it also contains a brief notice that Paul "resolved in the Spirit" to go to Macedonia and Achaia, then to Jerusalem, then to Rome (see Rom 1:10, 15; 15:22-29). The Greek here is ambiguous; what the NRSV renders as "resolved in the Spirit," suggesting the guidance of the Holy Spirit, others would translate as "formed the intention," taking *pneuma* to refer to Paul's own spirit of reflection or decision (Barrett 1998, 915; Cosgrove 1984, 178). Several factors in Lukan usage argue strongly in favor of the NRSV's rendering. To begin with, Luke routinely draws attention to the role of the Holy Spirit, so it would seem odd for Paul suddenly to begin making his own travel plans. (Earlier, an attempt to do that was rebuffed by the Spirit; see 16:6-10.) Second, the word "spirit" appears without the modifier "holy" in several places where the context nevertheless makes it clear that the Holy Spirit is meant rather than an individual's own spirit (e.g., 6:10; 8:18, 29; 10:19; 11:2; see also 11:28; 20:22; 21:4). Third, Luke seldom employs "spirit" to refer to a human being's state of mind (Acts 17:16 [obscured in NRSV]; perhaps Luke 1:17, 47; Campbell 2000, 172). Most important, when Paul adds "I must also see Rome" (v. 21), he speaks Luke's language for the divine plan, using the word *dei* (as at 1:16, 21; 4:12). Journeying to Rome reflects neither Paul's personal desire for travel nor his own discernment of what the witness requires but the divine will, conveyed to him by means of the Holy Spirit. This announcement parallels Luke 9:51, where Jesus "set his face toward Jerusalem," and the parallel underscores the sense that Paul's journey to Rome will eventuate in his death (cf. 9:16).

◊   ◊   ◊   ◊

This first stage in the Ephesian witness depicts the gospel as it instructs Jewish believers as well as conflicts with evil in the form of Jewish exorcists. The second stage will show the gospel in collision with the devotees of Artemis, a crucial figure in the religious and cultural life of Ephesus. Even in this first stage, however, it is clear that the gospel extends to all. The geographical spread represented here itself conveys that universality, from Apollos's Alexandria to Paul's Rome. It also comes to expression in 19:10 where "all the residents of Asia," Jew and Greek, hear the word of the Lord. Such hyperbole serves an important theological end, that of depicting the gospel's universal extent.

Sometimes this section of the book is characterized as the climax of Paul's mission as a free man (Tannehill 1990, 236), but understanding Paul in such near-heroic terms is mistaken. As throughout Acts, Luke makes it quite clear that Paul's activity is not his own. The miracles accomplished here, however extravagant, are explicitly attributed to God. Paul's itinerary is set by the Holy Spirit. In addition, Ephesus not only shows the labor of Paul, but that of Apollos and of Priscilla and Aquila, all of whom are depicted as effective teachers. Indeed, given the response to the downfall of the Jewish exorcists, even they serve evangelizing ends. It is Paul's gospel but not Paul's person that is crucial, as will also be clear in the conflict that follows, where even Paul's absence does not still the storm created by the gospel.

Defenders of Artemis of the Ephesians (19:23-41)

The scope of the witness expands in Ephesus. In addition to Paul, new figures preach and teach the gospel (18:24-28), and "all the residents of Asia" hear (19:10). It should not come as a surprise, then, to find that resistance to the witness also emerges and with force. This is not the first time Gentiles have initiated action against Christian witnesses (see 16:19-21), but the attention lavished on the scene makes it significant; it is also the most extensive scene in Acts that attends to human characters who are not believers. Even when the Jerusalem authorities convene and listen to the speech of Gamaliel, Peter and others are present and speak (5:17-42). One of the startling features of this final event in Ephesus is that believers scarcely appear, and they never speak.

Three distinct units comprise this scene; the first and last are speeches, and between them there is a riot. First, Demetrius objects to Paul's activity (or to its effect) and vividly depicts its dire consequences before a group of artisans (vv. 23-27). That speech prompts the second unit, the riot of vv. 28-34 with its enthusiastic chorus, "Great is Artemis of the Ephesians!" In the final unit, the town clerk delivers a speech in which he also considers the consequences for Ephesus, but this time the consequences stem from the actions of Demetrius and his cronies, since the town clerk presents the Christians as acting within the law and, by implication, unable to damage the great Artemis (vv. 35-41).

Paul's own letters mention Ephesus as a place of serious trouble (1 Cor 15:32; see also 1 Cor 16:8-9; 2 Cor 1:8-9). Beyond confirming Paul's work in Ephesus, however, those references offer little information, and attempts to fund a biography of Paul by combining the letters and Acts remain highly speculative.

◊ ◊ ◊ ◊

"She Will Be Deprived of Her Majesty" (19:23-27)

Verse 23 serves as a transition into the story, but it also indicates that danger is imminent. The *litotes* of "no little disturbance" anticipates the outbreak. Even the reference to "the Way" underscores the difficulty, since this Lukan manner of referring to followers of Jesus often occurs in connection with moments of resistance or persecution (e.g., 9:2; 19:9; 22:4).

Luke's first readers probably knew Ephesus and the city's association with Artemis well enough to imagine the direction from which the danger would come. Ample evidence confirms that the cult of Artemis occupied a central place in the life of Ephesus, as it had done since the eleventh century BCE (Strabo, *Geography* 14.1.22-23; Herodotus, *History* 1.26; Achilles Tatius, *Clitophon and Leucippe* 7.13-8.14; Xenophon, *Ephesian Tale* 1.2, 5). Artemis was understood to protect the young, those who sought sanctuary in her temple, and the city itself. The temple of Artemis was ranked as one of the wonders of the ancient world; it served also as the financial and banking center of Asia. For wide-ranging and obvious reasons, then, the citizens of Ephesus invested considerable pride in the administration of the cult of Artemis (Oster 1976, 24-44; LiDonnici 1992, 389-415; Strelan 1996, 41-94). A comment by Pausanias lauds the extent of her standing beyond Ephesus: "All cities worship Artemis of Ephesus, and individuals hold her in honor above all the gods" (4.31.8).

By contrast with earlier episodes, in which Luke depicts opposition to the witnesses with a brief statement about jealousy (5:17; 17:5) or loss of income (16:19), here he lingers over Demetrius and his speech. Demetrius is "a silversmith who made silver shrines of Artemis, [who] brought no little business to the artisans" (v. 24). The fact that such silver shrines have not been located does not undermine the verisimilitude of the description, since shrines from less expensive materials have been found, suggesting that precious silver items were recycled into other objects (*NewDocs* 4:7-10; Strelan 1996, 135). What is more important, especially in view of its repeated stress here, is that Demetrius and his colleagues depend on devotion to Artemis for their livelihood, which may well have been true directly or otherwise for many residents of Ephesus.

Demetrius gathers the workers and begins his speech with two assertions already made by the narrator, but, in Demetrius's restatement of them, Artemis of Ephesus collides with the Christian witness (vv. 25*b*-26). Demetrius first reminds the workers of what the narrator has already said in vv. 24-25*a*: Their prosperity derives from the Artemis industry. Then he repeats the narrator's statement from 19:10 that Paul has been persuasive not only to Ephesians but throughout the province of Asia. Demetrius characterizes Paul's teaching as "that gods made with hands are not gods" (v. 26). In Paul's sermon on the Areopagus, similar statements generate no opposition (17:24-25; and see also 7:48); the audience of philosophers would have agreed with them. Unlike the Athenians, however, the artisans in Ephesus earn their living by virtue of devotion to Artemis.

Since Luke often portrays the danger of false attachment to possessions (e.g., 1:18; 5:1-11; 8:9-24; 16:19-21), it is natural to interpret Demetrius's outcry as self-interest and nothing more. Although that interpretation of this passage goes back at least to Chrysostom (*Homilies on Acts* 42 [NPNF 11:258]), v. 27 indicates that more is at stake than greed alone. In Demetrius's view, Paul's attack on idolatry threatens not only the income of these workers, but the temple of Artemis and, indeed, even the greatness of the goddess herself. This conclusion reflects the extent of Artemis's reach into religious, civic, and economic life and amply explains the chaos that follows.

"Great Is Artemis of the Ephesians" (19:28-34)

The eruption set off by Demetrius's speech generates confusion, both within the narrative itself (v. 32) and for the reader attempting to understand it. The one thing that emerges with clarity is the unified response, "Great is Artemis of the Ephesians!" Despite its origin with the workers and their outrage, the cry is probably a hymnic cry, invoking the power of the goddess herself over the city and against the outsiders and their gospel (Strelan 1996, 143-44).

Luke underscores the nightmarish quality of the scene. People "rushed together," an expression earlier used of the mob that stoned Stephen (7:57) and made their way into the theater. The introduction of the theater may be jarring to contemporary readers, but it was the venue associated both with political assembly and with riots (MacMullen 1966, 168-73; Strelan 1996, 84). Since the theater at Ephesus could contain as many as 25,000 people, the potential for riot was serious. Verse 32 further enhances the sense of chaos, with many not even knowing the cause for the mob's formation. Even the sight of the hapless Jew Alexander, whose motives remain unstated, sets off the crowd for a two hour chorus in Artemis's honor. Scenes of this sort appear in a number of ancient writers (e.g., Heliodorus, *Ethiopians* 4.19; 7.8-9; 8.9; 10.8, 17; Chariton, *Chaereas and Callirhoe* 1.5; 3.4; Achilles Tatius, *Clitophon and Leucippe* 7.9), reflecting at least to a certain extent the reality of social protest (MacMullen 1966, 163-92; Pervo 1987, 37-38).

If the mob is confused, readers may also find this scene confusing. Nothing explains why the crowd seizes Gaius and Aristarchus, said to be traveling companions of Paul but otherwise unidentified (v. 29). The "officials of the province of Asia" join with believers to protect Paul. These significant local officials are said to be friendly to Paul, but no reasons explain their disposition (vv. 30-31). Alexander's involvement is also unclear; perhaps he is well-disposed to Paul, at least to the extent of upholding the oneness of God; it is equally possible that he wishes to distance himself and other Jews from Paul and the gospel message (v. 33). The fact that the crowd will not tolerate the voice of a Jew betrays a hostility that threatens all Jews in Ephesus (Stoops 1989, 86-87). These multiple ambiguities play in the story to enhance the sense of chaos.

"Citizens of Ephesus" (19:35-41)

The riot ends with the appearance of the town clerk and his speech. Commentators often dwell on his implied defense of Paul and his colleagues in v. 37 ("these men . . . are neither temple robbers nor blasphemers of our goddess"), but the speech begins with Artemis rather than with the accusations. In his own way, the town clerk also asserts the greatness of Artemis and her city, the keeper of the temple and of "the statue that fell from heaven." This reference to the legend that a statue of Artemis fell from heaven counters Paul's claims, insisting that Artemis herself does not come from human hands (Stoops 1989, 87). "Who is there that does not know" and "since these things [about

Artemis] cannot be denied" function as a theological counter-argument to the hysteria generated by Demetrius. In the clerk's view, Artemis and her city can prevail over all challengers, and such fears as Demetrius has stirred up have no foundation in reality. Historically speaking, the town clerk proves to be right, since the temple of Artemis continued to be a dominant presence in Ephesus even in the third century (Oster 1976, 29).

Beginning from this strong assertion, the clerk comments on "these men," without specifying who is included. If the town clerk here defends Paul, the defense is slight. He simply comments that they have not violated Artemis's name or her temple. (On the restraint of Jews regarding idols and shrines, see Josephus, *Ant.* 4.207; but see also *Ag. Ap.* 1.249, 311.) The clerk finally offers an alternative to Demetrius as well as a threat to the mob. Demetrius and the artisans can take advantage of legal procedures if they have actual complaints (vv. 38-39). And all present must understand the danger that the entire city would be accused of rioting; however prominent a city, none could ignore the threat that Rome would find such an uprising dangerous and would be quick to punish the city itself (Dio Cassius 54.7.6; Tacitus, *Annals* 14.17; Dio Chrysostom, *Discourses* 34.39). The verb Demetrius used (*kindyneuō*) to describe the danger to Ephesus (NRSV: there is danger) is now used to describe the danger these Ephesians pose to themselves (NRSV: we are in danger). As in earlier episodes, there is irony here in that the accusers of Christians are actually the ones disrupting public life, even as they charge Christians with doing so (see 16:19-24, 37; 17:5-9). It is not Paul but Demetrius who threatens Ephesus's standing. With this warning, the clerk dismisses all, and apparently they comply.

◊ ◊ ◊ ◊

A time-honored reading of this story understands it as a triumph for Christianity. In the face of a massive and popular religion in a leading city, Paul and his colleagues make such inroads that they constitute a threat. Even a mob cannot defeat them, because they find protection in provincial officials who warn Paul not to enter the theater and in the town clerk who declares believers innocent of any wrongdoing. No harm comes to anyone through this attack by the devotees of Artemis.

In startling ways, however, Paul and his colleagues do not triumph in Ephesus. Instead, the gospel appears to be silenced by this event. Paul himself does not succeed in speaking, since he cannot even reach the theater. Alexander attempts to speak but the crowd shouts him down. Nothing suggests that Demetrius or the crowd is satisfied by the outcome or alters its perspective, since the story ends with the clerk's dismissal. In the very next verse, Paul leaves Ephesus for Macedonia (20:1). Such silence regarding the Christian response may simply reflect the reality of a riot: there is no opportunity to speak. Even the narrator remains silent, however, with nothing at this point to indicate a continuing Christian community in Ephesus beyond the vague "the disciples" of 20:1 (although see 20:17).

This silence, taken together with the speeches of Demetrius and the town clerk, suggests that the riot in Ephesus has less to do with Christianity's triumph than with the implacable opposition between the God proclaimed by Christian witness and the gods whose regions that witness entered. In a powerful sense, Demetrius's speech is accurate: Paul does proclaim that the shrines are not God; that proclamation is in fact a threat to the local industry, to Artemis, and to an Ephesus entangled with her.

The silence of Paul allows that claim to stand uncorrected. Unlike Athens, where Paul could begin with shared convictions and move in the direction of the gospel (see above on 17:22-31), in Ephesus there is no common ground. Translation of the gospel into philosophical terms is one thing; translation into the language of Artemis's cult is quite another, since there can be no accommodation for another deity. No speech of Paul's can ameliorate the conflict Demetrius rightly perceives (Gaventa 2001).

At several important points prior to this, it has appeared that one of Luke's concerns may be the strengthening of those Gentile Christians who live under constant pressure from an environment teeming with gods (see Introduction and on 15:1-35).

Generally, the narrative approaches that issue from the vantage point of Israel's relationship with God, the only one who exists (13:15-17; 17:23-25), and the one who tolerates no practices tainted by idolatry (15:19-20, 29). Demetrius and fellow Ephesians demonstrate that, also from the side of the pagan cults, no compromise is possible. The tolerance that generally characterized Greco-Roman religious life ceased when religious behavior was perceived to threaten the local civil religion.

STRENGTHENING BELIEVERS (20:1–21:17)

This section comprises an extensive account of the journey of Paul and his coworkers from Ephesus to Jerusalem. If the focus of 19:23-41 is on Ephesian pagans and their perception of the gospel as a threat to their wealth, their city, and their goddess, at 20:1 the narrative turns to believers and the upbuilding of their faith. Only after Paul arrives in Jerusalem at 21:17 and then meets with James does attention return to nonbelievers. This extended account of life within the believing community alternates episodes narrating Paul's travel with episodes narrating discrete dramatic events, as follows:

20:1-6	Travel
20:7-12	Event (Gathering of believers in Troas)
20:13-16	Travel
20:17-38	Event (Farewell speech in Miletus to Ephesian elders)
21:1-7	Travel
21:8-14	Event (Gathering of believers in Caesarea)
21:15-17	Travel

Although numerous references to travel have appeared already in Acts, most of those are brief and to the point (e.g., 13:4-6, 13-14; 15:39-41; 17:14-15; 18:1). None is as elaborate as the itineraries in this section of the book, where Luke provides the names of traveling companions, precise locations on the itinerary, number of days involved, and even references to cargo. The detail lavished on these travel sections and the interspersing of them with scenes of community life suggest that they may have particular significance for Luke (see below).

Going Up to Jerusalem (20:1-16)

The journey begins as Paul travels first from Ephesus to Troas (vv. 1-6) and then from Troas to Miletus (vv. 13-16). Between these two travel narratives stands a vignette of community life which contains the vivid story of the healing of Eutychus (vv. 7-12). Another important literary feature in this initial section is the reintroduction of first-person plural narration. "We" appears in v. 5 and will continue through 21:8, except for the speech in 20:17-38 (see also 16:10-17; 27:1–28:16).

◊ ◊ ◊ ◊

Travel (20:1-6)

These initial verses find Paul and his companions departing Ephesus for Macedonia, then traveling south to remain in Greece for three months. Forced to travel through Macedonia instead of sailing directly for Syria, Paul leaves from Philippi and arrives in Troas. The locations recall various places Paul has already visited. Perhaps most important, the move toward Macedonia and then eastward in the direction of Jerusalem begins to fulfill the Spirit's direction of Paul to journey to Jerusalem and then to Rome (19:21).

In addition to the place names that pepper this section, new companions join Paul. Luke mentions Sopater, Secundus, and Tychicus only here (cf. the name Tychicus at Eph 6:21; Col 4:7; 2 Tim 4:12; Titus 3:12). Aristarchus and Gaius appeared for the first time at 19:29, although here Gaius is identified with Derbe in Asia Minor rather than with Macedonia. Trophimus is mentioned again only at 21:29 (and cf. 2 Tim 4:20). Timothy has appeared often, beginning in 16:1. Perhaps more important than any slight information that might be gleaned about Paul's companions is the fact that they represent many of the areas of Paul's witness (Tannehill 1990, 246). That Paul's entourage continues to grow is also important, as is the resemblance to Jesus' disciples who journeyed with him to Jerusalem (Spencer 1997, 191).

Another character returns here, namely, "we." Given that Luke does not identify the other travelers beyond their names and places of origin, perhaps it should not surprise readers that he also does not identify "we." Elsewhere "we" appears in contexts of considerable urgency, and the situation here is also demanding as Paul endeavors to consolidate believers while he himself journeys away toward captivity in Jerusalem and then Rome. The presence of "we" seems to support Paul's labor, serving as a replacement for the role Barnabas played earlier in Acts (e.g., 9:27; 11:25; 12:25; see Campbell 2000).

Frequent references to time mark this travel interlude, as the group remains in Greece for three months (v. 3), departs Philippi after the Feast of Unleavened Bread, reconvenes in Troas after five days, and remains there for seven days (v. 6). Attempts to construct the chronology of Paul's journeys and reconcile it with the Pauline letters rely heavily on these notices, but their significance extends beyond chronology. They also indicate that the work of consolidating groups of believers requires spending time with them (as earlier at 14:28; 15:32-35; 18:11). In addition, the reference to Passover further enhances the journey's associations with the journey of the Lukan Jesus to Jerusalem for Passover (Luke 22:1, 7-8, 15; Spencer 1997, 190).

Numerous features of this brief travel narrative reflect the effort of Paul to strengthen the gathered believers. In addition to the spending of time and the identification of Paul's enlarged number of traveling companions, twice in this brief passage Luke specifically refers to Paul as "encouraging" believers (vv. 1, 2). The reference to the plot against Paul presages the imprisonment of Paul, and it indicates the growing danger to the community as well (v. 3; and see 9:24; 20:19; 23:30).

Eutychus Restored to Community (20:7-12)

Interrupting the travel itinerary at this point is a brief account of a gathering of believers for worship and instruction. Despite earlier references to Paul's continuing concern for believers in various locations (e.g., 14:22-28; 15:36, 40-41), and despite the numerous occasions on which Paul preaches, only a few passages concern the worship of believers, and those are summaries rather than dramatic scenes (2:42-47 and 4:32-37, although see 4:23-31). The fascinating and somewhat humorous details of the Eutychus incident should not obscure the fact that this vignette concerns believers at worship. Luke locates the gathering on Sunday, "the first day of the week," consistent with other early writings that connect Christian worship with the day of Jesus' resurrection (1 Cor 16:2; *Did.* 14). Whether by this reference Luke intends Saturday night and early Sunday or Sunday night and early Monday remains unclear. Luke also places the story in the room upstairs (*hyperōon*) recalling the upper room (*hyperōon*) in which the disciples awaited the coming of the Holy Spirit (1:13; see also 9:37, 39). The act of breaking bread, mentioned here for the first time since 2:46, both begins and ends the story (vv. 7, 11), firmly connecting it to the life of the gathered community.

It is important to read the story about Eutychus within this context rather than as an isolated incident (Trémel 1980, 361). The story evokes associations with earlier incidents, since Luke–Acts includes stories of Jesus and Peter raising the dead (Luke 7:11-17; 8:40-42, 49-56; Acts 9:36-43). The story also recalls the miracles of Elisha and Elijah, although the parallels are inexact (1 Kgs 17:17-24; 2 Kgs 4:18-37).

Numerous details within the story bear noticing. Paul talks through the night, that is to say, in the darkness, but Luke notes that the room has many lamps, that is to say, it is well-illuminated (vv. 7-8). Commentators often connect the presence of the lamps with Eutychus's sleepiness, as lamps would generate warmth or foul the air, but that view neglects the fact that Eutychus is also said to be sitting at a window, therefore closer to fresh air (Bulley 1994, 176). Sometimes the lamps are viewed as playing an apologetic role, since ancient writings associate nocturnal gatherings with immorality (Talbert 1997, 183-85), yet little else in this story points in that direction. Both these explanations overlook the many ways in which language about light and darkness, sight and the lack thereof, pervades Luke–Acts. As early as the canticle of Simeon, whose eyes "see" salvation in Jesus and who interprets Jesus as "a light for revelation to the Gentiles," sight and light play an important role in Luke's story (Luke 2:29-32; see also Luke 12:35; Acts 9:1-19; 13:4-12; 26:18). In Luke's narrative, Christians are those who can and do see what God has done in Jesus Christ. Eutychus's fall out of the realm of the lamps and his restoration to it surely continues this motif of the light-giving power of the gospel.

Another compelling feature of the story is the role played by sleep, which figures almost as a character in the story. Although obscured in the NRSV, v. 9 twice describes Eutychus as being "brought down" by sleep (Bulley 1994, 176). Two important scenes in Luke's Gospel find sleep threatening the disciples in their role as witnesses (Luke 9:32; 22:45-46), and a number of eschatological texts employ wakefulness and sleep in a figurative sense to refer to watchfulness (e.g., Mark 13:33-37; Luke 12:37, 21:36; 1 Thess 5:6). Eutychus's sleepiness probably reflects those associations, so that his succumbing to sleep is simultaneously a succumbing to separation from the community of believers.

The spatial language in the text underscores the separation between Eutychus and the community. Luke writes that Eutychus *"fell* from the third floor *down* and was taken up dead" (v. 9 AT). Then "going *down* Paul *fell* upon him" (AT) to restore his life. Eutychus's life is restored, but the incident ends only when he is also restored to community. The customary response to a miracle comes, not immediately after Eutychus is restored to life, but at the very conclusion of the event, after Paul has broken bread and after he has finished instruction (v. 12; Bulley 1994, 178), further reinforcing the communal significance of the event.

Travel (20:13-16)

A second itinerary follows the story of worship in Troas. Leaving Troas, the group sails south for Assos, also on the northwest coast of Asia Minor, although Paul makes the trip alone and on foot. Why Paul separates from the group and travels to Assos on foot, and why Luke includes this detail, remains unanswered. United again in Assos, they continue south to Mitylene, Chios, Samos, and then Miletus. The travel report concludes with another reminder that the group is *en route* to Jerusalem and that Paul wishes to be there for Pentecost.

Both travel sections here have some reference to a separation. In the first, Paul and a few companions are separated from the "we," and join them again in Troas (vv. 3-5), while in the second Paul travels to Assos by land and his companions by ship (vv. 13-14). Certainly these notices may reflect historical travel sequences, but it is nevertheless interesting that Luke elects to include these details. Perhaps the separations and reunions themselves underscore the separation and reunion between Eutychus and his community.

◊   ◊   ◊   ◊

This passage marks a turning point in the narrative. At 20:1, Paul sets out relentlessly for Jerusalem, with no further occasions for introducing the gospel into previously unvisited cities. That fact thrusts his impending separation from the churches into the spotlight, especially for readers who hear echoes of Jesus' journey to Jerusalem (Luke 9:51; 13:22; 17:11). All of this passage, as well as the remainder of this section (20:1–21:17), shows Paul preparing the churches for his absence. The care with which he does that comes to expression here in the time he spends, the encouragement offered, and in the lengthy (even soporific) sermon he delivers (Tannehill 1990, 246).

At least one commentator characterizes Luke as having little interest in the interior life of the church, as a result of his strong concern for evangelism (Witherington 1998, 606). That characterization trips over this text, however. In the first place, it is by no means obvious that Luke would have recognized a distinction between "domestic" and "foreign" work of the church, between the church's own interior life and its proclamation of the gospel. Even granting such a distinction, however, this passage clearly evidences the importance of the life of the believing community. Eutychus's fall and restoration exemplify Luke's concern. Even if Eutychus's sleep is understood nonsymbolically, as a mere physical response to a long day and a tiresome sermon, Paul's return of him to the group and the group's comfort at that return confirm the story's focus on the wholeness of the community.

The focus on the interior of the church may also explain Luke's provision of a detailed travel itinerary at this juncture. However much or little the detail coincides with historical events, the fact that Luke includes such detail here in a condensed fashion merits attention. By providing three vignettes of community life (20:7-12, 17-38; 21:8-14) and alternating them with travel accounts, Luke knits these disparate groups together. In the early chapters of Acts, as he described the emerging church in Jerusalem, Luke depicted the community worshiping together, supporting each other materially, spending time together in the temple. The Jerusalem community even tends together to the threatened fracture regarding treatment of the widows (6:1-6). The communities scattered from Philippi to Miletus cannot be gathered together in one place, for obvious geographic reasons. Instead, by showing Paul and his colleagues traveling from place to place, Luke ties these disparate and distant groups together. Even as the Spirit pulls Paul to Jerusalem and Rome, and therefore away from these small groups of Christians, the journey itself pulls them together.

Among the many gaps in this story, those questions that remain unanswered, is the question whether the separation that threatens Eutychus and the community results from his own failing or from some external source. The only clue the text offers is that "sleep" weighs him down; nothing is said to chastise or castigate Eutychus himself. This is consistent with the speech that follows, in which Paul anticipates wolves who will come in to harm the flock. The shepherds must stay awake ("Keep watch," 20:28) so as to protect the sheep.

Paul's Labor, the Church's Future, and God's Grace (20:17-38)

At the center of this extended section that focuses on the upbuilding of believers in the churches established through Paul's labor (20:1–21:17) stands what is usually referred to as Paul's farewell address to the Ephesian elders. As the book's most extended speech for those who are already Christian (cf. 11:5-17; 15:7-11, 13-21) and the last speech prior to Paul's captivity, this address occupies an important place in the book as a whole.

Brief narratives mark the transition to (vv. 17-18*a*) and from (vv. 36-38) the speech itself. Analyses of the structure of the speech abound, including those that employ chiasmus, significant ideas, and time references as structural tools (Kilgallen 1994). One striking feature of the speech is its repetition of the Greek phrase *kai nun idou* ("and now behold") or *kai ta nun* ("and now") at vv. 22, 25, and 32. That repetition serves to identify shifts in subject matter, so that the following structure emerges:

vv. 18*b*-21   Review of Paul's labor in Asia
vv. 22-24   Paul's impending journey to Jerusalem
vv. 25-31   Warning about the church's future
vv. 32-35   The church commended to God

The speech shares a number of features with ancient farewell addresses. Common in ancient literature, a farewell address involves a setting of impending separation (either death or departure), in which a significant figure reviews the past and the present context, instructs successors, and offers exhortations to faithfulness (Kurz 1985; Fitzmyer 1998, 674). Examples abound both within the Old Testament and other Jewish literature (e.g., Gen 49:1-32; *T. 12 Patr.*; Josephus, *Ant.* 4.309-26) and in non-Jewish sources also (e.g., Diogenes Laertius, *Life of Epicurus* 10.16-22).

Many rhetorical flourishes enhance the speech. Although English translations scarcely do justice to them, emphatic pronouns sprinkled throughout the speech enhance its intimacy, as does the familiar but nevertheless effective use of the shepherd and wolf imagery in vv. 28-29. The series of pairs in vv. 20-21 likewise elevates the discourse ("in public and at home," "to Jews and to Greeks," "repentance," and "faith," AT). The repetition of "behold" and "this very day" lends urgency to the call for watchfulness (vv. 22, 25, 32 AT).

At a number of points the speech echoes the concerns if not the language of Paul's own letters (e.g., the emphasis on Paul's captivity, disavowing an interest in preserving his own life, reference to grace, and recollection of working with his own hands). This pattern causes some scholars to suggest that the speech comes to Luke from a Pauline source, or even from Luke's own eyewitness account (Bruce 1990, 419). It is perhaps equally important to see how this, the most Pauline sounding of the speeches of Acts, nevertheless serves the shape of Luke's story. In that sense, the Miletus address is analogous to Acts 17; each appears unusual by comparison with other speeches in Acts, the Areopagus because it so carefully addresses the philosophically-inclined Athenians who have no acquaintance with the gospel, and the Miletus speech because it addresses believers whose teacher is to be separated from them. Despite the uniqueness, however, each speech also deeply coheres with larger Lukan concerns.

Verses 17-18a provide the setting for the speech. Since he was bypassing Ephesus himself (see v. 16), Paul sends for the elders of the church to come to him. Luke employs the term "elders" for local church leaders in a variety of places (e.g., 11:30; 14:23; 15:2; 16:4). If it remained unclear what became of the Christian community at Ephesus following the riot generated by Demetrius and his cronies (19:23-41), this episode suggests it has been led by elders whom Paul now summons.

"From the First Day" (20:18b-21)

This compact recollection of Paul's labor in Ephesus moves from the time spent in Asia (v. 18*b*) to the character of Paul's service (v. 19) and then to the context and content of his testimony (vv. 20-21). The emphatic reference to time spent ("the entire time from the first day") both reinforces earlier notices about the time Paul spent in Asia (19:8, 10, 22) and implies that the work of the witness requires serious expenditure of time (as evidenced in other such references in 14:28; 15:33, 35; 18:11). Verse 19 introduces the characterization of Paul's labor as "serving the Lord," or more literally, "serving as a slave [*douleuō*] to the Lord." Paul's letters speak of him as a slave of Christ (Rom 1:1; Gal 1:10; Phil 1:1), but the notion has been present in Luke–Acts since the opening lines: Mary responds to Gabriel's annunciation by declaring herself the Lord's slave (obscured in the NRSV; Luke 1:38; see also Acts 2:18; 4:29; 16:17).

Paul describes his slavery with three words or phrases: he serves "with all humility, with tears, and with trials that came upon me through the plots of the Jews" (AT). The third phrase recalls the Lukan pattern of resistance in city after city, although it is curious that he specifies only Jewish opposition here when the riot at Ephesus is so immediately in mind. Humility and tears have not previously been mentioned in Acts (although see 2 Cor 2:4; Phil 2:3), and it is significant that struggles rather than triumphs find their way into the speech (see 19:11-20; Spencer 1997, 193).

In vv. 20-21, this recollection of Paul's personal difficulties yields to a rehearsal of the gospel. Although the speech is not kerygmatic in the sense of proclaiming the gospel in a new territory or even detailing its content (Fitzmyer 1998, 674), it nevertheless contains an epitome of the gospel itself. Paul begins in v. 20 with "I did not shrink from," another Lukan *litotes* that negatively states what Luke elsewhere affirms about the boldness of the apostolic witness (e.g., 4:29, 31; 9:27; 28:31). The series of pairs that marks the remainder of vv. 20-21 ably summarizes the witness:

proclaiming . . . to you and teaching you
publicly and at home
to Jews and to Greeks
repentance toward God and faith toward our Lord Jesus (AT)

Taken together, the pairs provide an all-encompassing claim about the witness, its content, its audience, and its persistence.

"On My Way to Jerusalem" (20:22-24)

"And now" marks the shift to the second part of the speech, and again Paul makes reference to the compulsion under which he labors: he is "bound in the Spirit" (see NRSV note). A small irony enters with this description, since it was Paul who set out to arrest believers and bring them "bound" to Jerusalem (9:2, 14, 21; Johnson 1992, 361). Despite the fact that Paul denies knowing what will happen in Jerusalem, several features of the speech assume his arrest and eventual death in captivity. To begin with the most immediate evidence, v. 23 anticipates that the future will resemble the past, with its "imprisonment and persecution." And the statement that follows in v. 25 ("none of you . . . will ever see my face again") suggests a separation more ominous than distance alone (see also v. 38). In the context of the repeated references to going to Jerusalem and then Rome (19:21; 21:13; 25:9-12; 28:14) and the parallels to Jesus' own journey to Jerusalem (Luke 9:51; 13:22; 17:11), the speech surely anticipates Paul's death.

In v. 23 Paul treats his own suffering and imprisonment as part of God's plan. He does not himself extrapolate from past to future experience, deducing that the logical outcome of his experience is imprisonment and death. Instead, the Holy Spirit is the agent who shows Paul what lies ahead. Not only is the Spirit the agent, but the activity of the Spirit consists of testifying. Given Luke's use of witness-language for proclamation of the gospel (e.g., Acts 1:8, 22; 2:32; 3:15; 5:32), this statement associates Paul's imprisonment and persecution with the gospel; as Paul's sermon in Pisidian Antioch includes the work of John the Baptist and the witness of the apostles (13:24-25, 31), here the trials of Paul themselves accrue to the gospel witness.

Verse 24 again places the question of Paul's future in its proper context. "I do not count my life of any value to myself" simultaneously prevents a misconstrual of the reference to Paul's future and shifts attention to the next statement. What is important is that Paul finish the "course," the ministry he received (see 13:25; 2 Tim 4:7). By identifying the ministry as one "received from the Lord Jesus," Paul again shifts the focus of attention from himself to the one who called him. That emphasis will be repeated in the defense speeches of chapters 22 and 26.

"Keep Watch" (20:25-31)

With the next *kai nun idou* ("And now behold" AT), Paul turns from his own future to the future of the Ephesian church. First, he gravely announces to his listeners that they will not see him again (see especially Luke 22:15-16; and also Gen 48:21; *T. Reu.* 1:4-5; *T. Dan* 2:1; *T. Naph.* 1:3; 2 Tim 4:6; 2 Pet 1:13-14). Second, he solemnly asserts his own blamelessness with regard to the church, since he has carried out his vocation of announcing "the whole purpose of God" (vv. 26-27). The language of these statements heightens the drama, some of which English translations cannot readily convey, such as emphatic pronouns (e.g., the verbs already contain the "I" and "you" of v. 25, but additional pronouns draw attention to them). As at 18:6, the claim to be innocent of the people's blood is a claim that Paul has fulfilled his vocation and has no further liability for their behavior.

Paul then turns his attention from his own commission to remind the elders of their responsibility "for the flock, of which the Holy Spirit has made you overseers" (v. 28). The metaphor of shepherds and their flocks is widespread both in Jewish and in early Christian writings (e.g., Ps 78:52, 70; Mic 5:4; Isa 40:11; Jer 13:17; 23:2; Ezek 34:12; Zech 10:3; *1 En.* 89:3–90:39; John 10:11, 14-16; 21:15-17; 1 Pet 5:2-3), but it is striking here because Paul asserts that the elders received their responsibility from the Holy Spirit. If this claim may seem to be at odds with

14:23, where Luke describes Paul and Barnabas as selecting elders for various churches, 14:23 also finds Paul and Barnabas entrusting those new leaders to the Lord through prayer and fasting. The speech repeatedly insists that Paul, the elders, and the church all exist only because of the guidance of God, Jesus, the Spirit. These leaders are not Paul's assistants, selected by him, but they are instruments of the Spirit. The speech says nothing about the selection of successors for these elders, presumably anticipating that the Holy Spirit would supply those also (Barrett 1984, 36).

The remainder of v. 28 is also challenging. As the note in the NRSV indicates, some important early manuscripts read "the church of the Lord" instead of "the church of God." The next phrase describes the church with an ambiguous phrase that may be translated either as "his own blood" or "the blood of his own." The first possibility makes it easy to understand why early scribes might have substituted "the Lord" for "God," so as to avoid the impression that the cross involves God's own blood. Yet even the phrase "the blood of his own" as a reference to Christ's death is unusual, for Luke does not elsewhere speak of the blood of the cross. Some students of Acts identify this as a Pauline element in the speech; as central as the cross is in Paul's letters, however, they seldom employ the language of blood in connection with the cross (Rom 3:25; 5:9; 1 Cor 10:16; 11:25, 27; Cousar 1990). Perhaps the phrase comes about here under the influence of the reference to blood in v. 26. Paul's innocence with respect to the blood of the elders prompts an identification of Jesus' death as an outpouring of blood. In addition, the intense pathos of this speech makes such a vivid expression less surprising.

With "the blood of his own," God is said to have "obtained" the church. Earlier treatments of Jesus' death in Luke–Acts interpret it as a human error that was nevertheless part of God's plan (e.g., Acts 2:22-24; 3:13-15, 17). Through the death and resurrection, repentance and faith are proclaimed to all (e.g., 2:38; 3:19-22). Nowhere else does Luke directly connect the death of Jesus with the church's own existence, and the fact that he does so here underscores the intense concern of the speech for the health and future of the church. The language of the verse is therefore unusual but important for what it says about the church. Assuming that "blood" here is a reference to the death of Jesus, then God, Christ, and Spirit all come into play here and on behalf of the church (Fitzmyer 1998, 680; Barrett 1998, 974). The church comes into existence by means of, is led by, and protected only by God.

Given the analogy of the church as a flock, imagining its enemies as wolves preying on the flock is understandable and appears elsewhere (Ezek 22:27; Zeph 3:3-4; Matt 7:15; *Did.* 16:3; Ign., *Phld.* 2.1-2; 2 *Clem.* 5:2-4). What is more striking is that v. 30 takes the threat a step further. Not only will wolves threaten from the outside, but "some even from your own group" will themselves constitute a danger. As with previous sections of the speech, this one also ends with reference to Paul's own labor. As Paul guarded the church for three years, he now enjoins the elders of the church to be alert.

"I Commend You to God" (20:32-35)

Although the responsibility of the elders is genuine and weighty, the final move of the speech assures the audience that the future of the church belongs neither with the "wolves" nor with the "shepherds," but with God. The transition to vv. 33-34, with its emphatic denial that Paul acted greedily and insistence on his responsible labor, borrows from the stock features of philosophical discourse. The genuine teacher is not one motivated by money (e.g., 1 Thess 2:5; Dio Chrysostom, *Discourses* 32.9, 11; Lucian, *Nigrinus* 25-26). This standard claim plays an important role in the Lukan narrative, which displays both the responsible use of possessions (e.g., 4:32-36; 16:15) and the devastating impact of greed (e.g., 5:1-11; 8:18-24; 16:19-24). In this particular passage, the move from v. 32 to v. 33 seems jarring, except that both statements have to do with the "building up" of the church. Such building up requires attention to the whole rather than to the profit of the individual. Verse 35 follows nicely in that it offers a theological warrant for Paul's example. The "must" of "we must support the weak" again is the divine *dei*; mutual support reflects God's own will. The final appeal to Jesus' words underscores the necessity of responsible action (O'Toole 1994).

The saying of v. 35 has generated considerable discussion, since these words that Paul attributes to Jesus do not appear in the Gospels (although, of course, the Gospels do not include all of Jesus' words). Parallels appear across a range of other literature, including Sir 4:31; 1 *Clem.* 2.1; 13.1; 46.7; Pol. *Phil.* 2.3; *Did.* 1:5; 4:5; Thucydides, *History* 2.97; Plutarch, *Sayings of Kings and Commanders* 173D; 181F; Plutarch, *Philosophers and Men in Power* 778C. More important than tracing the genealogy of the statement is the fact that the single time a teaching of Jesus is quoted directly in Acts it pertains to the proper use of possessions. Finally, what is important is not Paul's example but God's will and Jesus' command.

The brief narrative frame in vv. 36-38 provides the appropriate outcome for the farewell and shows that Paul's farewell address properly ends in prayer. The outpouring of affection reinforces Paul's anticipation that this parting is final (see Gen 46:29).

Treatments of this speech frequently identify it as a retrospective account of Paul's ministry in which he is the church's exemplary missionary who speaks for the last time as a free man. Although that is an understandable characterization of the speech, it is far from sufficient theologically. To begin with, the example Paul offers is not heroic in any generally recognized sense of that term. Paul's ministry is characterized by humility, tears, trials, long years of labor, and an uncertain future. No reference recalls the earlier dramatic healings or the vanquishing of magicians. He speaks, not as a free human being whose capture is imminent, but as one already a captive of the Lord. Even as Paul speaks about his own labor, he does so in language that points away from himself and toward the gospel, toward God. The language of witnessing, preaching, and teaching is dense here; what is important about Paul is not Paul the individual actor, but Paul the witness to God's gospel.

As the centerpiece of a larger section of the book that focuses on the church itself (20:1–21:17), the speech makes some powerful claims. Verse 28 inextricably connects the church's life with the crucifixion of Jesus. The elders are urged to conform to Paul's "example," bearing in mind that Paul's example is one of trial and uncertainty. They are to guard against those who would harm the church, but also against themselves as potential misleaders of the flock.

Finally, however, the speech has as its subject not the mission of Paul or the future of the church, but God. References to God, Jesus Christ, and the Spirit spill over one another here, ranging from the testimony of the Spirit to spoken words of Jesus to the grace of God. If Paul is an example, he is an example of God's action. Similarly, if the church remains faithful, it will be because of God's own care.

Final Steps Toward Jerusalem (21:1-17)

This account of a journey completes the cycle of travelogue and scene that opened in 20:1 (see above on 20:1-16). Here again Luke moves from a travel account (21:1-7), to a scene involving a gathering of believers (vv. 8-14), and then concludes with another travel account (vv. 15-17). Although the NRSV places v. 17 with the following scene in which Paul visits James, it belongs with vv. 15-16 as part of the final movement toward and into Jerusalem (as in the REB). The time reference at the beginning of v. 18 marks a new scene, and the references to Jerusalem in v. 15 and v. 17 belong together.

As in the earlier travel accounts in this section, Luke provides the itinerary in considerable detail. In the first seven verses alone, he refers to Cos, Rhodes, Patara, Phoenicia, Cyprus, Syria, Tyre, and Ptolemais—not to mention Jerusalem. Even the unloading of cargo merits inclusion (v. 3), as does the moment when Paul and his colleagues board ship and their fellow-disciples go home (v. 6). Even if Luke is making use of a written itinerary, as some scholars argue (e.g., Haenchen 1971, 600; Barrett 1998, 986), it would have been quite simple to consolidate the details into a far briefer account, suggesting that they bear some significance. Here, as in 20:1-16, that significance may lie in the consolidation of believers in a number of locations.

Another notable literary feature of this passage is that it recalls a number of persons and events from the early chapters of Acts that have their setting in Jerusalem. Philip reappears, who first enters the story as one of those chosen for work among the widows in Jerusalem (6:1-6). His prophesying daughters recall the words of Joel in Peter's Pentecost sermon (2:17). Agabus announces that Paul will be bound, just as he set out in 9:2 to bind believers and take them to Jerusalem. Paul declares that he is prepared to die in Jerusalem "for the name of the Lord Jesus," as earlier the apostles rejoiced to suffer in Jerusalem "for the name of the Lord Jesus" (5:41).

◊ ◊ ◊ ◊

Travel (21:1-7)

The first verses transport Paul and his companions from Miletus to the coastal city of Tyre. Although Luke has not previously mentioned Tyre in Acts, there are disciples in the city, and the travelers locate them. The text offers no information concerning these disciples, except for the puzzling statement that "through the Spirit" they told Paul not to go to Jerusalem. Since Paul initially decided to go to Jerusalem through the Spirit's guidance (19:21; see also 20:22-23), an apparent contradiction emerges. Varying interpretations emerge also, with some scholars concluding that the Spirit tells these believers what lies ahead, from which they draw their own conclusion that Paul should not go (Bruce 1990, 439). Others see in this conflict the necessity of discerning among messages from the Spirit (Tannehill 1990, 262-67). Luke does not treat it as a conflict, and it may be that the disciples' pleas largely underscore the danger and the fact that Paul continues undeterred.

That this discrepancy causes no tension between the two groups becomes clear in v. 5. As Paul and his colleagues leave the city, the believers of Tyre accompany them. Luke specifies that the "women and children" (NRSV: wives and children) go also. Elsewhere Luke refers to "men and women" among believers (e.g., 8:3, 12; 9:2; 22:4), and this reference to women and children breaks that pattern (Seim 1994, 21). The implication is not that only men are present elsewhere in the story, but that the seriousness of the occasion requires reference to the entire company. Similarly, the reference to prayer underscores the importance of the occasion. Luke early reckons prayer among the characteristics of the church's life (e.g., 1:14; 2:42), and he often makes specific reference to prayer at significant points of danger or decision (4:24-31; 13:3; 20:36).

Prophecy in Caesarea (21:8-14)

In Caesarea Luke reintroduces Philip, whom he describes as "the evangelist, one of the seven." Only here does Luke use the noun "evangelist," although the related verb describes Philip's activity (8:12, 35, 40) and that of other witnesses, including Paul (5:42; 11:20; 13:32; 16:10; 17:18). His work in Samaria concludes with the conversion of the Ethiopian eunuch, following which Philip finds himself in Azotus and then preaches his way to Caesarea (8:40). That he is "one of the seven" distinguishes him from the apostle Philip (1:13) and reminds readers of his commission to assist in distribution of food among the widows in Jerusalem (6:1-6). Although the narrative never depicts the seven in that activity, here Luke shows Philip engaging in a related work of hospitality. Moreover, Philip receives into his home the man whose former labor as persecutor had forced Philip from Jerusalem and into Samaria (8:1-5).

In Acts, most such references to the hospitality extended to Christian travelers refer only to an individual and possibly that individual's household (e.g., Cornelius, the mother of John

Mark, Lydia, the Philippian jailer, Mnason), but Luke comments that Philip had "four virgin daughters who prophesy" (AT). Given the paucity of instances in which other household members are mentioned, this one has intrigued interpreters at least since Eusebius, who reports that Papias had visited with the daughters in Hierapolis (*Church History* 3.31). The NRSV translates *parthenos* as "unmarried" rather than "virgin," but it is important to notice the connection to Mary, who is also called *parthenos* (Luke 1:26). It is unclear whether Luke wishes to indicate simply that they are unmarried or whether he assumes a connection between sexual abstinence and prophecy. The fact that a present participle depicts their prophetic activity connotes its ongoing character.

Because it is Agabus whose words Luke includes and the daughters themselves do not speak, it might be argued that Luke elevates this male prophet over the four women (O'Day 1998, 397). Agabus arrives from Judea, however, which implies that he has an awareness of the situation in Jerusalem not available to them (Reimer 1995, 249). Prophetic groups and individuals are not competing for honors in this scene. Indeed, the identification of Philip as an evangelist and his daughters as prophets conveys the strength of the community at Caesarea (Seim 1994, 183); the Spirit is not narrow in the extent of its gifts.

Apart from the geographical association of Agabus with Judea, Luke provides no introduction of him and no notice about his greeting of believers in Caesarea or his warm reception there (cf. 21:17). With an immediacy that suggests the urgency of his oracle, he goes to the gathering of believers and begins. As in his earlier appearance, Agabus brings a specific oracle (11:27-28), but here it is one he performs as well as speaks. Taking Paul's belt, Agabus ties his own feet and hands in an acted oracle reminiscent of those of Old Testament prophets (1 Kgs 11:29-31; Isa 8:1-4; 20:2-4; Jer 19:1-13; 27:2-13; Ezek 4:1-8). Paul's earlier description of himself as "bound in the Spirit" (NRSV: captive to the Spirit, 20:22) here echoes ominously.

Agabus claims that Jerusalem Jews will bind Paul and "hand him over to the Gentiles." The narrative that develops in

Jerusalem does not precisely conform to this statement, since Roman agents arrest Paul (21:33) and keep him in custody. Yet they do so because of a riot by Jews who are incensed by what they believe to be Paul's actions. And, as Luke has drawn the larger picture, frequently Jews are the ones who provoke Gentile action against Paul (e.g., 14:2; 17:5, 13; 18:12). The wording of the oracle also parallels that regarding Jesus in Luke 24:7 and what Paul will say of himself in 28:17.

Verses 12-13 constitute the climactic point of this entire section (20:1–21:17). First, the sense of foreboding that surrounds Paul's journey to Jerusalem takes its strongest form yet. In Miletus, the elders wept and embraced Paul (20:37); in Tyre, disciples who had presumably not known him before that encounter escorted him to his ship and prayed with him, having already urged him not to go to Jerusalem (21:4-6). Here, even the narrator joins the foreboding, as "we and the people" together try to stop Paul from completing the trip. Paul responds to the community's fears with his own fierce emotions, reflecting once again the depth of affection among believers.

Finally, Paul restates his determination and in the strongest terms yet: he is willing both "to be bound" (see 20:22) and "even to die in Jerusalem for the name of the Lord Jesus." The attempt to stop Paul only underscores the determination and the seriousness of the journey. The phrase "the name of the Lord Jesus" recalls scenes in Jerusalem, where preaching and healing occurred in Jesus' name (see 2:21, 38; 3:6, 16; 4:7). It also recalls the apostles in Jerusalem, who rejoiced when they suffered for Jesus' name (5:41) and especially the declaration of the Risen Lord that Paul would suffer on behalf of the name (9:16). In the face of this resolve, both the narrator and the believers acknowledge the primacy of God's will, echoing Jesus' words on the Mount of Olives (see Luke 22:42).

Travel (21:15-17)

A final brief report takes Paul and his companions the relatively short distance from Caesarea to Jerusalem. Joined now by believers from Caesarea, they arrive at the house of an otherwise unknown Mnason, whom Luke describes as a native of Cyprus and "an early disciple." Verse 17 characterizes the reception in Jerusalem as warm, bringing to an end this lengthy journey contemplated in 19:21 and begun in 20:1.

◊ ◊ ◊ ◊

The interspersing of travel and scenes of community life in 20:1–21:17 serves to draw remarkably dispersed groups of believers together in a single narrative, believers who could not gather as did Christians in Jerusalem but who nevertheless are connected by the gospel's activity among them (see above on 20:1-16). The painful emotional quality of this scene enhances the picture of the unity of this otherwise diverse group. In addition to the strengthening of these communities achieved by the very fact of Paul's journey, Luke depicts these small gatherings as themselves venues of the operation of the Spirit. Paul does not bring Spirit-filled speech to Tyre; instead, disciples with whom he has previously had no contact speak to him through the Spirit (21:4). In Caesarea, he finds both evangelism (Philip) and prophecy (Philip's daughters as well as Agabus). Everywhere, he finds hospitality. These communities are strengthened by the visit, but they are themselves the recipients of God's gifts and claims. Having received, they also share.

The intense emotional connection that comes to expression in this scene contrasts strikingly with developments that will quickly follow in Jerusalem. Although received warmly and greeted by James, Paul will soon find himself cut off from believers. In the chapters that follow, Paul deals with Jewish leaders, Roman officials, and a host of other characters in near isolation from this strong community of believers. That he is not entirely alone, however, is attested by nothing less than words from the Lord (23:11).

The journey of Paul to Jerusalem parallels that of Jesus to Jerusalem at a number of points, several of which occur in this passage. Like Jesus, Paul is to be bound by Jews and handed over to Gentiles (21:11; Luke 24:7). The will of God is involved in both cases (21:14; Luke 22:42). The sheer repetition of the intent to go to Jerusalem also reinforces the parallels. Yet describing Paul as the "hero" of this part of Acts severely misconstrues Luke's story, in which Paul is bound by the Spirit long before he is bound by chains. He is prepared to die, not to preserve his own honor or reputation, but for "the name of the Lord Jesus."

THE PERSECUTED AND VINDICATED PROCLAIMER (21:18–26:32)

At 19:21, through the Spirit's guidance, Paul declares that he will travel to Jerusalem and then to Rome. This major section of Acts begins with Paul's arrival in Jerusalem and ends with the authoritative decision to send him to Rome (26:32). Resistance to Paul's proclamation reaches its pinnacle in these chapters, where only the confinement of Roman custody prevents the completion of plots to kill him. The persecution of Paul finds him isolated, not only by virtue of his confinement, but also by the unexplained absence of other believers following his arrest. If resistance to Paul comes to a head in these chapters, so does his vindication and that of the gospel he proclaims; indeed, the character Paul and his gospel can scarcely be distinguished from one another. The speeches of chapters 22 and 24 prepare for the climactic speech of chapter 26 and the final pronouncement of Paul's innocence (26:31-32). Here second half of Acts culminates in the defense, not of Paul alone but of the divine plan that has both sent the Messiah Jesus as the fulfillment of Israel's hope and extended that hope to include the Gentiles.

Paul in Peril (21:18-36)

Two distinct scenes comprise this unit. In the first, Paul and his companions meet with James and the Jerusalem elders; the accusations against Paul are reported and a response determined (vv. 18-26). In the second, Paul is seized by rioters at the temple and finds himself in Roman custody (vv. 27-36). Although distinctive in place and personnel (apart from Paul), the charges against Paul hold the two scenes together. In addition, construing the two scenes as one unit provides a way to address some of the difficult questions regarding vv. 18-26 (see below).

◊ ◊ ◊ ◊

Paul Accused (21:18-26)

Initially well received in Jerusalem (v. 17), Paul and his companions quickly seek out James and the elders (v. 18, which is also the final appearance of "we" until 27:1). The scene generally resembles the arrival of Paul and Barnabas in Jerusalem in chapter 15, where they are welcomed and report on their labor (15:4). Paul greets James and the elders, although no reciprocal greeting is mentioned, and then relates "one by one the things that God had done among the Gentiles through his ministry." This summary of Paul's report resembles earlier such reports (see 14:28; 15:3, 12). As in those earlier reports, the work is attributed to God rather than to Paul or any other human agent. And the work is described as taking place "among the Gentiles." That phrase was more understandable earlier, where the preceding episodes had focused precisely on Gentile believers. Here, however, in the wake of Paul's persistent witness in synagogues (e.g., 17:1-4, 11-12, 17; 18:4) and several stories that prominently feature Jews who share in Christian faith (18:2, 24; 19:1; 21:8-10), depicting the mission as "among the Gentiles" is striking.

Luke reports that Paul visits James in the presence of "all the elders," but the voice that addresses Paul in v. 20 is that of an unidentified plural, with James not distinguished from the remainder of the group. Although some commentators see this as the third in a series of conflicts about the inclusion of Gentiles (along with 11:1-18; 15:1-35), no one present lodges a question about Paul's behavior (cf. 11:3), and no one makes a demand that he alter his practice or instruction (cf. 15:1, 5). Instead, the group voice delivers a brief speech consisting of three parts: a problem in the perception of Paul by Jewish Christians (vv. 20-21), a proposal that Paul should undertake to correct the problem (vv. 22-24), and a restatement of the earlier decision about requirements for Gentile believers (v. 25).

The speech forcefully articulates the serious challenge Paul faces in Jerusalem. There are "many thousands" of Jewish Christians who are zealous for the law (see 2 Macc 4:2; Gal 1:14), and they have been told that Paul teaches "all" Diaspora Jews not to follow the law. By describing the audience as it does, the speech predicts a hostile reception in Jerusalem, even among disciples. The report also reinforces the charge that Paul teaches Jews "to forsake Moses" by adding the phrases "not to circumcise their children or observe the customs." Although it is often claimed that Acts makes quite clear that the charge is false (Johnson 1992, 375; Fitzmyer 1998, 693), the narrative is tantalizingly silent on these points. It is true that Luke does not show Paul ever offering any such instruction, yet it is also true that reports of Paul's preaching in Acts say nothing about the continuing observance of the law. Paul does circumcise Timothy, but the narrator explicitly notes that he does it on account of the Jews (16:3) and does not connect the action with respect for the law. The vow Paul undertakes at Cenchreae shows his general faithfulness to Judaism, or at least to this particular vow (18:18). Turning to the Pauline letters to solve this question only complicates matters, since the comments about the law contained therein overwhelmingly pertain to the question of whether Gentile believers must conform to Jewish law. What is clear is that the situation is exceedingly dangerous if even Jewish believers have heard disturbing reports about Paul and must be satisfied (v. 20). The echoes of earlier charges against Stephen (6:11-14) underscore the ominous tone.

The response that the speech proposes is a rite of purification. Paul is to join with four men who are already under a vow, and he is to pay for the required shaving of their heads as a sign that the charges are false. Despite numerous attempts to connect this proposal to Nazirite vows or other acts of purification described in the Old Testament (Num 6:1-21; 8:21; 19:12; 31:19; 1 Chr

15:12, 14; 2 Chr 29:16; and see Josephus, *Ant.* 4.72-73; 19.294), the situation is quite unclear except that the speech anticipates a public enactment of Paul's respect for the law of Moses. The stipulation that Paul would pay the expenses for the shaving of the heads would itself be generous indication of his piety.

The last section of the speech returns to the Gentiles, who have been mentioned already in v. 19 and v. 21, and repeats once more the decree of 15:20-29. Since Paul was present at the Jerusalem Council, this element of the speech comes as a surprise and accounting for it is difficult. Some scholars see in its inclusion evidence that Paul actually had not been present at the Council (Achtemeier 1987, 14-15, 32-33); others see it as reflecting growing distrust of Paul's endeavors, especially if the emphatic "we" of v. 25 excludes Paul (Spencer 1997, 199-200). Perhaps its function is less ominous; having just addressed the situation of Jewish believers, the elders reinforce the agreed-upon understanding regarding Gentile believers. They must abstain from those practices that associate them in any way with idolatry. Although Paul makes no comment in response to the speech, with the action of v. 26 he conforms to the proposal of vv. 22-24, thereby setting the stage for the riot and seizure of Paul that follows (vv. 27-36).

This passage is the final reference to James or the Jerusalem church in the entire book of Acts; that fact, coupled with the many gaps within this scene, has produced a variety of interpretations, ranging from James defending Paul (Jervell 1972, 185-207) to James colluding in a plot against Paul (Mattill 1970, 115-16). Yet the scene shows no conflict between Paul and Jewish believers, and James's role is quite minimal. He may serve here less as the leader of the Jerusalem church than as a connection back to the Jerusalem council and even to the gathered believers in the earliest days in Jerusalem (1:13-14).

Paul Seized (21:27-36)

Conflict erupts, and when it does it comes not from Jewish believers but from "Jews from Asia," a place where Paul had both left the synagogue and taken others with him (19:9); it was also in Ephesus of Asia that Jewish exorcists found themselves powerless and humiliated (19:13-20). Seizing Paul and calling for help, the Asian Jews declare that Paul is teaching "everyone everywhere" against "the people and the law and this place" (AT). Both the accusation against Stephen and the previously reported accusation against Paul refer to the place and the law, and the charge against Jesus in Luke's Gospel is that he is leading the nation astray (Luke 23:2). Nowhere else, however, is someone said to teach against the people (*laos*), which may have to do with a perceived undermining of the boundaries of Israel through the Gentile mission.

The specific charge that follows brings together all three aspects of the accusation against Paul (people, law, and place). Although Gentiles could enter into the temple's Court of the Gentiles, a Gentile who went beyond that outer court was liable to death (Josephus, *J.W.* 5.193-94; 6.124-25; *Ant.* 15.417; Philo, *Embassy* 212). Warning inscriptions at the temple itself served as an inescapable reminder, if such a reminder was needed (*OGIS* 598; also in Barrett 1987, 53; Segal 1989). Trophimus, a Gentile from Ephesus, had been spotted in Jerusalem with Paul, leading to this dire accusation (20:4; see also 2 Tim 4:20).

As at Ephesus, where charges of undermining the *polis* and its god sparked a riot, so also in Jerusalem. The description of the riot that follows is vivid and frightening. Given reports in Josephus about the volatility of crowds in Jerusalem, especially at festival times (see 20:16), the portrait Luke renders has considerable verisimilitude (Josephus, *J.W.* 1.88-89; 2.8-13, 42-48, 169-74, 223-27). The specifics Luke provides are revealing. Verse 30 claims that "all the city" is around and the "people" rush together, and v. 31 asserts that "all Jerusalem" is in uproar over Paul. In addition to the hyperbole employed here, the terms "people" (*laos*) and "Jerusalem" signify more than numerical strength alone; this scene constitutes rejection of Paul by Israel itself.

The chaos recalls the riot of Ephesus (Fitzmyer 1998, 696-97), but it also reverses the early scenes in Jerusalem, particularly the

Pentecost account. There crowds came together, both residents of Jerusalem and Diaspora Jews, to understand a dramatic event (2:5-6; 3:11). They stayed to listen to Peter, and many believed. Here again both Jerusalem residents and Diaspora Jews come together, but there is no listening. Instead, the temple doors are shut to keep Paul out (v. 30), and the people attempt to kill him (see 22:22; 28:19; Luke 23:18; John 19:15; *Mart. Pol.* 3.2; 9.2).

Only the intervention of the tribune prevents Paul's death. The Fortress Antonia adjacent to the temple precinct allows the tribune, later identified as Claudias Lysias (23:26), to be informed and to intercede almost immediately (Josephus, *J.W.* 5.238-47). Perhaps because the Romans perceived him to be a threat to public order, Paul is bound with chains (see 12:6). Even that does not quell the riot, since the tribune's demand for an explanation prompts yet another uproar. The drama continues with soldiers carrying Paul away to keep the crowd from destroying him.

As the scene closes, three "characters" are in view: the mob of Jews who demand Paul's death, the Roman representative Claudius Lysias together with his soldiers, and Paul himself. Unlike the Ephesus scene, where other believers prevent Paul from going into the theater and concerned local officials warn him away, here Paul has no allies. Neither James nor any elder stands by. Not even the four men whose vow he had joined appear to be on the scene.

◊ ◊ ◊ ◊

Studies of Acts attuned to questions of ecclesiology, and particularly questions of the human leadership of the church, often see in this passage further evidence of the importance of the Jerusalem community and specifically of James as its undisputed leader (e.g., Bruce 1990, 444; Conzelmann 1987, 180). The historical role of James in the Jerusalem church may surface here, yet James's name appears in the passage once, he speaks only as one among the elders, and no decision is attributed to him. Concern with who rules the church seems out of place at this point in the narrative; instead, the reference to James connects this passage with the Council in chapter 15 and with the gathering of Jesus' disciples and family in 1:14. All of these are critical moments in which the believing community is threatened, whether by Jesus' absence, internal conflict, or external resistance.

Here the threat comes from those Jews who have been told that Paul teaches against the people, the law, and the temple. Luke portrays the threat in sharp terms in the riot scene itself, but he has carefully anticipated it with the solemn warning of James and the elders. In addition, the highly emotional tone of 20:1–21:17, in which believers all across the Mediterranean world are knit together by Paul's visit and their fears for him, sharpens the sense of conflict that erupts almost as soon as Paul arrives in Jerusalem.

The ambiguity of Jerusalem in Luke–Acts comes to a crisis point in this story and the events that follow. Luke begins his two-volume work with the priest Zechariah in the temple (Luke 1:5-23), and Luke shows the infant Jesus welcomed into the temple in his parents' arms (2:22-36; see also 2:41-51). Similarly, Acts opens with believers daily going to the temple (Acts 2:46) and Peter and John healing in its vicinity (3:1-10). Yet temple authorities conspire against Jesus (Luke 22:2) and endeavor to silence the apostles (Acts 4:1; 5:17). Here, the temple doors shut, not only protecting the precinct against rioters, but excluding Paul and his witness.

Apart from his initial greeting of James and the elders and his report about God's actions among the Gentiles, Paul utters not a single word in these two scenes. His silence in the face of the accusations against him serves to sharpen the question about his loyalty to people, law, and place—questions he will begin to address in the speech that follows.

Defense Before a Jerusalem Crowd (21:37–22:29)

This long passage comprises three distinct sections. The first (21:37-40) and last (22:22-29) are transitional narratives framing the defense speech (22:1-21). Following a conventional introduction and response in vv. 1-2, the body of the speech consists of four parts: (1) Paul's credentials as a zealous Jew (vv. 3-5), (2) Jesus' appearance to Paul on the Damascus road (vv. 6-11), (3) Ananias as healer and commissioner (vv. 12-16), and (4) Paul's vision in the temple (vv. 17-21). Couched in language designed to appeal to a Jewish audience, the speech moves from matters with which the narrative audience would agree (strict observance of the law and zeal for God) to matters that would provoke sharp disagreement (the call to the Gentiles), making its general movement similar to that in Stephen's speech (7:2-53) and Paul's speech at the Areopagus (17:22-31).

Because Luke has already narrated Paul's conversion in chapter 9 and will return to it again in the defense speech of chapter 26, numerous questions arise about the complicated set of similarities and differences among the three accounts. This particular account is distinctive in that it omits Ananias's vision and expands his words to Paul (cf. 9:10-19). In addition, only this account includes Paul's vision in the Jerusalem temple. Attempts to derive the three accounts from different sources are not persuasive; the differences largely reflect the changes in narrative setting (for details, see below). Paul is now addressing a Jewish audience that has been led to believe he teaches against people, law, and temple (21:28), and the speech responds to that misinformed view of him. (On the comparison of Luke's reports with the comments in Paul's letters, see above on 9:1-30.)

Not a Revolutionary from Egypt but a Citizen of Tarsus (21:37-40)

This transitional narrative involves the Roman tribune in securing for Paul the possibility of addressing the crowd. The various actions, including seeking the tribune's permission to speak with him, seeking again his permission to address the people, motioning for silence, and identifying Paul's language, heighten the drama of the occasion. Along the way, the exchange between the tribune and Paul focuses on Paul's identity, an issue that recurs in the speech and again in the exchange between Paul and the tribune following the speech. The confusion over Paul's identity emerges when his request to speak prompts the tribune to ask two questions, whether Paul knows Greek and whether he is a notorious Egyptian. The first may imply an insult, since Greek was the *lingua franca* of the age. The second question certainly implies an insult since there was great condescension and suspicion toward Egyptians (Strabo, *Geography* 17.1.12; Philo, *Dreams* 1.240; 2.255; *Alleg. Interp.* 2.84; 3.13, 37-38, 81, 87; Lentz 1993, 29-30). Regarding this particular incident, Josephus reports on an Egyptian who proposed to take control of Jerusalem away from the Romans, as well as on the swift Roman response (Josephus, *J.W.* 2.261-63; *Ant.* 20.169-72). Not surprisingly, then, the tribune's second question reveals what he suspects—that Paul is a threat to public order. Paul responds by identifying himself first and emphatically as a Jew, thereby sounding a main theme of the speech itself (see also 22:33). Only then does he give his place of origin as the important city of Tarsus, a city associated with learning, and one identifying Paul as the polar opposite of an uneducated Egyptian revolutionary (Strabo, *Geography* 14.5.12-15; Lentz 1993, 30-32).

"You Will Be His Witness" (22:1-21)

The Greek that catches the attention of the tribune yields to "the Hebrew language," probably to be understood as Aramaic, when Paul addresses his audience. Here the assertion "I am a Jew" works itself out before a Jewish audience, beginning with the respectful direct address employed also by Stephen (7:2), "Brothers and fathers."

"I Am a Jewish Man" (22:3-5): The speech begins with another emphatic assertion of Paul's identity (cf. 21:39): "I am a Jewish man" (AT) followed by a conventional explanation of Paul's credentials. He was "born in Tarsus in Cilicia, but brought up in this city at the feet of Gamaliel, educated strictly according to our ancestral law" (van Unnik 1973b; Du Toit 2000). The final statement in v. 3 moves to the present tense, "being zealous for God, just as all of you are today." Like those described in 21:20, Paul also is zealous, but his zeal is "for God" by contrast with those who are zealous for the law. Here the goal of this first section comes into view: Paul wants to identify himself as a good and loyal Jew, in every way like his audience.

When Paul narrates his persecution of believers in vv. 4-5, he builds on this identification by offering his activity as an example of the zeal described in v. 3. The Greek syntax itself confirms this observation, for v. 4 begins with a relative pronoun linking it to the antecedent "I" in v. 3: "I am a Jew . . . who persecuted." The details in vv. 4-5 largely repeat Acts 8:3 and 9:1-2, but the differences are revealing. Here Paul claims that he persecuted "to the point of death," thereby increasing the ominous character of his activity. In v. 5 Paul invokes the high priest and "the whole council of elders" to witness to his veracity, even though the personnel would scarcely have remained the same over the intervening years (Gaventa 1986a, 69-70).

"I Am Jesus of Nazareth" (22:6-11): The second part of the speech takes up the event that reversed Paul's attitude to the "Way." This part closely follows 9:3-9, but again there are revealing differences of detail. Perhaps the most striking differences pertain to the language of light. Verse 6 specifies that the light appeared "about noon," implying its unusual brilliance. Luke also notes that it was a "great" light, and later explains that Paul could not see "because of the brightness of that light" (v. 11). This emphasis underscores the reality and significance of Paul's experience. Paul also says that his companions saw the light (v. 9), thus introducing a conflict with 9:7:

The men who were traveling with him stood speechless because they heard the voice but saw no one. (9:7)

"Now those who were with me saw the light but did not hear the voice of the one who was speaking to me." (22:9)

Close attention to the role of each statement within its narrative context minimizes the apparent difficulties. Verse 22:9 appears at a different point within the recollection than does 9:7. In the first account of Paul's conversion, the companions' response *follows* the dialogue between Jesus and Paul. Their response contrasts with Paul's in that they do not perceive what has happened. The second account, on the other hand, inserts the response of the companions *within* the dialogue of Jesus and Paul. Placed in the middle of the dialogue, the comment once again calls attention to the light and heightens the drama of the encounter by emphasizing that only Paul heard the voice. Although the encounter had a character that all could see, only Paul heard what was said, particularly the words that point forward to his commission. This explanation of the function of 22:9 in its context does not eliminate the contradictions between 22:9 and 9:7, but it suggests, instead, that Luke has two somewhat different points to make with the same story; the minor contradictions that arise are a result of those different points.

This second account of Paul's encounter with Jesus also presents a slightly altered understanding of Paul's response to the event. Here Paul continues as an active participant, never quite as incapacitated as 9:8-9 would suggest. In Acts 9, Paul's only words at the encounter are, "Who are you, Lord?" Here he manages to add, "What am I to do, Lord?" Although in v. 11 Paul concedes that he could not see and was led by the hand, he still says, "I went into Damascus" (obscured in the NRSV). The first account, on the other hand, specifies that Paul's companions took him by the hand and led him into Damascus (9:8). Acts 22 also makes no reference to a period of fasting, so that the scene ends with Paul still waiting for the fulfillment of Jesus' words in v. 10.

One further feature of this passage calls for attention. Jesus' words in 22:8 repeat those in 9:5 almost exactly, with the addition of "the Nazarene" (NRSV: of Nazareth) as the only exception, a term Luke employs in Jewish settings (Luke 18:37; Acts 2:22; 3:6; 4:10; 6:14; 24:5; 26:9). Its appearance here further indicates that this account serves the defense of Paul in Jerusalem (Gaventa 1986a, 71-72).

To See the Righteous One (22:12-16): The commission comes into prominence in the third section of Paul's speech, the visit of Ananias (vv. 12-16). Because there is no description of Ananias's vision or Ananias's objections regarding Paul (as in 9:10-16), some scholars contend that Paul did not know of Ananias's experience or that Luke is employing a different source here, but the variation probably derives from the narrative context. Acts 9 emphasizes the believers' resistance to Paul, an issue that is absent in the second account. Acts 22 does not explicitly identify Ananias as a believer, in contrast to the term "disciple" in 9:10. Instead he is "a man pious with respect to the law, as witnessed by all the Jewish inhabitants" (AT). The adjective "pious" also identifies Simeon (Luke 2:25), the Jews present at Pentecost (Acts 2:5), and those who mourned the death of Stephen (Acts 8:2). His piety is "according to the law," further enhancing his credibility with the audience. The final element in Ananias's description also appeals to that credibility: "all the Jews" in Damascus attest to Ananias's faithfulness.

Apart from the greeting, "Brother Saul," Ananias's words to Paul in Acts 22 bear little resemblance to his words in chapter 9. In 9:17, Ananias announces that he has been sent by the Lord so that Paul might receive both his sight and the Spirit; here, by contrast, the emphasis falls on Paul's calling, particularly on its origin in the "God of our ancestors" (see, e.g., Gen 43:23; 46:1; Exod 3:13; Deut 1:11; 1 Chr 5:25; 12:17). It is the God of Israel who chose Paul, and Ananias amplifies that choice: "to know his will, to see "the Righteous One" and to hear his own voice." Knowing God's "will" (*thelēma*) replays the prominent Lukan concern with the plan or will of God (Schubert 1968a, 14). Employing the phrase "the Righteous One" both delays the introduction of Jesus' name in this volatile context and draws on a familiar title for David's offspring (Jer 23:5-6; 33:15). Ananias's statement reaches its main point with the claim that God chose Paul as a "witness for him to all persons of the things you have seen and heard" (AT). The term "witness" links Paul with the mission given to the apostles in 1:8 and with their activity throughout Acts (e.g., 1:22; 2:32; 3:15; 5:32; 10:39; 13:31). Identifying Paul as a witness to "all persons" implicitly includes Gentiles, but it does not yet name them explicitly. In v. 16 the role of Ananias comes to an end as he tells Paul to rise, be baptized, and wash away his sins. This part of the speech once again puts Paul's experience in language designed for a Jewish audience. Paul first learned that he was to be a witness from Ananias, a pious Jew acceptable to the whole Jewish community. Ananias described the one who called Paul as the God of Israel, never mentioning the name of Jesus. In other words, everything in this section seeks to maintain the identification between Paul and his hearers that was established as early as v. 3 (Gaventa 1986a, 73-74).

To the Gentiles (22:17-21): The final part of the speech continues to affirm Paul's loyalty to Judaism, but it also presents the occasion for the sharp rejection of Paul by his audience. Perhaps because Paul's vision in the temple is unique to this account, commentators sometimes treat it as an appendix to the conversion event, something not integral to the story itself; however, the connections between vv. 17-21 and the rest of Paul's speech are such that the temple scene is not only a part of the speech, but its climax. The final section in Paul's "call" takes place in Jerusalem, where he began his persecution (vv. 4-5), and where he now defends himself. Paul is not only in Jerusalem when he has his vision: he is in the temple praying, further reinforcing his identification as a faithful Jew.

What follows in the dialogue of vv. 18-21 is, at first glance, perplexing. Paul hears the command: "Hurry and get out of Jerusalem quickly, because they will not accept your testimony about me." For the first time in the speech, tension between Paul's message and the Jews enters. Until this point, the speech implies their agreement. Paul's response neither consents to the order to flee nor refuses that order. Paul appeals to his past and to the Jewish understanding of that past by rehearsing his activity as a persecutor. In this way, Paul argues that Jews know what he once did against the church; the implied connection is that they will accept his witness because they know his past (Gaventa 1986a, 75-77).

Verse 21 restates the call: "Go, for I will send you far away to the Gentiles." Here the specific nature of Paul's witness comes to expression for the first time. Not surprisingly, here also the speech breaks off or, rather, is interrupted by the audience.

A Roman Citizen by Birth (22:22-29)

How little Paul's defense has persuaded the crowd becomes clear in vv. 22-23. Verse 22 picks up the "Away with him!" that preceded the speech (21:36) and makes the violent intent of that cry explicit: "Away with such a fellow from the earth! For he should not be allowed to live." The actions of v. 23 reinforce the cries, as the mob prepares for violence.

By contrast with the crowd, which understands the speech but rejects it, the tribune still does not understand what has brought about the uproar. While the delegated centurion prepares to have an explanation beaten out of Paul, as was common practice, Paul introduces yet another category of identification. His appeal to Jewish birth and loyalty have failed with Jews and will be of no help at all with Roman soldiers (Spencer 1997, 211), and so Paul again introduces his Roman citizenship (see 16:37-38), however indirectly. Since there has been no legal proceeding against Paul, as a citizen he cannot be beaten (Livy, *History* 10.9.3-6; Cicero, *Against Verres* 2.5.66). The brief exchange with the tribune confirms that Paul's citizenship derives from birth, making his claim superior to that of the tribune himself. The tribune still has no answer about the reason for the crowd's violence against Paul, but this newly revealed element in Paul's identity provokes fear (as in 16:38-39; see Rapske 1994b, 139-45).

◊ ◊ ◊ ◊

In one sense this narrative turns on the question of Paul's identity. For the tribune and his colleagues, the fear that Paul is an Egyptian revolutionary yields to knowledge that he is a Jew from Tarsus. And that knowledge in turn yields to the awareness (and new fear) that he is a Roman citizen. For the crowds that demand Paul's death both before and after his speech, Paul is a destroyer of the people, law, and temple. Paul identifies himself as a loyal Jew, who received a calling from the risen Messiah to be a witness to the Gentiles.

Yet the speech shows that the question of identifying Paul does not fall within the purview of the Romans or of the crowd, not even within the purview of Paul himself. The speech begins with Paul identifying himself as God's zealot, one who made his own decisions about the "Way" and acted upon them. The vision of the risen Lord, however, took that question of identity out of Paul's hands. He is now to be a "witness to all the world" (v. 15). If Paul's response to the temple vision constitutes a mild resistance to the Lord's will (v. 19; see also Exod 3:11; Jer 1:6), the prerogative of God to send Paul on his way reasserts itself clearly in v. 21.

Paul's defense, then, shifts the grounds of the argument. He has been accused of teaching against the people, the law, and the temple. His speech affirms his strong bond with the people, invoking his birth (v. 3), his alignment with the leaders in Jerusalem (v. 4), and even his initial agreement with their assessment of the Way (vv. 4-5). It also reflects his strict education regarding the law (v. 3) and places him in the temple in prayer (v. 17). Yet the movement of the defense from Paul's initiative to that of the Lord shows that Paul does not so much defend himself as proclaim God's actions.

The early speeches in Jerusalem provoked the demand that the apostles cease preaching in the name of Jesus (4:16-18; 5:40). Here it is not Jesus who produces the outrage, since references to him appear early in the speech, and the audience continues to listen. Instead, murderous rage follows upon Paul's claim that his own prophetic vocation is to the Gentiles (Porter 1999, 154). The fact that that vocation is first announced explicitly in the temple only exacerbates the reaction. Luke has announced the universal scope of the gospel since the infancy narratives, but it continues to prompt outrage.

From the Crowd to the Council (22:30–23:11)

Having learned from Paul a number of things about his identity, but having failed to ascertain with any specificity the accusations made against him, the tribune now takes Paul to the official body that ought to be able to clarify the charges. Not only are these the leaders of the Jewish people, but Paul has said that they can testify on his behalf (22:5). What follows is the final appearance of Paul in Jerusalem, which ends not with a list of charges nor with an acquittal, but with a brawl among religious leaders.

The action of the tribune in 22:30 introduces the scene, and the vision in 23:11 marks the end of Paul's witness in Jerusalem. Two remarks by Paul introduce the two brief scenes before the council. First, Paul's declaration of his own good conscience (23:1) provokes a sharp exchange with the high priest Ananias (23:2-5). Second, Paul's declaration of his Pharisaic convictions about the resurrection (23:6) provokes a sharp exchange between Pharisees and Sadducees, which forces the tribune to deliver Paul from yet another mob (23:7-10).

◊ ◊ ◊ ◊

Despite his efforts, the tribune still has not determined what prompted the outrage against Paul in the temple precincts, and therefore he orders "the chief priests and the entire council to meet" (22:30). Whether a Roman tribune actually had the authority to convene the council has been the subject of debate, but the evidence on which to base a conclusion is slender (Josephus, *Ant.* 20.202; Tajra 1989, 91; Fitzmyer 1998, 716). However realistic or unrealistic, Luke's narration places Paul before two authorities, both the acknowledged leaders of the Jewish people and the Roman officials who convene them. Here Paul might reasonably anticipate a fair hearing.

Paul Before the Council (23:1-5)

Paul begins to speak without invitation or question from the council, which again strains verisimilitude. The fact that he opens with "Brothers," rather than "Brothers and fathers" as in 22:1, could suggest a lack of respect for this authoritative group, but the statement that follows is straightforward; Paul has lived "with a clear conscience before God." That statement serves less as a proper introduction to a speech than as a synopsis of the speech in chapter 22. It was "before God" that Paul lived prior to the revelation of Jesus Christ, even as he was involved in the persecution of believers; and it is "before God" that he now witnesses in Jerusalem (see also 24:16).

Any hope that the council would respond with more hospitality than did the crowd in the Jerusalem streets evaporates abruptly with the high priest's response. By ordering that Paul be struck on the mouth, Ananias emphatically rejects Paul's claim (see John 18:22). Where earlier the Jerusalem leadership had ordered the apostles to be silent and found that their order was rejected (4:13-22; 5:27-32), here Ananias directly silences Paul. This harsh picture finds confirmation in Josephus's reports about this particular high priest and his actions (Josephus, *Ant.* 20.103, 205-210, 213-14).

If Ananias's treatment of Paul replays the earlier treatment of the apostles in Jerusalem but at an increased volume, Paul's response replays that of Stephen before his accusers. By addressing the council as "stiff-necked," and "uncircumcised in heart and ears," Stephen offers an important precedent for Paul's outburst (7:51; Cassidy 1987, 64). Paul's own epithet, "whitewashed wall," conjures up a cosmetically enhanced exterior that conceals faulty construction or impurity within (as in Ezek 13:10-16; Matt 23:27). The most damaging comment, however, is that Ananias violates the very law he is supposed to be upholding. This accusation puts Ananias in the same company as earlier accusers of Paul, who commit the very acts of which they accuse him (see, e.g., 16:20; 17:1-9; 19:23-41).

The final exchange between those around the high priest and Paul proves especially difficult to understand. They ask whether Paul dares to "insult God's high priest," and he responds that he did not know that the individual with whom he has just had the exchange was high priest, quoting Exod 22:28 against his own action. It is difficult to imagine that Paul does not recognize Ananias as the high priest, or at least as a prominent member of the council, and none of the various explanations offered for this anomaly is entirely satisfying. One long-standing interpretation argues that Paul here speaks ironically; i.e., Ananias's behavior makes it impossible to perceive him as high priest (Calvin 1966, 229; Cassidy 1987, 64-65). This winsome possibility fails, since the address, "Brothers," and the quotation from scripture are difficult to reconcile with an ironic tone (Haenchen 1971, 638). Other interpreters read the exchange as further evidence that Paul is law-observant, but it is a peculiar form of evidence, since it first places Paul in a highly compromised position and then rescues him (Conzelmann 1987, 192).

A reading that addresses first the question in v. 4 may prove illuminating. The question of v. 4 virtually invites Paul to give vent to disrespect for the high priest. Hearing Paul's outburst against Ananias, the bystanders goad him to repudiate the high priest and, therefore, the people, the temple, and the law (21:28). By claiming that he did not know Ananias was the high priest, and by quoting Exod 22:28, Paul demonstrates that he is not guilty of such disrespect. It is not Paul who makes the separation from the Jewish leadership, but they who separate from him.

"I Am a Pharisee" (23:6-10)

The exchanges that focus on the high priest in vv. 1-5 do not come to a clear end, but Paul begins a second exchange in v. 6. Once again Paul introduces himself, this time with the carefully chosen expression, "I am a Pharisee, a son of Pharisees. I am on trial concerning the hope of the resurrection of the dead." Invoking Pharisaic connections signals his tie to one group, but it also recalls his claim in chapter 22 to be a faithful Jew.

Paul presents himself here as defending the "hope of the resurrection of the dead." As the note in the NRSV indicates, literally Paul speaks about "hope and the resurrection," but the phrase is a *hendiadys*; the two terms do not refer to distinct issues but to a single concern with the hope of resurrection (see 24:15). Because the appeal to the resurrection of the dead provokes a fight within the group, Paul is seen employing a "divide and conquer" technique that is highly manipulative. Despite the discomfort that action causes some readers, the comment at the outset of v. 6 seems to make it clear that that is exactly what Paul is doing. He speaks as he does precisely because he knows the impact it will have on his audience. The action may recall Luke's praise of the dishonest manager who acts shrewdly in a context of crisis (see Luke 16:1-9).

On one level, then, the appeal to the resurrection is simply a strategy for deflecting controversy, and one that succeeds dramatically for a moment. On another level, the appeal to the resurrection hope attempts to begin from mutually-held convictions. As with the earlier speech in chapter 22 (and see 7:2-53; 17:22-31), Paul starts at a point that he understands will be acceptable to at least part of the audience, but disruption among those present prevents even this slender effort. Paul never has an opportunity in this speech to reach the point of disagreement with the Pharisees, which concerns the specific resurrection Paul proclaims, that of Jesus of Nazareth and its consequences for Jew and Gentile alike. The speeches in this section of Acts work together and will culminate with that full explanation of hope in 26:23 (Tannehill 1990, 286).

Before the chief priests and the council, the response to Paul's initial claim is sheer turmoil. Lest readers miss the cause, Luke provides an explanation in v.8, but the explanation itself contains an apparent difficulty. He reports that "the Sadducees say that there is no resurrection, or angel, or spirit," while the Pharisees affirm all. According to Josephus as well as the Gospel accounts, the Sadducees do not believe in the resurrection of the dead, since they are strict interpreters who regard only the Pentateuch as authoritative (Josephus, *J. W.* 2.165; *Ant.* 18.16; Matt 22:23; Mark 12:18; Luke 20:27). Angels appear even in the Pentateuch, however, which requires further attention to what Luke means by "angel" and "spirit" here. Apparently he intends angel and spirit not in a general sense, but specifically in reference to beliefs that individuals who have died exist in the state of an angel or a spirit prior to their resurrection (Daube 1990).

Luke draws attention to the conflicting views of Pharisees and Sadducees and also to the chaos that greets Paul's statement. Four times Luke depicts the difficulties: "a dissension began," "the assembly was divided," "a great clamor," and "when the dissension became violent." Paul never again has the opportunity to speak, but v. 9 shows some of the Pharisees speaking, ostensibly in Paul's favor. Yet their very language does less to support Paul than to inflame the situation: "What if a spirit or an angel has spoken to him?" Given that the Sadducees have just been said to deny the existence of both spirit and angel, there must be some suspicion that the question intends to provoke the Sadducees and little surprise at the melee that follows (Fitzmyer 1998, 719).

When introducing Paul's provocative statement about the resurrection, Luke comments that Paul knows that the council contains both Sadducees and Pharisees. Since Paul would certainly have known that both Sadducees and Pharisees sit on the council before he ever appeared there, the comment prepares readers for the conflict to follow. Taken together with the aside regarding Sadducaic belief in v. 8, this explanation also provides a possible glimpse into the implied audience of Luke's work. Jewish readers would scarcely need to be informed about the participation of Sadducees and Pharisees on the council or their major distinguishing beliefs, but Gentiles might well require such assistance (see Introduction).

Because of the several difficult questions posed by the details of this text, readers may lose sight of the overall impact of the scene. Paul's initial speech in Jerusalem takes place in the presence of a mob that quiets only long enough to permit him to reach the main point, his calling to the Gentiles (22:21). Rescued from the mob's wrath by an official of Rome, which is to say in a highly tenuous situation, Paul then finds himself before the rightful religious authorities, where he should expect decorum and fairness. What he finds instead is clamorous and chaotic resistance. First, the high priest has him struck for an opening remark that seems entirely innocent. Then, his alignment with the Pharisees that might allow him a different entry into the council's hearing provokes utter chaos. Even the one ostensibly favorable response, that of Pharisees who suggest that an angel or spirit has spoken to Paul, proves more damaging than helpful. The council unmasks itself as the location, not of justice, but of yet more violence. Once again the tribune must intercede in order to protect Paul from physical harm.

The concluding statement in v. 11 provides an important clue to this part of Luke's narrative. It, of course, recalls that Paul's trials and testimony in Jerusalem are part of God's plan (19:21). It also reassures the reader that Paul will give testimony in Rome, even if Luke's narrative does not include an account of that testimony (Haenchen 1971, 639). In addition, the Lord's instruction reinforces Paul's claim that he stands blameless before God, since he is doing only what he has been commissioned to do (22:1-21; 23:1).

Paul's initial assertion of his "clear conscience" may seem odd, coming as it does from a man who has just the previous day recounted his persecution of believers. From Luke's perspective, the recitation of Paul's actions is not the stuff of biography; Paul is not a reformed persecutor who must somehow come to grips with his guilty past. Instead, Paul's actions as a persecutor align him with numerous agents who resist God's plan. The particular resistance Paul once engaged in has been defeated, and recounting it inspires thanksgiving rather than remorse.

Just as Paul's speech in chapter 22 pointed to God's actions rather than to Paul's own, this incident also reminds readers who is the proper subject of Acts. Despite the emphasis on finding out what accusations there are against Paul and despite the furor he creates, when the scene concludes the Lord says, "You have testified *for me* in Jerusalem" (emphasis added). With that brief phrase, Luke reminds readers that these scenes finally concern far more than the defense of an individual believer. Paul is not testifying for himself but for the Lord.

From Jerusalem to Caesarea (23:12-35)

Earlier in the narrative Luke reported plots against Paul that prompted specific responses (see especially 9:23-25, 29-30;

20:3), but here he provides an extended account that makes for a highly dramatic interlude between Paul's appearances before Jewish audiences—the Jerusalem mob and the council—and before Roman authorities. The passage opens with a brief account of the plot to kill Paul (vv. 12-15), which stimulates a report to the tribune (vv. 16-22), which in turn stimulates the tribune to send Paul and a letter of transfer to the governor Felix in Caesarea (vv. 23-30). As the passage ends, Paul arrives in Caesarea, where Felix places him under guard once more (vv. 31-35).

The use of repetition and detail extend and vivify this story, which shares some features with other ancient narratives of intrigue and conspiracy (Pervo 1987, 32-34; Talbert 1997, 203). Three times Luke reports on an oath taken by a number of Jews, who will not eat until they have killed Paul (vv. 12, 14, 21). Twice he explains how the conspirators hope to gain access to Paul by involving the chief priests and elders (vv. 15, 20). Vocabulary of conspiracy appears several times (vv. 12, 13), as does that of accusation (vv. 28, 29, 30, 35). Details abound as well, such as the depiction of the tribune taking Paul's nephew "by the hand" in order to speak with him privately, the precise accounting of the guards who accompany Paul, and the division of the journey at the midpoint, Antipatris. Such particulars have the effect of slowing the story down. What could have been reported in a sentence and passed quickly from the reader's awareness lingers because of the time required to read this account, and thereby Luke heightens the sense of danger encompassing Paul.

◊ ◊ ◊ ◊

An Oath to Kill Paul (23:12-15)

The two previous scenes have found Paul attempting to demonstrate his faithfulness before, first, a Jewish mob and, second, their religious authorities. Here the two come together in a deadly plot. Initially, Luke narrates a plot by "the Jews," who take an oath not to eat or drink before killing Paul. The hyperbole involved in the phrase "the Jews" is modified only slightly when v. 13 indicates that more than forty people take this vow, since forty people make for a large conspiracy. The severity of the vow they undertake is clear: either Paul's life or their own must end. Despite Luke's repetition of this oath in vv. 14 and 21, he demonstrates no interest in the consequences for the conspirators when the plot in fact fails (cf. *m. Ned.* 3.1).

Replaying Paul's own earlier initiative with the authorities (9:1-2; 22:5; 26:10), the mob goes to the "chief priests and elders" and repeats their oath, this time explaining the role they expect the leaders to play, that of requesting that the tribune bring Paul for their questioning. Between the Antonia Fortress and the council, the conspirators intend to kill Paul. Given the earlier conflicts in Jerusalem between Jewish leaders and the witnesses of Jesus, the involvement of the leaders comes as no surprise (e.g., 4:5-7; 5:17-18; 7:1), although two features of this proposal merit attention. First, no one in this brief exchange refers back to the chaos Paul unleashed in the council on the previous day, which need not mean that the present story is an independent unit (Conzelmann 1987, 194), but may only mean that all parties now agree on the need to silence Paul. It may be important that neither the Pharisees nor their scribes are mentioned here, since they appear somewhat favorably disposed to Paul in 23:6-10 (assuming that their comments are not calculated to offend the Sadducees). Second, it seems unlikely that the tribune would again risk Paul's safety by taking him back to the council (Haenchen 1971, 649), unless the "thorough examination" the chief priests and elders are to propose stands in marked contrast to the failed hearing of the previous day.

The Plot Disclosed (23:16-22)

The second scene, vv. 16-22, might have been passed over with a brief comment that the tribune learned of the plot and therefore sent Paul off to safety in Caesarea. The sheer fact of its presence underscores the crisis underway in Jerusalem. As often elsewhere, Luke introduces a new character, Paul's nephew, with the barest of identification (e.g., 12:13; 17:5-8; 19:29; 21:16). Nowhere else does Luke refer to this young man or how he came to know of the plot, but he takes word of it directly to Paul. Despite the fact that other texts assume the possibility of visiting prisoners (Matt 11:2; 25:36; Phil 2:25; 2 Tim 1:16-17; *Acts of Paul* 18-19; Lucian, *Peregrinus* 12-13), the tumultuous circumstances make it unlikely that the tribune would welcome visitors for Paul (Rapske 1994b, 149). That may explain the otherwise puzzling silence of the text on the involvement of Jerusalem Christians in caring for Paul or interceding on his behalf.

Through a circuitous route that builds suspense, word of the plot finally reaches the tribune; the nephew tells Paul, who asks a centurion to take the young man to the tribune, who takes him aside privately so that the young man can repeat the plot in detail once more.

Claudias Lysias Writes to Felix (23:23-30)

The tribune's swift and emphatic response conveys the seriousness with which he receives this report. Having sent Paul's nephew off without a single additional question, he gives orders to two centurions (the use of two messengers being frequent in Acts; e.g., 11:30; 15:27; 19:22). The two are instructed to take Paul to the governor Felix in Caesarea, the capital of the province of Judea, as well as a place of considerable importance earlier in Acts (see, e.g., 8:40; 10:1–11:18; 12:19; 21:8-16). In addition, they are to take a massive force consisting of "two hundred soldiers, seventy horsemen," as well as two hundred of what the NRSV translates as "spearmen." The obscure Greek word *dexiolabos*, which appears nowhere else before the sixth century CE, presumably refers to military personnel who carry something in their right hands (v. 23; BDAG 217).

Judgments vary about the verisimilitude of the figures Luke provides for the personnel accompanying Paul. On the one hand, this seems an outlandishly large number of men to protect a single individual; on the other hand, the tensions in first-century

Palestine ran high among opposing Jewish factions and between Jews and the Roman occupiers, and frequently involved large numbers of people, as Josephus reports in considerable detail (Josephus, *Life* 200; *J.W.* 2.224-31, 417-24; 4.128-34, 326-33; *Ant.* 20.108-17). Whether or not the tribune's orders are credible, they underscore the sense of impending danger throughout this passage. Only a large force traveling secretly at night can hope to deliver Paul from what, in Luke's portrait, is a city set upon his destruction.

The tribune also sends a letter to the governor, which serves the legal function of transferring Paul to Felix's authority and the literary function of reviewing the situation once again. Because the letter delicately varies from the narrative that precedes it, it merits particular attention. The tribune reports that, having learned that Paul was a Roman citizen, he rescued Paul from Jews who were about to kill him, but it was the tribune's own officers who learned of Paul's citizenship as they were about to flog him on the tribune's orders (22:22-29). The letter then reports on the tribune's efforts to learn the charges against Paul and reveals his own conclusion for the first time, that Paul has been accused of no capital crime. Finally, it explains that the plot against Paul prompts sending him to Felix and adds that he has instructed the accusers also to report to Felix, something readers learn only from the letter. The letter also reveals for the first time the name of the tribune, Claudius Lysias.

The recipient of the letter will play an important role in the next stage of the narrative (24:22-27). A Roman freedman, whose brother Pallas was an important associate of the emperors Claudius and Nero, Antonius Felix became procurator of Judea, Samaria, Galilee, and Perea. The historians Josephus and Tacitus both report on Felix (Josephus, *J.W.* 2.247, 252-70; *Ant.* 20.137, 141-44; Tacitus, *History* 5.9; Tacitus, *Annals* 12.54). In some respects their accounts of Felix differ, but neither account treats him favorably. In a frequently quoted passage, Tacitus observes that Felix "practiced every kind of cruelty and lust, wielding the power of king with all the instincts of a slave" (*History* 5.9).

From Jerusalem to Caesarea (23:31-35)

Verses 31-35 complete the story with the journey to Caesarea and the initial appearance of the governor Felix. The careful narration of the trip finds the company first at Antipatris, roughly halfway between Jerusalem and Caesarea. A reduced guard then continues with Paul to Caesarea, where they present both the letter and Paul to Felix. Felix's single question of Paul concerns his province, since Felix might have chosen to send the case to the governor of Cilicia (Tajra 1989, 116-17; Fitzmyer 1998, 729). Felix then states that he will hear Paul when the accusers arrive. Despite the letter's identification of Paul as a Roman citizen and its assessment that the charges against Paul are not serious, Felix displays no interest in listening to Paul without the presence of his accusers as well.

The many vivid details in this story give rise to a number of historical questions, but they should not obscure its overall effect. It strikingly depicts the danger confronting Paul in the form of both the Jewish mob and the religious authorities. By rescuing Paul from this plot, Claudius Lysias puts him one step closer to Rome. He also brings about the final separation of Paul from Jerusalem.

◊ ◊ ◊ ◊

The saying of the Lord in 23:11 prophesies Paul's witness in Rome and anticipates that more danger is in store for him, since courage will be needed (Spencer 1997, 214). That saying also stands as an ironic introduction to the mad act of the Jewish mob that swears to kill Paul, as if his life somehow belonged to them (Calvin 1966, 238). Despite their numbers and their rage, the mob is powerless because God's plan involves a witness for Paul in Rome and, more fundamentally, because Paul's life belongs to God. In that sense, this story recalls the defeat of Herod, who similarly thought he controlled the life of Peter and lost his own instead (12:1-23).

Reading this story in light of the persistent charge that Paul does not uphold Jewish law brings another issue to the surface:

the very people who accuse Paul and who are charged with interpreting the law here receive and apparently comply with a plot to violate the law by murder. Luke's language is unequivocal: what the mob intends is to kill Paul. The law-protectors reveal themselves to be less interested in observing the law than in their own convictions about Paul as they prepare to violate one of the most sacred of the commandments.

Although the letter of Claudius Lysias never directly declares him innocent, it does report that Paul is "charged with nothing deserving death or imprisonment" (Cassidy 1987, 100). Again Paul conforms to the pattern of Jesus, who is said to be innocent (Luke 23:4, 14-15, 22). The assessment is repeated several times, as Paul's case proceeds through higher levels of Roman authority (25:18; 26:31-32), forming an important motif of this part of Acts. Paul must testify in Rome, and he will do so as a prisoner, but he is never depicted as deserving his imprisonment.

Claudius's actions play an important role in this story. His repeated attempts to learn the charges against Paul and his protection of Paul's life stand in contrast with the behavior of Paul's fellow-Jews, who pay little attention to his speech in chapter 22 and who plot to kill him. That contrast does not imply that Claudius is favorably disposed toward Paul or that Luke is thereby defending or appeasing the Roman government, however. Claudius's letter reflects little more than the careful response of one who knows that his own authority is limited and ever-fragile and who is keenly aware of the firm Roman intention to maintain order and thwart any attempt at insurrection.

As earlier in Acts, this aggressive resistance will not silence the gospel. The assurance given Paul in 23:11 means that he will certainly witness in Rome; neither the hostility of Jerusalem nor the indifference of Caesarea will finally contain him. If the earlier chapters of Acts offer clues for reading these developments, this resistance will only increase the volume of the witness (see, for example, 4:13-22; 5:17-42; 8:1b-8).

The Accusers and Paul Before Felix (24:1-27)

Not only has the location of Paul shifted from Jerusalem to Caesarea, but the context has changed as well. Now Paul defends himself, not before Jewish authorities, but facing Roman officials. Three major sections comprise this initial Roman proceeding in Caesarea. First, the accusers arrive and Tertullus presents their case against Paul (vv. 2-9) in a speech notable for its extended *captatio benevolentiae* (the solicitation of the audience's favor). Tertullus employs other favorite rhetorical conventions as well, such as opening the speech with the word *pollēs* (NRSV: long; cf. *polymerōs* in Heb 1:1) and employing alliteration in the phrase "in every way and everywhere" (*pantē te kai pantachou*; see also Luke 1:1). Paul then presents his own defense speech, which both begins (vv. 10-13) and ends (vv. 17-21) with his version of developments in Jerusalem and his refutation of charges. The middle of Paul's speech (vv. 14-16) returns to his continuity with Israel's faith. Finally, Felix responds with actions that reveal his weaknesses and prolong Paul's custody (vv. 22-27).

◊ ◊ ◊ ◊

Tertullus Speaks for Paul's Accusers (24:1-9)

The escalation of the hostility against Paul may be seen in the characters who arrive in Caesarea as accusers. No longer does Luke refer to unidentified "Asian Jews" (21:27) or an unnamed mob (23:12-13), but the high priest Ananias himself (see 23:2) heads a delegation that also includes a professional orator, Tertullus. The use of professional advocates is well attested (Rapske 1994, 159), and here it signals the deadly seriousness of those opposed to Paul. Luke leaves it unclear whether Tertullus is a Jew or a Gentile. In the speech itself, he employs first-person plural, which may signal a genuine identification between Tertullus and the viewpoint of the Jewish leaders, or it may only convey his professional association with them. The very ambiguity of Tertullus's identity underscores the danger to Paul, who now faces not only Jewish authorities but a professional orator (Tannehill 1990, 297).

Tertullus's *captatio benevolentiae*, the most extensive in Acts, praises Felix for his establishment of peace, for reforms he has made, and for his foresight or providence. Reports about Felix in both Tacitus and Josephus stand in considerable tension with this generous assessment (see above on 23:12-25), although Josephus does credit Felix with clearing the revolutionaries known as Sicarii from the land (Josephus, *J.W.* 2.52). Tertullus's remarks may contribute something more than mere flattery, however. By drawing attention to the establishment of the peace, Tertullus signals that one of the charges he will bring against Paul concerns disrupting the civil order. Here also Tertullus employs a rhetorical convention, that of introducing elements of the accusation itself early on, even in the introduction (Winter 1991, 508).

In v. 5, the prosecutor turns directly to the charges, characterizing Paul as "a pestilent fellow, an agitator among all the Jews throughout the world, and a ringleader of the sect of the Nazarenes." Paul is said to upset the peace Felix has labored so hard to build. This accusation echoes the charges against Jesus in Luke 23:2, but it also recalls earlier accusations made against Paul by both Jews and Gentiles. In Philippi, the owners of the fortune-telling slave, presumably Gentiles, accuse Paul of "disturbing" the city (16:20); Thessalonian Jews claim that Paul is "turning the world upside down" (17:6); Demetrius and his fellow Ephesians similarly accuse Paul of undermining their god's worship and thereby the entire life of their city (19:26-27). In addition, the language chosen—"pestilent fellow," "agitator," "ringleader"—is calculated to play upon Roman anxiety about the possibility of unrest.

Tertullus does not stop with echoing the charges that have been brought against Paul earlier in the narrative, but in v. 6 includes one of the central accusations made against Paul in Jerusalem, that he tried to profane the temple. That Paul had taught against the law and the people's customs (see 21:28) would not concern Felix, for whom those would be matters internal to Jewish religious practice. That he might have defiled the temple, however, would be a different matter, since the Romans had shrewdly agreed to enforce strongly held Jewish convictions about restricting the temple from Gentiles (Rapske 1994b, 162). Given Jewish sensitivities about the temple, this particular charge would serve as evidence for the more general characterization of Paul as troublemaker in v. 5.

Tertullus cleverly concludes his charges with the comment, "and so we seized him." Just as Lysias's letter to Felix carefully omits the fact that Lysias's centurion was on the verge of beating Paul when he learned of his Roman citizenship, so Tertullus omits the fact that a riot in Jerusalem prompted the tribune to take Paul into custody (Bruce 1990, 277). By claiming that Jews were the ones who initially arrested Paul, Tertullus also may be hinting that Paul's case should properly be decided by Jewish leaders rather than by Felix (Johnson 1992, 411). Certain early interpreters must have understood Tertullus in that way, since some ancient manuscripts expand the speech in that direction, faulting Lysias for his intervention (see footnote in NRSV). Acting as a Greek chorus, "the Jews" who are present reinforce Tertullus's prosecution with their own assent.

Paul's Defense Before Felix (24:10-21)

Because Paul begins with a shorter and less ornate *captatio benevolentiae* than that of Tertullus, readers might regard his approach as less calculated to win Felix's favor, but Paul's introduction also hints at the agenda of his defense (v. 10). By recalling Felix's "many years" as a judge over Judea, Paul indicates an important line in his defense: this is a dispute about things that pertain to the Jewish people, and therefore it does not threaten Roman power.

The body of the speech begins (vv. 11-13) and ends (vv. 17-21) with reference to the innocence of Paul's activity in Jerusalem, with the center of the speech devoted to an affirmation of Paul's association with the Way. First, Paul takes up the charges of Tertullus by replaying Tertullus's own words. Tertullus had invited Felix to find out (lit. "you will be able . . . to ascertain" AT) about Paul, and Paul now invites Felix to find out (lit. "you are able to ascertain" AT; Tannehill 1990, 298). Paul recalls that he went up to Jerusalem to worship "not more than twelve days" earlier. Reconciling "twelve days" with the preceding narrative is somewhat difficult, but the point is clear: Paul had not been in Jerusalem long enough to stir up the sort of trouble imputed to him by Tertullus. In addition, he went to Jerusalem "to worship" (as did the Ethiopian in 8:27), an activity Felix would not have found troubling. Verses 12-13 directly rebut Tertullus's charge by insisting both that Paul was not disputing with anyone anywhere in the city and that no proof exists of the charges. The specification of Jerusalem is important, since Paul did in fact dispute with Jews in other cities and trouble often ensued (e.g., 17:1-9; 18:5-17).

Paul appears to be on the verge of a confession of guilt with v. 14 ("But this I admit to you"), but he turns instead to a confession of faith, the centerpiece of the speech (Tannehill 1990, 298). Identifying himself and all that follows as "according to the Way" (see 9:2; 18:25; 19:9, 23; 22:4), Paul asserts his belief in the "God of our ancestors." Specifying the patriarchs Abraham, Isaac, and Jacob would be meaningless before Felix (cf. 2:13; 13:26), who would not know those names but who would understand the importance of honoring the deities of one's ancestors.

Paul amplifies his worship of God in two ways, employing two participial phrases. First, he describes himself as believing "everything laid down according to the law or written in the prophets," that is, in Israel's Scripture (see Luke 16:16; 24:44; Acts 13:15; 28:23). Second, he describes himself as hoping in God for the coming resurrection. English translations customarily make v. 15 into an independent sentence, but it is a subordinate clause, depending on the initial phrase, "I worship the God of our ancestors," just as does the second part of v. 14. Verse 15 is not an independent item in Paul's belief structure, therefore, but is part and parcel of his belief in God and in the Scriptures of Israel. The connection between Scripture and the resurrection of

Jesus appears already in Luke 24:27, 44-47 (Haenchen 1971, 658), but is now extended to include the resurrection of both the righteous and unrighteous.

This brief statement of Paul's convictions picks up where his explosive assertion before the Jerusalem council necessarily left off (23:6), but it also contributes to Paul's defense by affirming that he belongs within the ancestral faith. He makes that claim explicit in his comment in v. 15 that Jews also believe in a resurrection, delicately neglecting the Sadducees at that point (see 23:8). And he concludes this section with the claim of v. 16 that he attempts to have "a clear conscience" not only toward God but toward all people. With v. 17, the speech returns to the initial narrative of events in Jerusalem. In a statement that parallels the assertion, "I went up to worship" (v. 12), Paul says that he went to Jerusalem to "bring alms to my nation and to offer sacrifices." Since the letters of Paul frequently comment on the collection for Jerusalem (e.g., Rom 15:25-28; 1 Cor 16:1-4; 2 Cor 8–9), commentators routinely understand this statement as referring to the collection, but there are serious problems with that view. Luke elsewhere shows virtually no interest in the collection (with the possible exception of 11:27-30). In addition, Paul's letters depict the collection as intended for believers, by contrast with the more general language of "my nation" in v. 17 (Tannehill 1990, 300). The very fact that v. 17 introduces comments about Jerusalem suggests that it repeats and expands on Paul's "worship," rather than alluding to a collection for poor Christians in Jerusalem. In this context, Paul's almsgiving signals to Felix his general commitment to charity toward his own people, a charity notably lacking in their dealings with him.

Verse 18 continues this parallel by restating the comment of v. 12; Paul was in the temple and had drawn no crowd and created no difficulty. And vv. 19-21 complete the parallel by amplifying the claim of v. 13 that there is no proof for the charges. He recalls the Jews from Asia, but pointedly observes that they are not present to testify. He then recalls the council's session in vv. 20-21 and the fact that they found him guilty of no crime. Paul's final statement reintroduces the topic of resurrection, one that could prove embarrassing to the Jewish leaders if the story of their chaotic session with Paul comes to Felix's attention.

Responses of Felix (24:22-27)

Both Tertullus and Paul having spoken, the story turns to Felix's responses: his initial response to the hearing and treatment of Paul (vv. 22-23); his summons of Paul (vv. 24-25); his hope of receiving a bribe from Paul (v. 26); and his final inaction in Paul's case (v. 27). Throughout this section, Felix is the subject of the action. Even in v. 25, which opens with a report on Paul's comments, Paul speaks in a subordinate clause that leaves Felix as the shaper of events.

The initial response of Felix in vv. 22-23 provides few clues as to his disposition. Although Luke comments that Felix was informed about "the Way," his attitude toward it remains veiled. That he delays judgment until the arrival of Lysias suggests that his primary concern is with public order, and Lysias will be able to indicate which portrait of Paul he should accept—innocent pilgrim or subversive pest. His apparently lenient instructions regarding Paul's custody do not necessarily betray a positive stance toward Paul, since prisoners routinely relied on those outside for assistance with even basic needs (Rapske 1994b, 171).

The second response of Felix introduces his wife Drusilla and finds the two of them listening to Paul's proclamation of the gospel. The introduction of Drusilla proves intriguing. Luke indicates that she is a Jew, but that by no means implies that she will be receptive to Paul, as Luke's story has made evident. Josephus's report about Drusilla's earlier marriage and Felix's role in securing her for himself contributes to the generally odious impression of Felix, but it is unclear that either Luke or his audience knows about the history of the relationship (Josephus, *Ant.* 20.141-44). Perhaps Luke's reference to her simply reflects his general interest in female characters, especially those of high standing (e.g., 17:4, 12; Haenchen 1971, 662).

Before Felix and Drusilla, Paul speaks about "faith in Christ Jesus," the logical next step after his earlier defense speech.

Although this general topic may have appealed to Felix's curiosity, the specific topics of v. 25 prove unsettling. When Paul takes up the virtues of justice and self-control, and then introduces judgment or accountability for those virtues, Felix "becomes frightened" and sends him away. The dissolution of this conversation recalls Paul's speech at the Areopagus, where he was also received with curiosity (17:16-21) and then dismissed as the topic turned to judgment (17:30-34). Felix may have particular reasons for fearing Paul's discourse; quite apart from the marital history of Felix and Drusilla, Luke's narrative displays a man lacking in both justice and self-control.

Up to this point, Luke's portrait of Felix is somewhat ambiguous, but the comment of v. 26 allows for no ambiguity. Luke has again and again depicted in harsh light those who would use money or other possessions for their own purposes (1:18; 5:1-11; 8:18-24; 16:16-24), and Felix's desire to profit from Paul's imprisonment surely signals Luke's scorn for him. Felix now emerges as an unjust judge (perhaps recalling Luke 18:1-8), and his fear in response to Paul's preaching is well-placed.

Felix's final action regarding Paul confirms this negative portrait. When he is succeeded by Porcius Festus (Josephus, *J.W.* 2.271; *Ant.* 20.182-97), Felix might reasonably be expected to release Paul (at least for a small fee; see *Ant.* 20.215). Instead, he allows him to continue in prison, having been there for two years, in order to secure the favor of "the Jews."

◊ ◊ ◊ ◊

In Luke 21:12-15 Jesus explains to his followers that they will be handed over to "synagogues and prisons," and brought to testify before "kings and governors" because of his name. In the initial account of Paul's conversion, the Lord tells Ananias that Paul will take his name "before Gentiles and kings" as well as before "the people of Israel" (9:15). Although this speech explicitly counters the charges made by Tertullus against Paul, it is also more than a defense speech; it fulfills the earlier prophecies by allowing Paul to testify in the presence of the Roman governor

Felix. Even the defense speech before a Roman official becomes an opportunity for the proclamation of the gospel.

Beginning with this scene, Paul is entirely under Roman jurisdiction. The plot of 23:12-35 to take matters into Jewish hands and Tertullus's rhetorical effort to regain custody have failed. Felix, like Gallio before him (18:12-17), as well as the town clerk of Ephesus (19:35-40), manifests little interest in the content of Paul's proclamation. Only the question of Paul's potential to create unrest matters to Rome. That indifference to Paul is itself another form of resistance to the gospel, a form perhaps more powerful than the active resistance from those Jews who bring accusations against Paul.

The brief remarks Paul makes here about his faith confirm what the story has insisted all along. It is the God of the ancestors whom Paul worships, but that God exists not only in the ancestral past. God also stands over the future resurrection of righteous and unrighteous alike (vv. 15, 16). And that God also is the God of Christ Jesus whom Paul proclaims in the present.

Paul Appealing to the Emperor (25:1-27)

Four brief scenes comprise this chapter, providing a dramatic interlude while Luke sets the stage for Paul's final and climactic defense speech in chapter 26. In two of these scenes, Paul himself appears, and in two others he becomes the subject of conversation as people ponder what should be done with him. First, Festus meets in Jerusalem with Jewish leaders and discusses Paul (vv. 1-5). In the next scene (vv. 6-12), Paul appears before Festus in Caesarea, and Paul appeals to the Emperor. Then Paul again becomes the topic of conversation as Festus confers with Agrippa and Bernice (vv. 13-22). Finally, Paul comes before all three and their courtiers, preparatory to making his defense speech (vv. 23-27).

The chapter constitutes an extended recapitulation of the action since Paul's arrival in Jerusalem. Among the earlier features that recur here are the plot to kill Paul (23:12-15), the charges against him (21:28; 24:5-6), his defense (22:3-21; 24:10-21), the insistence that accused and accusers confront one another (23:30, 35), the declaration that Paul was not charged with serious crimes but with religious disagreements (23:28-30), the resurrection as a disputed point (23:6), and the need to specify charges against Paul (21:33; 22:24; 23:28-29). The only novel development comes about when Paul appeals to the emperor (vv. 10-11), an appeal that both secures his journey to Rome and introduces his opportunity to witness before King Agrippa.

Many questions of Roman law and the situation in first-century Palestine come into play here. The political struggles involving various Jewish factions, their religious leaders, and Roman officials may be reflected in Luke's treatment of Festus, as well as in his reference to Bernice. The appeal Paul makes to Caesar raises questions about the nature of such an appeal and Festus's options for dealing with it. Questions about Luke's historical accuracy become acute, particularly when Luke narrates a private conversation between Festus and Agrippa, an event scarcely accessible to Luke or any of his sources. These important concerns should not obscure the function played by this chapter. A far briefer account would have sufficed to report simply that Paul appealed to Caesar, and Festus agreed to the appeal. By repeating and elaborating earlier events, Luke prepares the audience for the major speech to follow.

◊   ◊   ◊   ◊

Festus and Jewish Leaders in Jerusalem (25:1-5)

Unlike Felix, who kept Paul in prison for two years, his successor Festus moves expeditiously, first by going to Jerusalem shortly after his arrival (v. 1), and then by returning to Caesarea promptly for a hearing concerning Paul (vv. 4, 6). About Festus himself little is known, apart from brief notice in Josephus about his procuratorship in Judea around 60–62 CE (Josephus, *J.W.* 2.271-72; *Ant.* 20.182, 185-94, 197, 200). Luke does little to amplify that knowledge, focusing entirely on the situation with Paul. The impression given by vv. 1-2 is that the chief priests and other Jewish leaders arrive simultaneously with Festus. Their request reveals that Paul's defense before Felix and in their presence changed no minds. They report "against" Paul, and they ask the "favor" of having Paul transferred to Jerusalem, where they plan to kill him. The earlier plot against Paul returns, instigated this time not by an unnamed mob with the cooperation of the leadership, but by the leaders themselves. Festus's response reveals nothing of his disposition; he merely agrees to a hearing but on his territory rather than their own.

Paul Appeals to Caesar (25:6-12)

If Festus does not accede to the wish to have Paul taken to Jerusalem, he also does not delay in granting a hearing. By taking "his seat on the tribunal," Festus signals the beginning of a formal legal action (Bruce 1990, 487; see also 18:12, 16-17). This time, however, there is no elegant Tertullus to issue a formal speech of accusation, but instead a group of unnamed Jews from among the authorities summoned by Festus (v. 5). Luke's graphic language here vivifies the scene, as Jews "surround" Paul and bring "many serious charges against him." In Luke's narration, they act as a single person, both physically and verbally enclosing Paul with their accusations. Even before Paul speaks, the narrator reminds readers that these charges cannot be proved (v. 7). Like those against Stephen, these charges also are false (6:13).

For the first time since the conclusion of the defense before Felix, Luke quotes Paul directly, and what he says here largely summarizes that defense. He insists that he is not guilty of an offense against "the law of the Jews, or against the temple, or against the emperor" (v. 8). The first two of these charges have been made repeatedly (e.g., 21:21, 28) and addressed explicitly in 24:11-21. The last charge returns to Tertullus's characterization of Paul as a troublemaker (24:5-6; see also 17:6), which Paul now explicitly identifies and rejects.

Although Festus's initial words in vv. 4-5 reveal nothing of his disposition and seem to have deflected the favor sought by the Jerusalem leaders, now the narrator describes him as "wishing to do the Jews a favor" and therefore asking Paul whether he wants to be tried in Jerusalem and before Festus himself. Commentators sometimes see in this move a change in Festus, who in a few days has come to understand better the importance of securing the goodwill of Jewish leaders (Tannehill 1990, 305-307), but it may be that no real change has taken place. In the first scene, he does not so much deny the leaders the favor they request as postpone it. Now he has an opportunity to grant their request and make it appear to be beneficial to Paul at the same time.

With vv. 10-11, a new element enters the story, as Paul responds to Festus's question. He opens his response with an emphatic rejection of the question Festus has posed. Festus asked whether Paul wanted to go to Jerusalem and there be judged "by" or "before" (*epi*) him, and Paul responds that "by" or "before" (*epi*) the judgment seat of the emperor he is standing and must be judged there. (The NRSV's "I appeal" obscures the parallels.) In other words, Paul already stands before Festus, the emperor's agent (Fitzmyer 1998, 745), and his case does not belong in Jerusalem.

The second part of the response returns to the question of the accusations against Paul, this time drawing in Festus as well as the accusers. Paul repeats his assertion of innocence, but adds the comment, "as you very well know," at least indirectly accusing Festus of acting duplicitously. An emphatic pronoun, "you" (*sy*) sharpens the barb. Paul then elaborates on his innocence by explaining that he is not afraid to die if he is guilty (see the parallel statement in Josephus, *Life* 141). Adding the comment that, absent his guilt, "no one can turn me over to them" completes the indictment of Festus, especially since the Greek verb *charizomai* (NRSV: turn . . . over) plays on the earlier word *charis* (NRSV: favor; v. 9). Paul declares that he is not to be a favor Festus grants to the Jewish leaders.

The final two words in Paul's response seem merely to repeat his opening comment in v. 10, but in fact they signal an important change. Although in both cases he presents himself before the Emperor's judgment, in the first instance he claims already to be standing before the Emperor's tribunal, since a decision by Festus in Caesarea is legally a decision by the Emperor. At the end of v. 11, however, he appeals to the Emperor. Luke says nothing about Paul's motives for appealing to Caesar. The situation may suggest that Paul perceives his chances of just treatment lie outside Jerusalem and beyond Festus's grasp (Spencer 1997, 223), and there is no little irony in the notion that Paul must escape his own people to find fairness. Yet the narrative's established expectation that Paul is to witness in Rome suggests another possibility. Paul may appeal to the Emperor because only in that way can he be obedient to his vocation, which includes witnessing in Rome (see 19:21; 23:11).

After consulting with his council, Festus concurs, "You have appealed to the emperor; to the emperor you will go." One historical question that plagues this passage is whether an appeal to the emperor automatically demanded assent. Some scholars think Festus has no choice but to grant Paul's appeal (Haenchen 1971, 690; Bruce 1990, 507), but that point is not clear from Luke's account either here or in his conversation with Agrippa (Lentz 1993, 151-52). Whatever the historical situation, Luke presents Festus as having the authority to decide about it (vv. 12, 25). Perhaps his agreement means simply that he is pleased to have Paul leave Caesarea; whether for Jerusalem or Rome is a matter of indifference. Ironically, even as he accedes to Paul's request, Festus's words unwittingly recall the divine plan that Paul should go to Rome (19:21; 23:11).

Festus, Agrippa, and Bernice (25:13-22)

Here Luke summarizes Paul's situation once more, this time against the background of the arrival of King Agrippa and Bernice. Agrippa is Agrippa II, son of the Herod Agrippa I of Acts 12, who had been educated at Rome and whose rule was marked by considerable conflict with the Jewish leadership (Josephus, *J.W.* 2.223). Bernice is his sister, about whom reports circulated that she and Agrippa carried on an incestuous relationship. Years later, she went to Rome as the companion of

Titus and appears in contemporary historians and satirists because of that association (Juvenal, *Satire* 6.156-60; Suetonius, *Titus* 7; Dio Cassius 65.15).

Although Luke's audience may well know about Agrippa and Bernice, especially given the public nature of the relationship of Bernice with the emperor Titus, Luke does no more than introduce them. Almost immediately, Festus draws Agrippa into the situation in a report that replays the developments in Paul's case. As with Lysias's earlier written report to Felix, however, this report summarizes events while presenting Festus's behavior in the best possible light. Festus introduces Paul as "a man left in prison by Felix," simultaneously recalling Felix's action (or inaction, 24:27) and focusing responsibility on Felix rather than on himself. Similarly, vv. 15-16 repeat the meeting of Festus with the Jerusalem leaders, although here Festus claims that he cited Roman policy to the Jews, thereby making himself appear to be the principled upholder of Roman law. With v. 17, the report shifts to events in Caesarea. Festus stresses that he acted expeditiously but found that Paul had been accused of no crimes. Instead, there were disagreements about "their own religion," an expression that conveys Festus's distance from the discussion. He has observed this quarrel with considerable detachment. The specific point Festus reports is that the parties disagreed about Jesus, "who had died, but whom Paul asserted to be alive" (v. 19). Again the language conveys the distance that separates Festus from the quarreling parties, neither of whom would have described the claims about resurrection in this way. More important, Festus's report reinforces Paul's claim that what is at stake is his belief in the resurrection (23:6-10; 24:21), but this time it also emerges that this is no abstract disagreement about whether there is to be a resurrection. What is as stake is the belief in the resurrection of Jesus, the point that becomes central to the speech of chapter 26.

Verse 20 recalls Festus's offer to send Paul to Jerusalem, but does so again in a way calculated to enhance Festus's image. An emphatic pronoun (*egō*) introduces the claim that Festus himself could not investigate further, implying that his proposal of a

Jerusalem venue came from an honest understanding of his limited knowledge. He carefully omits to mention that a move to Jerusalem would have allowed him to please the Jewish leaders. Verse 21 completes the report, recalling Paul's appeal to the Emperor and Festus's decision to comply. The conversation comes to an end as Agrippa asks to hear Paul himself (see Luke 23:8).

Paul Before Agrippa and the Prominent (25:23-27)

This scene conveys little by way of new information, but it briefly reviews the situation once again and powerfully leads into Paul's speech in chapter 26. Agrippa and Bernice enter Festus's audience hall with a group of tribunes and important residents of Caesarea. In terms of the social standing and influence of the audience, nothing in Acts compares with this gathering. Festus introduces Paul with yet another description of the situation. Here he indicates that "the whole Jewish community" both in Jerusalem and in Caesarea has agreed that Paul should not live. This represents a considerable expansion of both earlier events (vv. 2-3, 7) and Festus's previous report to Agrippa (v. 15), where nothing has been said about the Jewish people as a whole or even about Jews in Caesarea. Festus contrasts himself with the judgment of the Jews, indicating that the challenge before him is to formulate a report to send to Rome.

The report for Rome serves as the justification for hearing Paul speak, and it marks a new development (although see Lysias's search for charges in 22:24, 28). Festus's final comment about the "unreasonableness" of sending a prisoner without indicating the charges against him is elaborate but misleading, since he could not send a prisoner without a statement of charges (Ulpian, *Digest* 49.6.1; Fitzmyer 1998, 753), a legal nicety of which Luke may have been unaware. Festus draws attention to the need to identify charges and therefore to the importance of the defense speech that is to come.

◊ ◊ ◊ ◊

This series of events figures prominently in attempts to assess the place of the Roman Empire in Luke's theological world. One time-honored view is that Acts constitutes a defense of Christianity to the Roman government, while a more recent view finds Luke defending Rome to the church (see Introduction). Without doubt, Rome and its power constituted an overwhelming force in Luke's world, but that does not mean that Luke's story has a stance toward Rome itself as even a subsidiary theme. Instead, this story features an official of Rome who acts in response to Jewish plots against Paul. Like Lysias and Felix before him, Festus stands between Paul and those who would destroy him and silence the gospel he preaches. In that sense, he is not an actual enemy of Paul. Yet his actions are aimed at gaining favor with local leaders and promoting himself with Agrippa and Bernice. However self-serving and even self-aggrandizing Festus's behavior with respect to Paul, he nevertheless serves the divine plan by sending Paul on his way to Rome and by allowing Paul to defend himself and his gospel in the presence of important citizens. In that sense, Festus becomes an unwitting tool of the gospel, which is silenced neither by its enemies nor by those who remain malignly indifferent to it.

From Defense to Proclamation (26:1-26)

In this chapter, Paul faces "a grand gallery for a grand finale" (Spencer 1997, 224). "Finale" is the right word, since the speech brings together a number of elements that have appeared in Paul's earlier defense speeches, puts those elements in the context of Paul's entire witness and, indeed, in the still larger context of the Lukan story as a whole. Literarily, this scene forms a second dramatic climax in Acts (the first being the conversion of Cornelius in 10:1–11:18; see Introduction), and the remainder of Acts constitutes the denouement working out the implications of this scene (as 11:19–15:35 works out the implications of the Cornelius episode). Although the powerful assembly anticipates Paul's defense, he makes no real defense but instead turns to proclamation. In that proclamation he sharply restates the gospel, in which for the first time it emerges that the risen Jesus is himself the proclaimer of salvation for Jew and Gentile alike.

Verse 1 comprises a brief narrative transition to the speech. Paul begins with a *captatio benevolentiae*, not insincere but conventional praise intended to gain the favor of the judge (vv. 2-3), followed by the body of the speech (vv. 4-23). After an initial appeal to his own character and to Jewish witnesses of that character (vv. 4-5), Paul turns with the "and now" of v. 6 to new material (as earlier in Acts 3:17; 20:22, 25). The "and now" section of the speech forms a chiasm, an inverted parallelism that emphasizes the reversal that came about following the christophany (Gaventa 1986a, 80). Paul first asserts that he is accused because of his hope, the hope of his forebears (vv. 6-8). He then narrates his earlier persecution of Christians (vv. 9-11). Verses 12-18 concern his commission as a witness. Verses 19-20 restate the commission, this time focusing on Paul's obedience. The topic of persecution is repeated in v. 21, although here it is Paul's persecution by Jews. Finally, vv. 22-23 restate Paul's opening claim that his belief in the resurrection is faithful to the prophets and Moses. The resultant chiasm emerges as follows:

1. Paul is faithful to tradition (vv. 6-8)
2. Paul persecuted Christians (vv. 9-11)
3. Paul commissioned as to witness (vv. 12-18)
4. Paul served as witness (vv. 19-20)
5. Paul has been persecuted (v. 21)
6. Paul is faithful to tradition (vv. 22-23)

The speech breaks off with Festus's outcry in v. 24, and a final scene displays the responses of Agrippa and Festus to the content of Paul's speech as well as the question of Paul's legal status (vv. 24-30).

Because the speech contains the third and final narration of Paul's conversion, literary questions also focus on the similarities and differences between this account and the previous two (9:1-19 and 22:3-21). As the discussion below will demonstrate, this rendition of Paul's conversion reflects its context. Unlike chapter

22, where Paul addressed a crowd of Jews outside the Jerusalem temple, in this passage he addresses powerful representatives of the Roman government, one of whom is also knowledgeable about Jewish people and tradition. In addition to this retelling of the conversion of Paul, words and phrases in the speech connect it with major concerns of Luke throughout the Gospel and Acts (e.g., witness, promise, hope, repentance, turning to God, light to the Gentiles).

As least since Paul's arrival in Jerusalem (21:17), events have been leading to this occasion, but the audience itself signals the speech's importance and also provides a way of understanding its content. Festus is a powerful governor of a Roman province; he is also a Gentile, as are presumably a number of those present. Despite Paul's address to Agrippa as someone knowledgeable about Jewish matters, Agrippa is also part of the Herodian family, a family that is not fully Jewish and is closely associated with Roman power. Paul appeals to Agrippa as one who shares traditions with him (vv. 26-27), but he also employs language that assumes the audience contains many who stand outside those traditions.

Paul's Final Defense (26:2-23)

The Opening (26:2-3): After Agrippa has given him permission to address the assembly, Paul stretches out his hand in the traditional pose of the orator (v. 1). In addition to the narrator's comment that Paul is defending himself, vv. 2-3 contain standard elements of a defense speech. Paul uses a term of direct address, "King Agrippa" (see also vv. 7, 13, 19). He explicitly states that he is about to defend himself, reinforcing v. 1. The *captatio benevolentiae* (the conventional opening in which the speaker praises the audience) credits Agrippa with knowing "all the customs and controversies of the Jews" (vv. 2-3). This remark has occasioned considerable speculation about Agrippa, particularly about whether Luke presents Agrippa as a Jew. What that speculation often overlooks, however, is how the comment functions in its context. Paul is about to present himself as the victim of an intramural quarrel regarding resurrection from the dead, and thus the appeal to Agrippa's knowledge serves to introduce the lines of Paul's defense. As Lysias and Festus have already concluded, the charges against Paul are not matters deserving death, but have to do with Jewish "customs and controversies" (23:29; 25:25)

Paul's Youth (26:4-5): As in chapter 22, Paul begins the body of his speech by reference to his past, hyperbolically invoking "all the Jews" as witnesses to his manner of living. In 22:5, he cites the high priests and council as potential witnesses to his earlier persecution of Christians, but here the witness list includes "all" Jews who are to testify to Paul's life "among my own people." The Greek word employed here is *ethnos*, which normally refers to Gentiles (and in the plural), but has appeared in the singular referring to Israel when Paul is addressing Roman officials (see 24:2, 10, 17). The description of Pharisaic life in v. 5 again demonstrates that the audience of Gentile outsiders has influenced this speech. Unlike 22:3, where Paul identifies himself with his Jewish brethren, here he employs terms slightly more distant, characterizing Pharisees as a party or sect, a term that an outsider might use (see Acts 5:17; 15:5; 24:5, 14; 28:22). Similarly, religion *(thrēskeia)* refers to cult or ritual, sometimes in a highly pejorative manner (e.g., Col 2:18; Wis 14:18, 27; Philo, *Spec. Laws* 1.315).

Faithfulness to Tradition (26:6-8): With the "and now" of v. 6, Paul turns from the past to which "all Jews" could testify and addresses a new situation. In this first section of the chiasm, Paul repeats an element of his earlier defense, namely, that he is accused concerning "hope and the resurrection of the dead" (23:6; 24:21). Yet vv. 6-8 also replay concerns that appear throughout Luke–Acts. Paul's description of the twelve tribes that served in hope recollects the prophet Anna, who served "night and day" (Luke 2:37). The promise, which here appears to be promise of the resurrection (as in 13:32), Luke earlier connects with the gift of the Holy Spirit (Luke 24:49; Acts 1:4; 2:33) and with the coming of Jesus as Messiah (2:39; 13:23). The question of v. 8—why anyone should regard it as impossible for God to raise the dead—may even recall Gabriel's word to Mary, "For nothing will be impossible with God" (Luke 1:37).

Paul's Persecution (26:9-11): In the second part of the chiasm (vv. 9-11), Paul takes up his activity as persecutor, introducing it with the elusive explanation, "I thought it necessary to do many things against the name of Jesus of Nazareth" (AT). An emphatic pronoun (*egō*) opens this statement, and it includes the word Luke has often used for God's plan (*dei*; lit., it is necessary; see, e.g., Luke 24:7, 26, 44; Acts 1:21; 3:21; 5:29), making it likely that Paul is presenting his actions as the result of his own calculations about the divine will. Instead of characterizing his activity in a general manner as "breathing threats and murder" (9:1) or persecuting the way "to the point of death" (22:4), Paul now itemizes his actions in vivid terms: he operated in Jerusalem (v. 10), where he not only locked up believers but voted against them when they were executed; in all the synagogues, he punished believers and compelled them to blaspheme (v. 11*a*); finally he pursued them "even into the outer cities" (AT). Again in v. 10 he uses the emphatic pronoun *egō*: these are all activities of Paul's own creation.

Paul Commissioned (26:12-18): Paul's speech turns to the christophany, the description of which again differs substantially from earlier accounts. This version moves quickly over its initial aspects and concentrates on Paul's calling (vv. 16*b*-18), with no reference to his blindness or to Ananias. Verse 13 closely parallels 9:3*b* and 22:6; in the middle of the day Paul sees a heavenly light. Here the phrase "brighter than the sun" makes explicit the significance of the element of time; that is, the light was strong enough to be impressive even in the midday sun. This light shone around Paul *and his companions,* and they all fell to the ground (v. 14*a*). Since blindness is not referred to here, the companions do not need to lead him into Damascus, and their role becomes that of sheer presence in vv. 13*b* and 14*a* (Gaventa 1986a, 82).

When all had fallen to the ground, Paul heard a voice "in the Hebrew language." Jesus' first words to Paul are exactly those of 9:4 and 22:7, but a new statement follows: "It is hard for you to kick against the goads" (26:14 AT). This Greek aphorism reflects the futility of resisting a greater power, in this case the power of God (e.g., Pindar, *Pythian Odes* 2.94-95; Aeschylus, *Agamemnon* 1624; Aeschylus, *Prometheus* 324-25; Euripides, *Bacchae* 794-95). The aphorism reveals the crisis: Paul has been acting upon *his own* perception of God's will, all the time resisting God's will.

Verse 15 closely parallels 9:5 and 22:8, but then the speech moves quickly to the result of the christophany. Jesus himself announces to Paul the nature of Paul's vocation. Jesus commands, "Get up and stand on your feet." Jesus underscores the importance of what he is about to tell Paul by saying, "For I have appeared to you for this purpose . . . ." The phrase "I have appeared" (*ōphthēn*) is almost a technical term for an experience of revelation (e.g., Luke 1:11; 22:43; Acts 7:2, 30). Although the earlier accounts of Paul's conversion are also revelatory (e.g., 9:17), this is the only one in which Jesus *announces* that he is revealing himself.

Jesus appears in order "to appoint [Paul as] servant and witness" (AT). The reference to servanthood recalls Luke 1:2, with its reference to "servants of the word." The conjunction "and" is epexegetical, meaning that the term "witness" describes Paul's servanthood (Rengstorf 1972, 542-43). Witness is, of course, a prime Lukan term for the work of the apostles (Luke 24:48; Acts 1:8; 22; 2:32; 3:15; 5:32; 10:39, 41; 13:31). For Paul to be called a witness (22:15) is for his work to be considered the same as that of the Twelve, even though he cannot properly be called an apostle (see the description in 1:21-22, but note 14:4, 14).

Jesus specifies that Paul is to witness to "the things in which you have seen me and to those in which I will appear to you," raising the question of how Paul can witness to things he has *already* seen if this is his first revelation of Jesus. Located in a narrative of Paul's conversion, this statement refers to the beginning of Paul's witness and mission. It also stands in Paul's final defense speech, however, where it summarizes Paul's activity. For that reason, the commission refers to "things . . . you have seen." Both the situation at the time of Paul's initial encounter with the risen Lord and the work Paul has done come to expression in the commission. (The personal pronoun "me" appears in some ancient manuscripts [*me*] and in the NRSV, but it probably did not appear in the original and represents a later scribe's clarification of the text.)

The initial words ("I will rescue you") of v. 17 similarly refer to the whole of Paul's witness rather than specifically to the time of his commission. Since Paul had not been in need of rescue at the time of his conversion, some have argued that the Greek word (*exaireō*) should be translated "choose" rather than "deliver." In Acts, however, *exaireō* never carries the connotation of selection (see 7:10, 34; 12:11; 23:27; cf. Jer 1:7-8). Here Luke compresses what has continually occurred with Paul as with other witnesses: God delivered him from danger.

The remainder of vv. 17 and 18 articulates Paul's calling, and in the most extended form of any of the three accounts of Paul's conversion (cf. 9:6; 22:10, 14-15). Each phrase not only reflects an understanding of conversion but powerfully reintroduces earlier and important motifs in Luke–Acts. First, Paul is to "open their eyes." This description of Paul's task complements the language of v. 16, where Jesus announces that he has appeared to Paul (lit. "I was seen") and refers to what Paul has seen and will see. Here, his own task is to open the eyes of others, in order that they also may see. Language about light and darkness, sight and blindness, is ubiquitous in Luke–Acts (Luke 2:30; 4:18; 24:16, 31; Acts 9:8, 18, 40; 13:11; 28:27; and see also Isa 42:6-7; 1 Pet 2:9; Philo, *Virtue* 179; *Jos. Asen.* 8.10; 15:13; *Odes Sol.* 11:18-19). Most important, the language here recalls the programmatic words of Simeon in Luke 2:32: "a light for revelation to the Gentiles and for glory to your people Israel."

Luke further heightens this stark contrast in the next phrase: "from the power of Satan to God." Although Luke elsewhere describes believers as "turning to God," this is the only instance in which he further describes them as turning from Satan. Yet the conflict with Satan figures early in Luke's Gospel in the temptation narrative (Luke 4:1-13), and numerous events in Luke–Acts involve struggles with Satan or those in Satan's control (Luke 22:3; Acts 5:3; 13:10; Garrett 1989). Transfer from the realm of Satan to that of God is central to Luke's understanding of salvation.

The conclusion of v. 18 takes up the consequences of turning to God: "That they may receive forgiveness of sins and a place among those who are sanctified by faith in me." Forgiveness of sins is another typically Lukan concern, appearing in the preaching of John the Baptist (Luke 1:77; 3:3) and in that of Jesus (Luke 4:18; NRSV: release). In the church's preaching, forgiveness of sins appears as one of God's central gifts through the coming of Jesus (Acts 2:38; 5:31; 10:43; 13:38). To receive "a place among those who are sanctified" is to be set apart by God to receive the positive gift of a share in the community (cf. Acts 20:32; LXX Deut 33:3; Wis 5:5).

Paul's Witness (26:19-20): This extensive statement of Paul's commission forms the center of the chiasm noted above. With vv. 19-20 the restatement of the earlier sections of the chiasm begins as Paul asserts his obedience to the commission, beginning with a *litotes* that emphasizes all that follows: "I was not disobedient." The sequence of v. 20 does not precisely follow Paul's itinerary, but it does reflect the promise of Jesus in Acts 1:8. Paul has not only obeyed the "heavenly vision"; he has participated in the fulfillment of the promise of the risen Lord to the apostles.

Paul's concise summary of his proclamation largely recapitulates vv. 17-18. The admonition to do "deeds consistent with repentance" introduces a topic not explicit in vv. 17-18. Repentance and turning are to be accompanied by deeds of repentance. The wording of this claim recalls Luke 3:8, in which John the Baptist addresses those who come to be baptized, "Bear fruits that befit repentance." We do not find the same formulation of this demand elsewhere in Acts; nevertheless, Luke does describe actions that illustrate repentance just following incidents of conversion (e.g., Acts 2:41-47; 4:4, 32-37). Thus, the admonition makes explicit what is assumed throughout the narrative.

Paul's Persecution (26:21): Verse 21 takes up the reaction to Paul's preaching by recalling the Jews' seizure of Paul in the temple precinct (21:27-36), and this "seizing" echoes that of Jesus (1:16) and Peter (12:3). In addition, it reverses the earlier persecution carried out by Paul. One who earlier voted for the death of believers (26:10) now becomes the object of similar action.

Paul's Faithfulness (26:22-23): The final section of the speech asserts that Paul has always had God's help as he witnesses to all people. His witness differs not from what was said by the prophets and Moses; that is, that Christ would suffer and would rise from the dead to proclaim light to the people and the Gentiles. This conclusion returns to Paul's opening remarks and thus completes the chiasm: Paul preaches only what has always been expected by Israel. It also returns to Luke's earlier claim that Scripture itself teaches the death and resurrection of Jesus (Luke 24:25-27, 44-45). Now, however, the witness of Scripture includes also the witness to Israel and the Gentiles alike (see 15:15). Most astonishing in the concluding statement: Jesus as the first of those to rise from the dead *is the one* who proclaims light to all. Here Luke takes a bold step, identifying Jesus as the proclaimer of light, salvation, to all people. Not only does Christ send Paul as a witness but Christ himself is the witness.

Responses Public and Private (26:24-30)

As is frequently the case in Acts, the speech is interrupted (e.g., 2:37; 17:32; 22:22), in this case by Festus's outburst, accusing Paul of madness. Perhaps Festus, like the Athenians (17:32), balked at the mention of resurrection, or perhaps his comment about "too much learning" reflects his own inability to comprehend Paul's argumentation (Fitzmyer 1998, 763). Whatever his motivation, his comment permits Paul a further appeal. Affirming the "sober truth" of his words, Paul turns from Festus to Agrippa, appealing again to his knowledge and conceding that he is speaking boldly (NRSV: freely), as is characteristic of the witness throughout Acts (e.g., 4:13, 31; 9:27-28; 13:46; 28:31). Paul himself is bold, and the events are known to Agrippa because this "was not done in a corner." With a stereotyped reference to public actions (Plato, *Gorgias* 485D; Epictetus, *Discourses* 2.12.17; Plutarch, *On Curiosity* 516B; Plutarch, *Philosophers and Men in Power* 777B), Paul characterizes not only himself but all of the Christian witness as open for inspection.

The exchange between Paul and Agrippa in vv. 28-29 is highly obscure (Lake and Cadbury 1933, 323), in large part because it is impossible to discern the emotional tone of Agrippa's remark. It could be a genuine statement of regard for Paul's appeal to his own belief in the prophets, or it could be a jeering rejection of the entire enterprise. Whatever the nature of Agrippa's response, Paul's rejoinder indicates that Agrippa understands him rightly: his intent is to bring Agrippa and all those present to the light of the gospel.

Paul's last appeal stands unanswered, and the scene closes with the departure of Agrippa and all his courtiers. As a single voice, they declare what has been clear since 23:29, that Paul is innocent of any charges. Agrippa reinforces that judgment with his final remark to Festus. Yet these declarations are cheap, made only out of Paul's hearing and as he is passing from their jurisdiction and into that of the Emperor (Tannehill 1990, 329).

◊ ◊ ◊ ◊

This final extended speech contains much that is familiar in Paul's defense. As earlier, he appeals to the shared belief in resurrection, and he introduces his own past actions as evidence of his loyalty to Israel. In addition, the speech is a virtual synopsis of Lukan theology. God's ancient promise to Israel finds its fulfillment in the death and resurrection of Jesus Christ, whose resurrection anticipates the resurrection of all. The witness to that risen Jesus boldly declares to Israel and also to the Gentiles that

God has acted to rescue them from Satan's grasp. All of this the prophets and Moses anticipate.

So familiar are these elements in the speech that they may obscure the ways in which it is also a turning point. Despite the apologetic introduction, Paul does not in fact defend himself in this speech. He responds directly to no charge made against him (cf. 24:10-21). Instead, the defense becomes an occasion for proclamation of the gospel (Kennedy 1984, 140; Crouch 1996, 341). Agrippa recognizes that fact, and Paul admits it with his closing remark: "I pray to God that not only you but also all who are listening to me today might become such as I am—except for these chains" (v. 29). Particularly coming as it does in the finale of Paul's defense, this insistence on proclamation signals a crucial feature in Luke's understanding. The only real defense available to Paul and to the church as a whole is that of proclamation. Responding to charges might relieve Paul from his imprisonment, but it would not constitute obedience.

Specifically, Paul proclaims the turn from his own decision about God's desire to his obedience to the call of the risen Jesus. The actions of vv. 9-11 focus on Paul's decisions and Paul's initiative. Those of the remainder of the speech attend to the Lord's bidding. He appears to Paul, commissions him, and God sustains him in his work (v. 22). Appropriately, Paul epitomizes himself with the words "I was not disobedient." Now the question is not Paul's own decision but Paul's faithfulness.

Most important is the striking move made in v. 23, where Paul identifies the risen Jesus as the one who is proclaiming "light" to Jew and Gentile alike. Earlier, Paul had persecuted the church, which the christophany identifies with Jesus himself (v. 14). Now Paul witnesses, but it is actually the Lord who proclaims. In a daring reversal of the classic line about the Gospels, here the proclaimed has become the proclaimer.

"And So We Came to Rome" (27:1–28:31)

Acts 27–28 serves as denouement for the climactic speech of Paul before Agrippa and Felix and, indeed, for the whole of Acts. The light preached by the risen Jesus to all people (26:23) now blazes in the dramatic story of God's salvation of Paul and company from certain death at sea. Rescued from death, Paul finally arrives at Rome, not as the initial bearer of the gospel, but as its captive witness, once more engaging in dispute with Jews but persistently preaching and teaching about Jesus.

Crisis and Confidence at Sea (27:1-44)

Given the number of voyages Luke has narrated that include Paul (e.g., 13:4, 13; 16:11; 18:18), the addition of yet another is in no way surprising, especially in view of the earlier indications that Paul himself would go to Rome (19:21; 25:9-12). What does come as a surprise is the detail Luke lavishes on this account. Earlier voyages are sketchy by comparison. Luke needed to mention the journey as part of his "orderly account" (Luke 1:1), but that requirement does not in itself explain the itemizing of locations, ships, and personnel, nor the extensive description of the storm.

Luke's contemporaries may not have found this chapter quite so surprising, since sea travel and the perils arising from it are a favorite theme in ancient Greek and Roman narratives (Homer, *Odyssey* 5.291-332; 9.62-81; 12.201-303; Virgil, *Aeneid* 1.34-156; Lucian, *Toxaris* 19-20; Lucian, *Navigium* 7-10; Lucian, *Verae historiae* 1.6; Achilles Tatius, *Clitophon and Leucippe* 3.1-5; Petronius, *Satyricon* 114-15; Chariton, *Chaereas and Callirhoe* 3.3; Josephus, *Life* 3.13-16). Audiences evidently enjoyed this sort of tale, just as contemporary moviegoers expect and enjoy car chase scenes in an action adventure movie. Specific details within the account have counterparts in other ancient narratives, including the storm, the attempt of those on board to protect themselves at the expense of others, the jettisoning of cargo, and the shipwreck.

The uniqueness of the story within Acts and the many parallels to features of it in other ancient literature prompt a variety of proposals about its sources, its historical accuracy, and most especially its role in Luke's larger story. Among the more prominent proposals are three: (1) chapter 27 derives from an eyewitness account composed by a traveling companion of Paul (Rapske 1994a, 22-47); (2) Luke has redacted an extant account of a voyage and shipwreck, into which he has inserted elements of the story pertaining to Paul (Dibelius 1956, 134-35, 213-14); and (3) Luke has largely created this story out of his own imagination in order to enhance Paul's standing (Haenchen 1971, 708-710). Resolution of this controversy is unlikely, since the same vivid details that persuade some interpreters of eyewitness accuracy strike others as the work of a fertile imagination. Whatever the literary background and historical content of the episode, in its Lukan context it dramatically enacts the confidence in God that Paul expresses before Agrippa and Festus.

Seven scenes comprise the story, which begins with the departure from Caesarea and ends with the safe landing at Malta:

(1) The initial stage of the voyage and its difficulties (vv. 1-8)
(2) Paul's failed intervention to halt the voyage (vv. 9-12)
(3) The storm and the loss of hope (vv. 13-20)
(4) Paul's intervention prophesying God's rescue (vv. 21-26)
(5) The drifting of the ship and further evidence of hopelessness (vv. 27-32)
(6) Paul's intervention with a meal (vv. 33-38)
(7) The shipwreck (vv. 39-44)

The scenes alternate between the physical realities of the voyage itself and Paul's interventions.

Yet another notable literary feature of this passage is the return of the first-person plural narrator, who appears in 27:1 and continues through 28:16. "We" last figured in Acts prior to Paul's arrest in Jerusalem (21:1-18; see also 16:10-17; 20:5-15). As before, "we" appears at moments of special urgency—the crossing into Macedonia, the final trip to Jerusalem, and now the long-awaited voyage to Rome (see above on 15:36–16:10).

◊ ◊ ◊ ◊

Difficulties from the Beginning (27:1-8)

Without further reference to the powerful Festus and Agrippa, Paul is transferred to the custody of an otherwise unknown centurion, Julius, who serves as part of the Augustan cohort, a unit established for the Emperor Augustus. Luke never indicates how large the contingent of prisoners is or how many soldiers oversee them (vv. 31, 42), although later he indicates that the entire ship contains 276 people. Among the passengers is Aristarchus, probably to be equated with the Aristarchus of 19:29 and 20:4, also identified there as a Macedonian. How Aristarchus comes to be with Paul and what has happened to the contingent that traveled to Jerusalem with Paul (20:4), Luke does not explain.

In addition to identifying the personnel on board ship, this scene attends to vessels and their stopping points along the way. They board a ship from Adramyttium, a port on the northwest coast of Asia Minor. Since that ship probably was returning to Adramyttium and was of only limited service to the centurion, he later finds an Alexandrian ship intent on Italy (almost certainly with grain from Egypt; see Suetonius, *Claudius* 18.2; Seneca, *Epistles* 77.1-2; Lucian, *Navigium* 1-9). Sailing up the coast to Sidon and taking advantage of the protection of Cyprus, Paul crosses to Myra in Lycia, and then, having boarded the second ship, begins the journey westward, stopping first at Fair Havens on Crete. The route attempts to avoid dangerous winds coming from the north by staying close to the southern coast of the island (Casson 1974, 152).

Two comments set the tone for the journey. First, the centurion presents himself as a decent individual. Although later he will ignore Paul's warning, Julius treats Paul well, permitting him to seek the help of friends at Sidon (v. 3). Presumably these friends are believers, although Luke has said nothing of a mission in Sidon (but see 11:19; 15:3). Without amenities for passengers on the ship, Paul would have needed food for the journey which these believers could help him secure (Casson 1974, 153). Second, and more pivotal for the story, even this initial stage of the voyage is marked by difficulty. The winds make travel slow and hint that more serious problems lie ahead.

Paul's First Intervention: A Warning (27:9-12)

Verse 9 signals that the strong winds of the first scene are only the beginning of the dangers. "The Fast" refers to the Day of Atonement, the tenth of Tishri (September/October). The season of dangerous navigation also begins at about that time, due to winter storms and the cloudy skies that restrict viewing the sun and stars (Casson 1974, 150). In one sense, what Paul says is not at all remarkable and would be obvious to anyone who knows that travel from October through April was considered risky. As the story unfolds, however, it becomes clear that Luke presents this warning as something more than an instance of conventional wisdom. Paul speaks not only as an experienced traveler (Ramsay 1925, 322) but as an agent of God who brings about the rescue of the ship.

Luke has characterized the centurion favorably, but here he shows himself more persuaded by the powerful than by the prophetic. The pilot and the owner (or perhaps the freight contractor, see BDAG 667), who may be mindful of inducements in bad seasons to those who produced and shipped grain for the huge demands of Rome, insist on continuing (Suetonius, *Claudius* 18.102). Verse 12 offers the additional view of the majority, supportive of the pilot and owner, that Fair Havens was unsuitable for wintering. The decision is to set out for Phoenix, another harbor on Crete.

The Storm Begins (27:13-20)

Quickly it becomes apparent that even hugging the shore of Crete will not ensure the vessel's safety. Among the desperate measures taken by the crew, Luke says that they attempted to "undergird the ship" (probably by the use of cables); later they throw both cargo and tackle overboard (see *1 En.* 101:4-5). That the sun and stars were hidden in the darkness of clouds indicates the severity of the storm and also the desperation of its crew without these essential navigational guides. Verse 20 drives to the heart of the matter: all hope had been abandoned.

The presence of the "we" narrator in v. 20 is intriguing. "We" seems to participate in the hopelessness of the ship's passengers as a whole, which provides an interesting contrast to Paul's confident assertion in the lines that follow. If even Paul's supporters give up hope, this may further indicate the severity of the crisis.

Paul's Second Intervention: God Will Preserve All (27:21-26)

The lack of food both symbolizes and provokes the hopelessness of those on board. The meal that follows and the discarding of grain in vv. 33-38 make it clear that the problem is not with availability—there is food to spare. Although the storm may well have induced seasickness and made food preparation difficult, in context of v. 20 the problem would seem to be lack of motivation. Those without hope have no reason to seek the sustenance of food.

Paul intervenes a second time, first with a forceful reminder that he had urged against the voyage. The "I told you so" rhetorically enhances his credibility as witness and also urges those present to attend to him in the crisis. The explanation Paul offers in vv. 23-24 is central to the passage, as Paul invokes "the God to whom I belong and whom I worship." Paul cannot assume that a contingent of Roman soldiers or the crew of an Alexandrian ship would recognize a reference to "the God of Abraham" (see 3:13), and he introduces God with an identification accessible to outsiders. The phrase does something more, however. It emphatically indicates that whatever follows by way of sustenance and rescue comes from God rather than from Paul. Paul is no more the hero of this event than he is the subject of witnessing earlier in Acts. The emphatic invocation of God may also imply a challenge to those on board who imagine that other gods govern the sea (as in, e.g., Jonah 1:4-16; Achilles Tatius, *Clitophon and Leucippe* 3.5).

The angel has reinforced once more the necessity of Paul's arrival in Rome. Three times in this short scene the familiar word *dei* is found, recalling not only the necessity of Paul's journey to Rome but its larger context within the divine plan (e.g., Luke 24:26, 44; Acts 3:21; 4:12; 23:11). Because of this necessity, God "has granted safety to all those who are sailing with" Paul (v. 24). Literally, what Luke says is that God has given them to Paul. This way of putting the matter contrasts with Paul's insistence that Festus could not "grant" him to the Jewish leaders as a favor (25:11; the verbs are the same). In both cases, the "granting" is connected with Paul's journey to Rome.

The Drifting Ship (27:27-32)

The hopelessness of the situation reappears here. Adrift on the "sea of Adria," the ship is far to the west of its intended safe harbor in Phoenix. Suspecting that they are nearing land, the crew tests the water's depth and finds it growing more shallow. Fearing a shipwreck in the night, they let down the anchors in order to slow the drifting. Luke next says that the sailors planned to escape by using the ship's boat, on the pretense that they were to lower additional anchors from the bow of the ship (v. 30). Such desperate measures betray deep fears and constitute an unspeakable betrayal of duty to the other passengers. Paul notifies the centurion, who now listens and has his soldiers cut the ropes so that the boat would float free.

Paul's Third Intervention (27:33-38)

In the face of dire hopelessness, Paul's urging of food seems absurd. The sailors who attempted to get away in the boat clearly expect the worst, and taking food constitutes an expectation that life continues, an expectation apparently not shared by Paul's other passengers despite his assurance in vv. 24-25. Now he urges food and again insists: "None of you will lose a hair from your heads."

Verses 35-36 have generated considerable controversy, with some interpreting the scene as an ordinary meal, and others drawing attention to its eucharistic overtones. Acts has earlier referred to believers sharing bread (2:46), but has not shown an explicit fulfillment of Jesus' instructions in Luke 22:14-20, making an exegetical judgment here difficult. The absence of wine, the fact that Paul does not himself distribute the bread, and the presence of nonbelievers further complicate the question. And that question itself may have overshadowed an important role for the text. Paul's insistence on taking food at this stage, when the very people charged with sailing the vessel have just demonstrated their own hopelessness, constitutes a sign of hope and confidence in God. Luke specifies that those who observe Paul are encouraged and then take food. If it is not the bread of the eucharist, it is the bread of hope.

Safely to Land (27:39-44)

The final scene brings all those aboard the ship back to safety on the land, but not without difficulty. With land in sight, the crew attempts to take the ship ashore but strikes a reef instead. As the ship begins to break up, another action threatens to undermine God's plan to rescue all who are on board. This time the threat comes from the soldiers, who decide to kill the prisoners. By preventing their escape, the soldiers presumably act to protect themselves, charged as they are with the keeping of these prisoners (see 12:19; 16:27). Julius intervenes, out of the desire to save Paul. Finally, swimming and floating on debris, group by dreary group, all collapse onto dry ground.

Coming on the heels of the declarations of Paul's innocence in 25:25 and 26:31-32 and presenting several interventions by Paul at important junctures in the voyage, this story invites interpretations that center on Paul's vindication or Paul's innocence (Miles and Trompf, 1976). Just as in the lengthy proceeding in Jerusalem and Caesarea, so also here, the Lukan Paul turns the spotlight away from himself and onto God. It has become increasingly clear that Luke can scarcely tell a story from which God is absent. Paul's guilt or innocence will enter the story briefly in the Malta episode (28:1-6), but here Paul serves as interpreter of God's plan. God's intention to have Paul witness in Rome is not to be thwarted.

It is not only Paul whom God delivers from the shipwreck, of course. The protection given him extends through the entire list of passengers. Here also Luke enacts a theme that has occupied his story from the oracle of Simeon (Luke 2:31-32) and the preaching of John the Baptist (Luke 3:6) through the speech of Paul before Agrippa and Festus (26:17-18, 23). It recurs even in the last lines of Acts (28:30-31): God's salvation extends to include all people.

Paul's God brings about this saving act on the sea. Among the established conventions of narratives involving voyages and their perils is the role of the gods who, from Homer on, protect ships, threaten them, and destroy them. Luke has already shown Christian witnesses venturing into this territory, but here Luke shows their God triumphing over the sea, perhaps even over the gods of the sea as well.

From Malta to Rome (28:1-15)

The final stage in Paul's journey to Rome takes him from shipwreck on the virtually unknown island of Malta to his long anticipated arrival in Rome (see 19:21). Three distinct stages complete the journey: the hospitality of the island's inhabitants and their double misunderstanding of Paul (vv. 1-6), the hospitality of Publius and Paul's healing of various inhabitants (vv. 7-10), and the final journey to Rome (vv. 11-15).

Features of this passage reflect the standard literary repertoire of Luke's day. Not surprisingly, given the multitude of stories about storms at sea, the friendly strangers who come to the aid of stranded sailors appear in a variety of narratives (e.g., Dio Chrysostom, *Discourses* 7.4-6; Petronius, *Satyricon* 114; Lucian, *Verae historiae* 1:28-29; 2:46). In addition, the notion of a personified Justice who seeks vengeance or retribution appears else-where (e.g., Wis 1:8; Josephus, *J.W.* 1.84; 4 Macc 18:22), as do anecdotes involving sudden death from the bite of a viper (Heliodorus, *Ethiopians* 2.20; *Greek Anthology* 290).

◊ ◊ ◊ ◊

Mistaken Identities for Paul (28:1-6)

Neither Julius and his soldiers nor the captain and his crew appear again. Their presence at the end of v. 44 ensures that all aboard ship do land safely, but now they vanish from the story. Inquiring about their presence at the fire or about how Publius later entertains all 276 people is something of an interpretive detour. Luke's attention continues to be fixed on Paul's role, pre-viously as that of interpreter of God's actions and here as the object of curiosity by the inhabitants of Malta.

Most scholars agree that the location is Malta, south of Sicily, an island under control of the Romans for over two centuries by the time this incident would have occurred. A glance at a map will show how far the ship was taken from its original destina-tion. Luke refers to the people initially encountered by Paul and others arriving on the island as *barbaroi*, those who are "non-Greek" either in language or in culture. Although the Greek word can have a sharply pejorative connotation, as in the English word "barbarians," it can also be a neutral reference to foreigners, as in the NRSV's translation, "natives." The context here suggests that the reference is neutral. The native inhabitants of Malta had some dialect of Punic as their primary language, but some would have understood either Greek or Latin or both.

The "unusual kindness" of the inhabitants recalls the human-ity of the centurion Julius (27:3). In this instance, the specific kindness mentioned is starting a fire to warm the newcomers drenched first from the sea and now from rain as well. This action in turn sets the stage for the events that follow, in which Paul twice becomes the victim of mistaken identity. First, as he is collecting wood for a fire, a "viper" attaches itself to his hand.

Luke does not specify that the animal is poisonous, although the conclusions drawn by the inhabitants suggest that they know it to be, and there is some evidence that all snakes were thought to be so (Pliny, *Natural History* 8.35.85-86). Less occupied with zoology than with theology, the natives immediately conclude that Paul is a murderer who has escaped from death at sea but who now meets his just reward (vv. 3-4). Second, when Paul emerges unscathed from this attack, the natives shift their position, concluding that he is not a murderer but a god (v. 6).

The fickleness of the Maltese recalls and reverses that of the residents of Lystra, who initially greeted Paul and Barnabas as gods because of their miraculous healing of a lame man, only to begin to attack them under the influence of Paul's opponents arriving from Antioch and Iconium (14:8-20). In neither situation is the judgment carefully formed, not to mention accurate. What is remarkable, however, particularly in light of the reaction of Paul and Barnabas at Lystra, is that Paul utters not a single word throughout the scene. He neither protests the accusation of murder nor rejects the more troubling label of deity. The silence may simply reflect the reprise-like character of Acts 27–28; by now the audience knows Paul's identity and does not require further confirmation. If some supplemental rejection of the label "god" is needed, it comes in the second part of the Malta story, where Paul prays at healings. Often commentators associate this scene with the earlier defense of Paul's innocence, but Paul has not been accused of murder and has no need to prove himself innocent of that charge (unless 9:1; 22:4; and 26:10 are to be considered evidence of murder).

For the natives of Malta, the viper is an instrument of justice. For Luke, however, something else may be at work here. In Luke's Gospel, Jesus delegates to the disciples the authority to "tread on" snakes and serpents, creatures associated with Satan, without themselves being harmed (10:17-20). Although the two passages employ different nouns for the creatures involved, a single association may be implied. Paul is not healed from the viper's attack so much as he is simply immune to it, and his immunity comes not from his own internal resources, but from the God who called him and delivered him safely from shipwreck (Spencer 1997, 235).

Mutual Hospitalities (28:7-10)

The introduction of Publius in v. 7 creates the occasion for reciprocal "hospitality," using the word in an extended sense to include the healings as well as the feeding and sheltering of Paul and others. Luke introduces Publius only by identifying him as the "leading man" of the island who owns property. The name strongly suggests that he is Roman, perhaps the Roman official charged with administration of the island. Luke does not bother explaining how Publius could have entertained an entire ship full of people, although commentators going back at least to Calvin have fretted over this difficulty (Calvin 1966, 302).

Luke does not linger over Publius's hospitality, nor over any of the events that follow. Briefly, v. 8 sketches the healing of Publius's father. Here Paul, whose laundry has earlier brought about healings (19:12), both prays and lays hands on the man. The detail is noteworthy, since elsewhere in Acts that combination of prayer and laying on of hands occurs when people are set aside for some task (e.g., 6:6; 13:3) and does not occur with healing. In Luke's Gospel, however, Jesus lays hands on some whom he heals (4:40; 5:13; 13:13), so that Paul's actions may constitute a reprise of the healings carried out by Jesus' disciples (Luke 9:1-6; 10:1-9). This action also serves as a correction, if one is needed, to the Maltese misunderstanding of Paul's identity, since a deity would have no need to pray for healing as Paul prays here.

Verses 9-10 round out the story by returning to the larger population of Malta. They now bring their sick to be healed through Paul. And, when the party is ready to depart, they grant them "many honors" and supply provisions for the last part of the voyage. "Honors" may refer simply to gifts or it may be money given in exchange for the healing, since the word *timē* can refer to a price (as in "proceeds" in Acts 4:34) or to "honor" (as in Rom 9:21). The exact nature of the honors is unclear, but with the term Luke depicts the completion of a cycle of reciprocity. Publius and the other residents of Malta have acted hospitably to Paul and his companions, and in return Paul has served as an agent of healing.

"And So We Came to Rome" (28:11-15)

The extent to which Luke is telescoping events becomes clear in v. 11, when he indicates that the group remains on Malta for three months before boarding another Alexandrian ship (see 27:6), presumably another vessel carrying grain for Rome. This ship Luke identifies as having the "Twin Brothers" as its figurehead. The title Dioscuri or "Twin Brothers" identifies the gods Castor and Pollux, twins to whom navigators looked for protection (Epictetus, *Discourses* 2.18.29; Lucian, *Navigium* 9; Casson 1971, 359). The reference to them here is puzzling. Because the pair occasionally figure as guardians of truth, it has been suggested that they provide yet another indication of Paul's innocence, since they would not tolerate a lawbreaker on "their" ship (Ladouceur 1980). This explanation might work for the inhabitants of Malta, but neither Luke nor the audience implied by his narrative would be persuaded by the judgments of the Twin Brothers. Closer to the Lukan story-world is the suggestion that there is a whiff of irony here, as those who seek the protection of the Twin Brothers have stayed ashore during the winter while the true God protected both Paul and those outside the community of believers (Talbert 1997, 224; Spencer 1997, 236). Perhaps nothing more is intended than vivid detail, such as the verses that follow also supply.

Departing Malta, the ship travels north, first to Syracuse and then to Rhegium, located in the "toe" of the Italian boot. From there, it journeys quickly to the central Roman port of Puteoli. The final segment of the journey by land to Rome takes the company along the Appian Way first to the Forum of Appius, a market town located forty-three miles from Rome, then to the Three Taverns, thirty-three miles from Rome. Finally, as Luke says with astonishing understatement, "we came to Rome."

Both in Puteoli and in Rome, there are believers who receive Paul. In Puteoli, they provide for the needs of the travelers, as has been done by fellow-believers throughout Acts (e.g., 10:48; 16:15; 21:7-8; 27:3). Luke says nothing about how these groups of believers came into existence, an omission that may reflect his relative lack of interest in the history of communities as such. As is evident throughout the story, Luke's concern with how believing communities come into existence has to do with God's initiative rather than with identifying their human teachers or tracking church development across the Mediterranean world.

The arrival of Paul in Rome distinguishes itself from his arrival in other cities throughout the book. Here he does not begin by entering the synagogue and preaching, but he is himself greeted by fellow-believers at the Forum of Appius (some forty miles from the city itself). The change may derive simply from the fact that he is still a prisoner of Rome, although reference to that fact has nearly slipped out of the narrative. In addition, however, the change enacts the fulfillment of the prophetic word announced in 19:21 and repeated in a variety of forms and from a variety of agents since that time: Paul must give witness in Rome.

◊ ◊ ◊ ◊

Much discussion of this passage focuses on the portrait of Paul, both on the island of Malta and as he arrives in Rome. Some interpreters understand this scene as the final declaration of Paul's innocence (Miles and Trompf 1982; Ladouceur 1980), while others perceive in Paul a full-blown divine man, no longer a prisoner but "a mighty superman, who spreads blessings around him" (Haenchen 1971, 716). Both views distort the conclusions of the fickle islanders of Malta, views by this point in the story so self-evidently wrong that Luke does not bother to correct them overtly. Instead, he relies on the story for the proper identification of Paul as God's agent rather than as a murderer or divine hero. Paul prays and lays hands on the sick in order to bring about God's healing. Paul thanks God for his arrival in

Rome. As throughout the story, responsibility is attributed to God rather than to any human agent.

Theologically, one of the most important features of the Malta episode is what does *not* happen, since nothing is said of Paul preaching and teaching there. This narrative gap almost demands response, which some interpreters provide from earlier in the story; since Paul has elsewhere preached, they assume that he preaches here also. Given the character of these chapters as a reprise of earlier elements of Acts, and given the clear declaration at the end of chapter 28 that Paul continues to preach and teach, the traditional view has some force. A more recent proposal is that the story displays the cooperative spirit Luke thinks should exist between Christians and pagans (Tannehill 1990, 340-41), but Luke's story is not about cooperating for some common human good. On the other hand, the reciprocity between the islanders and Paul, standing as it does so near the close of the volume, may hint at reciprocity still to come (Gaventa 2001).

Having anticipated Paul's arrival in Rome since 19:21, the actual event seems anticlimactic. No crowd gathers for Paul's preaching, and no description illumines the situation of those believers who journey out to meet him. That minimalistic assessment should not obscure the importance of Paul's thanksgiving in v. 15. The journey all along has less to do with what will happen in Rome than with the God who directs Paul to that place.

"When We Came into Rome" (28:16-31)

The first section of the denouement of Acts (27:1–28:15) narrates the voyage to Rome. Although the necessity of Paul's journey has been established as early as 19:21 (and see also 23:11), the trip itself involves new territory, both geographically and dramatically. In this second part of the denouement, however, there is a return to the familiar debate with Jews. In those scenes (vv. 17-22 and 23-28) as well as in the conclusion (vv. 30-31), Luke returns to themes that extend through the Acts of the Apostles as well as the Third Gospel.

Structurally, this final section of Acts constitutes an inclusion or ring. It both begins (v. 16) and ends (vv. 30-31) with summary comments characterizing Paul's Roman custody. Two scenes stand between these summaries, in both of which Paul engages in discussion with Jews of Rome (vv. 16-22, 23-28). A major feature of the second scene is Paul's quotation of Isa 6:9-10, the interpretation of which poses major problems for identifying Luke's understanding of the Jewish mission.

Many readers find the conclusion of Acts abrupt and unsatisfying. Paul does not receive the opportunity to defend himself before the emperor, and the outcome of his captivity is never told. Luke indicates nothing of what took place following Paul's two-year stay in Rome. Readers always experience "gaps" in narration, but the gap at the end of Acts threatens to widen into a canyon. In an attempt to account for the gap, interpreters have employed strategies either historical or theological. Among historical explanations are the suggestions that Luke planned but never completed his third volume (or that the third volume was subsequently lost), that he stopped where he did because the trial was still underway, or that he wrote no further than the extent of his own eyewitness knowledge. All of these theories presuppose that the current ending is, in fact, unsatisfactory or temporary, while the theological explanations accept the current ending as the one Luke intended and seek to understand it within Luke's overall plan. Among these explanations is the notion that Luke did not wish to glamorize the martyrdom of Paul, or that the arrival of Paul in Rome marks the fulfillment of 1:8 and so the completion of Luke's program. As the discussion below will indicate, the present ending does bring together a number of important Lukan motifs, which makes it seem unlikely that vv. 30-31 constitute only a mere pause before undertaking a new volume. In addition, the reference to a two-year period suggests that Luke knows what happened at the end of that time. (On the theological implications of this ending, see below.)

◊ ◊ ◊ ◊

Verse 16 briefly characterizes Paul's custody in Rome. Because it begins with the phrase "When we came into Rome," it appears to repeat the announcement of v. 14 ("And so we came to Rome"), but the two serve different purposes. Verse 14 concludes the long journey, and v. 16 introduces events that take place in Rome. Paul's "house arrest" may reflect an awareness of his relatively high social standing or it could simply indicate that he is not regarded as dangerous (Skinner 2003, 165), and it makes possible the scenes that follow.

A First Meeting with Roman Jews (28:17-22)

The introduction to this scene raises some logistical questions. Although Christians from Rome have already journeyed to meet Paul (see v. 15), nothing more is heard of them. Instead, Paul calls together leading Jews of the city, who come despite the fact that they later claim not to have heard about Paul (v. 21). Luke's inattention to such questions of consistency reveals less about the historical situation in Rome than it does about his eagerness to get to the heart of the matter, namely, Paul's witness.

In vv. 17b-20 Paul recapitulates the events in Jerusalem. (That he says nothing of the difficult voyage may provide further indication of its standing as part of the book's denouement rather than as its climactic event.) He begins with an emphatic personal pronoun (egō) and a direct denial of wrongdoing: "I had done nothing against our people or the customs of our ancestors" (see 23:1; 24:10b-13; 25:10-11). The second half of the verse telescopes the complex events in Jerusalem, where Paul was not so much handed over to the Romans as delivered by them from the rage of Jerusalem Jews (21:27-36). Verse 18 similarly replays earlier declarations by Roman officials that Paul was accused of nothing that warranted his death (23:29; 25:25; 26:31-32).

The brief phrase at the beginning of v. 19 reinterprets earlier events, as Paul claims that the Jews "objected" or "contradicted" (antilegō), presumably speaking against the official declaration of his innocence. Nothing in the proceedings in Jerusalem or Caesarea coincides precisely with this claim, especially since the various Roman declarations of Paul's innocence take place outside of public view (23:29; 25:25; 26:31-32), so that Jewish objections would be difficult. What the phrase may reflect is the pressure on Festus to take Paul to Jerusalem, a pressure that apparently prompts Festus to propose a change of venue for Paul's hearing (25:9). As a result, Paul appeals to Caesar (v. 19; 25:11).

Paul carefully adds that he had "no charge" to bring against the Jews. This claim has been construed as a legal statement, since individuals falsely charged could in turn bring accusations against those who so charged (Witherington 1998, 798). Yet the larger context seems far less concerned with Paul's legal standing than with his standing among his own people, which suggests that the statement is rhetorically shaped. Paul carefully words his report in order to secure the hearing of Roman Jewish leaders for a few minutes more.

With v. 20, Paul turns from this rehearsal of events in Jerusalem and Caesarea to the present. "For this reason" he has asked to speak with Jewish leaders, "since it is for the sake of the hope of Israel that I am bound with this chain." The connection between the two parts of this verse is important. The reference to "the hope of Israel" recalls, of course, Paul's identification of that hope with Israel's past, as well as with the resurrection of Jesus and the declaration of saving light to all people (26:6-8, 22-23). He has asked to "speak with" the Jewish leaders, in order to put that hope before them.

When the Jewish leaders speak, they do so as a group with a single voice, and they make two distinct statements, one about Paul and the other about what they refer to as "this sect." About Paul, they report that they have received no information from Judea, either in writing or in person (v. 21). Not only does this statement offer the possibility for Paul to gain a fresh hearing in Rome, where the heated accusations of Jerusalem apparently have not followed him, but it indicates that the discussion that follows will have to do with the content of Paul's teaching rather than with Paul himself. Here the issue is not Paul's observance or non-observance of the law (cf. 21:28; 24:5-6), or Paul's posture toward his own people, but the gospel.

The final statement of v. 22 hints that there will nevertheless be difficulties. The Jewish leaders want to hear from Paul, because "this sect" is "everywhere" spoken against. Several details in this comment are significant. Just as Paul said in v. 20 that he wanted to talk with them "since" or "because" (*gar*) of the hope of Israel, so here the leaders want to hear Paul "for" or "because" (*gar*) the sect is everywhere spoken against (Koet 1989, 24-25). What Paul has spoken of as "Israel's hope" here is reduced to "the sect," language elsewhere used to designate a group set apart by its opinions and judgments (e.g., 5:17; 15:5; 24:5). Although Paul has said that he is "contradicted" by the Jews (v. 19; NRSV: objected), here it is the "sect" that is "contradicted" (*antilegō*). The leaders' wish to hear from Paul is already undermined by the hyperbolic claim that the community he represents is "everywhere" spoken against, recalling earlier charges that Paul and his colleagues were turning the world upside down (17:6).

Hearing and Refusing to Hear: Division Persists (28:23-29)

Luke signals the importance of this scene by the deliberation with which Paul and the leaders agree on a day, as well as by the arrival of "great numbers" to meet with him (v. 23). Concisely, Luke summarizes Paul's action: for the entire day he was "testifying to the kingdom of God and trying to convince them about Jesus both from the law of Moses and from the prophets" (v. 23). As will be the case in v. 31, this summary distills both Lukan volumes. The phrase "kingdom of God" appears earlier in Acts (e.g., 8:12; 19:8), but it appears far more often in the Gospel as the content of Jesus' own proclamation (e.g., Luke 4:43; 8:1; 16:16; and also see Acts 1:3). In addition, the notion that Scripture teaches about Jesus appears in both Luke and Acts (Luke 24:44, 46; Acts 26:22-23). The verbs that characterize Paul's instruction (witness and persuade) similarly have served in Acts as indicators of the activity of Jesus' witnesses (e.g., 2:40; 8:25; 20:21; 17:4; 18:4).

If v. 23 condenses the Lukan understanding of the gospel, v. 24

does the same for human response: some are persuaded, but others do not believe. This division has occurred throughout Acts among both Jews and Gentiles (e.g., 13:43-45; 17:32). Verse 25 sharpens the division by describing the group as disagreeing with one another. The term employed here is *asymphōnoi*, "voices in disharmony." They leave, quarreling among themselves, but only after Paul pronounces a single word (NRSV: one further statement).

By contrast with the disharmonious voices of the Jews, Paul's introduction to his final statement emphasizes a kind of harmony. He assesses the Holy Spirit as speaking rightly when speaking through the prophet Isaiah, in this way signaling the unified voice of the Holy Spirit, Isaiah, and now Paul himself. Further, the voice that once spoke to the ancestors now speaks in Rome.

Early Christian interest in this passage from Isa 6:9-10 is widespread (see Matt 13:14-15; Mark 4:12; John 12:40; Rom 11:8). The Gospel of Luke quotes only a brief portion ("looking they may not perceive, and listening they may not understand," 8:10), but here Luke quotes the two verses in full and includes even the introductory instruction to the prophet: "Go to this people and say. . . ." That word of instruction seems, at first glance, not quite appropriate to the current context. In addition, Luke closely follows the LXX, except for one slight modification in this introductory instruction. Where LXX Isa 6:9 reads, "Go and say to this people," Luke reads, "Go to this people and say," an alteration that places "this people" at the beginning of the quotation. The phrase "this people" appears again in v. 27, and the expression stands in contrast with that other people, the Gentiles, in v. 28.

The introductory instruction also implies a further division among Jews. As it stands in Acts 28, the introductory instruction appears to address, not Isaiah (through whom the Holy Spirit is speaking), but the ancestors themselves. In Paul's comment, the Holy Spirit commands *the ancestors* (not Isaiah) to speak to the people. Perhaps Luke implies that the division among the people who gather to speak with Paul resembles a division of the past, in which some listened and others refused to do so.

The bulk of the quotation from Isaiah focuses on perception and the unwillingness to perceive. Verbs of hearing, looking, and understanding lead relentlessly to the conclusion that the people will not in fact "turn" to God's healing. The quotation's language of hearing fits particularly well with the context, in which the Jewish leaders have claimed that they want "to hear" Paul. Despite his day-long proclamation, he concludes that many will not listen.

The "then" (*oun*) of v. 28 presents the conclusion to be drawn from the quotation, and the phrase "Let it be known to you" signals an important disclosure to follow: "to the Gentiles has been sent this salvation of God, and they will listen" (AT). "Let it be known" also contrasts with the phrase "it is known to us" in v. 22 (NRSV: we know; Dupont 1979, 469). The Jewish leaders claim to know only that Christian faith is universally spoken against, but Paul makes known to them the salvation of the Gentiles. Twice earlier Paul has uttered pronouncements similar to this one, and following both pronouncements he continues to preach and teach in synagogues (13:46-47; 18:6-7). The extended and severe quotation from Isaiah, taken together with the place of this third statement near the closing of the book, makes its indictment unavoidable. Verse 29 does not appear in the NRSV because the earliest and best manuscripts of Acts do not include it, but its sentiment seems consistent with the entire scene.

"With All Boldness and Without Hindrance" (28:30-31)

Verses 30-31 return to the fact of Paul's captivity, employing a brief summary of his situation that serves also to recall most of the Lukan narrative. First, Luke reports that he lived "at his own expense," or "in his own hired dwelling." The Greek word refers to the contracted price for something (BDAG 654), perhaps a flat in the endless, crowded tenements of the great city. This tiny detail serves less to display Paul's living environment, however, than to recall Luke's theme of the responsible use of possessions. As in the farewell address to the Ephesian elders, Luke wants it known that Paul does not take advantage of others (20:33-34).

Paul also "welcomed all who came to him." Given the harsh language of vv. 25-28, the question whether "all" includes both Jews and Gentiles naturally arises. That the question is not a recent invention is clear from the fact that a few Greek manuscripts add the words "both Jews and Greeks" at the end of the verse. Since Luke allows "all" to remain ambiguous, perhaps interpreters must do the same, but not without noticing that one of the tasks of Paul as a witness is to welcome without question those who come.

Paul's activity is further described in v. 31. He preaches "the kingdom of God" and teaches "about the Lord Jesus Christ," apt summaries of the proclamation and instruction of both the Gospel and Acts. The final words, "with all boldness and without hindrance," further typify the appropriate character of Christian witnessing. Throughout Acts, the witnesses to Jesus' resurrection have spoken "boldly" (4:13, 29-31). "Without hindrance" intensifies the description. Not even the fact of his captivity causes Paul to soften his proclamation (Skinner 2003, 166-70). This final phrase is sometimes taken to refer to an external hindrance, such as that which might be imposed by the Roman authorities (Lake-Cadbury 1933, 348; Haenchen 1971, 726), but that view places far more stress than is warranted on the Roman captivity. Paul's bold speech gives evidence, not of Roman permission, but of divine design.

◊　◊　◊　◊

Much discussion of this passage focuses on the question of Luke's view of the Jewish mission, attempting to discern whether or not the conclusion of Acts assumes that the Jewish mission has now come to an end and further work will continue only among Gentiles. (It is important to distinguish that question from the task of identifying Luke's own audience or the situation of the church as he knew it; see Introduction.) On the one hand, the harshness of the text cannot be ignored. Not only the quotation but the framing of it as the Holy Spirit's speech and the juxtaposition of it with the receptivity of Gentiles make the indictment unmistakable.

On the other hand, even in chapter 28 it is clear that some Jews do listen. Also, earlier indictments have been followed by further witnessing, and v. 30 leaves open that possibility. In addition, prophetic speech regularly stings its intended audience, without signaling a final rupture between God and God's people. And the repeated emphasis on Paul's faithfulness to Israel and Israel's hope in God, both backward and forward, suggests that the story is not finished. If the speech of chapter 26 is climactic, then its insistence on Jesus as proclaimer of light for all people is not negated even by this troubling conclusion.

The aftermath of the Holocaust inevitably draws interpreters, as it should, to this question of Luke's understanding of the Jewish mission. That question is not the only important theological question in this passage, however. Luke closes his two volumes with language that evokes much of the content of those volumes—the kingdom of God, the Lord Jesus Christ, the salvation of God. Yet the sense that the story is not finished summons readers to supply the ending themselves (Marguerat 1999). Luke has strongly hinted at Paul's death (e.g., 20:22-24, 25, 38), so that "gap" fills itself from the narrative. The gap that remains is how readers will respond, and whether they also will join the witness to God's salvation in the person of Jesus Christ. Paul's witness in captivity is "unhindered," and the gospel will continue to be "unhindered" as well.

SELECT BIBLIOGRAPHY

WORKS CITED (EXCLUDING COMMENTARIES)

Achtemeier, Paul J. 1987. *The Quest for Unity in the New Testament Church*. Philadelphia: Fortress.

Alexander, Loveday. 1993. *The Preface to Luke's Gospel: Literary Convention and Social Context in Luke 1.1-4 and Acts 1.1*. SNTSMS 78. Cambridge: Cambridge University Press.

———. 1995. "'In Journeyings Often': Voyaging in the Acts of the Apostles and in Greek Romance." In *Luke's Literary Achievement: Collected Essays*, edited by C. M. Tuckett, 17-49. JSNTSup 116. Sheffield: Sheffield Academic Press.

Allen, O. Wesley, Jr. 1997. *The Death of Herod: The Narrative and Theological Function of Retribution in Luke–Acts*. SBLDS 158. Atlanta: Scholars Press.

Aune, David E. 1987. *The New Testament in Its Literary Environment*. LEC 8. Philadelphia: Westminster.

Barclay, John M.G. 1996. *Jews in the Mediterranean Diaspora: From Alexander to Trajan (323 BCE-117 CE)*. Edinburgh: T. & T. Clark.

Barrett, C. K. 1984. "Apollos and the Twelve Disciples of Ephesus." In *The New Testament Age: Essays in Honor of Bo Reicke*, edited by William C. Weinrich, 1:29-39. 2 vols. Macon, GA: Mercer University Press.

———. 1987. *The New Testament Background: Selected Documents*. Rev. and exp. ed. San Francisco: Harper and Row.

Bassler, Jouette M. 1982. *Divine Impartiality: Paul and a Theological Axiom*. SBLDS 59. Chico, CA: Scholars Press.

———. 1985. "Luke and Paul on Impartiality." *Bib* 66:546-52.

Bauckham, Richard. 1995. "James and the Jerusalem Church." In *The Book of Acts in Its Palestinian Setting*, edited by Richard Bauckham, 415-80. BAFCS 4. Grand Rapids, MI: Eerdmans.

Bechard, Dean Philip, S.J. 2000. *Paul Outside the Walls: A Study of*

Luke's Socio-Geographical Universalism in Acts 14:8-20. AnBib 143. Rome: Pontifical Institute.

Black, C. Clifton. 2001. *The Rhetoric of the Gospel: Theological Artistry in the Gospels and Acts.* St. Louis: Chalice.

Brown, Raymond E. 1994. *The Death of the Messiah: From Gethsemane to the Grave.* 2 vols. ABRL. New York: Doubleday.

———. 1997. *An Introduction to the New Testament.* ABRL. New York: Doubleday.

Brown, Schuyler. 1969. *Apostasy and Perseverance in the Theology of Luke.* AnBib 36. Rome: Pontifical Biblical Institute.

Bulley, Alan D. 1994. "Hanging in the Balance: A Semiotic Study of Acts 20:7-12." *EgT* 25:171-88.

Burchard, Christoph. 1985. "A Note on ῥῆμα in Josas 17:1 F.; Luke 2:15, 17; Acts 10:37." *NovT* 4:281-95.

Cadbury, Henry Joel. 1932. "The Hellenists." *Additional Notes to the Commentary,* edited by F. J. Foakes Jackson and Kirsopp Lake, 59-74. BC 4. Reprint 1979, Grand Rapids: Baker.

———. 1958. *The Making of Luke–Acts.* 2nd ed. New York: Macmillan.

Campbell, William Sanger. 2000. *Who Are We in Acts?: The First-Person Plural Character in the Acts of the Apostles.* Ph.D. diss., Princeton Theological Seminary.

Carroll, John. 1988. *Response to the End of History: Eschatology and Situation in Luke–Acts.* SBLDS 92. Atlanta: Scholars Press.

Cassidy, Richard J. 1987. *Society and Politics in the Acts of the Apostles.* Maryknoll, NY: Orbis.

Casson, Lionel. 1971. *Ships and Seamanship in the Ancient World.* Reprint 1995, Baltimore: Johns Hopkins University Press.

———. 1974. *Travel in the Ancient World.* Reprint 1994, Baltimore: Johns Hopkins University Press.

Chrysostom, St. John. 1886. *Homilies on the Acts of the Apostles and the Epistle to the Romans.* Translated by J. Walker, J. Sheppard, H. Browne. NPNF 11. Reprint 1980, Grand Rapids, MI: Eerdmans.

Cohen, Shaye J. D. 1986. "Was Timothy Jewish (Acts 16:1-3)? Patristic Exegesis, Rabbinic Law, and Matrilineal Descent." *JBL* 105:251-68.

Conzelmann, Hans. 1961. *The Theology of St. Luke.* Translated by Geoffrey Buswell. New York: Harper and Row.

Cosgrove, Charles H. 1984. "The Divine ΔΕΙ in Luke–Acts." *NovT* 26:168-90.

Cousar, Charles B. 1990. *A Theology of the Cross: The Death of Jesus in the Pauline Letters.* OBT. Minneapolis: Fortress.

————. 1992. "Council of Jerusalem." *ABD* 3:766-68.

Crouch, Frank. 1996. "The Persuasive Moment: Rhetorical Resolutions in Paul's Defense Before Agrippa." In *Society of Biblical Literature Seminar Papers*, 333-42. Atlanta: Scholars Press.

Croy, Clayton. 1997. "Hellenistic Philosophies and the Preaching of the Resurrection (Acts 17:18, 32)." *NovT* 39:21-39.

Crump, David Michael. 1992. *Jesus the Intercessor: Prayer and Christology in Luke–Acts*. WUNT 2.49. Tübingen: J. C. B. Mohr (Paul Siebeck).

Dahl, N. A. 1958. "'A People for His Name' (Acts xv.14)." *NTS* 4:319-27.

Daube, David. 1990. "On Acts 23: Sadducees and Angels." *JBL* 109:493-97.

Davies, W. D. 1974. *The Gospel and the Land: Early Christianity and Jewish Territorial Doctrine*. Berkeley: University of California Press.

Dibelius, Martin. 1956. *Studies in the Acts of the Apostles*. Translated by Mary Ling. Edited by Heinrich Greeven. Reprint 1999, Mifflintown, PA: Sigler.

Dinkler, Erich. 1975. "Philippus und der *anēr aithiops* (Apg. 8.26-40): Historische und geographische Bemerkungen zum Missionsablaud nach Lukas." In *Jesus und Paulus: Festschrift für Werner Georg Kümmel*, edited by E. E. Ellis and Erich Grässer, 85-95. Göttingen: Vandenhoeck und Ruprecht.

Du Toit, Andrie B. 2000. "A Tale of Two Cities: 'Tarsus or Jerusalem' Revisited." *NTS* 46:375-402.

Dupont, Jacques 1979. "La conclusion des Actes et son rapport à l'ensemble de l'ouvrage de Luc." In *Les Acts des Apôtres: Traditions, rédaction, théologie*, edited by J. Kremer, 359-404. BETL 48. Leuven: Leuven University Press.

Fitzmyer, Joseph A. 1981. *The Gospel According to Luke (I-IX)*. AB 28. Garden City, NY: Doubleday.

Fowl, Stephen E. 1998. *Engaging Scripture*. Challenges in Contemporary Theology. Oxford: Blackwell.

Gamble, Harry Y. 1995. *Books and Readers in the Early Church: A History of Early Christian Texts*. New Haven: Yale University Press.

Garrett, Susan. 1989. *The Demise of the Devil: Magic and the Demonic in Luke's Writings*. Minneapolis: Fortress.

————. 1990. "Exodus from Bondage: Luke 9:31 and Acts 12:1-24." *CBQ* 52:656-80.

Gaventa, Beverly Roberts. 1978. *Paul's Conversion: A Critical Sifting of the Epistolary Evidence*. Ph.D. diss., Duke University.

———. 1982. "The Eschatology of Luke–Acts Revisited." *Encounter* 43:27-42.

———. 1986a. *From Darkness to Light: Aspects of Conversion in the New Testament.* OBT. Philadelphia: Fortress.

———. 1986b. "To Speak Thy Word with All Boldness. Acts 4:23-31." *Faith and Mission* 3:76-82.

———. 1995. *Mary: Glimpses of the Mother of Jesus.* Columbia, SC: University of South Carolina Press.

———. 2001. "Traditions in Conversation and Collision: Reflections on Multiculturalism in the Acts of the Apostles." In *Making Room at the Table: An Invitation to Multicultural Worship,* edited by Brian K. Blount and Leonora Tubbs Tisdale, 30-41. Louisville: Westminster John Knox.

Green, Joel B. 1998. "Salvation to the Ends of the Earth: God as the Saviour in the Acts of the Apostles." In *Witness to the Gospel: The Theology of Acts,* edited by I. H. Marshall and David Peterson, 83-106. Grand Rapids, MI: Eerdmans.

Harrill, J. Albert. 2000. "The Dramatic Function of the Running Slave Rhoda (Acts 12.13-16): A Piece of Greco-Roman Comedy." *NTS* 46:150-57.

Hemer, Colin. 1989. *The Book of Acts in the Setting of Hellenistic History.* WUNT 49. Tübingen: J. C. B. Mohr (Paul Siebeck).

Hill, Craig C. 1992. *Hellenists and Hebrews: Reappraising Division Within the Earliest Church.* Minneapolis: Fortress.

Hirsch, Emanuel. 1929. "Die drei Berichte der Apostelgeschichte über die Bekehrung des Paulus." *ZNW* 29:305-12.

Hock, Ronald. 1980. *The Social Context of Paul's Ministry: Tentmaking and Apostleship.* Philadelphia: Fortress.

Horsley, G. H. R. 1992. "Double Names." *ABD* 4:1011-17.

Horst, P. W. van der. 1976. "Peter's Shadow: The Religio-Historical Background of Acts v.15." *NTS* 23:204-12.

Jervell, Jacob. 1972. *Luke and the People of God: A New Look at Luke–Acts.* Minneapolis: Augsburg.

———. 1988. "The Church of Jews and Godfearers." In *Luke–Acts and the Jewish People: Eight Critical Perspectives,* edited by Joseph B. Tyson, 11-20. Minneapolis: Augsburg.

Juel, Donald H. 1992. "Hearing Peter's Speech in Acts 3: Meaning and Truth in Interpretation." *WW* 12:43-50.

Kennedy, George A. 1984. *New Testament Interpretation Through Rhetorical Criticism.* Chapel Hill: University of North Carolina Press.

Kilgallen, John J. 1994. "Paul's Speech to the Ephesian Elders: Its Structure." *ETL* 70:112-21.

Koet, B. J. 1989. "Paul in Rome (Acts 28:16-31): A Farewell to Judaism?" In *Five Studies on Interpretation of Scripture in Luke–Acts*, 119-39. SNTA 14. Leuven: Leuven University Press.

Kraabel, A. T. 1981. "The Disappearance of the 'God-Fearers.'" *Numen* 28:113-26.

Kurz, William. 1977. "Acts 3:19-26 as a Test of the Role of Eschatology in Lukan Christology." In *Society of Biblical Literature Seminar Papers*, edited by Paul Achtemeier, 309-23. Missoula, MT: Scholars Press.

———. 1985. "Luke 22:14-38 and Greco-Roman and Biblical Farewell Addresses." *JBL* 104:251-68.

Ladouceur, David. 1980. "Hellenistic Preconceptions of Shipwreck and Pollution as a Context for Acts 27–28." *HTR* 73:435-49.

Lentz, John C., Jr. 1993. *Luke's Portrait of Paul*. SNTSMS 77. Cambridge: Cambridge University Press.

Levinskaya, Irina. 1996. *The Book of Acts in Its Diaspora Setting*. BAFCS 5. Grand Rapids: Eerdmans.

LiDonnici, Lynn R. 1992. "The Images of Artemis Ephesia and Greco-Roman Worship: A Reconsideration." *HTR* 85:389-415.

Llewelyn, S. R. 1997. *New Documents Illustrating Early Christianity*. 8 vols. Grand Rapids, MI: Eerdmans.

Lohfink, Gerhard. 1976. *The Conversion of St. Paul: Narrative and History in Acts*. Translated by Bruce J. Malina. Chicago: Franciscan Herald.

MacMullen, Ramsay. 1966. *Enemies of the Roman Order: Treason, Unrest, and Alienation in the Empire*. Cambridge: Harvard University Press.

———. 1984. *Christianizing the Roman Empire (A.D. 100–400)*. New Haven: Yale University Press.

MacRae, George W., S.J. 1973. "'Whom Heaven Must Receive Until the Time': Reflections on the Christology of Acts." *Int* 27:151-65.

Marguerat, Daniel. 1995. "Saul's Conversion (Acts 9, 22, 26) and the Multiplication of Narrative in Acts." In *Luke's Literary Achievement: Collected Essays*, edited by C. M. Tuckett, 127-55. JSNTSup 116. Sheffield: Sheffield Academic Press.

———. 1999. "The Enigma of the Silent Closing of Acts (28:16-31)." In *Jesus and the Heritage of Israel: Luke's Narrative Claim Upon Israel's Legacy*, edited by David P. Moessner, 284-304. Harrisburg, PA: Trinity.

Marxsen, Willi. 1968. *Introduction to the New Testament: An Approach to Its Problems.* 3rd ed. Translated by Geoffrey Buswell. Philadelphia: Fortress.

Mattill, A. J. 1970. "The Purpose of Acts: Schneckenburger Reconsidered." In *Apostolic History and the Gospel: Essays Presented to F. F. Bruce*, edited by W. W. Gasque and R. P. Martin, 108-22. Exeter: Paternoster, 1970.

Miles, Gary B., and Garry Trompf. 1976. "Luke and Antiphon: The Theology of Acts 27–28 in the Light of Pagan Beliefs About Divine Retribution, Pollution, and Shipwreck." *HTR* 69:259-67.

Mitchell, Alan. 1997. "'Greet the Friends by Name': New Testament Evidence for the Greco-Roman *Topos* on Friendship." In *Greco-Roman Perspectives on Friendship*, edited by John T. Fitzgerald, 225-62. SBLRBS 34. Atlanta: Scholars Press.

Murphy-O'Connor, J. 1992. "Lots of God-Fearers? *Theosebeis* in the Aphrodisias Inscription." *RB* 99:418-24.

Neirynck, F. 1984. "Acts 10, 36a τὸ λόγον ὄν." *ETL* 60:118-23.

Nobbs, Alanna. 1994. "Cyprus." In *The Book of Acts in Its Graeco-Roman Setting*, edited by David W. J. Gill and Conrad Gempf, 279-89. BAFCS 2. Grand Rapids, MI: Eerdmans.

Nolland, John. 1980. "A Fresh Look at Acts 15.10." *NTS* 27:105-115.

Oster, Richard. 1976. "The Ephesian Artemis as an Opponent of Early Christianity." *JAC* 19:24-44.

O'Toole, Robert F. 1994. "What Role Does Jesus' Saying in Acts 20,35 Play in Paul's Address to the Ephesian Elders?" *Bib* 75:329-49.

Palmer, Darryl. 1987. "The Literary Background of Acts 1:1-14." *NTS* 33:427-38.

———. 1993. "Acts and the Ancient Historical Monograph." In *The Book of Acts in Its Ancient Literary Setting*, edited by Bruce W. Winter and Andrew D. Clarke, 1-29. BAFCS 1. Grand Rapids, MI: Eerdmans.

Pearson, Birger. 1992. "Alexandria." *ABD* 1:152-57.

Pervo, Richard I. 1987. *Profit with Delight: The Literary Genre of the Acts of the Apostles.* Philadelphia: Fortress.

Porter, Stanley E. 1999. *The Paul of Acts: Essays in Literary Criticism, Rhetoric, and Theology.* WUNT 2.115. Tübingen: J. C. B. Mohr (Paul Siebeck).

Ramsay, William M. 1925. *St. Paul the Traveller and the Roman Citizen.* 14th ed. Reprint 1982, Grand Rapids, MI: Baker.

Rapske, Brian. 1994a. "Acts, Travel and Shipwreck." In *The Book of Acts in Its Graeco-Roman Setting*, edited by David W. J. Gill and Conrad Gempf, 1-47. BAFCS 2. Grand Rapids, MI: Eerdmans.

————. 1994b. *The Book of Acts and Paul in Roman Custody.* BAFCS 3. Grand Rapids, MI: Eerdmans.

Reimer, Ivoni Richter. 1995. *Women in the Acts of the Apostles: A Feminist Liberation Perspective.* Minneapolis: Fortress.

Rengstorf, K. H. 1972. "ὑπηρέτης, ὑπηρετέω." *TDNT* 7:530-44.

Richard, Earl. 1984. "The Divine Purpose: The Jews and the Gentile Mission (Acts 15)." In *Luke-Acts: New Perspectives from the Society of Biblical Literature*, edited by Charles H. Talbert, 188-209. New York: Crossroad.

Riesenfeld, H. 1979. "The Text of Acts x.36." In *Text and Interpretation: Studies in the New Testament Presented to Matthew Black*, edited by Ernest Best and R. McL. Wilson, 191-94. Cambridge: Cambridge University Press.

Routh, Martin Joseph. 1846-48. *Reliquiae Sacrae.* 5 vols. Reprint 1974, Hildesheim, NY: Georg Olms.

Sanders, E. P. 1990. "Jewish Association with Gentiles and Galatians 2:11-14." In *The Conversation Continues: Studies in Paul and John in Honor of J. Louis Martyn*, edited by Robert T. Fortna and Beverly R. Gaventa, 170-88. Nashville: Abingdon.

————. 1992. *Judaism: Practice and Belief 63 B.C.E.-66 C.E.* London: S.C.M.

Schubert, Paul. 1968a. "The Final Cycle of Speeches in the Book of Acts." *JBL* 87:1-16.

————. 1968b. "The Place of the Areopagus Speech in the Composition of Acts." In *Transitions in Biblical Scholarship*, edited by J. Coert Rylaarsdam, 235-61. Chicago: University of Chicago Press.

Schürer, Emil. 1973-87. *The History of the Jewish People in the Age of Jesus Christ.* Revised and edited by G. Vermes, F. Millar, and M. Black. 4 vols. Edinburgh: T. & T. Clark.

Segal, Peretz. 1989. "The Penalty of the Warning Inscription from the Temple of Jerusalem." *IEJ* 39:79-84.

Seim, Turid Karlsen. 1994. *The Double Message: Patterns of Gender in Luke–Acts.* Nashville: Abingdon.

Skinner, Matthew L. 2003. *Locating Paul: Places of Custody as Narrative Settings in Acts 21–28.* SBLAB 13. Atlanta: Society of Biblical Literature.

Snowden, F. M., Jr. 1970. *Blacks in Antiquity.* Cambridge: Harvard University Press.

————. 1983. *Before Color Prejudice.* Cambridge: Harvard University Press.

Soards, Marion L. 1994. *The Speeches in Acts: Their Content, Context, and Concerns.* Louisville: Westminster John Knox.

Stanton, Graham. 1978. "Stephen in Lucan Perspective." *StudBib* 3:345-60.

Stenschke, Christoph W. 1999. *Luke's Portrait of Gentiles Prior to Their Coming to Faith.* WUNT 2.108. Tübingen: J. C. B. Mohr (Paul Siebeck).

Sterling, Gregory E. 1992. *Historiography and Self-Definition: Josephos, Luke–Acts and Apologetic Historiography.* NovTSup 64. Leiden: E. J. Brill.

———. 1994. "'Athletes of Virtue': An Analysis of the Summaries in Acts (2:41-47; 4:32-35; 5:12-16)." *JBL* 113:679-96.

Stoops, Robert F., Jr. 1989. "Riot and Assembly: The Social Context of Acts 19:23-41." *JBL* 108:73-91.

———. 1992. "Simon." *ABD* 6:29-31.

Strelan, Rick. 1996. *Paul, Artemis, and the Jews.* BZNW 80. Berlin: de Gruyter.

Tajra, Harry W. 1989. *The Trial of St. Paul: A Juridical Exegesis of the Second Half of the Acts of the Apostles.* WUNT 2/35. Tübingen: J. C. B. Mohr (Paul Siebeck).

Talbert, Charles H. 1977. *What Is a Gospel? The Genre of the Canonical Gospels.* Philadelphia: Fortress.

Throckmorton, B. H. 1973. " Σώζειν, σωτηρία in Luke–Acts." In *Studia Evangelica, Vol. vi,* edited Elizabeth A. Livingtone, 515-26. TU 5.57. Berlin: Akademie Verlag.

Trémel, Bernard. 1980. "A propos d'Actes 20, 7-12: Puissance du thaumaturge ou du témoin?" *RTP* 112:359-69.

Tyson, Joseph B., editor. 1988. *Luke–Acts and the Jewish People: Eight Critical Perspectives.* Minneapolis: Augsburg.

———. 1999. *Luke, Judaism, and the Scholars: Critical Approaches to Luke–Acts.* Columbia, SC: University of South Carolina Press.

Unnik, W. C. van. 1973a. "Der Befehl an Philippus." In *Sparsa Collecta. Part 1,* 328-39. NovTSup 29. Leiden: E. J. Brill.

———. 1973b. "Once Again: Tarsus or Jerusalem." In *Sparsa Collecta. Part 1,* 321-27. NovTSup 29. Leiden: E. J. Brill.

Von Wahlde, Urban C. 1995. "The Problem of Acts 4:25a: A New Proposal." *ZNW* 86:265-67.

Walaskay, Paul W. 1983. *"And So We Came to Rome": The Political Perspective of St. Luke.* SNTSMS 49. Cambridge: Cambridge University Press.

Wall, R. W. 1991. "Successors to 'the Twelve' according to Acts 12:1-17." *CBQ* 53:628-43.

Wenham, David. 1993. "Acts and the Pauline Corpus II. The Evidence of Parallels." In *The Book of Acts in Its Ancient Literary Setting*, edited by Bruce W. Winter and Andrew D. Clarke, 215-58. BAFCS 1. Grand Rapids: Eerdmans.

Wilder, Amos. 1983. "Story and Story-World." *Int* 37:353-64.

Wilson, S. G. 1983. *Luke and the Law*. SNTSMS 50. Cambridge: Cambridge University Press.

Winter, Bruce W. 1991. "The Importance of the *Captatio Benevolentiae* in the Speeches of Tertullus and Paul in Acts 24:1-21." *JTS* 42:505-31.

———. 1994. "Acts and Food Shortages." In *The Book of Acts in Its Graeco-Roman Setting*, edited by David W. J. Gill and Conrad Gempf, 59-78. BAFCS 2. Grand Rapids, MI: Eerdmans.

Zwiep, A. W. 1997. *The Ascension of the Messiah in Lukan Christology*. NovTSup 87. Leiden: E. J. Brill.

SELECT COMMENTARIES ON ACTS
(CITED AND NOT CITED)

Barrett, C. K. 1994. *A Critical and Exegetical Commentary on the Acts of the Apostles I-XIV*. ICC. Edinburgh: T&T Clark. A massive treatment of the Greek text by one of the leading commentators in the English-speaking world. Perhaps daunting for beginners, but a volume to be consulted regularly for reference.

———. 1998. *A Critical and Exegetical Commentary on the Acts of the Apostles XV-XXVIII*. ICC. Edinburgh: T&T Clark. See above.

Bruce, F. F. 1987. *Commentary on the Book of the Acts: The English Text with Introduction, Exposition and Notes*. NICNT. Revised ed. Grand Rapids, MI: Eerdmans. An historically oriented commentary on the English text.

———. 1990. *The Acts of the Apostles: The Greek Text with Introduction and Commentary*. 3rd ed. Grand Rapids, MI: Eerdmans. A meticulous guide to the Greek text and historical questions from a conservative scholar.

Calvin, John. 1965. *The Acts of the Apostles 1–13*. Translated by John W. Fraser and W. J. G. McDonald. Calvin's Commentaries. Grand Rapids, MI: Eerdmans. Although necessarily dated in many respects, Calvin's perspective on Lukan theology and occasionally his comments on individual exegetical questions make this an important volume.

————. 1966. *The Acts of the Apostles 14–28*. Translated by John W. Fraser. Calvin's Commentaries. Grand Rapids, MI: Eerdmans. See above.

Conzelmann, Hans. 1987. *Acts of the Apostles*. Hermeneia. Translated by James Limburg, A. Thomas Kraabel, and Donald H. Juel. Philadelphia: Fortress. The outworking of Conzelmann's influential understanding of Luke as a theologian of salvation history, the volume is suitable largely for advanced students and scholars.

Dunn, James D. G. 1996. *The Acts of the Apostles*. Narrative Commentaries. Valley Forge, PA: Trinity. A concise commentary, based on the Revised English Bible, and intended for ministers and students.

Fitzmyer, Joseph A. 1998. *The Acts of the Apostles*. AB 31. New York: Doubleday. An impressive and reliable resource on text-critical, linguistic, and historical questions. Helpful also for its extensive bibliography.

Haenchen, Ernst. 1971. *The Acts of the Apostles: A Commentary*. Translated by Bernard Noble and Gerald Shinn. 14th ed. Philadelphia: Westminster. A major commentary reflecting the influence of Martin Dibelius and Hans Conzelmann, somewhat dated in its approach but nevertheless insightful.

Jervell, Jacob. 1998. *Die Apostelgeschichte*. Meyer K. Göttingen: Vandenhoeck und Ruprecht. Jervell's long-standing thesis about Luke's preoccupation with Israel comes to vigorous expression here in the prestigious Meyer commentary series.

Johnson, Luke Timothy. 1992. *The Acts of the Apostles*. Sacra Pagina 1. Collegeville, MN: Liturgical. An accessible commentary that gives special attention to Luke's use of the Old Testament and explores the theme of prophecy and fulfillment throughout Acts.

Kee, Howard Clark. 1997. *To Every Nation Under Heaven: The Acts of the Apostles*. New Testament in Context. Harrisburg, PA: Trinity. Focus on the social, cultural and historical contexts of the Lukan narrative, composed in a nontechnical style.

Krodel, Gerhard A. 1986. *Acts*. Augsburg Commentary on the New Testament. Minneapolis: Augsburg. A readable and engaging commentary, intended for laypeople and students.

Lake, K. and H. J. Cadbury. 1933. *English Translation and Commentary*. BC4. Ed. F. J. Foakes-Jackson and K. Lake. London: MacMillan and Co. Nearly seventy-five years after its publication, the work of Lake and Cadbury continues to be important for its extensive observations about the text of Acts and its translation. A major contribution to twentieth-century scholarship.

O'Day, Gail R. 1998. "Acts." In *Women's Bible Commentary*, edited by Carol A. Newsom and Sharon H. Ringe, 394-402. Expanded ed. Louisville: Westminster John Knox. Not a full commentary, but an important and accessible introduction to feminist questions about Acts.

Spencer, F. Scott. 1997. *Acts*. Readings. Sheffield: Sheffield Academic Press. A brief and engaging commentary focused on literary questions, notable for its consistently fresh observations about the Lukan story.

Talbert, Charles H. 1997. *Reading Acts: A Literary and Theological Commentary on the Acts of the Apostles*. New York: Crossroad. Follows the author's earlier thesis that Acts is a narrative about the successors of Jesus. The commentary offers helpful observations about the structure of individual units in Acts, and it also finds many parallels to elements of Acts in other literature of the Greco-Roman world.

Tannehill, Robert. 1990. *The Narrative Unity of Luke–Acts. Volume 2: The Acts of the Apostles*. Minneapolis: Fortress. As reflected in the title, this is not a conventional commentary but a study of the story of Luke–Acts as a literary whole. Both in its overall approach to Luke–Acts and in its remarks about individual texts, it is among the most important contributions to Lukan studies in the last quarter-century. A contemporary classic.

Walaskay, Paul W. 1998. *Acts*. Westminster Bible Companion. Louisville: Westminster John Knox. A concise and lucid commentary on the NRSV, intended for use by lay readers.

Wall, Robert W. 2002. "The Acts of the Apostles." In *The New Interpreter's Bible*, edited by Leander E. Keck et al. 12 vols. Nashville: Abingdon. 12:3-368. A provocative reading of Acts which attempts to locate its story of Jesus' successors within the larger canonical framework not only of Luke's Gospel but also of the Pauline as well as the Catholic Epistles.

Witherington, Ben III. 1998. *The Acts of the Apostles: A Socio-Rhetorical Commentary*. Grand Rapids, MI: Eerdmans. A lengthy compilation of scholarly views on standard exegetical questions, largely concerned with the historical reliability of Acts.

INDEX

Abraham, 28-29, 86, 117, 121-22, 124, 128, 130, 133, 135, 195-96, 198, 213, 258, 327

Acts of the Apostles
audience of, 49-51, 120-21, 316, 341
author of, 49-50
date of composition, 51, 133
ending of, 31, 45-46, 65-66, 363, 370
genre of, 26, 42-43, 54-55, 58, 69, 175
and Gospel according to Luke, 52-53
purpose, 51-52, 110, 121, 222-23, 226-27, 275-76
sources of, 57-58, 95, 97, 103, 106, 117, 119, 133-34, 147, 162-63, 165, 178, 206, 230, 284, 304, 308, 319, 350
See also literary features

Agrippa II, King, 48, 331-32, 335-41, 347-50, 356

almsgiving, 85, 87, 164, 328

angels. *See* divine messengers

Antioch, 38, 101, 162, 176-82, 187-89, 191, 194-95, 205, 208-11, 213-14, 224-25, 227, 231-32, 263

apostle(s), 37, 41-42, 44, 62-66, 68-74, 77-78, 81, 88, 91-93, 95, 97, 99-101, 104-7, 109-11, 114-17, 122-23, 127, 132, 157, 162, 175, 182-83, 189-90, 202, 205-6, 209-10, 214-15, 264, 295, 311, 313
See also authority, apostolic; witness, and apostles

Apostolic Decree. *See* Jerusalem, Council of

atonement, 35, 82, 90, 146

authority, apostolic, 101, 114-15, 134, 161, 172, 175, 181, 186, 188, 217, 220
See also church, governance of; leaders, Christian

baptism, 26, 34, 37, 42, 53, 65, 71, 80-82, 118, 139-40, 144-46, 153, 159, 168, 171-75, 194, 237, 240, 242, 258, 262, 264-66, 308
See also Holy Spirit, and baptism

Barnabas, 38, 99, 101, 132, 154, 176-80, 187-92, 195, 197, 202-3, 205-7, 210, 213, 217, 224-25, 230-31, 278, 288, 298, 358

blindness and sight, 79, 149-50, 153, 189, 193-95, 280, 306-7, 342, 344

boldness (*parrēsia*) 27, 40, 91, 94, 97-99, 154, 202, 204-5, 258, 264, 285, 347, 368-69

breaking of bread. *See* food

Caesar. *See* Rome, emperor of

Christology, 89-90, 200
as absentee, 34-35, 90, 162
as subordinationist, 32

christophany. *See* theophany

church (*ekklēsia*)
community life, 41, 43, 54, 63, 67-68, 73-74, 77, 81, 85, 88, 95, 98-100, 103-5, 111-12, 114-16, 138, 154, 156-57, 159-61, 163, 170, 181, 183, 190, 240, 256, 276-77, 279-83, 289-91, 294-96, 320, 345, 361
and God's action, 30, 39-40, 81, 99, 103, 105, 122, 133, 170, 190
governance of, 33, 44, 53-54, 71, 73,